The Cinema of Poetry

The Cinema of Poetry

P. Adams Sitney

OXFORD
UNIVERSITY PRESS

OXFORD
UNIVERSITY PRESS

Oxford University Press is a department of the University of Oxford.
It furthers the University's objective of excellence in research, scholarship,
and education by publishing worldwide.

Oxford   New York

Auckland   Cape Town   Dar es Salaam   Hong Kong   Karachi
Kuala Lumpur   Madrid   Melbourne   Mexico City   Nairobi
New Delhi   Shanghai   Taipei   Toronto

With offices in

Argentina   Austria   Brazil   Chile   Czech Republic   France   Greece
Guatemala   Hungary   Italy   Japan   Poland   Portugal   Singapore
South Korea   Switzerland   Thailand   Turkey   Ukraine   Vietnam

Oxford is a registered trademark of Oxford University Press
in the UK and certain other countries.

Published in the United States of America by
Oxford University Press
198 Madison Avenue, New York, NY 10016

Library of Congress Cataloging-in-Publication Data
Sitney, P. Adams.
The cinema of poetry / P. Adams Sitney.
p. cm.
Includes index.
ISBN 978–0–19–933702–6 (hardcover)—ISBN 978–0–19–933703–3 (pbk.)   1. Experimental films—
Europe—History and criticism.   2. Experimental films—United States—History and criticism.
3. Poetry in motion pictures.   4. Motion pictures—Aesthetics   I. Title.
PN1995.9.E96S48 2014
791.43'6—dc23
2014002191

1 3 5 7 9 8 6 4 2
Printed in the United States of America
on acid-free paper

In token
of my admiration of their geniuses
this book is inscribed
to
SUSAN HOWE
DANIEL HELLER-ROAZEN
OLEG TCHERNY

{ CONTENTS }

{ PREFACE }

Just as my book *Eyes Upside Down* (2008) returned to the matter of *Visionary Film* (1974, 1979, 2002), some thirty-four years after the initial writing of that book, *The Cinema of Poetry* revisits the themes and issues of *Modernist Montage* (1992) twenty years later. Since 1961, when I began to write on cinema and to edit and publish the texts of filmmakers and critics, the relationship of film to poetry has been my central focus. In the term *poetry* I include the works of poets, dead and alive; the theory of poetry; the poetics of lyric, epic, and dramatic verse; and the poetics of cinema, especially but not exclusively as formulated by filmmakers. Of the ten filmmakers I discuss in detail here, six have been treated in my other books, although Pasolini, from whom I derive the title of the volume, previously appeared in and also provided the title for my *Vital Crises in Italian Cinema* (1995, 2012), the one book I have written in which poetry played almost no role.

Because I have been writing on poetry and cinema throughout my career, it is natural that this volume incorporates, in some of its chapters, texts I have published earlier in periodicals or anthologies. I am particularly grateful to Don McMahon, my editor at *Artforum*, who encouraged me to write on a number of the filmmakers discussed here and who has always given me superb editorial advice.

I wrote the bulk of *The Cinema of Poetry* in the spring of 2011 while I was the Anna-Maria Kellen Berlin Fellow at the American Academy in Berlin. I am deeply grateful to Dr. Gary Smith, its director, and Pamela Rosenberg, the dean of Fellows and Programs, for inviting me and for their hospitality, and to Susan Howe, Susan Stewart, and Leonard Barkin for supporting my nomination. The remarkable librarian of the Academy, Yolanda Korb, procured every book, article, and photocopies of manuscripts that I required with lightning efficiency. The hospitality of Daniel Heller-Roazen and Oleg Tcherny, Robert Beavers and Ute Aurand, and the constant support of The Institute for Cultural Inquiry (Berlin) made my research on Pasolini and Markopoulos efficient and remarkably pleasurable. It was my good fortune that my former student Beau Madison Mount was a fellow at the ICI during the period I was in Berlin. Through his efforts I was generously welcomed by the director, Christolph Holzhey; the associate director, Manuele Gragnolati; and Dr. Holzhey's academic assistant, Luca Di Biasi, while they were in the midst of an extended examination of Pasolini's achievements. That forum provided an invaluable sounding board for my speculations on Pasolini's film theory.

My study of Gregory Markopoulos's *Eniaios* would not have been possible without the generosity of Robert Beavers, who not only gave me access to the Temenos Archive in Zürich each time I could arrange to visit it but also patiently answered hundreds of my questions. The Stanley J. Seeger Hellenic Fund at Princeton University permitted me to attend the Temenos screenings in Lyssaraia, Greece, in 2004, 2008, and 2012. Likewise, Marilyn Brakhage and the Stan Brakhage collection in the archives of the library of the University of Colorado in Boulder (and its knowledgeable curator, Brad Arnold) considerably enriched my study of the filmmaker. But without the help of Don Yannacito I would not have been able to spend two months going through Brakhage's papers.

In addition to writing the chapters on Pasolini, Bergman, Tarkovsky, Brakhage, and Markopoulos in Berlin, I reworked during those months earlier essays I published on *Ménilmontant, Nostalghia,* Joseph Cornell, Nathaniel Dorsky, and Lawrence Jordan. Short essays I had published on Ingmar Bergman's films *Tystnaden* [*The Silence*] and *Visningar och rop* [*Cries and Whispers*] became my starting point for a longer study of his *Fanny och Alexander.* I also incorporated essays I had published on Stan Brakhage's "Faust" series and his Modernism in the chapter largely devoted to his Vancouver series. Don McMahon asked me to write an essay on Jerome Hiler's *Words of Mercury* soon after I returned from Berlin. Immediately upon completing it, I felt it belonged with the consideration of Dorsky's films in the penultimate chapter.

With the encouragement of my editor at Oxford University Press, Brendan O'Neill, and drawing on the generous comments of two unidentified readers of the manuscript, I wrote the autobiographical introduction and, in writing it, came to realize how long I had been nurturing this project. Robert Haller of Anthology Film Archives, Fred Camper, Marilyn Brakhage, Nina Zurier, Nathaniel Dorsky, Sebastian and Jonas Mekas, Jerome Hiler, John Borruso, Linda Levinson, and Richard Pilaro helped me make or acquire the illustrations. Valerie Borchardt at Georges Borchardt, Inc., deftly and kindly handled all the contractual negotiations for me.

The friendship of filmmakers and poets has inspired many of the pages of this book in ways they may not recognize. This book would not exist without the conversations of the filmmakers Nathaniel Dorsky, Jerome Hiler, Lawrence Jordan, Robert Beavers, Ernie Gehr, Peter Kubelka, and Saul Levine or the poets Robert Kelly and Susan Howe, and certainly not without the constant support of Jonas Mekas, who is both poet and filmmaker.

{ ACKNOWLEDGMENTS }

Parts of this book first appeared in the following:

"The Cinematic Gaze of Joseph Cornell," in *Joseph Cornell*, ed. Kynaston McShine (New York: Museum of Modern Art, 1980) pp. 69–89.

"Ingmar Bergman's *The Silence* and the Primal Scene," *Film Culture*, no. 76 (June 1992): 35–38.

"Liksom en saga av Broderna Grimm," trans. Joel Ohlsson, *Chaplin*, no. 222 (June 1989): 124–25, 164; "Color and Myth in *Cries and Whispers*," *Film Criticism* (Spring 1990): 37–41. (Originally published in Swedish translation in *Chaplin*).

"*Ménilmontant* de Dimitri Kirsanoff, figures et syntaxe de l'avant-garde," trans. Pierre Gras, in *Jeune, dure et pure!: Une histoire du cinéma d'avant-garde et expérimental en France*, ed. Nicole Brenez, Christian Lebrat, (Paris: Cinémathèque Française, 2001) pp. 138–140.

"Andrei Tarkovsky's *Nostalghia*," in *The Hidden God*, ed. Mary Lea Bandy and Antonio Monda (New York: Museum of Modern Art, 2003) pp. 161–166.

"Idyll Worship: Gregory J. Markopoulos's *Eniaios*," *Artforum* (November 2004): 187–191; "Further Orders" [on Temenos 2008], *Artforum* (October 2008): 135–140.

"Brakhage's Faustian Psychodrama," in *Stan Brakhage: Filmmaker*, ed. David E. James (Philadelphia: Temple University Press, 2005) pp. 153–167.

"Brakhage and Modernism," in *Masterpieces of Modernist Cinema*, ed. Ted Perry (Bloomington: University of Indiana Press, 2006) pp. 159–178.

"Tone Poems: The Films of Nathaniel Dorsky," *Artforum* (November 2007): 341–347.

"Moments of Illumination: The Films of Lawrence Jordan," *Artforum* (April 2009): 162–69.

© Artforum, March 2012, "Labor of Love," by P. Adams Sitney pp. 55–56.

"Temenos 2012," *Artforum* (October 2012): 67–68.

"Markopoulos and the *Temenos*," *Framework* (Fall 2012): 331–340.

"Andrey Tarkovsky, Russian Experience, and the Poetry of Cinema," *New England Review*, 34, no. 3–4 (2014): 208–241.

Selections from the *The Cantos* by Ezra Pound (copyright 1970 by Ezra Pound), *The New Collected Poems of George Oppen* (edited by Michael Davidson, copyright 2008 by Linda Oppen), and *The Selected Poems of Federico Garcia Lorca* (edited by Donald M. Allen, copyright © 1955, 2005 by New Directions Publishing Corporation) reprinted by permission of New Directions Publishing Corporation.

Selections from *My Vocabulary Did This to Me: The Collected Poetry of Jack Spicer*, edited by Peter Gizzi and Kevin Killian, published by Wesleyan University Press, copyright © 2008 by the estate of Jack Spicer and used here by permission.

Selection from *Stanzas in Meditation* by Gertrude Stein, copyright © 1956, 2010 by the Estate of Gertrude Stein, reprinted by permission of Yale University Press.

Selections from *Life, Life: Selected Poems* by Arseny Tarkovsky (translation copyright © 2007, 2010/ by Virginia Rounding) reprinted by permission of Crescent Moon Publishing.

ARK "Beam 1" by Ronald Johnson reprinted by permission of Derek Johnston for Flood Editions, copyright © 2013.

The Cinema of Poetry

Introduction

AN AUTOBIOGRAPHY OF ENTHUSIASMS

In completing *The Cinema of Poetry*, I have written a version of the book I wanted to read more than fifty years ago, when the magnetic attraction of the two domains, poetry and cinema, first seized hold of my attention. It was 1960. I was sixteen years old. The terms *cine-poem* and *film-poem* were still being used to identify the avant-garde cinema. *Film-poem* was nearly interchangeable with *experimental film*. But the nature and history of avant-garde cinema were not the only things that fascinated me. Larger questions, unanswerable but ineluctable, about film and poetry were regularly discussed in the pages of *Film Culture*, the journal I had just discovered and whose five years of back issues I read avidly, hardly dreaming that two years later I would be invited to join its editorial board.

I had heard that in 1953 Cinema 16 had held a round table on "Cinema and Poetry" in which Maya Deren, Parker Tyler, Willard Maas, Dylan Thomas, and Arthur Miller participated. I knew no one who had actually witnessed it, nor was I able to find a single written account of it. Instead, I read all that I could find by each of the participants, and I tried to imagine what they might have said to each other about cinema and poetry. My regret over having missed the panel was almost as intense as my fantasies of what it must have revealed.

I was not searching for a coherent theoretical formulation of the relationship between the two arts, or even a synthetic statement of positions on the subject. I wanted, instead, to know the range of what had been thought, especially by filmmakers, on the nature of poetry, on its place in cinema, and on its use in particular films. Fortunately, I had access to Yale University's Sterling Library, where I could find Maya Deren's pamphlet, *An Anagram of Ideas on Art, Form, and Film* (1946), and her summa "Cinematography: The Creative Use of Reality" that had just appeared in *Daedalus* (Winter 1960). That same year, Parker Tyler published *The Three Faces of the Film*, containing eighteen essays on "The Art," "The Dream," and "The Cult" of cinema.

Issues of *Film Culture* between April 1958 and Spring 1962 (issues 18–24) nurtured the seeds from which *The Cinema of Poetry* eventually grew. Parker Tyler contributed short studies of avant-garde filmmakers in many of these issues: Brakhage, Peterson, Maas, and one combining Markopoulos, Harrington, and Boultenhouse. When I started *Filmwise*, a mimeographed journal of which each issue was devoted to one or two filmmakers, Tyler graciously extended the series with new essays on Deren, Brakhage, and Markopoulos and allowed me to reprint the one he had given *Film Culture* on Maas. I always regretted that he did not continue in that vein after *Filmwise* came to an end in 1964. In a sense, my articles for *Artforum* (on Morgan Fisher, Peter Hutton, Saul Levine, Ken Jacobs, Nathaniel Dorsky, Jerome Hiler, and Lawrence Jordan—the last three of which have been reworked for this book) sought to exercise what I learned from those early studies by Tyler.

It was *Film Culture* yet again that led me to the theoretical work of Pier Paolo Pasolini. I served on its editorial board beginning with issue 24 (Spring 1962). In that number one of my coeditors, Louis Brigante, translated a text he titled "Literary and Stylistic Figures" (originally "Cinema e letterature: appunti dopo 'Accatone,'" initially published as the appendix to the script of *Accatone* [FM Roma 1961]). It was my first acquaintance with Pasolini's writings. Incidentally, it was also the author's preliminary venture into the film theory that would climax four years later in "Il 'cinema di poesia.'" In "Literary and Stylistic Figures" I discovered an enticing example of the very sort of speculation on the relationship of poetry to narrative cinema I had been hoping to find as a complement to the theoretical work of Tyler and the avant-garde filmmakers (especially Deren, Brakhage, and Markopoulos) regularly published in *Film Culture*. Without that anticipatory lure, I might never have seized upon "Il 'cinema di poesia'" just as I was learning to read Italian in 1965. I have been rereading it, and teaching it, ever since.

Pasolini's critical and theoretical opposition to the notion of the cine-poem, that is to say, to a cinema analogous to that of lyric poetry, commanded serious attention if one were to consider the full range of intersections between the theory of poetry and the theory of film. Yet for two decades his writings on cinema were eclipsed by the temporary triumph of his polemical agonists, the French semioticians and, immediately following their decline, the longer reign of Lacanian theories of spectatorship. Although they lacked the obscurity cultivated by Lacan's followers, Pasolini's arguments were anything but transparent. The labor of unpacking them waited for the scholarship of the turn of the twenty-first century. By then the films to which they referred and in which they were grounded had been forgotten or ignored. I have attempted to restore that context in my opening chapter. For him, the "cinema of poetry" was first of all a historical phenomenon, a rhetorical shift he observed in films by Antonioni, Olmi, Bertolucci, and Godard. As a historical phenomenon, it had a precise political dimension, which meant, for Pasolini, an orientation toward both class and language.

When I began this book, I set myself the task of explicating the context of "Il 'cinema di poesia,'" stressing its relevance in film history and applying it to the films of Ingmar Bergman. Whereas Pasolini had attempted to interpret free indirect discourse in terms of class perspective, I read it psychoanalytically. Bergman too had turned to what Pasolini was calling the cinema of poetry in 1963 with *The Silence*, although Pasolini ignored the modification in his style; he preferred to cite Bergman's 1960 film *The Devil's Eye* as an example of an earlier mode of "poetic" cinema, before the dominance of free indirect point of view. But it was not until *Persona* (1966) that the shift in Bergman's stylistic system could not be ignored. For Tarkovsky, Bergman was already a crucial precursor. He made *Andrey Rublev* the same year as *Persona*, under the influence of earlier Bergman films, but it was with *Mirror* (1975) and the films that follow that he moved into the formal mode Pasolini called "the cinema of poetry." *Persona* itself inflects the imagery and theme of Tarkovsky's *Nostalghia* (1983).

My interest in psychoanalysis coincided with my fascination with avant-garde cinema. When *Film Culture* published Sigmund Freud on "dream work" in issue number 21 (Summer 1960), between essays by Tyler and Luis Buñuel, I rushed to buy a paperback of *The General Introduction to Psychoanalysis,* from which Mekas had excerpted it. However, it was not until fifteen years later, when the psychoanalyst Dr. Leon Balter pointed me to essays on the primal scene by Freudians Jacob Arlow and Henry Edelheit, that my work on the poetics of Ingmar Bergman and Andrey Tarkovsky slowly began to take shape.

In reviewing the latent sources for this book, I was naturally surprised to realize how these formative influences have clung to my critical imagination and played out over half a century. But even more than that, I was astonished to find, in rereading Tyler's *The Three Faces of the Film* for the first time in fifty-two years, the stimulus of my entire critical project. For there I discovered *in nuce* the principles of the film analysis I have practiced over the past five decades.[1] I had forgotten that Tyler points his reader to the centrality of his essay on *Dead of Night*, "Film Form and Ritual as Reality" (orig. *Kenyon Review*, 1948). In that chapter he interprets the common elements of the frame story and its several embedded episodes as an allegory of filmmaking and film viewing:

> What I wish to point out about these independent minor plots is the significance of their *form* rather than of their *substance*. We can analytically identify their substance, as I say, with pathological mental phenomena. The peculiarity of their form in this movie, internally connected with the over-all plot (itself explicable on psychoanalytic grounds), is *that the supernatural element can in all cases be interpreted in terms of film itself, that is, in terms of its technical forms, its quality of illusion.*[2]

Then he reads the opening of a curtain and the view through a window, in one episode, as a metaphor for the film screen; a magical mirror, in a second episode, as a declaration of the reflexivity of the screen; the ventriloquist's dummy, in the third and crucial episode, as the paradigm of a film actor; and the architect around whose dream the whole film circulates as representing the filmmaker.

It is no accident that the strongest critic of the avant-garde cinema of the 1940s and 1950s was also the first great psychoanalytic interpreter of cinema at large. However, it was Tyler's defense of the film-poem that brought me to reread his book after such a long time. In the chapter "Dream Structure: The Basis of Experimental Film," which he wrote specifically for *The Three Faces of the Film*, we find the following reflections on "the cine-poem":

> The orthodox criticism of so-called "Surrealist craziness" in these films is that, however ingenious or "pretty," this dominant element divorces itself from "reality." I would ask: Is a poem "real"? And answer: Yes, but it is seldom "realistic," even in narratives, for normally it uses many figures of speech, time-elisions (equivalent to a type of montage), and as a rule follows no rigid logical or temporal order. Modern poetry is especially complex and "irregular"; its basic order, like that of dreams, is the psychic order of association and suggestibleness. A "poem," one might remark, is what a cine-poem normally sets out to be.... [3]
>
> ... It is a truism that the film camera is active as well as passive; that all we know as "film technique" is a product of cinematic inventiveness and manipulation formally parallel with the structural theory of actual magic. But cannot this widely known faculty of the camera to imitate magic, dreams, and hallucinations—cavalierly used by Hollywood as it pleases—be used to express reality primarily as *imaginative* reality, as poetry, and—in that visual style to which Experimental films give prominence—particularly a sort of dance ritual, a ritualistic pantomime? The only element the dream finds necessary to reach order is *rhythm*. Art supplies this.... [4]
>
> ... [P]oetic creators in all media have perennially "dreamt strange dreams" as did Psyche of Greek legend, the subject of one of Gregory Markopoulos' films, and enriched vision with eternal ambiguity thereby. In dreams and spontaneous wild imaginings, man hunts down his innermost secrets, and by ritualizing this vein of the imagination, grows familiar with his inward, less conspicuous self....On the contrary [to the dream sequence in Hitchcock's film of psychoanalysis, *Spellbound*], in the work of the Experimental film makers, the same sort of supernatural or magical condition as operated in the dream-sequence is used, without psychoanalysis, as the means *through which the protagonists are able to recognize their ultimate desires*. To know, as an audience, this supreme distinction, we must learn to interpret the symbols in Experimental films not as psychoanalytic, but as *poetic*, material. [5]

Toward the end of 1963 Jonas Mekas entrusted two issues of *Film Culture* (numbers 29 and 30) to me. The latter was entirely devoted to the first publication of

Stan Brakhage's *Metaphors on Vision*. The other contained everything I could assemble at the time relating to poetry and cinema: articles by Willard Maas, Sidney Peterson, Charles Boultenhouse, poems by Parker Tyler (who also contributed an essay) and Jonas Mekas, an essay by the poet Michael McClure on Brakhage, and above all the text of the Cinema 16 round table.[6] Amos Vogel had allowed me to borrow the precious wire recordings for one night. I typed and edited the first of the two sessions into one as I was listening to it. (My hasty, amateur transcription contains several errors. The symposium as a whole can now be heard on http://www.youtube.com/watch?v=HA-yzqykwcQ.)

Ken Kelman wrote "Film as Poetry" especially for that issue. He discussed the opening dream in *Sawdust and Tinsel* (aka *The Naked Night*): "In this, one of the greatest passages in all film, we are presented with an apocalyptic vision, in which a clown and his bear-trainer wife become transfigured into symbolic creatures of poetry."[7] Kelman's essay, together with Pasolini's remarks on *The Devil's Eye* in "Il 'cinema di poesia'" and Noel Burch's discussion of *Persona* in his *Theory of Film Practice*,[8] confirmed for me the relevance of Bergman's vision in a discussion of this matter, despite the filmmaker's silence on the question of poetry.

The present book is not merely an isolated return to the obsessive concerns of my initiatory period as a critic. Poetry and cinema have been central to all of my books except *Vital Crises in Italian Cinema*. Romantic poetry (especially that of Blake, Wordsworth, and Shelley) plays a crucial role in *Visionary Film*. In *Modernist Montage* I wrote on Milton, Mallarmé, Desnos, Khlebnikov, Stein and Olson. *Eyes Upside Down* returned to the subject matter of *Visionary Film* with an emphasis on the American artistic and literary tradition, with massive doses of Emerson (on poetry) and Whitman and attention to Nin, W. C. Williams, the Language poets, and the French poet Paul Valéry. The relationship of *Visionary Film* to *Eyes Upside Down* corresponds crudely to one between *Modernist Montage* and this book.

It is likely that fewer readers will read this book from beginning to end than turn to individual chapters for the discussions of particular filmmakers and their films. This is to be expected, insofar as my work has always been centered on the interpretation of specific films and texts. Nevertheless, it might be useful for such readers to have an overview of a number of interlocking themes and theses that run through the book. So I shall set out in capsule form the gist of each of the nine chapters. In this distillation I have been greatly assisted by the reports on the manuscript by the two anonymous reviewers solicited by Oxford University Press. Their insights have generously given me perspectives on my project that I might otherwise have missed.

The argument of *The Cinema of Poetry* begins as a response to Pasolini's essay from which I take my title. There the filmmaker adapts the literary device of "free indirect discourse" (which accentuates the subjective point of view in "objective" prose narratives) to "free indirect point of view" as the signal

mode of ambitious narrative cinema in the early 1960s. In Pasolini's formulation the subjective perspective does not correspond to the point-of-view shot
of earlier cinema but to a range of rhetorical tropes *indirectly* linking the whole
film to the perspective of its protagonist. Consequently, the film spectator is
drawn into the mental states and even the dreams of a character. Without in-
tending it, Pasolini thereby broke down the conventional distinction between
the self-conscious, montage-oriented, avant-garde cinema and the European
realist cinema, as André Bazin theorized it, with its emphasis on the long take
and depth of focus. Pasolini even privileged the sequence shot in his taxonomy
of poetic tropes. The sequence shot is a long take, usually entailing camera
movement, that incorporates the elements of establishing shots, close-ups, and
medium shots without the breakdown of montage. At times, it even replaces
shot-countershot exchanges, as, famously, in Carl Th. Dreyer's *Ordet* (1955)
and *Gertrud* (1964).

The density and allusiveness of Pasolini's text requires careful analysis. He
supports his radical case for the historical shift in narrative film style with
extraordinary claims for the semiotic nature of reality itself. Gilles Deleuze
was the only major theoretician of cinema to acknowledge the importance of
Pasolini's position. He propounded a similar historical shift, locating it more
than a decade earlier, from what he called "the movement-image" to "the
time-image." Deleuze grounded his argument in an ontological claim (drawn
from a fusion of Henri Bergson's and C. S. Peirce's writings) even more radical
than Pasolini's: that light and movement are the primary factors of the material
world and that perception precedes perceiving agents.

In subsequent theoretical articles Pasolini elaborated on principles inherent in "Il 'cinema di poesia.'" As I emphasize in "Poetry and the American
Avant-Garde Cinema," he clarified the previously unstated idea that for him
cinema has inherent affinities to narrative poetry and resists the lyric. Yet he
introduces the notion of "a 'structure that wants to be another structure,'"
which accounts for extended passages of lyric within a narrative film (among
other structures). Although he never addresses directly the suggestion that the
"stylemes" of the "cinema of poetry" can often operate on a barely conscious
level, the attention he gives to nuances of color, reframing of an otherwise
insignificant object, and the entries and exits of characters in the frames of *Il
deserto rosso* might have escaped the notice of a less astute observer. To illuminate these implicit dimensions of Pasolini's text, I have discussed in more
detail than Pasolini did the films to which he alludes. This exfoliation entails
the speculation that passages in the work of Bertolucci and Godard exemplify
structures "that want to be other structures."

The next chapter, on Dimitri Kirsanoff's 1926 masterpiece, *Ménilmontant*,
challenges Pasolini's historical schema by showing how elaborately the
tropes of free indirect point of view orchestrate this narrative of the life of
two orphan sisters from rural France in lower-class Paris. The ambiguities

and ellipses in the cinematic narrative come to represent uncertainties and confusions in the perspectives of the sisters as they learn to negotiate the perils of urban lowlife after the traumatic loss of their parents. Kirsanoff's technique requires the spectator to attend closely to a range of innovative figures of montage whose meanings are frequently suspended until later in the film.

"Ingmar Bergman's Primal Scene," which follows, considers *The Silence, Cries and Whispers*, and *Fanny and Alexander* as examples of the "cinema of poetry." Bergman's model would be the dramatic poem rather than narrative poetry. This is most explicit in the extensive passages from *Hamlet* in *Fanny and Alexander*. But it is more subtly manifested in what the psychoanalyst Henry Edelheit called "libidinal theater": the variety acts and puppet play of *The Silence*, the magic lantern performances of *Cries and Whispers* and *Fanny and Alexander*, and the latter's climactic exploration of the puppets and magical curiosities of Isak's shop. Whereas the psychoanalytic current was latent in Pasolini's theory, it is manifest in Bergman's version of the "cinema of poetry." Thus I use psycho-analytic literature (Bruno Bettelheim's *The Uses of Enchantment*, Jacob Arlow's "The Revenge Motif in the Primal Scene," and Edelheit's "Crucifixion Fantasies and Their Relation to the Primal Scene" and "Mythopoeisis and the Primal Scene"—See notes 3 and 4 to Chapter 3.) to explore how Bergman marshals a cinematic indirect discourse to articulate the subjectivity of his protagonists. In the case of Bergman, Pasolini's historical argument is pertinent: in the early 1960s his cinema demonstrated a stylistic transformation in which oneiric and realistic elements merged; the domains of dream and reality ceased to be clearly circumscribed (as they had been in *Wild Strawberries* [1957]).[9]

Bergman rarely mentions poets or poetry. Yet from the few times he does we can glean that he associated poetry with the dissolution of narrative, as when he speaks of the pretitle sequence of *Persona* as a poem. Similarly, he writes in *Images: My Life in Film* of the failed plan for *Face to Face*: "it would have been a sacrosanct cinematic piece of poetry...Here, finally, all forms of storytelling are dissolved"[10] and of the genesis of *Cries and Whispers*: "I believe that the film—or whatever it is—consists of this poem: a human being dies, but, as in a nightmare, gets stuck halfway through and pleads for tenderness, mercy, deliverance, something...I believe this is the poem or the invention, or whatever you want to call it".[11] The freedom from storytelling that the poem represents for Bergman leads ineluctably to overcoming his "reluctance" to touch "on a number of my own inner conflicts..." (*Images*, p. 70).

In Bergman's films, the cinematic free indirect point of view is the site of the coalescence of autobiographical poetry with the perspectives of his pro-tagonists. For Pasolini such a fusion can only mean that the filmmaker is con-fessing his identification with his "neurotic, bourgeois" characters. Andrey Tarkovsky, who was profoundly influenced by Bergman's art, did not share his precurser's "reluctance" to let fiction fuse with autobiography. In contrast to

Bergman, he had an intense and explicit relationship to poetry. So, in the final chapter of this book's first part, "Andrey Tarkovsky's Concept of Poetry," I draw on the filmmaker's writings to examine his claim that poetry is fundamental to the nature of cinema.

He wrote, "the proper viewing of film requires the spectator to organize the disparate elements of film by intuiting the poetic linkages of its construction, guided by the fundamental metonymy of cinematic images." For this filmmaker poetic thinking weaves an intuitive, associative web within the infrastructures of his films. More than projecting the indirect point of view of his protagonists (although it does do that as well), poetic thinking "sculpts time," revealing "otherwise indiscernible movements of Being." The primary influence on his concept of poetry was the work of his father, the poet Arseny Tarkovsky. In *Mirror* he not only offers a thinly disguised cinematic autobiography but also incorporates at crucial moments his father's voice reading his own poems.

He also incorporates documentary images to mark the passage of historical time. However, Tarkovsky's quarry is ontological rather than psychological. His preference for using sequence shots stems from his intuitive sense of a connection between the articulations of temporality available to a filmmaker and the nature of the poet's primal apprehension of reality. The factual time that cinema, alone of all the arts, is able to "imprint" on a film is a "cluster" that brings together the very linkages Pasolini reads as tropes of free indirect point of view. But for Tarkovsky, the temporality that cinema reveals is what dictates the rhythm and the editing of particular films, rather than the other way around. So, in chapter 4, I attempt to show what this poetics means for *Mirror* and *Nostalghia*.

The second part of *The Cinema of Poetry* proposes overviews of the careers of a number of American avant-garde filmmakers. In the prefatory essay, "Poetry and the American Avant-Garde Cinema," I return to Pasolini to show how his viewing of an exhibition of the New American Cinema challenged his account of poetry in film. He responded by denying the aesthetic viability of a cinematic analog to lyrical poetry. The chapters that follow describe the works of filmmakers who embraced the very models Pasolini repudiated. Each of these chapters marks the affinities of the filmmakers for particular poets: Joseph Cornell for French symbolists (especially Mallarmé), Federico Garcia Lorca, and Emily Dickinson; Lawrence Jordan for Robert Duncan, Michael McClure, and H.D.; Stan Brakhage for Gertrude Stein, Ezra Pound, Robert Duncan, and Ronald Johnson; Nathaniel Dorsky for John Ashbery, George Oppen, and Jack Spicer; and Jerome Hiler for Ashbery and Shakespeare. For Gregory Markopoulos the poets of classical Greece were essential, as was the structure of the Greek language itself.

Unlike the four filmmakers of the first part of this book, I have known all those of the second part personally. Consequently, I have drawn on our conversations as liberally as I cite and analyze what they have written. The first filmmaker I discuss in the second part of the book is the collage artist Joseph Cornell. He was an avid filmgoer, and he amassed a large collection of 16mm films, some of which he reedited into films of his own. He also employed filmmakers Rudy Burckhardt, Stan Brakhage, and Lawrence Jordan to photograph scenes under his direction. As an adult convert to Christian Science, he made artworks that instantiated Mary Baker Eddy's claim: "That which material sense calls intangible is found to be substance." His conception of cinema entailed various aesthetic mediations of visual experience to invoke the intangible. I discuss a scenario he wrote and illustrated with stereoptic plates ("M. Phot"), an essay he wrote about Hedy Lamarr, some of his collage films, and others that he conceived and directed. For Cornell, to encounter an object in fullness is to acknowledge its evanescent temporality, that is to say, its absence or its recession into the past. When he reedited Hollywood genre films and documentaries, he instilled the characters he found in them with what Pasolini thought of as free indirect point of view, transforming all the images he retained of the original drama into the character's dreamlike associations. Sometimes when he directed a film he organized the shots as if they were the impressions of a poet (Lorca, Dickinson) wandering through his favorite New York neighborhoods.

Lawrence Jordan, the focus of the sixth chapter, worked with Joseph Cornell, helping him give shape to several collage films and to incorporate lines from Lorca's "Your Childhood in Menton" into his *A Legend for Fountains*. That experience may have sparked Jordan to adapt H. D.'s "Hermetic Definition" to film. But unlike Cornell, Jordan did his major work in cutout animations. In both his animated and live-action films the filmmaker "transforms" his images into a dilation of time in which "the so-called Present moment is always the same moment." Whereas Cornell pushed his films toward evocations of evanescence, Jordan sought to manifest his trinity of "time/Moment/change" through the rhythms of editing and camera movement to a paradoxical image of "timelessness." I read his "alchemical autobiography," *Sophie's Place*, as a poem of his aesthetic education, or election, as an artist, particularly under the tripart guidance of Cornell, the poet Robert Duncan, and the collage artist Jess. Duncan's own "essential autobiography" instructed Jordan to accept his spontaneous thoughts and free associations as instruments for the discovery of "an enduring design" in his work. Later, in his *H. D. Trilogy*, he displaced the self from the center of his work through a version of "free indirect point of view" in which the words of H. D.'s poem, the perspectives of a woman wandering through Greek and Roman sites, and the perceptions of the filmmaker coincide and separate.

Stan Brakhage was a high school friend of and collaborator with Jordan. He, too, assisted Joseph Cornell and was tutored by Robert Duncan. His relationship to poetry was so intense and complex that the chapter devoted to him, the longest in this book, is a mere sketch of its intricacy. After outlining the course of his early career and the massive influence of both Gertrude Stein and Ezra Pound on his cinematic poetics, I concentrate on two serial projects, both tetralogies: the "Faust" films he made between 1987 and 1989 and the "Vancouver Island films" of 1991, 1994, 2000, and 2002.

Brakhage had made more than 200 films, the great majority of them silent, before the "Faust" series. So his employment of voice-over in the first, second, and fourth of them was a radical departure into narration and free indirect discourse. In turning to the myth of Faust, Brakhage was updating an abandoned project from his youth, originally inspired by Duncan's masque, *Faust Foutu* (in which Jordan played Faust). The dissolution of his first marriage had engendered a crisis in his work that brought him to reexamine his "election" as an artist in the series. Then his second marriage, to Marilyn Jull, a Canadian, brought him several times to Vancouver Island (where he eventually relocated just before his death). There he retraced, yet again, the iconography of his cinematic coming of age.

A prolific writer and theorist, Brakhage formulated the notion of "moving visual thinking" during these years. It is the culmination of his lifelong polemic against the priority of language in perception and thought. Although he never succinctly defines "moving visual thinking," he uses the formula to refer to both the moiling, granular field of liminally visible electrostatic charges that he takes to be the ground of all visual experience and to the perpetual scanning movements and refocusing of the eyes. According to Brakhage, peripheral vision, phosphenes, dream images, and noetic pictures all respond to the biofeedback and "synaptic" pulses of that ground. In an interview with Suranjan Ganguly, he described "moving visual thinking" as "a streaming of shapes that aren't nameable—a vast visual 'song' of the cells expressing their external life."[12] He told the audience of the Millennium Film Workshop: "There's thinking with words, numbers, symbols, which is essentially left-brain thinking; there's thinking musically, gestalt-composition which is right-brain thinking. Then, there are streaming of unnameable, or resistant to nameable, shapes, forms, even colors which I believe is the largest part of thinking. It is composed of the electrical synapting neuron feedback of the entire body. I am attempting to give as close to representation as I can get in the form of film of that kind of thinking. I believe that this is coming direct from the grid upon which all original vision is made."[13]

Despite the profound influence of Cornell and Duncan on Brakhage's thought, he always resisted mystical interpretations of a suprasensible universe beyond the parameters of human perception. Instead, he drew from the unlikely fusion of Gertrude Stein and Charles Olson a poetics of bodily dynamism. By the time he came to make the Vancouver tetralogy, he found a similar inspiration in Ronald Johnson's long poem *ARK*. Yet contravening Brakhage's ideological commitment to living poets, I argue that he found in Johnson's poem a restatement of topoi they both inherited from Walt Whitman's sea chants.

The visual tropes of the "Faust" series reflect the filmmaker's earliest films, his psychodramas of the middle and late 1950s, while its theme recalls the poetic enthusiasms of Brakhage's youth: Goethe, Marlowe, Valéry, Duncan. The free indirect discourse of the soundtrack takes up the burden of aligning the concepts of "moving visual thinking" with the imagery of these films. In contrast, the Vancouver series are silent films; their photography, montage, and, in the final film, handpainting on celluloid *presuppose* the principles of the filmmaker's mature theories.

Nathaniel Dorsky and Jerome Hiler began to make films in the shadow of Brakhage's preeminence. Through most of the 1960s they showed each other, and a few other young filmmakers, the footage they were shooting and talked of making films in "open form" in which "the montage moves from shot to shot outside of any other necessities, except of course the accumulation of being." Dorsky was inspired by John Ashbery's poetry in this aspiration. In chapter 8, "Nathaniel Dorsky, Jerome Hiler, and the Polyvalent Film," I trace the evolution of Dorsky's cinema first to the point in 1996 at which he "found a way around Brakhage" (in the words of filmmaker Phil Solomon) with the achievement of that open form that he called "polyvalent film." This led him to a sustained period of productivity: the polyvalent form released and focused the energies driving the previous thirty years of his career. Then I discuss several of his most notable achievements. Hiler's cinematic evolution was as private as Joseph Cornell's. He had continued to shoot films and share them with Dorsky, but he had been loath to finish and exhibit them until enticed by the New York Film Festival in 2011 to complete and show *Words of Mercury*.

In Dorsky's films each shot is a monad; the editing sequence discovers a harmony latent among them. In his book *Devotional Cinema*, he calls the harmony a "balance point" and asserts that it "unveils the transparency of our earthly existence." Hiler, by contrast, works with superimpositions interlarded with monadic shots. There are subtle differences between their versions of open form: Hiler's film is elegiac, whereas Dorsky tends toward celebration.

At the start of their careers, both Dorsky and Hiler were mentored by Gregory Markopoulos to make films outside of the commercial system. He influenced their work, particularly as colorists. Markopoulos himself eventually abandoned the idea of making individual autonomous films. Instead, he reedited nearly everything he had made and shot massive amounts of new material to construct an eighty-hour-long film, *Eniaios*. Furthermore, he insisted that it be exhibited only in a designated site in the mountains of central Peloponnese, Greece, which he called the *Temenos* (the ancient Greek term for a sacred precinct). He was also a prolific writer of visionary film theory, diaries, and annotations of his vast reading, all of which is preserved in the Temenos archives in Zürich.

In the final chapter, "Gregory J. Markopoulos and the Temenos," I examine the filmmaker's reading of Plato and ancient Greek poetry and their influence on his final project in conjunction with an examination of his film theories. Because *Eniaios* has yet to be projected in its entirety, I discuss the various systems he proposed for its organization into twenty-two cycles and look closely at the eight cycles exhibited so far.

I applied Pasolini's ideas of a cinema of poetry to the films organized around the centrality of a protagonist in the first four chapters of this book. The allusions and associations of an entire film were grounded in the free indirect point of view of the betrayed sister in *Ménilmontant*, Johan in *The Silence*, the four women of *Cries and Whispers*, Alexander in *Fanny and Alexander*, and Alexei in *Mirror*. Because free indirect point of view imbued all the images and references in those films with resonant associations, the films were particularly responsive to psychoanalytical interpretation. Above all, the violence (manifest and repressed) and the enigmas figured by the cinematic tropes of Kirsanoff, Bergman, and Tarkovsky made the application of primal scene schemata fruitful.

Conversely, the disappearance of visible protagonists from the screen in many of the films of Jordan, Brakhage, Dorsky, Hiler, and Markopoulos displaced the free indirect point of view to the creative persona of the filmmaker behind the photography and editing (and, in some cases, the voice-over). Often the scenes of instruction and of artistic initiation played roles parallel to those I found for primal scene fantasies in the European narratives. Many of Cornell's films, especially his collage films, and the first two of Brakhage's "Faust" series occupy a transitional stage between these two poles. In all the examples from the American avant-garde cinema, I located a quest through cinematic tropes for a transcendent dimension inaccessible to direct representation. In Cornell's work, it would be called the intangible, Jordan names it timelessness, Brakhage "moving visual thinking," Dorsky (and implicitly Hiler) transparency, and Markopoulos "Eternity."

PART I

Poetry and the Narrative Cinema in Europe

Bernardo Bertolucci: *Prima della rivoluzione* (1963)
Puck's ode to the River Po

Pier Paolo Pasolini and "The 'Cinema of Poetry'"

Pier Paolo Pasolini delivered the initial version of his most widely discussed, and highly controversial, theoretical essay on cinema, "The 'Cinema of Poetry'" ("Il 'cinema di poesia'") at a round table discussion on "Critica e nuovo cinema" during the First Mostra Internazionale di Nuovo Cinema at Pesaro, Italy, May 31, 1965. At that festival none of his colleagues addressed issues of style or semiology in a comparable manner, but in the two years following, the Tavola rotunda at Pesaro followed Pasolini's lead almost exclusively. On both of those occasions he offered extensions and refinements of his theoretical position, with renewed polemical vigor.

Part of the essay appeared in *Film Critica* 156–157 (April–May 1965). The art journal *Marcatrè* (9–20–21–22) included it when it published all the speeches at the Tavola rotunda in 1966. That year Pasolini himself appended the essay to his publication of the script for *Uccellacci e uccellini*. Then, in 1972, he collected his theoretical essays and brief notes on cinema as the concluding section of three in *Empirismo eretico*. The surviving typescript of "Il 'cinema di poesia'" is titled "Di un possible discorso libero indiretto nel cinema" ("Concerning a Possible Free Indirect Discourse in Cinema"). At Pesaro he called it "La mimesi dello sguardo" ("The Mimesis of the Glance"). Although it bears no title at all in the Tavola rotunda presentation in *Marcatrè*, by the time of the earlier *Filmcritica* publication, the essay was called "Il 'cinema di poesia,'" the title it has retained in all its subsequent publications. This history indicates both the centrality of the text for its author and the uncertainty, even for him, of its primary subject.

It has been by far the most elaborately studied of Pasolini's essays on the cinema. The most detailed reading, by John David Rhodes, claims that it is really a study of "art cinema" in the early 1960s. Rhodes's careful charting of the intricate twisting of the argument is impressive. I shall have occasion to refer to it again here. However, I cannot accept his reductive proposition that "poetry" is essentially a placeholder for a narrative genre, which he anachronistically aligned to David Bordwell's 1979 essay "The Art Cinema as a Mode of Film Practice." Long before Rhodes's open-minded and sympathetic engagement with Pasolini's text, a number of critics dismissed its use of semiology, its free play with logic, and its apparent incoherence: Christian Metz, Umberto Eco, Stephen Heath, Pio Baldelli, Emilio Garroni, Gianfranco Bettitini, and Antonio Costa represent a formidable coalition of opponents to Pasolini's first foray into film theory. A decade later its defenders, including Teresa De Lauretis, Gian Pier Brunetta, Sam Rodhie, Roberto Turigliatto, Christopher Wagstaff, and Giuliana Bruno, began to publish reconsiderations of the essay. Most influentially, Gilles Deleuze took up Pasolini's use of free indirect point of view to articulate what he called "the perception-image" in *Cinéma 1: l'Image-Mouvement* (1986). However, he ignores utterly the issue, or metaphor, of poetry in his adaptation of free indirect discourse.

Yet by all accounts "Il 'cinema di poesia'" is a confusing and even contradictory text. Rhodes, writing here of the "opening movement" of the essay, nicely formulates its mode of argument "characterized by the language logic of deductive reasoning, prone to reversals, false dead ends, surprising paths that seem to emerge from the thicket of language."[1] The nature of that thicket might be illuminated if we consider some of the unstated notions on which the essay is grounded. The two domains that are particularly relevant would be Pasolini's evolving ideas about poetry and free indirect discourse.

Pasolini himself wrote poetry in both Friulian and standard Italian. He published nineteen volumes of poetry during his lifetime. He might have thought of his more than twenty volumes of stories, novels, plays, and film scripts as either poetry or prose. Certainly, he would have referred to the seven books of essays he lived to see in print and the two that appeared the year of his death as prose. The distinction between poetry and prose as a function of dividing the work of creative intuition and expression from the arguments of reason reflects the abiding influence of Benedetto Croce on Italian aesthetics. Several of the most astute readers of Pasolini's writings on the cinema have mentioned or expounded upon the residue of Crocean ideas in his theoretical work.[2] For Croce, poetry, as ποίησις (*making*), founds all art. It is the manifestation of an equation between intuition and expression. Furthermore, as the subtitle of his *Estetica* (1902) indicates, he believed that aesthetics is the "science of expression and general linguistics." In a 1935 article he summarized his thought on poetry:

> To poetry is attributed the sphere of the imagination, of dream, of unreality. Such is the generally accepted view, but we cannot merely accept this as it stands. By dint of revision and correction we must show that poetry precedes the distinction between real and unreal... The sphere of poetry is that of sheer quality lacking the predicate of existence; void, therefore, of the thought and criticism which distinguish and thereby convert the world of fancy into the world of reality. The expression of prose is distinguished from the expression of poetry purely and simply, as fancy, poesy, are distinguished from thought, philosophy...

In its character as symbol or sign, prose expression is not properly speaking language, any more than the natural manifestation of feeling is language, the only true language or word being poetic utterance, whence the deep truth in those old sayings that poetry is the mother tongue of humanity, and that "poets came into the world earlier than prose-writers."[3]

Heidegger concurs with Croce's identification of poetry as ποίησις when he writes: "*All art*, as the letting happen of the advent of truth of what is, is, as such, *essentially poetry [Dichtung]*."[4]

Pasolini gave the Crocean-Heideggerian position a semiological and Marxist inflection without fundamentally altering the etymological argument. He sees the world in which man finds himself as constituted by poetry. That world perpetually expresses itself in verbal and nonverbal languages. Therefore, in Pasolini's peculiar diction, "poetry" and "expression" are ontological categories before they become terms of artistic semiology. The interplay of these two levels of meaning causes some of the difficulty in reading "Il 'cinema di poesia.'"

A second, and perhaps more thorny, problem arises from Pasolini's use of "free indirect discourse." Although he was conversant with the critical literature on the parameters and the history of this literary technique, and although he had employed it extensively in his novels and stories, his lengthy review of Giulio Herczeg's *Lo stile indiretto libero in italiano* (which includes a discussion of Pasolini's use of the device) deliberately ignores the grammatical details which dominate Herczeg's book and those of his major predecessors. He focuses instead on the class implications of employing free indirect discourse. But in doing so, Pasolini loses sight of the specificity of the technique and treats virtually all narrative as free indirect discourse by compounding it with first-person narration, interior monologue, indirect discourse, and even dialogue. Not content with expanding the idea to include virtually all literature, he writes of Pop Art as free indirect discourse in painting. At this point his conception of free indirect discourse approaches the trope of irony, which theorists from Friedrich Schlegel to Georg Lukács found at the heart of the novel. His review of Herczeg's book, "Intervento sul discorso libero indiretto," appeared in *Paragone* the very month that Pasolini presented the first version of "Il 'cinema di poesia'" at Pesaro. Later, Pasolini included the review in the volume *Empirismo eretico* at the head of the section on "Litteratura" preceding his collection of theoretical essays on cinema.

Many of the points that Pasolini makes in the discussion of Herczeg's book on free indirect discourse have echoes in the discussion of the cinema of poetry. So in the film essay he repeats a version of the claim that "[i]t is certain that every time one has Free Indirect this implies a *sociological consciousness*, clear or otherwise, in the author, which seems to me the fundamental and constant characteristic of the Free Indirect."[5] Furthermore, he contends that it "lends its internal structure to almost every narrative form" (p. 89) so that "entire novels are no more than entire Free Indirects in that either there is a total identification of the author with the character, or the characters are a pseudo-objectification of the author, or the characters are devices for expressing the thesis of the author in a substantially different language, or finally—unconsciously—the characters perfectly inhabit in the same way the social and ideological world of the author (who in this manner often behaves with an arbitrariness conferred on him by his 'superiority')" (pp. 90–91). Finally he invokes "the language of poetry" as one extreme terminus of first-person narration and interior monologue (pp. 88–89). This is clearest in the "post scriptum" (omitted from the definitive text that appears in *Empirismo eretico*), in which he identifies the "crisis of the Free Indirect" as "a problem of Marxism," referring to recent prose texts by Roversi and Volponi as narratives in the language of poetry.[6]

The text of "Il 'cinema di poesia'" begins with a polemical statement of the urgency of seeing cinema as a system of signs: "I believe that it is no longer possible to begin to discuss cinema as an expressive language without at least taking into consideration the terminology of semiotics." Consequently, at first Pasolini apes semiological discourse, distinguishing verbal signs (for which he coins the term *l'insegno* as if he were about to present a systematic taxonomy) from visual signs (*im-segni*). But no sooner does he mention the "lin-sign or language sign," as Barnet and Lawton translate *linsegno,* than he qualifies it by pointing out that an accompanying gesture can change or even reverse the meaning of a word.

So from the start the system of linguistic signs is superimposed onto another system of mimetic signs, which is said to be more original for the cinema: it derives "its own practical possibility of existence" (my translation) from it.

A closer inspection of the opening sentence of the essay would demand a reading that is both more literal and more ironic in the light of what follows. The author is obliged merely to take *some* account of the terminology of semiotics as a starting point of what would be more primarily a discussion of "cinema as an expressive language." Unstated, however, is the conclusion that the obligatory semiological opening is merely a foil for a deeper analysis of the subject. His consideration of the diction of semiology will be confined to the repeated use of the term *syntagma* in the first third of the essay and to making reference to "signs" throughout.

At this moment in his theoretical speculations, Pasolini believed that cinema was fundamentally a visual mode of communication. Later, he will repudiate that claim, calling film an "audio-visual technology." At this stage, however, he is eager to assert that as a mode of visual communication through *im-segni,* cinema represents the world of memory and dreams. The evocation of memory and dreams has several functions. In the first place, it displaces or mediates cinematic images. The referent in a memory or a dream is not present to the subject. There are voluntary acts that can be performed before a present object that often cannot be done to images, such as counting the details—say, the number of houses in a dreamed or remembered village. Certainly one cannot move about at will in a dream or a memory in order to have a clearer view or to examine a detail. Thus, even though he will later provocatively assert that reality expresses itself or writes in *im-segni*, he begins by distinguishing his theory of cinematic mediations from earlier forms of filmic realism.

Furthermore, Pasolini wants to attribute to cinema an oneiric dimension. The dreamlike quality of films has been a recurring theme of film theory since the first decade of cinema. He attributes the artistic success of Buñuel and Dalí's *Un chien andalou* not to its surrealistic program (insofar as he utterly rejects surrealism as a literary movement) but to its dreamlike montage. In this "limit-case," as he calls it, the "poetical quality of its [cinematic] language" is "crazily demonstrated." As Pasolini interprets their achievement, the filmmakers utilized the original poetical dimension of cinema. In one crucial, if extravagant, sentence, he asserts the primal nature of cinematic language: "Tanto la mimica e la realtà bruta quanto i sogni e i meccanismi della memoria, sono fatti quasi pre-umani, o ai limiti dell'umano: comunque pre-grammaticali e additrittura pre-morfologici (i sogni avvengono al livello dell'inconscio, e così i meccanismi mnemonici; la mimica è segno di estrema elementarità civile ecc.)"[7] (As much gesture and brute reality as dreams and the mechanisms of memory, [the bases of cinematographic language] are pre-human facts, or at the limits of the human: in any case [they are] pre-grammatical and absolutely pre-morphological (dreams form at the level of the unconscious, and so do the mnemonic mechanisms; gesture is a sign of extremely elementary social behavior, etc.)).

His positing of the primitive nature of cinematic language thus reflects Croce's theories and ideas of the origins of speech inflected with a psychoanalytic nuance. Even more directly than from Croce, these notions derive from the speculations of Giambattista Vico, whose work Croce revived and extolled. Significantly to the domains of gesture, dreams, and memories, Pasolini has added "brute reality." But he will soon qualify that.

He distinguishes the activity of the poet from that of the filmmaker by means of the metaphor of a dictionary; that is to say, the writer draws his words from a finite pool with traditional meanings, but the filmmaker creates his im-signs from chaos. Yet these im-signs have "a common patrimony." Throughout the first part of the essay he returns to the image of a railroad train as conventionally represented in films: "All of us, with our eyes, have seen the famous steam engine with its wheels and its pistons. If we see it in the real world, 'it says something to us'" (HE, p. 171).

Here the function of memory in films plays a role. Because we have seen trains, we understand the imagery of the engine and pistons in a film. But now he will elaborate on the complexity of our associations and interpretations of the train in different contexts:

Its apparition in a barren wasteland, for example, *tells us* how touching mankind's industriousness is, and how enormous is the capacity of industrialized society and, therefore, of capitalists to annex territories of new consumers. At the same time, it *tells* some of us that the train engineer is an exploited man who nevertheless performs his job with dignity for a society which is what it is, even if it is his exploiters who are identified with it. As object the steam engine tells us all these things as a possible cinematographic symbol in direct communication with us; and indirectly, with others, as part of the common visual patrimony.[8]

This extraordinary fantasia on the significance of a filmed train sets up the conclusion that "brute reality" is an insufficient description of the fourth element in his synthesis: "'Brute objects' therefore do not exist in reality. All are sufficiently meaningful in nature to become symbolic signs." The "syntagmas" the filmmaker chooses when he films people, places, and things *"have an already lengthy and intense pregrammatical history."* (HE, p. 171; Pasolini's italics.) This is the first formulation of what will later become the most controversial irony of Pasolini's film theory, the idea of cinema as the written language of reality in which "brute objects" are always expressing themselves. Insofar as "Il 'cinema di poesia'" is concerned, the four roots of cinematic discourse—mimetic gestures, dreams, memories, and brute reality—are all interlocked primal language systems. He sometimes calls the images they produce *archetypes*, which he further defines as "habitual and thus unconscious observation of the environment, gestures, memory, dreams" (p. 171).

The poetic basis of cinema entails a double movement, according to Pasolini. On the one hand, *"Lo strumento linguistic su sui si impianta il cinema è dunque di tipo irrazionalistico*: e questo spiega la profunda qualità onirica del cinema, e anche la sua assoluta e imprescindibile concretezza, diciamo, oggetuale."[9] (*The linguistic instrumentality on which the cinema is based is therefore of the irrational kind*: and this reflects the profoundly dreamlike quality of the cinema, and also its absolute and ineluctable specificity; let's call it, its objectability.) The irrational, premorphological, almost prehuman language of cinema is a modern reemergence of the irrational "poetic wisdom" of primitive humanity as described in Vico's *Scienza Nuova*. On the other hand, corresponding to Vico's concept of the *sensus communis* as a "mental dictionary," the im-signs already have accumulated a long "pregrammatical" history that accounts for the elaborate range of connotations they evoke. He hesitates and waffles about calling these connotations "etymologies." In short, the linguistic status of the *poeticità* at the heart of cinema is problematic for Pasolini.

However, neither the semiology of cinema nor the underlying poetry of the medium is the author's quarry in this essay. He is out to engage the common visual rhetoric he sees operating in the films shown at the Mostra del Nuovo Cinema, its raison d'être. Before hitting his stride, he must invoke a version of Croce's discrimination between the languages of prose and poetry. So he divides the "cinematographic tradition" into the "language of poetry" and the "language of prose," or at least that of a "language of prose narrative," arguing that the narrative tradition has suppressed until now the inherent "language of poetry" at the base of cinema. Yet the medium did not quite lose "all its irrational, oneiric, elementary, and barbaric elements." Rather, they were "forced below the level of consciousness," where they could be deployed for shock effect or persuasion.

In a discussion with Oswald Stack, Pasolini presented his thesis with uncharacteristic clarity:

> In my view the cinema is substantially and naturally poetic, for the reasons I have stated: because it is dreamlike, because it is close to dreams, because a cinema sequence and a sequence of memory or of a dream—and not only that but the things in themselves—are profoundly poetic: a tree photographed is poetic, a human face photographed is poetic because physicity is poetic in itself, because it is an apparition, because it is full of mystery, because it is full of ambiguity, because it is full of polyvalent meaning, because even a tree is a sign of a linguistic system. But who talks through a tree? God, or reality itself. Therefore the tree as a sign puts us in communication with a mysterious speaker. Therefore, the cinema by directly reproducing objects physically, etc. etc. is substantially poetic. This is one aspect of the problem, let's say pre-historic, almost pre-cinematographic. After that we have the cinema as a historical fact, as a means of communication, and as such it too is beginning to develop into different subspecies, like all communications media. Just as literature has a language [*lingua*] for prose and a language [*lingua*] for poetry, so does the cinema. That's what I was saying. In this case you must forget that the cinema is naturally poetic because it is a type of poetry, I repeat, which is pre-historic, amorphous, unnatural. If you see a bit of the most banal western ever made or any old commercial film, if you look at it in a non-conventional way, even a film like that will reveal the dreamlike and poetic which there is physically and naturally in the cinema, but this is not the cinema of poetry. The cinema of poetry is the cinema which adopts a particular technique just as a poet adopts a particular technique when he writes verse. If you open a book of poetry, you can see the style immediately, the rhymes and all that: you see the language [*lingua*] as an instrument, or you count the syllables of a verse. The equivalent of what you see in a text of poetry you can also find in a cinema text, through the stylemes, i.e. through the camera movements and the montage. So to make films is to be a poet.[10]

In the text of "Il 'cinema di poesia'" the distinction between films emphasizing the language of poetry and films emphasizing the language of prose led Pasolini to a further discrimination between im-signs that engender "communication with ourselves" and those archetypes directed primarily to others. Images of dreams and memories constitute the first category; gestures and "visually observed reality" make up the second. In terms of the poetics of filmmaking, this would mean that a filmmaker somehow invests his images with his subjectivity, redefined as his "ideological and poetic vision of reality at that moment." However, the "brief stylistic history of cinema" has evolved so that the subjective visions congeal into conventional syntagmas, having quickly created "a tradition of the 'language of narrative prose'" by suppressing the immanent poetry of cinema. Within that tradition the poetic and the prosaic tendencies were interlocked. Yet—and here Pasolini finally comes to the heart of his argument—since the end of the Second World War the narrative cinema, or at least the most ambitious narrative films, have tended toward the "language of poetry." At the time of the first Mostra del Nuovo Cinema Nuovo Pasolini thought that tendency had reached a climax. From this point until the end of the essay, the author focuses on the stylistic characteristics of these recent, radically poetic films and reflects on the importance of the phenomenon.

At this point Pasolini makes an astonishing move: after posing the question "how is the 'language of poetry' theoretically explicable and practically possible in cinema?" he proposes that it is through a filmic version of free indirect point of view. For the audience at Pesaro in 1965, or for the readers of the text of his presentation as it appeared in *Filmcritica* and *Marcatrè*, presumably unfamiliar with his long review of Herczeg's book (not yet published at the time of the Mostra del Nuovo Cinema), this proposition must have seemed extraordinarily strange; for free indirect discourse is an issue in the criticism of prose narrative, rather than of poetry, even though Pasolini immediately and elliptically claims that Dante used the technique in *Inferno*.[11]

Without explaining his peculiar use of the term, he leaps right away into a discussion of the sociological implications of free indirect discourse as a "pretext" for an author to express "a particular interpretation of the world" indirectly through a character. The very indirection of this method is what drives the filmmaker to incorporate massively the "language of poetry" (HE, p. 176). Although Pasolini held an antigrammatical interpretation of free indirect discourse and showed no interest in stylistic details when discussing Herczeg's work, he is determined to lay out the stylistic taxonomy of what he calls "free indirect point of view" when it comes to cinema.

In the first place, he identifies the point-of-view shot with direct discourse (exemplified, significantly, by a citation of Dante's *Purgatorio* 4.136–139). His cinematic example comes from Carl Dreyer's *Vampyr*, in which a window in the lid of a coffin allows the filmmaker to alternate shots of the corpse carried to its burying place with the corpse's point-of-view shots of the undertakers and the moving landscape through the coffin window. The acknowledged "extravagance" of these subjective shots provides a marked contrast to the more elusive identification of other "free indirect point-of-view shots." To prepare his audience for his elaboration of that category, he compares free indirect discourse to interior monologue. In literature, he points out, the author of interior monologues can take advantage of the "abstract terms" stored in his dictionary. Cinema utterly lacks that power of abstraction, he asserts. Therefore, he concludes, "a 'free indirect point-of-view shot' will never correspond perfectly to the interior monologue in literature" (p. 177). Furthermore, the various linguistic means a writer has to indicate the peculiar language of a character have no cinematic equivalent. The camera cannot distinguish the way one character looks at things from the perspective of another or from the gaze of the filmmaker. Only a "stylistic" strategy can generate tropes to suggest such differences. "Thus," he reasons, "the fundamental characteristic of the 'free indirect point-of-view shot' is not linguistic but stylistic. And it can therefore be defined as an interior monologue lacking both the explicit conceptual elements and the explicit abstract philosophical element...In fact, it causes it to free the expressive possibilities compressed by the traditional narrative convention through a sort of return to the origins until the original oneiric, barbaric, irregular, aggressive, visionary quality of cinema is found through its technical devices" (p. 178). The repetition of the epithets—oneiric, barbaric, and so forth—underlines the author's manner of stating that the inherent "language of poetry" latent within cinema is actually identical with what he has been calling "free indirect point of view." The burden of the subsequent section of the essay is to delineate the specific "technical devices" that manifest the "language of poetry."

It was this latter part of the essay that appeared first in print in nos. 156–157 of *Filmcritica* (April–May 1965).[12] With its detailed allusions to specific films and film techniques, it would have been the section of the essay most interesting to the journal's readers. Actually, the paragraphs devoted to his primary film example, Antonioni's *Il deserto rosso,* came almost unchanged from the Communist journal *Vie Nuove,* in which Pasolini conducted *dialoghi* with its readers nearly every week between June 25, 1960, and September 30, 1965. On January 7, 1965, he answered a letter from a self-described "communista cristiana" distressed that Antonioni's film had won the Golden Lion at the Venice Film Festival instead of Pasolini's *Il vangelo secondo Matteo.* In his answer Pasolini graciously defended Antonioni's film, admitting that until *Il deserto rosso* he had little esteem for his colleague's formalism. But now because Antonioni no longer depicted alienated characters from a "vaguely sociological" perspective but rather thoroughly identified his own aestheticism with the neurotic viewpoint of his heroine, he made what struck Pasolini as "a very beautiful film." Comparing Antonioni's technique to that of an author's using free indirect discourse, Pasolini coined the expression—which he never used again— "visione libera indiretta" for Antonioni's breakthrough. Significantly, he does not refer to this technique in terms of the "language of poetry," but he does call filmmakers "poets" when explaining the technique:

> Through this stylistic mechanism, Antonioni freed himself: finally he could see the world with *his own* eyes, because he identified his own delirious aesthetic vision with the vision of a neurotic woman. It's true that such an identification is somewhat arbitrary; but the arbitrariness in this case is a part of his poetic freedom: having once discovered the liberating mechanism, the poet can get drunk on his freedom. It doesn't matter that it is a fallacy to make his "frames" of the world as it appears to a real neurotic coincide with the world as it appears to a neurotic poet; to the extent that this fallacious operation has become the non-poetic and uncultivated residue of the film, to that very degree on the contrary his "poetic drunkenness" is appropriate. The important point would be that there is a substantial possibility for an analogy between the neurotic vision of the poet and that of his neurotic character. There's no doubt that the possibility for an analogy of this kind exists. And its contradiction is then a cultural fact, which instead of objectifying itself in the character, subjectifies herself in the author. Therefore precisely through the extraordinary formalistic success this time the imposition of the sociological theme of alienation isn't in the least fallacious or worthless.[13]

It is quite possible that the idea of "free indirect point-of-view shots" first came to Pasolini when he saw *Il deserto rosso*, for he interprets Antonioni's experimental use of color as the perspective of the explicitly neurotic protagonist, although in both the *Vie Nuove* text and in "Il 'cinema di poesia'" he uses a paralipsis ("I don't want to linger on those aspects of the film which are universally recognized as 'poetic'") to spell out those color effects while pretending to pass them by.

In examining Pasolini's citations of technical examples, it is important to remember that he did not have access to copies of the film when writing his theoretical essays. Before the advent of video reproduction, all writers on film had to depend on their memories for details. Despite minor errors, Pasolini was remarkably accurate in his recollections. He recalls an image of the violet flowers outside the apartment of a worker Corrado seeks to recruit "aggressively in focus" as he leaves. This isn't the case. But Pasolini's attention to the reframing of the flowers and their reappearance later (actually in the background) is an astute observation of Antonioni's use of details; his interpretation of the reframing as neurotic obsession is a brilliant piece of criticism. The same can be said of the other two examples: the shift of color stock for what he calls a dream sequence, which may be that or Giuliana's recollection as she tells a story from her childhood to her son. He dropped the speculation that the filmmaker had used a 300mm telephoto lens here to give the episode a documentary "and therefore realistic" emphasis when he rewrote the text for

Pesaro. Finally, when he attributes "an insane pan from the bottom up along an electric blue stripe on the whitewashed wall of the warehouse" to "a deep, mysterious, and—at times—great intensity in the formal idea that excites the fantasy of Antonioni" (pp. 178–179), he seems to have found a perfect example of a free indirect point-of-view shot, unless we assign the camera movement as a countershot to the distracted glance of Corrado (which it might be in the somewhat ambiguous montage). In that case, the shot would be an instance of what he analogizes as "direct discourse" without any reference to the neurotic protagonist. Similarly, many of the mysterious shots of fleshlike rock formations in the so-called "dream" sequence might be construed as point-of-view shots as seen by the girl as she swims around them. Perhaps his extension of free indirect discourse to cover an entire work, of fiction or of film, is intended to bracket precisely such ambiguous cases.

The example of Antonioni, however, remains problematic, for Pasolini asserts that he "does not want to linger" on the particularly "poetic" examples because, more fundamentally, two aspects of "an extremely meaningful stylistic operation" can be seen in *Il deserto rosso*. They are (1) successive reframings of the same object or field from different distances, with different lenses, or from slightly different angles, and (2) camera setups in which characters enter and leave the otherwise empty frame. These strategies can be found abundantly in Antonioni's films, but they are actually less frequent and less prominent in *Il deserto rosso* than in several of the black-and-white films that preceded it. Yet in those films, which Pasolini rejected for their formalism and their concentration on the problems of advanced modern societies, he would not have been able to locate a patently neurotic protagonist with whom the filmmaker's aesthetic vision might be identified. In sum, Pasolini seems to reinvigorate his earlier disquisition of Antonioni in "Il 'cinema di poesia'" because he needs the figure of the neurotic protagonist to make his peculiar interpretation of free indirect point of view explicit and he needs the obsessive use of reframing and entrances and exits around empty space for his taxonomy of the tropes of the "cinema of poetry."

In some ways Bernardo Bertolucci's *Prima della rivoluzione* serves both of his purposes better, but he did not have ready-made an analysis of its stylistics at the time he was preparing his Pesaro talk. The three paragraphs he devotes to this film compare and contrast the meaning of its "obsessive immobility of the frame" to Antonioni's style and introduce an important new notion: that within the film there is "*the temptation to make another film.*" In essence, the other film would be one in which the substantial poetry of the cinema would express itself without the "pretext" of a protagonist and a narrative. Bertolucci provides the locus for this idea because, unlike Antonioni, he does not thoroughly substitute the point of view of his neurotic heroine for his own. Rather "we have a mutual contamination of the worldviews of the neurotic woman and the author. These views, being inevitably similar, are not really distinguishable—they shade into each other; they require the same style" (p. 180).

By avoiding concrete examples of Bertolucci's style, Pasolini alludes to the fixity of his framing images as a catchall category of the language of cinematic poetry: "The immobility of the frame of a piece of reality (the river Parma, the streets of Parma, etc.) testifies to the elegance of a deep and uncertain love, precisely for that piece of reality" (p. 180). He compounds the ambiguity of this stylistic attribution by mentioning "expressively sharp moments in the film" in which the "emphasis [insistenze] of the framing and the montage rhythms," informed by the neorealism of Rossellini and "mythic realism of some un-named young modern masters," by means of editing and unusually long shots, "explodes in a sort of technical scandal."[14] Yet again, Pasolini is a very perceptive and eloquent reader of the film, but his reference to an immobile camera seems inaccurate. Bertolucci shot the streets of Parma and the Po with a dramatically moving camera and even aerial photography from a helicopter. Pasolini's elliptical references to images of the *Prima della rivoluzione* point indirectly to the opening sequences and the remarkable ode to the river and the woods given by the character Puck late in the film, as he decries the immi-nent industrial development of the zone. The highly stylized opening stands out for its avoidance of fixed camera shots. Instead, the narrator, Fabrizio, is introduced first by his voice-over, then by the alternation of moving tele-photo close-ups of him rushing to find a young woman, intercut with views of the city from a moving car or the helicopter. In the opening ten minutes the camera moves in all but ten of the forty-seven shots, although that number includes two sequence shots containing substantial fixed moments. The first of the fixed images does not appear until the fourteenth shot, and after that, most of the fixed images are quick inserts, between one and four seconds long.

Puck's envoi to the Po and its woods comes an hour and twenty minutes into the film, and its twenty-seven shots last only two minutes and ten sec-onds: Bertolucci rapidly moves between Puck wading into the river as he addresses a boatman, the trees, and the unseen wildlife; a painter naming the things he is painting on his canvas; and images of the fog-bound woods and landscape (including a sequence of three aerial jump cuts). The audio-visual poem within the film ends with the pathos of Puck bidding "Ciao fucile! Ciao fiume! Ciao Puck!" When Pasolini mentions the "elegiac" dimension of Bertolucci's film, he may have had this eloquent episode in mind. It certainly illustrates the "sudden inspiration" tempting the filmmaker to make another film: "It is, in short, the presence of the author, who transcends his film in an abnormal freedom and who constantly threatens to abandon it, detoured by a sudden inspiration which is, finally, the latent inspiration of the love for the poetic world of his own vital experiences" (p. 180).

Actually, we know more than Pasolini tells in "Il 'cinema di poesia'" about what he means when he speaks of the poetry of *Prima della rivoluzione* because he returned to Pesaro the next year for the second Mostra del Nuovo Cinema to follow up his initial theoretical foray with a talk on "The Written

Language of Reality" (originally titled and first published as "La lingua scritta dell'azione"). There he showed an excerpt from Bertolucci's film to exemplify "the language of poetry," contrasting it to the opening shots of Ermanno Olmi's *Tempo si è fermato* in order to use the latter to illustrate "the language of prose." In preparing the talk, Pasolini examined both films on an editing table, so the description of the shots is impeccably accurate. He selected a ninety-second-long sequence of thirteen shots of Gina, the neurotic aunt and lover of the narrator, alone in her bedroom. Ten of these shots are static; two are point-of-view pans of photographs she has laid out on the bed; and one the author describes as a "motionless master shot, and therefore active, but rendered passive by the qualification of the editing, because of the absurdity of the addition with the preceding moneme; followed by the passive movement of the zoom on the bed."[15] In this essay Pasolini introduces the analogy of the "active voice" for continuities of action that do not call attention to themselves through editing or camera peculiarities (which would be markers of the "passive voice"). The jump cuts throughout the passage render the sequence passive, as does the unmotivated zoom to the bed, after Gina leaves the room at the end of the ninth shot. These indications of the "passive voice" show the sequence to be made in "the language of poetry," whereas the "active voice" that provides continuities in Olmi's film show it to be "prose… even if a prose gently soaked in 'the poetry of things'" (HE, p. 221).

The focus on Gina and the choice of a sequence without Bertolucci's typical camera movements may be the consequence of Pasolini's desire to retain the two ideas central to his earlier essay: the prevalence of the fixed camera and the free indirect point of view of the neurotic heroine. John David Rhodes, who found the brief discussion of Godard that follows that of Antonioni and Bertolucci in "Il 'cinema di poesia'" "one of the most incisive descriptions of [his] poetics," dissented from Pasolini's statement that "Godard's protagonists are also sick; they are exquisite flowers of the bourgeoisie." Rhodes's point is that "Godard does not need the pretext of the sick protagonist. Rather, Pasolini does if he is going to make his theory of the 'cinema of poetry' stick to Godard."[16] As I have implied, Rhodes's criticism might have been addressed to the interpretation of *Prima della rivoluzione*, perhaps even more cogently than to his reading of Godard; for it seems to me that Pasolini's recognition of how Godard skews the perspective of his early films through the use of obsessive protagonists—middle-class thieves, prostitutes, a stripper, an adulterous wife—is another of his acute critical insights.

The two paragraphs "Il 'cinema di poesia'" devoted to Godard make no mention of a particular film. In an interview with Luigi Faccini and Maurizio Ponzi published in the same issue of *Filmcritica* as the section of "Il 'cinema di poesia,'" Pasolini claimed to have seen very little of Godard's work, although the French filmmaker had released seven feature films and participated in three compilations by that time: "I know Godard and I like his work very much even if until now I have seen only *A bout de souffle* [1961] and *Il nuovo mondo* [1962], the episode of *RoGoPaG* [a compilation film to which Pasolini himself contributed *La ricotta*]. I like him because Godard destroys certain previous stylistic conventions…He does everything with such a vitality, with such a figurative ability that it seems truly poetic to me."[17] The references to other films that Pasolini makes in the interview shows that it could not have been conducted before 1964, yet it is possible that between that time and the composition of "Il 'cinema di poesia'" he might have seen more of Godard's work, as the scope of his generalizations about it suggests.

After claiming that as a Parisian Godard is too cynical to resort to the "formal classicism" of Antonioni or the elegiac mood of Bertolucci, Pasolini defines his kind of formalism thus: "His vitality is without restraints, modesty, or scruples. It reconstitutes the world within itself. It is also cynical toward itself. The poetics of Godard is ontological—it is called cinema. His formalism is thus a technicality which is intrinsically poetic: everything that is captured in movement by the camera is beautiful. It is the technical, and therefore poetic, restoration of reality" (p. 181). Then with another paralipsis he concludes:

> His pretextual "free indirect discourse" is a confrontational arrangement, which does not differentiate between the thousand details of the world, without a break in continuity, edited with the cold and almost self-satisfied obsession (typical of his amoral protagonist) of a disintegration reconstituted into unity through that inarticulate language. Godard is completely devoid of classicism; otherwise, one could speak of neocubism in reference to him. But we would speak of an atonal neocubism. Beneath the events of the film, under his long "free indirect point-of-view shots" which imitate the state of mind of his protagonists, there is always a film made for the pure pleasure of restoring a reality fragmented by technique and reconstituted by a brutal, mechanical, and discordant Braque. (pp. 181–182)

If Pasolini had seen Godard's most recent film, *Bande à part* (1964), he would have found a concise illustration of his point in the poem-song of Odile as she rides the metro with Arthur, one of the two men in love with her. As the sequence of twelve shots progresses over nearly two minutes, she moves from reciting the lyrics of a song to singing them. Godard cuts away from her, first to other metro riders and then, intermittently dropping the ambient sound of the subway, freely to the "details of the [city] without a break in continuity"—a woman alone at a sidewalk café, a clochard sleeping over a warm vent, the tile sign "Liberté" of a metro stop, a busy street at night, a man asleep alone, a train platform, a couple sleeping. The lyrics of the song, a melancholy declaration of identification with the passive endurance of banal lives ("things are what they are"), ends with a series of metaphors heard over the image of the sleeping couple: "like you, like a grain of sand, like blood forever spilt, like fingers always wounded, yes, I am your fellow creature."[18] Here the lyrical film running beneath the events of *Bande à part* is a poem to daily life in Paris in the mode of Agnes Varda's sixteen-minute-long *L'opéra mouffe* (1958).

Godard's deployment of what Pasolini identifies as free indirect point of view usually requires a counterpoint between what we see on the screen and what we hear on the soundtrack.

Early in the film Godard used a very long sequence shot (almost four minutes) of Odile dancing in a café with both her suitors, Arthur and Franz, in which the filmmaker breaks into the soundtrack four times for an exercise of simple indirect discourse: the first time he explains, "Now is the time for a digression ["parenthèse"] in which to describe our heroes' feelings"; then, in the three subsequent interruptions, he articulates, in order, Arthur watching his dance steps and thinking of Odile's kisses, Odile wondering if the men are noticing her breasts, and Franz wondering "if the world is becoming a dream or if the dream is becoming the world." Both of these language-centered examples from Godard's film point to a development that can be found in Pasolini's later essays in film theory in which he shifts his focus from cinema as a visual art to an "audiovisual technique."

In "Il 'cinema di poesia'" the author contrasts his three filmmakers who use "free indirect point-of-view shots" with three masters of "great film poems" in prose—Bergman, Chaplin, and Mizoguchi—but he offers examples only from the first two. Their "common characteristic was that 'the camera was not felt'" (p. 183). In particular, they did not employ any of the techniques he summarizes a bit later in the essay as the anarchic, rule-breaking gestures that have become the stylemes of the "Nuovo Cinema" as it can be seen in the opening Mostra of Pesaro: alternating shots from wide angle to telephoto on a face; excessive zoom movements "expanding [things] like excessively leavened bread"; shooting against the light flashing into the camera; handheld shots, annoying tracking shots, montage mistakes for expressive reasons, irritating splices, disorienting opening shots, endless static shots of one image,and so on (p. 184).

Perhaps Mizoguchi's very long takes and elaborate tracking shots stood in the way of Pasolini's remembering any particular scene from his work that would clearly make his case. But his examples from Chaplin's *City Lights* (1931) and Bergman's *Djävulens öga* (*The Devil's Eye*, 1960) are revealing in this respect. The former example is a comic tour de force at the heart of Chaplin's film, but the latter is a transitional moment in Bergman's; Pasolini's keen eye as a filmmaker allows him to isolate it and expound on its poetry. In these cases, Pasolini contends, the camera was not felt; it was simply "there, motionless, filming whatever 'totality' was in front of it" (p. 183). Actually, the camera in *City Lights* is not quite still. Pasolini does not remember, or may not have noticed, that in recording his "ballet, those symmetrical, useless steps taken first here and then there" within the boxing ring, Chaplin made subtle use of the opposition between still shots and those in which the camera followed his movements, keeping them "symmetrical" within the frame of the screen.

The episode breaks down into fourteen shots, but only four of them show Charlie boxing the champion. In the first three of those the camera moves to follow the boxers and referee, but its presence is not felt because the action—the "ballet"—is so absorbing. The ten others, all unmoving and much shorter, show the referee, the bell, and Charlie in his corner before and between rounds.

The slight panning movements to keep him at the center of the frame underscore Chaplin's directorial skill at keeping the referee between himself and the champion and his exquisite timing as an actor in finding opportunities to get in a punch. It is only in the third of these shots of boxing that the camera halts its incessant reframing, as first Chaplin and then the champion go down for a count. The final static shot shows the ring at a slightly greater distance: Charlie has so thoroughly entangled himself in the string to the bell that he stops and starts the rounds every time he staggers under the champion's blows. The fixed camera achieves its comic punctuation more effectively than intercutting would have done; it reveals his mastery of the gag while lending pathos to his ultimate defeat. After the interplay of slight camera movements and pugilistic dancing that brings us to identify with the tramp, the insertion of a distant, still frame momentarily separates us from his antics. In essence, the shift from the shots in which the camera followed Chaplin's movements to the still frame subtly announces his inevitable defeat after delighting us with his hilarious evasions of the professional boxer. Yet this brilliant fusion of mise en scène, camera movement, and editing has disappeared from Pasolini's memory. Films made before 1960 do not command his intensive scrutiny in "Il 'cinema di poesia.'" They merely represent the negative moment in the theoretical-historical argument for the emergence of "free indirect point-of-view shots."

The example from *Djävulens öga* is more to the point than that from *City Lights*. But even there the accurate description of the unfelt, static camera does not entirely account for the effect Pasolini remembers. He neglects the crucial labor of the soundtrack. This is how he describes the scene from Bergman's film:

> ...when Don Giovanni and Pablo leave [Hell] after three hundred years, and see the world once again, the apparition of the world—something so extraordinary—is presented by Bergman as a "long shot" of the two protagonists in a somewhat wild stretch of springtime country landscape, one or two extremely ordinary "close-ups" and a great "establishing shot" of a Swedish panorama of disturbing beauty in its transparent and humble insignificance. The camera was still; it framed those images in an absolutely normal manner. It was not felt.
>
> The poetic nature of classical films was thus not obtained using a specifically poetic language. This means they were not poems, but stories. (pp. 183–184)

There are actually two long shots in the sequence he picks out and then one medium close-up. In the first of them Pablo enters so excited he is almost dancing, while an unmoved Don Juan slowly follows behind him. Two horses stand to the left: we also see a tall pole indicating a well, a wooden house, trees, and clouds. Pablo rushes to the right, then the left, turns around, gazes out left over the landscape, then comes to the right center beside his master. All the while the voice-over continues from the previous shot of a narrator whom we had seen sitting at a desk explaining Hell, Heaven, and Earth as the essential realms of a comedy: "And so Don Juan and Pablo appear in the spring sun of this comedy. They dive out of a dry, bottomless well which goes down to Hell on a hidden elevator. Blinded by the sun, blinking, they are dazed in the earthly paradise." The shot changes as Pablo speaks, showing us his view by means of a point-of-view shot looking over a village from the hill on which they are standing. In the foreground there are trees, then fields with a road to the left going straight to a lake; in the center, farther back, there is a church with a steeple and a few buildings with the lake beyond them. Cumulus clouds give shape to the sky. The image is not remarkable in itself. Pablo says: "Look, Sir. Trees, flowers, and clouds...." A subsequent medium close-up of Pablo and Don Juan grounds the point of view as Pablo continues with unabashed enthusiasm: "More clouds and grass, water, trees.... Look over there! More trees, grass, flowers...." Then the appearance of a laughing devil ends his rapture. In short, the dramatic situation underlined by Pablo gushing over seeing the world for the first time in centuries invests the otherwise pedestrian landscape shot with its "poetic nature."

Pasolini does not use a linguistic analogy to characterize Bergman's fragment, but he might have; for this is not free indirect discourse, or even indirect discourse, but direct discourse in the two senses in which Pasolini had adapted that linguistic terminology: the static shot of the village nested between two images of Pablo and Don Juan is what he called a "subjective point-of-view shot," and Pablo's cataloguing of elements of "the apparition of the world" is direct speech. The naming of the "humble" sights brings to the fore the "disturbing beauty" of the townscape. Thus in this case the poetic undercurrent of the classical cinema of prose is a result of verbal pressure on the images of the unfelt camera. Perhaps Bernardo Bertolucci was conscious of this effect as well, for he heightens the intensity of Puck's ode by having the painter name what he is seeing during the pauses in Puck's effusive elegy.

Of course, the inaccuracies of memory pale beside Pasolini's illumination of aspects and details of films no one else has noticed. The shortcomings in describing the Chaplin and Bergman films, to which he did not have convenient access in 1965 when all critics and theoreticians of the cinema had to rely on memory, do not vitiate his central argument that in "the great film poems" made before 1960 "the general and common characteristic was that 'the camera was not felt'... It was transparent to perfection; it did not superimpose itself on

facts, violating them through insane semantic deformations that are attribut-
able to its presence as continuous technical/stylistic awareness" (p. 183). Here,
as throughout "Il 'cinema di poesia,' " Pasolini demonstrates his supreme critical insight and originality.

Yet he was not writing as a critic or a historian. Near the end of the essay
he asked himself: "Of what use is it to have singled out and, in some way, to
have baptized this recent technical/stylistic tradition of a 'cinema of poetry'?"
(p. 184). Then, putting the tendency he observed at the first Mostra del Nuovo
Cinema in a cultural and political context, he interpreted the prevalence of a
"cinema of poetry" as one aspect of the revival of formalism in the arts: a "part
of that general attempt on the part of bourgeois culture to recover the ground
lost in the battle with Marxism and its possible revolution" (p. 185).

Pasolini was always more of a prophet than a philosophical or historical
analyst. However, the continuing, and perhaps even growing, significance of
"Il 'cinema di poesia' " as a work of film theory and analysis has resulted from
readings that put aside its prophetic fervor and even overlook or excuse its semiological inflection. At the time Pasolini wrote it, he was hardly familiar with
the writings of the French semiologists of the cinema. His semiology ultimately
derived from a reading of Charles Morris rather than Ferdinand Saussure. The
Pesaro Mostra was, in fact, his first direct encounter with the French school.
His absorption and virulent reaction to their work, especially that of Christian
Metz, fueled many of his subsequent essays in film theory, beginning with
his text for the second Mostra del Nuovo Cinema, "The Written Language of
Reality." But there, too, his contribution to the stylistic study of cinema out-
weighed his linguistic analysis. Like most of the major film theoreticians of the
period (Stan Brakhage and Stanley Cavell were significant exceptions), he was
swept up in the search for a linguistic model; his previous writing on poetry
and fiction may have tempted him further into this arena of dispute; his heretical temper and his irrepressible originality made him so marginal at the time
that his theoretical work was quickly dismissed as "amateur."

His polemical position helps us to understand his reaction to the advo-
cates of pure cinematic poetry within the American avant-garde as he came
to know it following the publication of "Il 'cinema di poesia' ". When he first
proposed "free indirect point of view" as the emergent mode of cinematic
poetry, the only alternatives to the dominant narrative genres that he knew
were the documentary and the silent avant-garde cinema (he makes allusion to *Un chien andalou*). He was not present at the July 1964 screening of
the Exhibition of the New American Cinema at the Mostra Internazionale
del Cinema Libero in Porretta Terme. But he did see the subsequent exhibition that Jonas Mekas brought to Torino, Rome, and the Pesaro Mostra in
1967. Yet the significance of some of the poets of the American avant-garde
cinema could not have escaped his attention even earlier than that; for
the very issue of *Marcatrè* that published the full text of "Il 'cinema di

poesia'" for the first time followed the round table of Pesaro with Juditte Sarkany-Perret's "U.S.A.—Cinema à New York" consisting of interviews with Jonas Mekas, Harry Smith, Gregory Markopoulos, Andy Warhol, Stan Vanderbeek, and Stan Brakhage (who speaks of the influence of the poets Ezra Pound, William Carlos Williams, and H.D. on his sequence of short, 8mm *Songs* [*Canzone*]). After seeing the 1967 exposition of such films at Pesaro and in Rome, Pasolini was "disappointed" and dismissive of them. The terms of that rejection will be pertinent to our discussion when we come to consider his 1967 essays "Essere è naturale?" and "I segni viventi e i poeti morti" in the second half of this book. In the latter of these, stimulated by his viewing of American avant-garde films, he acknowledged: "speaking of a cinema of poetry, I always meant to speak of narrative poetry" (HE, p. 251).

Dimitri Kirsanoff: *Ménilmontant*

[Left] Reaction to finding murdered parents; [right] reaction to seeing sister with her lover.

Dimitri Kirsanoff's *Ménilmontant*

The most perfect example to my knowledge—and one of the earliest instances of systematically employed free indirect point of view in cinema—predates Pasolini's historical schema by four decades. Dimitri Kirsanoff's *Ménilmontant* (1926) fulfills all his rubrics for "the cinema of poetry."

All great films manifest evidence of their historical origins and leave in their wakes the repercussions of influence. Yet, to a remarkable degree, *Ménilmontant* seems an autonomous creation, as sophisticated and demanding as any narrative film of the silent period, without obvious imitators. Although Richard Abel has astutely called attention to aspects the film shares with Abel Gance's *La Roue* (1923) and Leon Moussinac's *Le Brasier ardent* (1923)—spectacular opening sequences of rapid montage—and with Jean Epstein's *Coeur fidèle* (1923)—the superimposition of water over a closeup of the heroine[1]—any comparison of the film as a whole with those admirable works would have to underline the intensity, uniqueness, and exceptional rigor of Kirsanoff's achievement.

In one important respect we can trace the film's pedigree. *Ménilmontant* was made as a film without intertitles, one that would convey its complex and subtle narrative wholly through images and cinematic tropes. As such it was indebted to Lupu Pick's *Sylvester* (1923) and to Charles Ray's *The Old Swimmin' Hole* (1921) and perhaps also to Lupu Pick's *Scherben* (also 1921, with just one title), as in Murnau's *Der Letze Mann* (*The Last Laugh*) (1924). Kirsanoff's first film, *L'ironie du destin* (1924), now lost, was said to be deliberately titleless as well. Only in Dziga Vertov's masterpiece, *Chelovek s kinoapparotom* (*The Man with a Movie Camera: A Film without Intertitles*) (1929), made at the end of the silent period as a monument to the capabilities of the mute cinema, do we find a more exhaustive catalogue of filmic rhetoric. Only Teinosuke Kinugasa's *Kurutta Ippēji* (*Page of Madness*) (1926) presses the wordless silent film to even more ambitious intricacies.

Kirsanoff's abolition of words from *Ménilmontant* (aside from those found in situ, such as "Notre mère" and "Notre père" on the graves of the protagonists' parents or the word "Maternité" carved in stone over the hospital portal from which one sister emerges with a baby) is consistent with his larger aesthetic

strategy of utilizing both ambiguity and rhetorical indetermination to maxi-
mize the connotative effect of his shots and cuts. The maturity of the plot that
Kirsanoff constructed is almost as remarkable as the film's tolerance for ambiguity and uncertainty and its exploitation of ellipsis in many forms. Its disregard for the sentimental conventions governing many of the most ambitious
French fictional films of the period and its insightful representation of seduction and prostitution are factors in its maturity, as is its radical modernism;
for Kirsanoff renders indirectly the subjective perspective and bewilderment
of a provincial orphan seduced and made pregnant in Paris. He does this by
means of what Pier Paolo Pasolini calls "the cinema of poetry," or the adaptation of free indirect discourse to cinema. Consequently, the unfolding of the
plot requires the active interpretation of innovative cinematic tropes, whose
meaning is often suspended for considerable stretches of time. Even at the end
of the film several crucial events remain ambiguous.

Conventionally, intertitles would clear up these ambiguities. But Kirsanoff
seems to want to preserve these uncertainties. In 1929 he told Marcel
Lapierre: "The intertitle is the bane of cinema. In the eyes of some people that
is the flagrant sign of the inferiority of cinema to the other arts…In absolute cinema [le cinéma absolu] intertitles shouldn't exist. It's a palliative…You
don't explain with words a symphony. A film should be comprehensible in
itself."[2]

The ambiguities Kirsanoff nurtured by refusing intertitles reflect blind
spots in the consciousnesses of the protagonists. Perhaps more important, the
ellipses and inexplicable but comprehensible tropes promote the web of connotations which make *Ménilmontant* "un film absolu." The most obvious example of this is the relationship between the opening and closing of the film.
In a series of quickly edited details *Ménilmontant* starts with signs of a violent struggle in a rural house: two men and a woman rush outside. One man,
catching sight of an axe, slays the other two people and escapes. Although
we never see these characters again, or learn anything of them, including the
motives for the violence, it is certain that the murdered couple are the parents
of the two sisters who are the film's protagonists.

Just before the end of the film there is a second murder, involving, yet again,
two men and a woman, with another weapon come upon by chance. Of the
three, only the victim is known to us: he is the young man who seduced both
sisters. His death is an irony: had he not happened to witness, by accident,
the reunion of the sisters—one homeless on the first night of her release from
the maternity hospital with his baby, the other a prostitute—the unidentified
woman and her accomplice who attacked him might not have found him. As
the two men struggle, the woman finds a loose cobblestone and hurls it at his
head, fatally.

These two patently interrelated episodes dramatically affect the lives of the
two sisters. The first effectively terminates their provincial life. They go to Paris

and find employment making boutons. After the concluding murder we see some images of the city at dawn and a closeup of a hand making a bouton. This metonomy of the earlier montage that represented their introduction and accomodation to Paris (the separate stages elliptically fused together) suggests that one or both sisters returned to their earlier employment.

The implications of the final shot are much more extensive than that. If the opening murder propelled them to Paris and to a precarious and vulnerable existence, the second ironic death could be said to have released them from the worst aspects of their fate. It opens the question of whether or not the dead man was the pimp of the sister who was prostituting herself. Such an interpretation would throw some light on his murder. Kirsanoff went to pains to show the woman who killed him as a figure of the criminal subculture. We see her surreptitiously drinking the dregs of abandoned wine glasses and stealing bills left on a table as payment or a tip. She too may have been seduced and led into prostitution by the pimp. Can we then see the opening of the film, at least in this retrospective light, as an erotic triangle? The furiously enraged character could not be the husband and father of the two sisters, but may be the adulterous lover, or merely an intruder.

Kirsanoff not only sets up parallel sequences for their connotations but also gives added weight to certain configurations of shots by isolation and repetition. The reaction of one sister to the sight of her parents' mutilated bodies is registered by a series of four shots along the same axis, each closer than the previous, ending in a closeup of her eyes as she raises her hand to block the sight. Kirsanoff uses this trope only one other time in the film. When the same young woman sees her lover taking her sister into his apartment, a series of three shots, closer and closer, reveals her shock, and now intimates an affective association with the moment of her orphaning.

Likewise a series of handheld shots of Paris street life forms a discontinuous unit within the film, linking and marking stages in the emotional life of the sisters. The first fulfills a double purpose: it introduces Paris, expressing the tumultuous rhythms of the metropolis as initially experienced by the provincial girls, in contrast to a long shot, punctuated by dissolves of them walking down a long country road; and at the same time it reveals that they are already settled in the city, have jobs, and are just at the point of finishing the work week, at noon, presumably on Saturday. Rhetorically, such double-functioning tropes are varieties of zeugma. One example might be syllepsis—a single verb with two incongruous objects: "He flew to New York and into a rage." The zeugma effect pervades *Ménilmontant*. Tropes and images recur with variations, giving them new meanings and forcing retrospective reconsiderations of the events previously represented. An unnamed author of a review of *L'ironie du destin*, clearly reflecting Kirsanoff's own view of the film, had argued: "It is true that the image isn't always immediately explicable. The same delay of comprehension occurs in the other arts...In the choice of the theme to be presented with an intertitle, Kirsanoff also told us, it isn't necessary to limit oneself to a simple subject."[3] The cinematic amplification of zeugma and ellipsis produces large- and small-scale "delays of comprehension" throughout *Ménilmontant*. The film's modernism is a function of the swiftness and compression of its narration intersecting with its retardation of comprehension.

Consider the following elaboration of connotations based on the initial associations of a cinematic trope: the second time the handheld camerawork appears, it is directed toward representing the subjectivity of the sister who will eventually become a prostitute. She is alone in the bed she usually shares with her sister, who, for the first time, has spent the night with her lover. The montage suggests the sounds of approaching cars and steps that might indicate the woman returning, while the superimposition of a naked female body seems to anchor the imagery in the erotic imagination of the waiting sister. Thus the trope that had initially intimated the excitement of the great city now comes to mark the exclusion from that excitement in the mind of the sister left behind.

A third variant of the trope accompanies the emergence of the first sister from the maternity hospital. This scene immediately follows her discovery of her lover's betrayal with her sister. The handheld camera depicts a busy, rainy Paris; amid the superimpositions we see a hearse. The excitement and seductions of the metropolis have turned to signs of bitter alienation for the destitute mother. Through her eyes we will see the fourth and final handheld sequences of Ménilmontant at night. Its neon signs of dance halls and hotels lead to the elliptical evocation of the business of prostitution. In this new context she will locate the sister she last saw entering the apartment with her lover.

The logic of the film hints that we may have to reconsider the designation "lover" by which I have indicated the principal male in the film. Kirsanoff's avoidance of titles eludes any verbalization of his role. In the initial seduction he does seem to be an aggressive lover, and even in his betrayal of the first sister he may be seen as a callous young man of robust sexual appetite. But the conclusion of the film implies that his initial preying upon these two provincial girls may have actually been the professional recruiting technique of a pimp. By carefully linking the narrative almost exclusively to the perspective of the sister who has the child, and by radically limiting all omniscient narration save the murder of the parents and the death of the young man, Kirsanoff directs us to chart the course of the love affair from the deluded point of view of the infatuated and betrayed woman.

Even the topology of Ménilmontant's street plan becomes an integral part of Kirsanoff's cinematic strategy. He films the meeting of the sisters with their lover in the maze of deserted narrow streets. The lover leaves a bar, starts in one direction, hesitates as he considers the opposite directions, then continues along the path he began. Or he looks in one offscreen direction, then in the other, where he hails someone; to our surprise it is the sister who had been waiting at home the first night that he escorts into the visible portion of the scene. The accumulation of such gestures, retrospectively considered, figuratively represents his balancing the seduction of the two sisters. But since Kirsanoff's camera keeps from our view the object of his intrigue until the last moment, the effect is that of a zeugma, because we do not even know there is an intrigue afoot until it is revealed. Had we known he was seducing both sisters, the effect would have been one of simple suspense. Which is he meeting? But because we assume he is heading toward the sister he has already seduced, we may read his vacillation as ambivalence until the more dramatic interpretation is forced upon us.

In the direction of his principal actress, Nadia Sibirskaia, Kirsanoff demonstrates a massive debt to D. W. Griffith. Sibirskaia's intimations of innocence, girlish enthusiasm, and despair, even the prominent bow in her hair to make her look very young, and the coy play of her finger at the edge of her mouth, derive from Mae Marsh's representation of The Dear One in the modern story of *Intolerance*. Yet although the social ambience of metropolitan poverty, prostitution, and crime is common to both films, Kirsanoff avoids Griffith's denunciation of societal malevolence, his sentimentality, his Christian piety, and his triumphalism.

Despite his insight and fascination with the erotic dynamics of the urban slums, Griffith conceived The Dear One and her family as an autonomous cell of innocence and virtue, resisting, with ultimate success, a complex network of economic oppression and sexual vice. By substituting for their sexuality their gradual entrapment by the desires, lies, and indifference of others, he could assert their autonomy only through a melodramatic reversal of fortune, at the cost of reducing his narrative to a simple chase. Hyperbolically amplifying suspense and last-minute restitution to epic proportions, Griffith preserved his protagonists from an authentic interaction with their milieu.

Kirsanoff critically dissected the ironies of sexual desire within a more dramatically fractured urban unit: two orphaned sisters and their shared lover. His sense of irony was both more intense than Griffith's and less benign. But above all, he put in the foreground of his film the tension between rhetorical figuration and its narrative implications, so that wherever the locus of his attention fell upon a local detail, a latent dimension of the story he has so strenuously condensed could expand. For instance, rather than follow the subjects of his film from their parents' graves, he enigmatically dwells on the gravesite itself, first overgrown with weeds, then with its markers in ruins, and finally eradicated in a swath of mud. This unexpected and unique prolepsis intimates that the sisters will never return to their provincial birthplace, the scene of their parents' murder. In place of suspense, with its emphasis on postponing the outcome of events, Kirsanoff structured his film around such an exfoliation of an asymmetrical series of tropes fusing psychological perspectives with often ambiguous narrative expositions.

 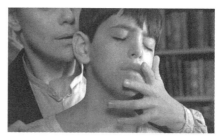

 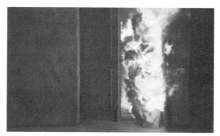

Ingmar Bergman:
[Left] *Tystnaden* (1963)
The dwarfs' Variety Show; dwarfs entertain Johan
[Right] *Viskningar och rop (1972)*
    The aunt's magic lantern
    Fanny och Alexander (1982)
      Ismail magically reveals fire in the bishop's house to Alexander

Ingmar Bergman's Primal Scene

At the time Pier Paolo Pasolini was developing his theory of the nature of narrative poetry in cinema, Ingmar Bergman was exploring the psychoanalytic ramifications of connotation in film construction. According to Robert C. Gordon, who reads Pasolini's essays on cinema as a theory of metaphor, the psychoanalytic dimension was already articulated in "Il 'cinema di poesia' ":

> The problem of "style indirecte libre" and inner monologue in cinema, resolved by recourse to the concept of "soggettiva indiretta libera" which ushers into existence the notion of "cinema di poesia," is stated in the same terms as the problem of abstraction: the inner monologue transcends the immediate and concrete, as does abstraction and, like the latter, the former can only be possible in cinema via metaphor. The characterization of the poetic and metaphoric as equivalent to a repressed subconscious of a prose narrative discourse contains strong inferences, via its psychoanalytic vocabulary and even the use of the oneiric, that what is termed subconscious is also a figure of latent subjectivity.[1]

Although there is no evidence that Bergman was ever engaged with Pasolini's films or his writings, Gordon's formulation of "a repressed subconscious of a prose narrative" aptly describes the infrastructure of many of Bergman's strongest films after 1962. But what can be determined of Bergman's attitude toward psychoanalysis suggests that it was a problematic issue for him. Nevertheless, his lifelong fascination with dreams, familial violence, magic, and mental breakdowns, often of a psychotic nature, makes his films particularly responsive to psychoanalytical interpretation. But above all his use of cinema to erase the distinctions between everyday "real" experience and the imagination makes the insights of Pasolini's film theory relevant to his films, particularly but not exclusively those made after 1962, in which the cinematic stylistic devices can be read as the "free indirect point of view shots" of his neurotic (and psychotic) protagonists and, following Pasolini's argument, of the filmmaker himself.

The pretitle scene of *Persona* (1966) might be a pure instance of what Pasolini means by a film that wants to be another film. It is a non-narrative string of some forty shots, most of them very brief, with no direct reference to the events or characters in the film to follow, except for the next-to-last image of a boy, awakened in a morgue, who touches a soft-focused screen on which the faces of the two women who will turn out to be the principal characters in the film slowly dissolve into each other. In fact, in *Modernist Montage,* I argued that *Persona* allegorically represents the process of a psychoanalysis, with Elisabet (an actress) as the silent psychoanalyst and Alma (her nurse) standing in for the neurotic patient. In this complex schema, Alma, in turn, stood for an unseen male figure, obscurely suggested by the allusions to Elisabet's unwanted, unloved son.[2] At the heart of the neurosis that generates the free indirect point of view of the film, I found a primal scene disturbance: a fascinating and terrifying fantasy of parental intercourse after which the analysand imagines himself as an unwanted byproduct, the survivor of an unsuccessful abortion.

Pasolini claimed that "The 'cinema of poetry'...produce[s] films with a double nature. The film that is seen and ordinarily perceived is a 'free indirect point-of view shot.'...Beneath this film runs another film, one that the filmmaker would have made even without the pretext of the visual mimesis of the protagonist—a film whose character is completely and freely expressive/expressionistic" (HE, p. 182). The stylemes of the "cinema of poetry" are, according to Pasolini, "proof of the presence of such an unrealized, subterranean film." However, the primary stylistic marker of the neurotic obsession that constitutes *Persona*'s matrix is not included in Pasolini's catalogue of stylemes of "the cinema of poetry." In this case, uniquely within Bergman's oeuvre, it would be his extraordinary ascesis of shot-countershot. The most unique or obsessive aspect of it is his nearly total avoidance of this most basic trope of narrative cinema. Its rare occurrences are so dramatic that the shot-countershot of *Persona* calls attention to itself and consequently underlines the psychoanalytical allegory at eight points in the film. In the first place, shot-countershot is withheld in the pretitle sequence until the moment that the boy, waking in the morgue, turns from his book—Mikhail Lermontov's *A Hero of Our Time*—to look directly into the camera; as he reaches out to touch it, the first countershot presents a screen on which the faces of Alma and Elisabet fuse into one another, before we have met them, and long before we can know that a similar image of fusion will mark the climax of the film, when at the conclusion of Alma's repeated act of projection, she accuses Elisabet of the very acts for which she feels guilty. Not only is the first countershot in the film that of a screen on which images are projected, but the awakened boy vainly attempts to make the images tangible. Here, as in Bergman's other scenes of plays, puppet theaters, television, burlesque shows, magic lanterns, and above all film projections, which recur throughout his oeuvre, the projected images are the loci of the eruption of the "irrational, oneiric, elementary, and barbaric elements" of the unconscious.

The climax of *Persona* is its *most* elaborate displacement of shot-countershot: Alma's fantasy of Elisabet's failed motherhood appears on the screen twice, in two series of four shots, first of the listener four times, then four countershots of the speaker. As the original script of the film does not indicate this rejection of intercutting, we can assume Bergman improvised this startling scene while editing the film. It is as if the raw materials of shot-countershot were shown to the viewer and the montage suppressed in the process of editing the film, tacitly acknowledging the construction of *Persona* as an act of self-discovery. The sequence's overall effect is both to emphasize the cinematic illusion and to call attention to the stylistic peculiarity of shot-countershot in this one film of Bergman's. A final exchange, in shot-countershot, shows Elisabet packing. Surprisingly, it will turn out to be the last time we see her with Alma, aside from flashbacks.

Seeing in the film the conjunction of a psychoanalytic allegory, an exploration of primal scene fantasies, the peculiar use of a basic cinematic trope, and the indices of improvisational editing led me to conclude that *Persona* explores Bergman's anxieties about the origin and nature of his creativity as a filmmaker. This is supported by a reading of the elaborate network of allusions in the pretitle sequence of the film. In my study I was greatly encouraged by two studies of the psychoanalyst Henry Edelheit, who interpreted crucifixion fantasies as functions of a primal scene schema and who also stressed the role of theatrical spectacles and composite creatures (his examples included centaurs, minotaurs, and other mythological beasts) as figures for the disturbing parental intercourse.[3] Naturally, I extended this to cover the fusion of Alma and Elisabet on the screen in the pretitle sequence and at the climax of Alma's projection.

The primal scene schema in *Persona* also illuminates the two films to which Bergman directly alludes, even quotes, within it: *Fangelse* (*Prison*) (1949) and *Tystnaden* (*The Silence*) (1963). Both in the pretitle sequence of *Persona* and in the sequence which follows the ripping of the filmstrip, there appear excerpts from a trick film that Bergman fabricated as a would-be circa-1905 comedy in *Fangelse*. (This moment, too, follows one of the rare shot-countershot exchanges between Alma and Elisabet.) The waking boy of the pretitle sequence is the same young actor who played in *Tystnaden*. In fact, he is reading the same copy of a Swedish translation of *A Hero of Our Time* that he was reading in the earlier film; it is almost as if in the morgue he picks it up from the very page he was seen reading in the middle of *Tystnaden*.

Again we find an emphasis on the rejection of children and physical and psychic violence toward them, as in both earlier films. Furthermore, they both have crucial episodes of a theatrical or cinematic spectacle in which primal scene confusions abound. Significantly, these spectacles are both preludes to explicit representations of sexual intercourse. Finally, the spectacles in both films evoke the suggestions of homosexual unions, such as that at the horizon of Alma's relationship to Elisabet.

Fangelse, the first film Bergman directed from an original script of his own, depicts the despair of a troubled writer and the suicidal anguish of a young prostitute forced to hand over her baby to her pimp, who murdered it. At the beginning of their liaison, they discover a projector and watch the primitive one-reel comedy already threaded on it. Bergman has claimed that this is a reconstruction of the first film he owned as a child. But this must be a "screen memory"; for the actions of the comedy are too intimately fused to the themes of the film in which it appears to be coincidental.

Insofar as the comedy narrates the disturbances that keep a man from sleeping, it corresponds to infantile, nocturnal anxiety engendered by primal scene experiences. The film within the film has three stages: the catastrophe of the man's attempt to warm his bed, the intrusion of a thief, and the farcical pursuit of the thief by a policeman. In the initial stage the would-be sleeper accidentally burns his buttocks, douses his smoking nightshirt in a water bucket, and is frightened back into bed by the stop-frame manifestations of a skeleton and a devil. Here the elementary displacement signals genital confusion, the substitution of pain for pleasure, and consequent punishment from archetypal creatures of the unconscious.

Both the thief and the policeman continue the idea of punishment, wielding phallic weapons, a knife and a nightstick. First the thief, frightened by a spider suspended over the sleeper, awakens him by accidentally whacking his protruding feet in his failed attempt to squash the spider, itself a displacement of intimidating female sexuality. The entry of the policeman initiates an acrobatic frenzy in which the thief whirls the sleeper around his body and through his legs, comically suggesting intercourse, before the policeman hurls him against the buttocks of the bent-over man, as if in a homosexual embrace. The comedy concludes with another appearance of the skeleton and the devil, scaring all three men into leaping out of windows.

A young boy who appears only once plays a pivotal role in the plot of *Fangelse* and provides further confirmation of the relevance of this film to the psychodynamics of *Persona*. While hiding in a cellar, the prostitute finds this boy also hiding in order to make his parents "believe he is dead and feel sorry." His father has demanded that he give up a sharp knife he uses as a toy, but to preserve it he has hidden it in the cellar. Later the prostitute will kill herself with this knife. In a sense, the boy in the pretitle sequence of *Persona* can be said to be pretending he is dead. Consequently, the entire film describes a fantasy of vengeance against the parents, in this case particularly the mother, as a variation on what Jacob Arlow has called "the revenge motif in the primal scene."[4]

In *Tystnaden*, Bergman's penultimate film before *Persona*, the preadolescent boy, Johan, traveling with his mother, Anna, and his aunt, Ester, has as central a role as Bergman will permit a boy in any of his films until the autobiographical *Fanny och Alexander* (1982), which is the most explicit of the filmmaker's primal scene scenarios. Anna, a rather cruel nymphomaniac, relishes the fact that the man she has picked up in her one-day stopover cannot understand a word she speaks. Ester, apparently dying of cancer, seems to have had a lifelong incestuous and masochistic fascination with her sister's erotic compulsions. Throughout most of the day in which the film takes place, Johan wanders through the corridors of the hotel where the three share a suite. At one point he peeks through a keyhole at his mother making love. Later, after he tells his aunt of this experience—this is the moment when we see he is reading *A Hero of Our Time*—she enters the couple's room and then whines and pleads outside their door. Within the economy of the primal scene schema, she is thus acting out part of the boy's anxiety.

Three episodes in the film may be said to be versions of what Edelheit called "libidinal theater." The first is the most elaborate: Johan wanders through the hotel corridors after taking a nap in bed with his mother. His cap gun, tucked into the front waistband of his shorts, bears an explicitly phallic association. Twice he stops to stare at a large copy of Rubens's *Rape of Deianira* showing the nymph and the centaur Nessus in an ambiguous but distinctly erotic posture. Following Edelheit's "Mythopoesis and the Primal Scene," I take the centaur's fusion of man and beast as an emblem of primal scene confusion. It is no accident that Johan is startled at this very moment by an elderly waiter, who will later show him photographs from a funeral and grotesquely play with and devour a phallic sausage for his amusement.

Bergman subtly underlines the relationship of the painting to Anna by parallel montage. Just after Johan has stared for a second time at the painting's naked figures, the scene cuts to a closeup of the mother's breasts as she washes after her nap. A panning movement of the camera reveals that Ester is watching her ablutions. The rhyming gesture of the montage here, and elsewhere in the film, is a styleme of "free indirect point of view." Johan's sexual confusion gets further amplification as he wanders into a hotel room where a company of acrobatic dwarfs (there are seven in all!) play dead to his cap pistol shots before they put a girl's dress on him. In another montage rhyme, Bergman cuts to Ester watching Anna dress, suggesting the boy's temporary sexual identification with the mother in the lascivious company of the male dwarfs. One of them, with a monkey mask, cavorts alone on a bed for his companions' and Johan's entertainment until their leader angrily enters, stops them, and, having removed Johan's dress, escorts him back into the corridor. No sooner is the boy alone than he urinates against the wall, ending the sequence.

Edelheit proposed five unresolved questions characteristic of what he calls the "double identification" of the primal scene. The "double identification" entails imagining both viewing parental intercourse and participating in it. They are relevant to the depicted mentality of Johan in this episode. The questions are:

1) What is happening? 2) To whom is it happening? Who is the victim and who the aggressor? 3) How many people are involved? One? Two? Several?

Or is it one composite creature? 4) What is the anatomy of the scene? If it is made up of more than one individual, which one has the penis? 5) Where am I (the observer)? Am I participating or am I excluded?[5]

In Johan's fascination with the painting the first phase of an alternation occurs: he is the anxious observer of a composite creature and a figure clearly identified, through montage, with his mother. But in the second phase, as he joins the dwarfs watching the antics on the bed, he, like Snow White, has become a substitute (or rival) mother and, although he still merely observes the composite creature (dwarfed man below, monkey above), he is symbolically a participant. The troubling question "which one has the penis?" compels him to his aggressive urination, which is linked to his spying on and shooting other males with his cap pistol.

The child-sized monkey-man performing on the bed is the first of several libidinal performances acted out in the film. Much later, while his mother is making love to a stranger, Johan performs a Punch and Judy puppet show for his aunt, making the frame of her bed his stage. His Punch repeatedly batters down Judy with his stick. According to the boy, Punch speaks a strange language because he is afraid, and he cannot sing because he is *so* angry. Here we see the fear and anger of the primal scene observer without the fascination and excitement. Those qualities are distilled in a third example of libidinal theater, which actually occurs in the film between the other two. Anna wanders into a Variety Theater, where the seven dwarfs perform. They jump over one another in an acrobatic act reminiscent of the thief, the cop, and the sleeper in *Fangelse*. Then they form a single composite creature, a caterpillar of interlocked bodies. Once the performance ends, Anna watches the only other couple in the theater have sex. Later she will lie to Ester, telling her she had intercourse with a stranger on the theater floor. In this episode Anna alternates between being an observer of first symbolical and then actual intercourse and fabricates a seductive story of her participation. Later, she not only fantasizes for her sister, but she also aggressively dramatizes her experience, making love to a man observed by her son; and finally she even has sex in front of her sister, while she explicitly tells her of her hatred for her stemming from her jealousy of Ester's relationship to their father.

A complex web of associations runs through Bergman's cinema from *Fangelse* to *Fanny och Alexander,* conjoining variations of the primal scene with representations of theater, cinema, and fairy tales. In his autobiography, *Lanterna Magika,* the filmmaker illuminates the Oedipal sources of his need to make films. Fittingly, he stresses *Fangelse* and *Tystnaden* as guides to its genesis and meaning. However, the psychodynamic role of fairy tales is most vividly represented by the symbolic structure of *Viskningar och rop* (*Cries and Whispers*) (1972), a film particularly remarkable for its use of color.

In the rare company of such films as *Marnie* (1964) and *Il deserto rosso* (1964), *Viskningar och rop* fuses its meaning to its controlled use of color.

Brilliantly simple, it is a film dominated by reds, even punctuated with redouts rather than blackening fades. Opening with crepuscular light in the sculpture garden of a nineteenth-century mansion, the film moves quickly indoors, where it settles, with a single exterior flashback, until its epilogue. The house is remarkable for its red upholstery: richly saturated red walls and furnishings set off the white gowns in which the three sisters, Agnes, Karin, and Maria (and their servant Anna) dress themselves following the model of their dead mother, who appears in a flashback.

Agnes lies dying, apparently of a cancer of the uterus or stomach. After her death the white motif shifts to black. Bergman's screenplay, which differs significantly from the finished film, offers fascinating hints about connotations of the color scheme. He presents it as a letter to his cast, telling them that "ever since my childhood I have pictured the inside of the soul as a moist membrane in shades of red."[6] Furthermore, the image of the four women in white moving against red wallpaper haunted him for more than a year before he started making the film.

So, after the brief, muted spectrum of the dawn, and a caressing pan of an antique clock in azure and gold, a concentration on red and white seizes and holds the film. Even when the mother appears, drawing us for a short time outside again into a very green world, she emerges first in her white dress (dissolving out of a close-up of a white rosebud), holding a small, very bright red book.

Perhaps the most brilliant and simple act of color organization comes from the dramatic placement of what I have called the epilogue, actually a final flashback motivated by Anna's reading of Agnes's diary after her death. The family has left the house, dismissing Anna from their service with the stingy offer of a gift she has refused. Instead, she takes what she knows she would not be allowed to have, although the others would not value it: Agnes's diary. As she reads of an ecstatic afternoon of perfect weather and sororal companionship, we hear Agnes's voice-over and see a final flashback of Anna rocking the three sisters on a double glider swing amid lush autumnal colors. The natural effulgence is all the more striking for being reserved and isolated at the end of the film. After the tonal contrast had shifted from white on red to black on red, the climactic oranges and ochres are lavished in a visual cadenza. The overall placement of blocks of colors transforms what would otherwise be a merely pretty range of scenes into a musical sequence and pictorial elegance into meaning.

What meaning? Let us begin at the end and work our way backward. The autumnal colors invoke the consummation of the seasons, a gorgeous dying of nature. It is fall (or Swedish summer); the penultimate flaring of color tonality, just before the vegetal death, corresponds to the recovery immanent in Anna's reading of Agnes's words. It is not a rebirth, a spring; rather, it is a repetition in a different register of the temporality of the whole film. But now we know Agnes from the perspective of her death, so the flashback describes a liminal

zone, where memory is under the sign of death even if it is gorgeous in its prolongation of the end.

This liminality is one key to the film. In its dramatic center, where the "free
indirect point of view" dreams hold sway, the corpse of Agnes elicits comfort
from the three surviving women. Resorting to a commonplace of decorum,
Karin refuses to get involved with the dead and insists that her uncanny experience is a dream; Maria temporarily shows more sympathy, remembering
how she huddled with Agnes once in a moment of childhood terror, but recoils
at the corpse's kiss; Anna alone cradles the dead body in an often reproduced
image that suggests a Pietà but shows as well a full breast beside the "dead" face
incapable of earthly nurture. As Mater Dolorosa, the servant has a religious
faith in the liminality of death itself. This is consistent with the very first sight
we had of her early in the film, waking and praying beside the fetishes of her
dead daughter.

Tracing the film farther back toward its beginning, we can see that this maternal, religious image of the fusion of death and life reverses the first flashback in which the white rose against the red wall triggered the memory of
its virtual negative: the red book like a spot of blood on the white dress of
the mother. In this memory Agnes recalls caressing her mother's face. (The
script adds that the mother later retracted this moment of affection, just as
Karin and Maria deny their earlier moment of reconciliation with each other
after Agnes's funeral.) The elaborate linkage of gestures, both rhyming and
reversing, throughout the film should not surprise us; for here, as often elsewhere in Bergman's work, the different characters of the film are vectors of a
single fantasy system which generates its narrative complexity by scattering
and redistributing its aspects among imagined persons who are in essence a
single haunting presence. Anna is as much the absent mother as is Maria (Liv
Ullmann plays both Maria and the mother); even the miserable Karin (who
may take her name from the filmmaker's own mother) is another version of
the mother, her most threatening face.

The most remote icon of the liminal zone between life and death may
be glimpsed in the very first shot of the film, at the quintessential moment
of liminality, dawn. Very briefly we see a classical statue of a man bearing a
lyre: Apollo, the god of poets, or, as I would prefer to believe, Orpheus, the poet
of life in death and of the power of language over nature. Agnes, Bergman's
surrogate in the film, is herself an amateur artist who crosses the barrier of
death and seems to return; her Eurydice, the mother, is associated with the
green world the only time it appears in the film. Without her, nature appears
in its decaying stage.

Language itself is multiform and ambiguous in this film: we never learn the
contents of the mother's bright red book, unless it is the red-bound copy of *The
Pickwick Papers*, the communal reading of which marks the height of familial
cohesion. Bergman seems to have carefully chosen Dickens's first masterpiece

for this function. Its comic world of male solidarity and chicanery, threatened by female plots for marriage, reflects in reverse the tragic female society of the film and its reprehensible but peripheral males.

The exchange of Karin and Maria that seems to indicate their reconciliation is muted by a musical passage from Bach; Karin's central utterance—"a tissue of lies"—repeated twice, apparently describing her marriage to Frederick but otherwise unexplained, fuses body and language in a metaphor of deception; the unctuous eulogy of the minister turns into a cry of agnostic alienation; the doctor gives voice to Maria's mirror in a cruel diagnosis of her nature; the corpse of Agnes talks and, more poignantly, her diary becomes a voice from beyond the tomb. The title of the film—"Whispers and Cries" would be a more literal rendering of "Viskningar och rop"—describes two limits of expressive language but comes from a review the filmmaker read of a composition by Mozart.[7]

The men of the film are all shadowy figures for the dead father, who is palpably absent here, as in *Tystnaden*. Alternately fierce and weak, they underline the missing male presence in Agnes's life. The doctor, Maria's sometime lover, and Frederick, Karin's husband, represent the punishing power of masculinity, whereas Maria's suicidal husband and the minister illustrate male weakness as self-absorption. Within the visual and color economy of the film the self-inflicted wound of Maria's husband (when he reacts to her hint that she has slept with the doctor) is part of a covert symbolical equation with the broken glass Karin inserts in her vagina and their visual echo: the red book against the mother's dress as a displaced menstrual stain. In this dreamlike, liminal world of the metamorphic woman, fusing fantasies of defloration, menstruation, and castration, the four men are versions of masculine self-hatred in sadistic and masochistic registers.

The central instance of the intrusion of the unconscious occurs, characteristically, in a magic lantern show. We know from Bergman's autobiography the fetishistic importance he gives to the magic lantern. In the flashback of the mother in *Viskningar och rop* there is a magic lantern associated with Christmas gifts, as in both the autobiography and *Fanny och Alexander*. In this case, the world represented in the magic lantern show comes from Grimm's fairy tales. We might even say that the magic lantern represents simultaneously the gift of fairy tales—and thereby the psychic-defense machinery for exteriorizing infantile and Oedipal terrors—and the gift of cinema for the incipient filmmaker.

In *The Uses of Enchantment*[8] Bruno Bettelheim points out the persistence of a red-white axis of symbolism in fairy tales, which marks the turn from sexual innocence to puberty and maturity in girls. We find it in the three drops of blood on the handkerchief of "The Goose Girl," the three blood drops in the snow that herald the birth of "Snow White" (in the conventional Italian version, there are three blood drops in milk), and the pricking of the finger of "Sleeping

Beauty." More sinisterly, the bleeding feet of the sisters of "Cinderella" reflect this same menstruation and defloration motif without the white contrast. In *Viskningar och rop*, the self-mutilation of Karin echoes these bleeding feet with more explicit recognition of their genital symbolism. The doctor's harsh analysis of Maria's mature beauty as she stares into the mirror may have its imaginative origin in the sadistic behavior of Snow White's narcissistic mother. The tale of "Hansel and Gretel," the actual subject of the magic lantern show, is particularly apt for refracting the complex of images generating *Viskningar och rop*. Bettelheim tells us:

> The mother represents the source of all food to the children, so it is she who is now experienced as abandoning them, as if in a wilderness. It is the child's anxiety and deep disappointment when Mother is no longer willing to meet all his oral demands which leads him to believe that suddenly Mother has become unloving, selfish, rejecting... [The gingerbread house] is the original all-giving mother, whom every child hopes to find again later somewhere out in the world, when his own mother begins to make demands and impose restrictions... The witch... is the personification of the destructive aspects of orality... When the children give in to untamed id impulses, as symbolized by the uncontrolled voraciousness, they risk being destroyed. (pp. 159, 161–162)

Oral gratification and oral aggression are prominent components of Bergman's film, whose very title brackets speech acts with labial (whispers) and dental (cries) suggestions. Maria's seduction of the doctor involves a sensual and somewhat greedy scene of eating; in direct contrast, the silent meal of Frederick and Karin, in which she spills wine and denies him sexual pleasure, precedes the horrific self-mutilation of her genitals, and that too ends with her rubbing the blood on her mouth and laughing; Agnes vomits, and Anna goes through a pantomime of breast-feeding her.

The fairy tale of Hansel and Gretel begins by positing the zone of liminality: "At the edge of the forest." That edge has become the threshold of life and death and the gingerbread house a womblike red interior. For Agnes, cancer is the witch, eating her up from within. As an amateur artist, she is at once the incarnation of the Orphic statue and the object of his poetic quest. Her death enacts a fantasy in which a minister (like Bergman's own father) must acknowledge her superior spirituality; her two siblings (Bergman had two) admit the shallowness of their affection; and the figure of the mother trisects into a nurturing Madonna incarnated as Anna, who has learned the painful lesson of losing a child (a fantasy echoing through Bergman's films from *Fangelse* to this one), a seducer, represented by Maria, who goads her victim to destroy himself out of jealousy and humiliation, and a castrating vagina dentata, Karin, laughing like the wicked witch at the destructive consequences of untamed erotic impulses.

So, in making *Viskningar och rop*, Bergman yet again reenacts his fantasy of dying and living to see the loss and remorse his death has caused. In the infantile imagination, this death represents the guilt for desiring the mother erotically. To counteract that desire, the frightening image of the mutilated vagina blocks the fantasy of intercourse with the mother. In fact, the ambiguity of the gesture—is she trying to repel Frederick or trap him into castrating himself?—collapses prohibition into punishment. In the fairy tale structure, Karin corresponds to both the mother and the witch.

In the story of Maria, that guilt is symbolically projected on the mother as a seductress, whose pursuit of pleasure would deprive her daughter (we can substitute "son"; for here, as in *Tystnaden* and *Persona*, Bergman has defended against autobiographical reference by transposing genders) of a father. Thus Maria fulfills the role of the mother in the fairy tale who fails to care for her children and abandons them to the forest. But in Anna we have the all-giving mother who has lost her daughter (again read "son"): the female-for-male substitution is blatant in the Pietà allusion.

The lesson of "Hansel and Gretel," according to Bettelheim, is that the child must learn to curb his infantile desires and win self-sufficiency through his own ingenuity. The ingenuity of *Viskningar och rop* is the Orphic transformation of terror into art, of the loss of the mother into the musical richness of autumnal color and the self-sufficiency of memory. Color, internal rhymes, the trisecting of the protagonist, and the subtext of the fairy tale contribute to what Pasolini called the "pretextual 'free indirect discourse'" of Bergman's "cult of the object as symbol of the lost world" (HE, p. 181).

The rhetoric of cinematic modernism that aligns *Tysnaden* and *Persona* with the films Pasolini identified as "the 'cinema of poetry'" is not as pronounced in *Viskningar och rop*. Aspects of the television style—long takes and the use of the zoom lens to reframe in place of cutting—begin to appear in Bergman's films after 1969, when he made his first film for television: *Riten* (*The Rite*). The television films he made after *Viskningar och rop, Scener ur ett äktenskap* (*Scenes from a Marriage*) (1973), *Trollflöjten* (*The Magic Flute*) (1975), and *Ansikte mot ansikte* (*Face to Face*) (1978), permanently altered the filmmaker's mode of production and style. That style reverses the principle that Pasolini called "the first characteristic of the cinema of poetry...[that is] allowing the camera to be felt" (HE, p. 183). The influence of television production on Bergman's filmmaking entailed something of a return to the transparency and theatricality of a more conventional representation of cinematic time and space, after the radical stylization of *Tystnaden, Persona, Vartimmen* (*The Hour of the Wolf*) (1968) and *Skammen* (*Shame*) (1968).

Nevertheless, the primal scene schema that drove the modernist structures of *Fangelse, Tystnaden, Persona*, and *Viskningar och rop* is explicit in Bergman's farewell film, *Fanny och Alexander*. In this case the Oedipal adolescent takes center stage. In both its forms, the 312-minute-long television version in four episodes and the 188-minute film given theatrical release, Alexander Ekdahl dominates the action. He is the son of a theatrical family, living in a sumptuous apartment in what seems to be Uppsala with his mother, Emelie, an actress, and his father, Oscar, an actor and theater manager. In the same building lives his grandmother, Helena, a retired actress, and the families of his two uncles, Gustav-Adolf, who runs the restaurant attached to the Ekdahl's theater, and Carl, a professor. Alexander has a younger sister, and Gustav-Adolf has three children. Seven live-in maids attend the extended family.

After Oscar collapses during a rehearsal of *Hamlet* and dies, Emelie remarries and removes her two children to the austere home of her second husband, Bishop Vergérus, who brutally disciplines Alexander and attempts to isolate his wife and her children from the Ekdahls. The Cabbalistic magician and antique dealer, Isak Jacobi, a friend of Helena and formerly her lover, spirits away Fanny and Alexander to hide them in his shop. When the bishop dies in a fire, caused apparently by the imaginative power of Alexander's will, Emelie returns to the Ekdahl apartment with the children and takes over the management of the theater.

Just as Bergman restructured Carl Dreyer's tragedy, *Vredens Dag* (*Day of Wrath*) (1943), as a comedy in *Sommarnattens leende* (*Smiles of a Summer Night*) (1955), he managed to transform his earlier primal scene dramas into a tragicomedy with *Fanny och Alexander*. He achieves this, I believe, by making the primal scene scenario more explicit than it has been in his earlier masterpieces. There was even a moment when he decided to make his protagonist describe witnessing his mother in the throes of sexual ecstasy. In the published script Alexander tells Fanny: "[The Bishop] was lying on top of Mama with his nightshirt drawn up over his skinny arse, jerking up and down and making the whole bed shake. Mama was calling for help and praying to God. God, oh dear God, she moaned just like this." However, the filmmaker did not include this speech in either version of the film. Nor did he make it clear, as the script indicates, that neither Alexander nor Fanny are Oscar's natural children, although in the longer version Helena refers to Oscar's indulgence of Emelie's infidelities. In *Fanny och Alexander*, as in *Sommarnattens leende*, adultery is a comic matter.

Viewers familiar with Bergman's 1987 autobiography will see in the Ekdahl family an idealized version of the filmmaker's background (and in the home of Bishop Vergérus a demonic parody of the household of his own father, a stern Lutheran minister). Transposing his maternal grandparents, the Åkerbloms, to the paternal side of the family, he modeled Helena Mandelbaum Ekdahl on his grandmother, Anna Åkerblom, who kept a statue of Venus de Milo in her opulent fourteen-room apartment. The young Ingmar liked to imagine it coming to life. Much later, he recognized a similar "secret terror" when he saw the statue in Cocteau's *Le sang d'un poète* come alive.[9] The exterior shots of the Ekdahl apartment were filmed near to the Åkerblom apartment in

Uppsala.[10] Emelie Ekdahl, like Karin Åkerblom, Bergman's mother, is an adulteress, but Oscar is far more understanding and tolerant of her sexuality than Erik Bergman was of his wife's. Like the filmmaker, Alexander has one sister of whom he is fond, but the older brother and rival whom Ingmar Bergman disliked has been eliminated from the fantasy. However, he retained the crucial Christmas present (given initially to his older brother, Dag, and swapped to Ingmar for toy soldiers) of a magic lantern. If the autobiographical allusions are to be strictly followed, the correspondence would make Alexander nine years old at the start of the film. The lame servant, Maj, comes directly from the Bergman household, her name slightly altered from Marit. "The best thing in the world," Bergman wrote, "was to lie on her arm in her bed with my nose pressed against her coarse nightgown" (*The Magic Lantern*, p. 20). Whereas the autobiographer writes of the fascinating urinating habits of his uncle, Carl Åkerblom, Carl Ekdahl amuses his nephews and nieces by extinguishing a candelabra with his flatulence. An aunt who staged family entertainments with Chinese shadow puppets was probably the source for the aunt with the magic lantern slides of Hansel and Gretel in *Viskningar och rop*, and her puppets may have suggested the Japanese puppets in Isak Jacobi's shop. In fact, many passages in the early chapters of *The Magic Lantern* read like a scenario for *Fanny och Alexander*.

The film idealizes many of the autobiographical reflections by transforming the "security and magic" (p. 18) of his grandmother's environment into the multifamily apartment building and fusing it with the displacement of what he described as his actual "searing experience" (p. 33) of accompanying a musician, night after night, who played backstage at a production of Strindberg's *The Dream Play* into a fantasy childhood as an extra in the Ekdahl theater. The free-thinking Ekdahls abound in the tolerance and indifference to social opinion that Pastor Bergman's family lacked. When the filmmaker was six, his mother had to fire a beloved servant because she became pregnant. The Ekdahls, in contrast, support Maj and celebrate the birth of her daughter, conceived from Gustav-Adolf's premature ejaculation on Christmas Eve. The cruelty and terror Bergman recalls in *The Magic Lantern* became the source of his representation of the bishop and his household. Alexander repeats a lie that the young Ingmar told his schoolmates: that his parents had contracted to sell him to a circus. When his teacher contacted his family, "There was a dreadful court scene. I was put up against the wall, humiliated and disgraced, at home as well as at school" (p. 11). Alexander's first sustained contact with the bishop occurs shortly after his father's death, when Emelie introduces him in order to reprove the boy for telling his schoolmates that she negotiated to sell him to a circus. Erik Bergman's punishments of his son—interrogations, forced confessions followed by kissing his ring, strokes of a carpet-beater, confinement in a dark closet—become the Dickensian tortures the bishop repeatedly inflicts on Alexander.

From the very start of the film, "the primal scene schema" as expounded by Henry Edelheit is operating. Although the greatest concentration of the ambiguities of Edelheit's five questions occurs late in the film (during the encounter of Alexander and Isak's sexually ambiguous nephew, Ismail), the very opening entails a fine example of the fifth point—the fusion of the observer with the observed. The prologue begins with a slow pan down the front of a child's cardboard theater, from the inscription "Not for Pleasure Alone" to a painted backdrop of a Greek landscape with temples and statues, which slowly rises to reveal a castle before which cutout figures show a young woman eyeing a young man, with two other men conversing off to the side. The rising backdrops clearly indicate an imaginary viewer watching the spectacle. So it is a surprise when the castle backdrop rises to reveal not another setting but a boy (Alexander) manipulating the figures. With a mild shock we experience the fusion and the separation of the observer and the observed.

Alexander places a regal female between the young lovers and then rests his head on his arm wistfully, as if bored with his theater. By placing his protagonist behind the scene rather than in front of it, as the first seconds of the shot would lead us to expect, the filmmaker locates the ambiguity of the observer and the participant in a theatrical space in which the drama is only implicitly libidinal. If we take the cardboard drama as a version of *Hamlet* (which is in rehearsal at the Ekdahl's theater at that moment, and for which the children of the house plead for walk-on roles), Alexander has interrupted the liason of Ophelia and Hamlet by inserting Queen Gertrude between them.

The subsequent twenty-seven shots of the prologue gloss the meaning of this cardboard mise-en-scène. In a sense they represent Alexander's first visual soliloquy, or what Pasolini might identify as his initial "free indirect point of view." A fluidly mobile camera, with a zoom lens, in Bergman's masterly television style, follows him as he goes from room to room, cutting as he passes each threshold and panning to show what he sees rather than introducing point of view shots. His speech is minimal; he calls out names, "Fanny" and "Mother" at first, as if obliquely naming the cardboard figures in his play theater, the names of two servants, and finally "Grandma." This onomastic ritual is not a conjuration but rather the precautionary assurance that he is alone in the rooms he is exploring. A telling pan to an ornate doorknob hints that he is about to invade a more restricted space. It turns out to be his grandmother's apartment. After calling her name to secure the space, he leaps onto her empty bed and buries his head under her pillow.

Right after this playful Oedipal gesture of superseding his father to take the place of his long-dead grandfather, we see the boy enthroned in an alcove and hear him speaking his only two complete sentences of the prologue: "I am the king of seventeen lands. Heed me." But no sooner does he initiate this impersonation of a king than he hears a rat (which suggests perhaps the moment when Hamlet kills Polonius, mistaking him for his hiding stepfather, but claiming to attack a rat). At this point the cinematic syntax shifts slightly. The filmmaker cuts from a long shot of the boy sitting in the alcove to a closer shot as he leaps, as if in fear for his genitals, and looks first under his seat and then beside him to discover the rodent trapped in a cage. In a close-up he studies the animal and then frees it. This socially aggressive gesture of kindness suggests an act of identification with the rat. In his autobiography Bergman wrote of his grandmother's apartment: "At the end of the long dark hall was an interesting room with four holes bored in the door near the floor, red wallpaper, a mahogany-and-plush thronelike chair with brass fitting and ornamentations. Two steps covered with soft carpeting led up to the throne and, when you opened the heavy lid of the chair, you stared down into a chasm of darkness and odours. Courage was required to sit on Grandmother's throne."[11] The rat and its liberation reflect the play of fear and courage the autobiographer recalled from his ventures onto the cloacal throne.

The next shot slowly reveals Alexander gazing out of a frosted-over window. The first point-of-view shot in the film shows what he sees: a man driving a horse cart loaded with furniture, grimly contrasted to the vivid colors of flowers for sale on the street. Apparently a family has been evicted on Christmas Eve. This first Dickensian moment in the film foreshadows Alexander's fate following the death of his father. His explicit usurpation of the role of the king, coupled to the oblique identifications with the humble victims of power, reflects the ambivalence and guilt Alexander feels as a result of his Oedipal fantasies.

Furthermore, this fusion of contradictory roles introduces the primal scene fantasy at the heart of the prologue. Bergman disguises the causes and effects inscribed in the sequence of shots by representing Alexander as aimlessly wandering from room to room, bored, seeking some form of amusement. So the connections between his failed role as an emperor, his vision of distress and poverty, and the daydream that follows seem at first merely paratactic. However, within the logic of the primal scene schema that covertly orchestrates the opening of the film as thoroughly, though less enigmatically, as the pretitle sequence of *Persona*, Alexander's transition to the role of the observer of simultaneously enticing and terrifying apparitions is determined by his inability to sustain the role of the omnipotent male. He dives under a table, where, alternately closing and rolling back his eyes, he *sees*, in the first sustained shot-countershot sequence of the film, a statue of Aphrodite beckon to him. There is an aspect of the opening of *Viskningar och rop* in this scene. The classical statue has been transferred from the Primal Garden of the earlier film to the grandmother's sumptuously decorated interior, and the mechanism of the antique clock is even more elaborate. It reproduces one described in the autobiography (p. 21). As three o'clock sounds, golden putti holding cymbals and a flute move in a circle, the chandelier tinkles to the reverberations of the clock's bells, and the statue of Aphrodite moves one of her hands as if beckoning Alexander toward her while an anchor-like spike moves across the floor.

A slow pan, as if charting the boy's reluctant gaze, stops at the skeleton head of a death figure receding behind tall plants. But just then the rumble of coal poured into a chute by one of the maids breaks the reverie at the moment that Helena, Alexander's grandmother, enters, turns toward the camera, and, spotting Alexander under the table, invites him to play a game of cards.

Until the statue moves, everything in the prologue conforms to the orders of realism. Thus the solicitation by the goddess of erotic love is the turning point and telos of the prologue as an elaborate introduction to Alexander's psyche. The postponement of the magical event brings into play the first ambiguity in Edelheit's schema. Because the opening shots tutored us to understand the camera movements as indices of Alexander's subjectivity, and because nothing in his passage through the apartments violated the patterns of realism, the transition to shot-countershot alone would not alert us to a shift of modality. The sudden movement of the marble arm and hand, then, pose Edelheit's first question: What is happening? The rest of the film will answer it by deepening and complicating the interplay of imagination and actuality. When Bergman cut down the film for its theatrical release, he eliminated both the emperor-rat sequence and the death figure, implying that his protagonist's fascination with observing the Aphrodisian mysteries is more essential to his film than the threatening images of the trapped rodent, the phallic spike, and the skeletal male. This emphasis is consistent with the comic resolution of the film and with its representation of the imaginative life of Alexander as a young artist; for, in the first episode proper, "The Ekdahl Family Celebrates Christmas," the boy transmutes his primal vision into a seductive (and aggressive) spectacle for his sister and cousins.

The toy that the young Bergman traded for was a primitive film projector that cranked a loop of film. In *Fanny och Alexander* the boy's gift projects slides, in keeping with the fictive time of the narrative, the end of the nineteenth century. After the children have been put to bed on Christmas Eve, Alexander assembles his magic lantern. However, the performance he will give is intricately connected to the events leading up to it. In bringing the children to the nursery, Maj, who seems to have drunk a good deal at Christmas dinner, indulges them in a massive pillow fight culminating in an explosion of feathers, an echo of the dormitory fight in Jean Vigo's anarchic *Zéro de conduit* (1933). As she is wrestling on the floor with Alexander, in a sexually suggestive manner, the tipsy mothers, Emelie and Alma, enter to end the ruckus. In a manifestation of ambivalence Alma slaps Maj's face and tells her to come to her for her Christmas present. Although the viewers must understand the slap as an expression of jealousy (for Gustav-Adolf has been openly flirting with the maid and is about to have intercourse with her), for the children, especially Alexander, who is emotionally attached to Maj, the conjunction of aggression and generosity would be a manifestation of the puzzling ambiguity of parental behavior characteristic of Edelheit's primal scene schema. His second and fourth questions are elided in the fusion of violence and affection between the women: Who is the aggressor? and Which one has the penis?

Before the mothers leave, they make the children recite their prayers and kiss them good night. Recognizing the preadolescent sexuality of the boys, Emelie, giggling, tells Alma that her son, Putte, "kisses like a man." As a night-light, Alma illuminates a transparency of the Nativity, replicating a memory from the autobiography: "Later in the evening I woke up. Gertrud was singing a folksong downstairs and the nightlight was glowing. A transparency of the Nativity scene and the shepherds at prayer was glimmering faintly on the tall chest-of-drawers. Among my brother's other Christmas presents on the white gate-legged table was the cinematograph..." (p. 15). Bergman meticulously recreates this moment in the film. Alexander can faintly hear Carl's German wife singing Schumann's leid, "Du Ring an meinem Finger," for the adults. He also inserts a revealing elaboration. Maj returns to show off the dress Alma has given her and to tell him that he cannot come to her bedroom that night because she will have a visitor. Distressed at this rejection, he spurns her attempts to soothe him. This is the clearest indication that the affair of Maj and Gustav-Adolf is a displacement of the primal scene trauma for the boy. Its logic is confirmed by the overdetermined conclusion of the film, with the simultaneous births of daughters to Maj and Emelie (who had been pregnant when Bishop Vergérus died). Furthermore, the film elaborates the displaced primal scene scenario when, following his impregnation of Maj, Gustav-Adolf has sex with Alma, conspicuously locking their adolescent daughter, Petra, out of the room as she brings them their breakfast. Completing the logic of primal scene retribution, it is Petra who subsequently persuades Maj to leave the Ekdahl family with her to set up a shop together, against her father's efforts to keep Maj and the baby in the household.

Thus it is within the context of an elaborate exfoliation of the primal scene schema that Alexander operates the magic lantern for the first time. He projects and narrates, at first reading from a book, the story of Arabella: "There she lies, the beautiful girl, poor Arabella. Little does she know what awaits her. She's alone in the whole house. Oh! Oh! Her mother is dead, and her father is carousing with loose companions. Who comes then as the clock strikes 12:00 in the castle tower? 'Fear seizes me. What is that terrifying white figure floating on moonbeams and drawing near my bed? It is my dead mother. My mother's ghost.'" Just as Bergman did in *Tystnaden*, *Persona*, and *Visningar och rop*, Alexander has feminized what will be his own story: a dead father and a mother carousing with an objectionable man. Likewise, the ghost of Arabella's mother prefigures the ghost of Hamlet's father, played by Oscar in the next episode of the film. In fact, Oscar dies during that rehearsal and returns as a ghost, appearing to both Alexander and Helena. The bishop's two drowned daughters, Pauline and Esmeralda, will later appear briefly, haunting Alexander, as does the ghost of Bishop Vergérus himself at the end of the film. In performing the ghost story Alexander is attempting to frighten the children of the nursery. One of the typical consequences of primal scene trauma is the tendency to perpetuate the disturbance by unconsciously contriving situations to expose others to versions of the primal scene. Thus, for Alexander, the magic lantern becomes a tool of mastery over his own humiliation at being excluded from Maj's bed (itself a displacement of his mother's bed) and the instrument through which he manipulates the emotions of others. In a parallel scene, at the climax of the film, he will experience terror and humiliation before the puppets of Aron, Isak's nephew and Ismail's brother.

There is another factor at play in the primal scene imagery of the nursery. Edelheit has shown that mythological beasts imaginatively fused from two creatures—such as sphinxes, centaurs, and griffins—are figures for the ambiguous and frightening coupling of the parents. Bergman's most explicit use of this imagery occurs in *Tystnaden* when the preadolescent boy is fascinated by the dwarf with a monkey mask jumping on a bed and by a replica of Rubens's painting of Deianira raped by centaurs. Just at the point in Alexander's magic lantern show when the ghost of Arabella's mother floats toward her, the audience of children is frightened by Putte, coming from behind them wearing an animal mask. Another mythological creature in *Fanny och Alexander* is an angel—half man, half bird. In the nursery an angel dominates the Nativity transparency. Significantly, in the Christmas pageant performed earlier in the Ekdahl's theater, Emelie, wearing wings as prominent as those in the transparency, played the Angel Gabriel. Admittedly, angels are so domesticated in Christian imagery that they hardly register as composite creatures. Yet such domestication and invisibility consistently mark the differences between the earlier primal scene manifestations in Bergman's cinema and *Fanny och Alexander*, in which festive comedy disguises the traumatic undersong and in which, conversely, the subterranean film of primal scene schemata is so near the surface. Oscar, appropriately, played Joseph in the pageant. The published film script makes quite clear what the film barely intimates: that Oscar was asexual or impotent. Alexander was the son of an actor who had been in their company and Fanny the daughter of a visiting archbishop.[12]

Alerted by the smell of paraffin from the magic lantern, Oscar enters the nursery to investigate, but rather than make sure the children go to sleep, he puts on a performance of his own, transforming a common object into a magical, and ambivalent, presence. His act, like his son's, shifts the Oedipal drama into a female register. He weaves a story around a nursery chair, asserting that it was once the throne of a diminutive Chinese empress, stolen by pirates from her tomb. He asserts that it is made of precious metals and is luminous in the dark (foreshadowing the mummy in Isak's shop). But after warning the children to treat it gently and to breathe on it at least twice a day, he ducks into their closet, reemerges as a nasty crone, and attacks the chair for biting him. Thus his magical fable reflects the brief moment in the prologue when Alexander played the emperor of seventeen lands only to be frightened by a rat under his throne.

The next time we see Oscar in the film he is rehearsing his role as Hamlet's father's ghost. In the published script the episode of the magic lantern does not end with Oscar's departure from the nursery. Instead, Alexander announces to Fanny that he will make his acting debut as Macbeth, and then he recites the famous soliloquy from Act V when he learns of Lady Macbeth's death ("Tomorrow, and tomorrow, and tomorrow..."). More than any other of Shakespeare's heroes, Macbeth is the figure of guilt. In identifying with this role, Alexander confirms a crucial dimension of Frank Gado's reading of the film. Gado writes that

> Oscar's dying...serves to suggest a deeper analogy with the psychological underpinning of Shakespeare's [*Hamlet*]. When the father calls his son to his bed for a final word, the boy resists. The other members of the family assume that the child is merely frightened by the strangeness of death, but one can infer from subsequent events that the real reason is guilt for having wished his father were out of the way so he can have his mother all to himself (just as he will later wish his stepfather's death into occurring)...The Bishop represents a surrogate self to be hated and punished for acting out Alexander's desires. More obviously, he is also the other half of the split father image—not the emasculated Oscar who makes the son feel guilty but the overpowering sexual rival who makes him feel impotent...Trying to extricate himself from his Oedipal trap, Alexander (or Bergman) in effect creates a new father for himself in Isak Jacobi...To create the appearance of continuity, Bergman inserted a brief scene, not found in the screenplay, in which Alexander is visited by the Bishop's ghost and put on notice that he will be haunted for the rest of his life. Yet, although this displacement of Oscar's ghost by the stepfather's further implies the two fathers' common identity and brings an awareness of the boy's guilt closer to the surface, it is essentially a gloss...Clearly, Bergman's fascination is with the psychosexual anguish expressed through the nuclear dream; the rest is a conjurer's trick performed both for his own diversion and to enlist an audience's sentimental approval.[13]

Here, as generally, I find Gado to be the best critic of Bergman's films writing in English, although I cannot subscribe to his judgment of the film as "actually two films"—a sentimental "outer layer" and a "chilling...core" (p. 498). *Fanny och Alexander* is as much about conjurer's tricks as it is an expression of psychosexual anguish. The bildungsroman of Alexander is the story of his apprenticeship as a conjurer; Oscar shows his superior skill as a conjurer in the transformation of the nursery chair; but the master conjurers of the film would be Isak Jacobi and his nephews, Aron and Ismail, who have mastered arts far exceeding those of the Ekdahls. Shakespeare, however, haunts the film as the greatest conjurer of them all.

The first play the Ekdahls' theater performed after Oscar's death was *Hamlet*; the last before it temporarily closed when Emelie married the bishop was *Twelfth Night*. One of Oscar's deathbed wishes had been that everything should go on as usual. Emelie tried to fulfill this wish, but another, that there be no pompous cathedral funeral, she ignored. It was the funeral that brought her into a relationship with Bishop Vergérus that eventually subverted the continuity of the theater. It also exiled Alexander from the magical realm of his grandmother's apartment building. The world of the theater is congruent with that of the Ekdahl apartment: Oscar's Christmas speech to his troupe matches Gustav-Adolf's final oration welcoming the two babies in the epilogue; theirs is the "little world," which reflects the big and evil world outside and still provides a refuge from it.

The televised version of the film, like a Shakespearean play, is divided into five acts: the prologue and first act form the first televised episode, the second and third acts make up the second, the fourth act corresponds to the third episode, and the fifth act and the epilogue appear as the fourth and final episode. There are subtle and intricate connections among the episodes. The panning movement down from the top of Alexander's play theater that opens the prologue recurs to open the second act, moving down the image of a similar theatre on the poster for *Hamlet*. The core of the prologue is further reflected in the next two shots: Alexander peers from behind the stage curtain to a countershot of Oscar as the ghost of Hamlet's father, reciting "My hour is almost come/When I to sulph'rous and tormenting flames/ Must render myself." More obliquely, the third act opens with Feste, bringing down the curtain of *Twelfth Night*, singing the song whose chorus line is "For the rain it raineth every day," while the fourth act opens with a montage of details of a rainstorm at the Ekdahl's summer house in the Stockholm archipelago. The lie Alexander invents in the third act—that the ghosts of the bishop's two daughters told him of how they and their mother drowned as they tried to escape from their father (and for which he is severely punished)—reverberates in the images of a turned-over doll carriage abandoned in the rain at the start of the fourth act and even more directly in the skeleton of a horse in the very river where they drowned at the opening of the fifth.

This act, subtitled "Demons," constitutes the turning point of Alexander's education and instantiates Edelheit's primal scene schema most fully. It is also the section of the film most marked by the agency of a styleme of what Pasolini might have called a "free indirect point of view," although the particular styleme—parallel montage—is not to be found in his catalogue of tropes of "the cinema of poetry." As the act progresses, Bergman pushes the parallel montage toward magical causality. Even if up to this point the film has induced us to accept the fictive validity of ghosts, a new degree of uncanny magic will raise all five of the questions Edelheit associated with the double identification of the primal scene schema. We might wonder, What is happening? when Isak, visiting the bishop ostensibly to purchase an antique chest from him, somehow manages by magic to whisk away the children inside it despite Vergérus's suspicion that that is his plan. Bergman seems to be deliberately playing with us by showing, at first, Isak's magic in a purely theatrical manner. Letting himself into the room where the children are locked with a skeleton key while the bishop is preparing a receipt, Isak gets them to hide in the chest. He puts a black cloth over them. When he opens the lid for Vergérus to show him he is not stealing anything, we can accept the theatrical convention that the bishop sees nothing, especially because the filmmaker does not give us a point-of-view shot of the inside of the coffer. But when the bishop rushes to the locked room to make sure Fanny and Alexander are still there, the shot of them lying on the floor, watched over by Emelie, baffles us. What is happening? Even if one reason is that Isak substituted puppets made by his nephew Aron for that purpose, there is nothing in the scene to indicate how he would have smuggled them into the room. Furthermore, the transition between the shot of Vergérus accusing the shopkeeper of stealing the children and the image of him looking at their bodies on the floor is startlingly enigmatic: as the bishop charges up the stairs, Jacobi makes two fists and lets out a scream, apparently causing a brilliant light to flood first his face and then the whole scene until the shot whites out. Neither the scream nor the blaze of light are mentioned in the published script.

When Isak's assistants carry the chest into his shop, the two children step out of it. Later Aron will gloss this mystery, and perhaps the whole film, when he tells Alexander: "If one is brought up as a magician, and has learned all the tricks in childhood, then one can do without supernatural interference! A sorcerer like me prefers to show what is understandable: it is up the spectators to provide what is not." If the prologue introduced the range of Alexander's native imagination, the scenes in Isak Jacobi's shop show how that imaginative power can be intensified and refined under the tutelage of the nephews. The initial parallelism of the two episodes involves the sequence of doors through which the boy passes when he wakes in the night, seeking to urinate and to explore the environs at the same time. Just as he cautiously called out names in the opening of the film, he talks aloud to himself in case Isak or Aron can hear him, even though he sees them asleep: "I must pee... Damn, I think I've lost my way... Now I'm lost, for sure..." Like Alexander, Aron has a puppet theater, but a much more elaborate one with monumental marionettes; like the vivified statue of Aphrodite, there is a mummy in the shop that moves, capable of turning its head at Aron's command.

Repeatedly as Alexander moves through Isak's shop, Bergman cuts to the bishop's residence. As the sequence progresses, the parallel montage becomes more and more precise, moving from an indeterminate temporal zone to simultaneous events, until simultaneity ultimately blends into causality. In the first instance, Isak starts to translate from Hebrew and then seems to be inventing a story for the children about a young man on a lonely quest for a salvific bath in the condensed tears of human hopes and despairs. As the children go to sleep, the scene shifts to an embassy by Carl and Gustav-Adolf to negotiate Emelie's freedom from her husband, but at his bidding and as if in fear of his reprisals, she begs the brothers to restore the children from Isak's kidnapping. The intercutting suggests this is going on the very night of their escape.

As soon as the failed negotiations end, we see Alexander awaken, needing to urinate. Failing to find a toilet, he relieves himself in a potted plant, recalling Johan, the boy of *Tystnaden*, who peed in the hotel corridor after his encounter with the dwarfs. His first sustained encounter in the shop is with his father's ghost, whom he chides for his supernatural impotence: "Why can't you go to God and tell him to kill the bishop? Or doesn't God give a damn about you, or any of us?" As Oscar urges a gentler spirit on the boy, the scene returns to Emelie and Vergérus, drinking tea because they cannot sleep. When the bishop articulates his surprise that anyone could hate him as Alexander does, we return to the boy who seems to wake from dozing in the shop just as a key magically turns in a door. Then he hears the voice of God answering his question, "Who is behind the door?" After giving him the Mosaic warning that no man can see God and live, the divine voice terrifies Alexander by announcing his imminent appearance. "This is the end of me," the boy whimpers as the whole shop rumbles and the large foot of a puppet God descends, followed by the massive bearded marionette, with Aron behind him, mocking Alexander's fright at his uncanny performance.

The screenplay makes the primal scene allusion much more concrete than the film does. In a passage of dialogue between Alexander and the voice of God, which Bergman eliminated, the boy answers the question "Is there anything greater than love?" with "Well, if there is it would be His Grace the bishop's cockstand." This response places the phallic power of Vergérus directly in opposition to the helpless ghost of Oscar. It also invokes the similarly suppressed scene in which Alexander told Fanny of how he had witnessed his stepfather and their mother having sex. Instead of including these explicit references to the primal scene, the filmmaker lets the parallel montage establish links between Alexander's meeting with Aron and Ismail and the intimate life of Vergérus and Emelie. A subtle clue to that interaction is the sudden shift to the boy and Aron drinking cups of coffee, after we had seen the bishop and his wife drinking tea in the previous shift of scene. In Ismail's chamber, where his uncle keeps him locked up, the prisoner immediately offers Alexander a drink of the coffee Aron has brought him. Between Emelie and Vergérus the shared drink is her ruse to drug him and escape, with the unanticipated consequence of his fatal inability to escape the fire his aunt starts. But for Aron, Ismail, and Alexander, the drink represents their Cabbalistic communion.

However, a more dynamic interaction occurs when Aron induces the mummy to turn its head toward Alexander. Bergman cuts on a matching movement to a very short scene of Elsa, the paralyzed, idiotic aunt of the bishop, turning her head toward the kerosene lamp by her bed and reaching out to it; as soon as she touches it, the inserted parallel ends. In the previous scene in the Episcopal manse her nephew had moved the lamp closer to her when she complained of darkness. This is the first, tentative suggestion of a magical and causal connection in which the events in the shop are affecting what goes on in the bishop's house.

Soon after that, Bergman steps up the indices of simultaneity as Aron leads Alexander into the forbidden chamber where the dangerous Ismail dwells. When he unlocks the outer of the two doors that hold his brother, the scene cuts to the bishop's bedroom, where he half-wakes, drugged, to hear Emelie tell him she is leaving. When we return to the shop, Aron knocks again, unlocks the same door, as if an instant of time had opened to expand into the dramatic confrontation of mother and stepfather.

Inside the chamber the scene between Ismail and Alexander recalls the climactic exchange between Elisabet and Alma in *Persona*. Ominously, Ismail asks to be left alone with Alexander. Before locking them in together, Aron gives his brother a long kiss on the lips. Bergman cast a woman, Stina Ekblad, as Ismail, making his sexual presence visibly ambiguous. That ambiguity underlines his mysterious identity. An onomastic ritual brings to a full circle the recital of names with which Alexander began the film. Once they are alone together, Ismail commands Alexander to write his name on a scrap of paper; but when the boy tries to read back what he wrote, he finds he has written "Ismail Retzinsky." In this symbolic equation (Alexander = Ismail), the biblical tag which Ismail applied to himself becomes true of Alexander as well: "And he will be a wild man; his hand will be against every man, and every man's hand against him."

To the boy's puzzlement over this trick, Ismail suggests: "Perhaps we are the same person. Perhaps we have no limits; perhaps we flow into each other, stream through each other, boundlessly and magnificently." The mysterious fusion of *Persona* thus becomes an explicit but substantially verbal theme in *Fanny och Alexander*, as Ismail's sorcery brings into play Edelheit's third question: "How many people are involved? One? Two? Several? Or is it one composite creature?" Ismail's gender ambiguity triggers the fourth: "What is the anatomy of the scene? If it is made up of more than one individual, which one has the penis?" The latter is particularly apt insofar as the filmmaker has invested the episode with a disturbing suggestion of pederasty. As Ismail reveals Alexander's own thoughts to him, he stands close behind him, having removed the boy's shirt. Alexander's discomfort during this scene is a masterpiece of Bergman's direction. Ostensibly, he is distressed because Ismail is forcing him to focus his mind on killing the bishop, but the mise-en-scène suggests the homosexual seduction of a frightened preadolescent.

It seems clear that Ismail can read the boy's mind. In the previous act, Alexander had tried to kill the bishop by a sheer naïve act of will. Together with Fanny, he had concentrated on their stepfather's death, vainly uttering the formula: "Die, devil, die!" But now, under Ismail's guidance, and through the magic of parallel montage, he succeeds, to his own horror. During the earlier attempt, the children could hear the bishop below playing his flute that signaled the failure of their efforts. Now, as Ismail whispers in Alexander's ear, the sound of the flute returns as a motif of the bishop's death. For the first time in the intercutting of scenes, the soundtrack of the action in the antique shop does not give way as the brief scenes from the bishop's house appear. When we see Elsa touching the lamp, continuing the very gesture which the earlier insert had suspended, we hear Ismail refusing Alexander's plea to stop: "It is not I talking. It is yourself." As we see Elsa's room engulfed in flames and the woman on fire staggering out of bed, Ismail uses the future tense: "The doors will be thrown open. A scream will echo through the house." Then, returning to images of Ismail and Alexander, the sorcerer revises the sequence in the present tense: "The doors are thrown open. No, wait. First, a horrible scream echoes through the house. A shapeless burning figure moves across the floor." The revision literalizes the temporal magic of cinematic montage that, as the sequence has already demonstrated, can suspend, repeat, and dramatically intensify actions or shift their illusionary mode from imagination to actuality.

In casting this spell, Ismail persistently frustrates Alexander's attempts to stop him, while assuring him of their fusion and of his spiritual authority: "I obliterate myself," he tells him. "I am your guardian angel." Thus the angelic presence that entered the film as a theatrical convention when Emelie put on wings to play in the Nativity pageant and that mutely presided over Alexander's playful conjuring of a ghost in his magic lantern debut culminates in the self-definition of the supernaturally powerful woman-man who is at once Alexander's projection, his double, and his demonic tutor.

It would be possible to read all the extraordinary events in the shop as Alexander's dream, if we take figuratively the moment when he lifts his head at the sound of the door opening in Aron's puppet theater. Such a reading would make the puppet show, the mummy, and the meeting with Ismail oneiric phantasms. Within the fiction we would still have to take the parallel scenes in the bishop's manse as actual, as they correspond to the report the police give Emelie the next morning when they interview her at Helena's apartment, where Alexander hears their account, although we have no indication of how he got from Isak's shop to his grandmother's house that morning. However, so long as the unexplained magic of Isak's rescue of the children remains unresolved, an argument for interpreting Aron's and Ismail's occult powers as Alexander's dream is weak.

Aron, true to his biblical namesake, is the spokesman for Bergman's relationship to his audience in this film that was intended to be the finale of his career. He tells Alexander, "Anything unintelligible makes people angry. It's much better to blame the apparatus and mirrors and projections. Then people start laughing and that's healthier from all points of view—particularly the financial one." Bergman first won an international reputation on his magical comedy *Sommarnattens Leende*. His success was sealed by the two films that followed it: *Det Sjunde Inseglet* (*The Seventh Seal*) (1957) and *Smultronstället* (*Wild Strawberries*) (1957). The former was clearly an allegory in the medieval mode, the latter a spiritual biography with dream sequences and flashbacks unambiguously depicted as the imaginary experiences of its protagonist. The mixture of genres and the ambiguous magical events would make *Fanny och Alexander* a riskier project, according to Aron's precepts.

In his most convivial moment with Alexander, as they share cups of coffee, the puppeteer humorously illustrates his point with a story about his parents, who operated a "conjurer's theater" in Russia. He relates how the ghost of his father's recently dead aunt showed up in the midst of a stage performance, lost in the maze of mirrors and projectors. "It was a fiasco and Papa had to refund admission." Ironically, the ghost balled up the carefully orchestrated illusionism. An audience is unprepared to pay for the genuine intervention of the uncanny.

Isak's shop embodies the aesthetical and metaphysical core of the creation and presentation of art. The men who inhabit it form a curious Trinity: Isak Jacobi, as Aron describes his beliefs, is a Spinozan metaphysician, who claims we are "surrounded by realities, one outside the other... [in which] the smallest pebble has a life of its own... [insofar as] everything is God's thought, not only what is good but also the cruelest things." Aron and Ismail correspond to Apollo and Dionysus, in Nietzsche's dichotomy: Aron is the craftsman of illusions and the principle of individuation, while Ismail represents the collective powers of the will. Even the eddy of biblical names they bear suggests a network of poetically productive fraternal and father-son tensions: Isak, Jacob(i), Ismail, Aron. In their shop, Alexander receives his initiation into the mysteries of the origins of representation, as well as a lesson in their economics. The final measure of Alexander's education is his introduction to Strindberg. In the prologue Helena proposed to play a game of cards with him. At the conclusion of the epilogue she reads aloud to him from the text of the new play that will bring her out of retirement: August Strindberg's *Ett drömspel* (*A Dream Play*) (1901, first performed in 1907). In his sixty-year-long career as a theater director, Bergman himself mounted many productions of Strindberg. He directed *A Dream Play* three times, twice before *Fanny och Alexander* and once after. Helena reads from the opening paragraph of the preface to the play: "...Time and space do not exist. On a flimsy foundation of reality imagination spins out and weaves new patterns..."; but she stops before Strindberg speaks of his cast: "Characters split, double, multiply, vanish, solidify, blur, clarify. But one consciousness reigns above them all—that of the dreamer."

Following his first encounter with the bishop's ghost, who knocked him to the ground and told him he would never escape him, Alexander put his head in Helena's lap. Thus the crucial phase of the haunted boy's education concludes with an aesthetic artifact that corresponds to his intense experience of the magic of the mind. The sentence Helena does not read, however, prefigures Pasolini's formulation of "free indirect points of view."

Andrey *Tarkovsky*:
Zerkalo (1975)
Dream of the mother in the crumbling dacha
The young and old mothers see each other in a mirror
Soviet soldiers crossing Lake Sivash.
The Leningrad orphan on a hill, in imitation of Pieter Brueghel's "Hunters in Winter"

Andrey Tarkovsky's Concept of Poetry

A documentary work is an attempt to recapture someone somewhere looking back. Looking back, Orpheus was the first known documentarist: Orpheus, or Lot's wife.

—SUSAN HOWE[1]

The first cinematic site of Andrey Tarkovsky's quotation of poetry is *Zerkalo* (*Mirror*) (1974). There he quotes in toto four poems of his father, Arseny Tarkovsky, without identifying him as the author, as well as a substantial passage from a letter by Pushkin. The protagonist of *Stalker* (1979) recites another of Arseny Tarkovsky's poems, attributing it to a fictional character. Then, in *Nostalghia* (1983), yet two more of his poems, yet again unattributed, can be heard in the mode of *Zerkalo*.

Tarkovsky's theoretical book, *Sculpting in Time* (*Zapechat lennoe vremi a'*, literally "Depicted Time," 1986, English translation by Kitty Hunter-Blair, 1989), is saturated with references to and quotations of poetry, not only the poems of his father but also of Pushkin, Dante, Pasternak, Valéry, Mandelstam, Goethe, Shakespeare, and Bashō, along with prose masters Cervantes, Gogol, Proust, Joyce, Mann, Hemingway, Dostoyevsky, Tolstoy, Hesse, and Kleist. But even before he cites any of these writers (aside from the ubiquitous Dostoyevsky), he meditates on the meaning of "poetry." When he writes, in the opening chapter, of the genesis of his first feature film, *Ivanovo detstvo* (*Ivan's Childhood*) (1962), he makes the following extraordinary claim: "I find poetic links, the logic of poetry in cinema, extraordinarily pleasing. They seem to me to be perfectly appropriate to the potential of cinema as the most truthful and poetic of art forms."[2] Here the filmmaker not only identifies poetry with a principle of linkage but also asserts hyperbolically that cinema is "more poetic" than literary verse. He adds that discovering poetic links as a creator (and, he will later add, as a viewer) provides an intensity of pleasure. His elaboration of this point entails the introduction of a new category: thought. The poetic linking of cinema, he asserts, is in opposition to any "rigidly logical development of plot." In a sense, poetry is opposed to the conventions of drama that have been massively adapted by feature-film makers. "But film material can be joined together in another way, which works above all to open the logic of a person's thought."[3] Poetry then organizes its pleasurable links according to the processes of thought.

The subtle effects of Tarkovsky's filmic practice may guide us in understanding his radical claims for the poetry of cinema. I take it that he means that films may exhibit all the verbal linkages of poetry—rhyme, assonance, tropes, and so forth—and at the same time offer complementary systems of linkages on the visual and auditory levels. Associations of color, shape, movement, noise, music, and gesture are available to the filmmaker to evoke nuances and touch on profundities beyond the logic of plot. Cinema's mode of thought is not a static system of ideas and perceptions but something that "develops" or changes with time: "In my view poetic reasoning is closer to the laws by which thought develops, and thus to life itself, than is the logic of traditional drama" (*Sculpting in Time*; hereafter ST, p. 20). So, it seems, poetry approaches truth insofar as it reveals the unseen nature of life. Because it recapitulates the logic of life itself, poetic linkage triggers the emotions: "Through poetic connections feeling is heightened and the spectator is made more active" (p. 20).

The revelation of life then gives pleasurable feelings to both the creator and the spectator of films. How? Tarkovsky tells us that this occurs through "associative linking, which allows for an affective as well as a rational appraisal" (p. 20). This seems to be a rephrasing of his initial observation. He repeats it because he believes that the cinema has very rarely utilized its poetic potential. "It possesses an inner power which is concentrated within the image and comes across to the audience in the form of feelings, inducing tension in direct response to the author's narrative logic" (p. 20). That species of narrative logic must be synonymous with poetic linkage. He explains how this works. The spectator is not passive. Instead, he is compelled by the author "to build the separate parts into a whole."[4] Tarkovsky will tell us in a later chapter that the "artistic image is a 'metonym'."[5] The proper viewing of a film requires the spectator to organize its disparate elements by intuiting the poetic linkages of its construction, guided by the fundamental metonymy of cinematic imagery. The tension raised by this activity releases feelings of pleasure in the recognition of the associated links.

Then he explains that he is not just considering verses when he uses the word *poetry*. "When I speak of poetry I am not thinking of it as a genre. Poetry is an awareness of the world, a particular way of relating to reality."[6] Here "the world" and what he had called "life itself" are equivalents. Suddenly, he unleashes a barrage of names, citing painters, poets, and filmmakers who showed such an awareness of the world: Grin, Van Gogh, Prishvin, Mandelstam, Pasternak, Chaplin, Dovzhenko, Mizoguchi. These artists show that poetry is more than an associative psychology; it is ontology: "Such an artist can discern the lines of the poetic design of being. He is capable of going beyond the limitations of coherent logic, and conveying the deep complexity and truth of the impalpable connections and hidden phenomena of life" (p. 21). In effect, the links with which he began his discussion of poetry are allegories of the otherwise indiscernible movements of Being. What Tarkovsky never states, but nevertheless implies, is that the indiscernible movement of Being is Time, and that as the artistic instrument most adequately equipped to render time, cinema is the art of poetry *par excellence*.

Yet he distances his work from "poetic cinema" as he understands the term to be commonly used.[7] With its emphasis on symbolic action, "poetic cinema" loses touch with concrete reality. In contradistinction, Tarkovsky insists that the "basic element of cinema, running through it from its tiniest cells, is observation." In fact, he quotes two haiku as examples of the poetic power of "pure observation" (p. 66). Although he explicitly distinguishes his use of haiku as analogy for cinema from that of Eisenstein, who saw in the condensed Japanese poetic form a model for montage, the chief representative of "poetic cinema" for Tarkovsky would be not Eisenstein but Stan Brakhage, although he does not name him. I understand him to be polemicizing against Brakhage when he writes: "But a faithful record, a true chronicle, cannot be made by shooting by hand, with a wobbling camera, even making blurred shots—as if the camera-man hadn't quite managed to focus—or any other gimmicks of that kind...where everything is deliberately made incomprehensible and the director has to think up explanations for what he has done."[8] Fortunately, Brakhage has left a thorough account of his meeting with Tarkovsky at the Telluride Film Festival in 1983. It is a hilarious and heartbreaking story of Brakhage's enthusiastic but unappreciated introduction of the Soviet filmmaker at the American premiere of *Nostalghia* and his subsequent attempt to screen a selection of his own films for him while Tarkovsky shouted nonstop objections and insults, translated at Brakhage's insistence by Krzysztof Zanussi.[9] Ironically, the aesthetics of *Sculpting in Time* is closer to the theoretical work of Brakhage, from *Metaphors on Vision* (1963) through *Telling Time* (2003), than to that of any other filmmaker, at least to my knowledge. Tarkovsky did put his finger on the central theoretical issue that separates them: Brakhage's commitment to the "truth" of eyesight led him to deny the objectivity of standard lenses and seek what Tarkovsky would see as "gimmicks" to simulate the movements and fluctuations of vision. This argument repeats one Maya Deren had with Brakhage when she wrote, in "Cinematography: The Creative Use of Reality" that "photography is a form of reality." She argued thus:

> [T]he camera has been conceived of as the artist, with distorting lenses, multiple superimpositions, etc. used to simulate the creative action of the eye, the memory, etc. Such well-intentioned efforts to use the medium creatively, by forcibly inserting the creative act in the position it traditionally occupies

in the visual arts, accomplish, instead, the destruction of the photographic image as reality.[10]

The poetry of cinema, for Tarkovsky as for Deren, depends on the ontological priority of the cinematic image as rendered "objectively" by the photographic apparatus. Elaborating on Paul Valéry's dictum that "poets are philosophers," Tarkovsky sees the common principle of film and literature as the arrangement of "the real world" in sequence. The advantage of cinema is that it need not describe the world because the world "manifests itself directly" to the camera. Yet Tarkovsky distinguishes himself from Deren (although it is unlikely he knew anything of her) by affirming that the greatest achievement of the apparatus is "*to take an impression of time*."[11] The nuance of his phrasing is important: Deren had argued, with an important inflection of difference, that the transfiguration of time was at the center of cinematic art. By this she meant that the filmmaker's freedom to retard, speed up, reverse, and freeze time allowed her to create cinematic rituals, in a mode of time unique to cinema. In practice Tarkovsky took extensive advantage of slow motion, but his theoretical stress on taking an *impression* of time indicates that he saw cinema as a means for the acute observation of a complex temporality that fluidly incorporated duration, memory, and dreams. For him, to "sculpt in time" was to unveil the truth of lived time, not to invent imaginatively new temporal structures. In other words, Deren has a magical view of the manipulation of time, whereas Tarkovsky's mysticism emerges from an immanent temporality. Unlike Deren or Brakhage, Tarkovsky understood the exfoliation of time *within a shot* to be the foundation on which the articulations of shot changes are based.

Zerkalo, his most patently autobiographical film, instantiates his theory of cinematic time and demonstrates his attitude toward poetry in film. Although the profession of its protagonist is never identified, it is clear from the pretitle sequence that the film is an account of artistic incarnation. In that opening a preadolescent boy (Ignat) turns on a black and white television. Then we see what he sees, unmediated by the television scan: in one long panning and tracking take, a psychologist hypnotizes a young man with a severe stutter. After she commands him to say "I can speak," he repeats her words clearly. This allegorical prelude, probably inspired by the pretitle sequence of Bergman's *Persona*, presents the entire film that follows as if it were the newly liberated speech of the filmmaker, represented by the narrative voice-over we hear in the first episode following the titles.

Johnson and Petrie succinctly describe the unique perspective of the film: "Even if this paradox [of a voice-over which is a matter wholly of direct memory] is not fully assimilated on a first viewing, it gives the film an unusual viewpoint, for the past which we are being shown is built up not simply out of direct experience but as a mosaic of what the narrator knew firsthand, what he was told, what he dreamed or imagined, and what happened around him as part of the historical process that he shared with millions of other people."[12] Even an unconventional first-person narration of this sort would fall under the wide umbrella of Pasolini's "free indirect point of view," but his theoretical apparatus fails to do justice to Tarkovsky's work. In the first place, the distinction between narrative poetry and "poetry-poetry" makes no sense to the Russian filmmaker, who would reject associating his genre with that of Pasolini's examples—Bertolucci and Godard (although Antonioni was one of the few filmmakers Tarkovsky openly admired). Moreover, he would abhor Pasolini's idea of viewing his films as indices of a class position. Instead, we must look closely at how he has constructed his work, and how it relates to his theoretical text, to grasp its uniqueness and its place in a poetic tradition.

The forward tracking movement of the first shot after the titles implies a narrating consciousness that is quickly confirmed and grounded in the voice-over, speaking in the first person plural. As the camera slowly zooms past a woman sitting on a wooden fence, smoking and looking out over a lush green landscape toward a distant figure approaching on foot, the voice-over says: "The road from the station lay through Ignatyevo turning off near the farmstead where we spent our summers before the war…and then on to Tomshino through a dark oak wood." Thus the adult male voice establishes the past tense: the image of the young mother is a memory. A reverse shot of her accompanies the announcement of the central theme of the absent father: "We usually recognized the family when they appeared from behind the bush. If he turns toward the house, it's Father. If not it isn't him, which means he'll never come again." But the figure who approaches is not the father but a flirtatious doctor looking for the road to his home. A subtle sound association announces the perspective of the child who once watched this scene and who is now recounting it.

Then we hear a creaking sound. When the woman turns to look at what is making the noise, a countershot shows, for the first time, the protagonist of the film, young Alexei at about five years old, rocking in a hammock. He seems to have just woken up; his younger sister still sleeps beside him. His mother then echoes the creaking by bouncing slightly on the stile of the fence. The doctor seems to take this gesture as an invitation despite her manifest indifference to his attentions. So he proceeds to sit next to her on the fence, breaking the rail with his added weight. The collapsing fence is a displaced primal scene allusion, reinforced by the words of the doctor, who says, laughing, "It is nice to fall with a pretty woman." Later, as he walks away into the field, a sudden gust of wind sweeps over the buckwheat. It is an Apollonian emblem of poetic inspiration, bridging the doctor's brief visit, enigmatic and vaguely threatening from the child's perspective, with the first recitation of a poem by Arseny Tarkovsky. It is "First Meetings," a love poem, collapsing the autobiographical fantasy of the filmmaker onto the fictive recollections of Alexei about the absence of his father. Like that of the narrator himself, his father's profession is never identified, but the use of three of the four recorded poems as keys to the interiority of the lonely woman fixes an association between the voice of the poet (actually that of Arseny Tarkovsky) and the fictive father. Throughout the film such figures of montage—image to image, and image to sound—resonate with allusions personal to the filmmaker. Thus the poem, in male voice-over, articulates the loneliness of the character of Maria, Alexei's mother; but insofar as it is Arseny Tarkovsky's poem, read by the poet, it highlights the Oedipal, primal scene schema as the undersong of the opening scenes, which the casting of Margarita Terekhova as both Alexei's mother and his wife, Natalia, drives home. Likewise, Ignat Daniltsev plays both the adolescent Alexei and his son, Ignat, with the effect of locating the generational identities within the memory and fantasy structure of a narrator rather than in the phenomenal world. For Tarkovsky these networks of association occupy poetic rather than psychoan-alytical realms, but, despite his polemical position, this distinction dissolves in his filmic practice.

The rhythm and camera movements correspond to the stanza breaks and emphases of "First Meetings" without slavishly following them, so that the poem maintains its autonomy while it is linked to what we see on the screen. It sublimates the parents' temporary erotic happiness into a religious event ("epiphany"). As the camera tracks behind Maria walking toward the dacha, the poet chants of an Edenic time in which "We celebrated every moment" as if there were no others in the world. Just before the stanza concludes, with an invocation of "your realm/ Beyond the mirror," she halts to look back. At that moment Tarkovsky cuts in a false countershot to the five-year-old Alexei, with the moving camera following him past his sleeping sister, and then, with an elliptical jump, we see the two children eating strawberries and milk on a bare wooden table within the dacha. Alexei pours a handful of sugar on a cat while she licks spilt milk off the table surface. The boy's unsupervised behavior points up his mother's distracted mood and constitutes the moment when the words of the poem diverge most clearly from the filmic image; so that when the camera slowly tracks past the table to stop on the mother leaning against the wall, absorbed in thought and indifferent to the mess her son is making, the words of the poem reconnect to her: "...eyelids brushed with blue/ Were peaceful, and your hand was warm." We might thus understand the poem as the mother's memory of her poet husband. The doctor's attentions, and the pleasure she derived from disdaining him, provoke the memory of the poetic intensity of her husband's initial passion.

The shot does not change as the third stanza commences, but Maria walks out of the frame. The camera slowly scans the room before finding her sitting by the window. After a brief pause during which we hear the poet address her—"...and the word *you*/ Revealed its new meaning..."—the camera tracks out the open window toward a bench on which we see an iron, a glass of water, and a piece of linen, nearly illustrating the lines "Even the simplest things—the jug, the basin—/ When stratified and solid water/ Stood between us…" There is even rainwater to be seen dripping from vegetation in the foreground of the shot. Furthermore, in an extraordinary intensification of the scene out of the window, the line "Mint leaves spread themselves beneath our feet" makes the carpet of grass more vivid as the camera tilts up for a wider view of the pine trunks and the landscape beyond them.

The dramatic climax of the recitation occurs when the filmmaker cuts to a close-up of Maria as we hear: "Fish leapt in greeting from the river,/ And the sky unfurled above…/ While behind us all the time went fate,/ A madman brandishing a razor." So, as the lyric poem unfolds, it turns out that the erotic-religious intensity was a foil for the final lines' acknowledgement of the insane violence with which time mutilates love. By the end of the recitation we have to revise our earlier impression: the mother is not so much longing for her husband who is away at war as mourning the loss of his passionate love for her. It is a poem that enacts its own temporal insight, leading us in one direction only to reverse course in the final couplet; it slashes away at its own lush imagery. The film itself will do likewise.

Rather than cut with the end of the poem, the filmmaker holds the image of the mother's face as she wipes away tears, then looks at a notebook (presumably the manuscript of the poem) while we hear cries from outside. We follow her through the dacha, past the children still eating, toward the commotion over a shed that has caught fire. The overlapping of events keeps the poem from marking a cleanly isolated episode, with the double consequence of letting it function at once as an indication of Maria's interior reflection and as a clue in the narrator's effort to penetrate the mystery of his mother's moods.

Tarkovsky's placement of "First Meetings" at this point in the film suggests that it was written by Arseny Tarkovsky to the filmmaker's mother, Maria Ivanova, around 1937. However, Natasha Synessios points out that it was written in 1962 and that the filmmaker originally intended to use in this place "Ignatevo Forest" (1935), a poem "directly about the mounting problems between Tarkovsky's parents."[13] By 1962 Arseny Tarkovsky had been married three times; the addressee of "First Meetings" might have been any one of his wives or another woman altogether.[14] The very generality of the pronouns "we" and "you" in the poem open the possibility of transferring the referent to another woman, complicating the cause of Maria's tears. Unless the filmmaker had knowledge unavailable to us about the genesis of the poem, he was employing it to fabricate an idealized moment in his parents' relationship (as he clearly does with two of the other three poems in the film). Yet the central point of the poem, at least insofar as it is an element in constructing the initial situation of the film, is concentrated in its final couplet. A savage fate has already run amok with the erotic idyll by the time the film opens. Furthermore, the inherent play of substitution in the poem's pronouns corresponds to the fluid transitions among subjects in the opening minutes of the film: stutterer—narrator—mother—doctor—father—Alexei—mother—and, as we shall see, an older mother.

Thus Tarkovsky has embedded the sequence of the poem within a haunting chain of memories and dreams. The borderlines between actual memories, screen memories, and dreams are fluid: early indicators of structural distinctions, such as the alternation of black-and-white and color film stocks, or repeated scenes of a sleeper awakening, are frequently annulled by later signals. For instance, the opening twenty minutes of the film can be seen retroactively as the very dream to which the narrator refers in a telephone call to his mother, in the first scene in his apartment in the present (1973). But once we think there is a stable discrimination between the realism of the present scenes and the oneiric penetration of the past, irrational occurrences take place in the apartment, such as Ignat's meeting with two elderly women who ask him to read aloud a letter of Pushkin's. The fluidity with which these domains interpenetrate is central to Tarkovsky's concept of poetry as "a particular way of relating to reality."

Immediately after the burning of the shed, young Alexei wakes twice in a row. Once the Apollonian wind—filmed in slow motion—awakens him, and the second time he stands up and calls "Papa." The black-and-white dream that follows begins as the mother's nightshirt flies across the room, a metonymy for parental intercourse. In slow motion, we see his father helping Maria wash her long hair in a basin. The father quickly disappears from the scene as the ceiling of the room begins to fall in—now an old apartment rather than the dacha, with a gas stove emitting two large jets of flame; it is as if the building were flooded, but Maria remains unperturbed and moves toward a mirror—the eponymous mirrors are abundant in all the interiors of the film—where a much older version of herself, played by the filmmaker's actual mother, looks back at her. The hair washing and falling plaster translate the primal scene displacement of the broken fence into more explicitly dreamlike metonymies, replacing the doctor-substitute with the father. In this intricate chain of associations, the Empedoclean universe of water, fire, earth, and wind highlights the ambivalence between attraction and threat that resonates as the child's perspective blends into the adult narrator's dream life and uncertain memories; for he has to ask his mother when his father left them and when the shed burned down in order to make sense of his dream. Both occurred in 1935, she tells him.

We do not actually see the narrator as an adult in the film until he is on his deathbed, and even then, we see only his hands and torso. Emblematically, Tarkovsky took this role himself and had to be persuaded by his director of photography not to have his face in the shot. Moreover, when we first enter the present time, as the camera scans the narrator's apartment while he talks to his mother on the telephone, a poster for the film *Andrey Rublev* appears prominently on the wall, followed by a photograph of Maria Ivanovna, apparently in her forties. Even if the poet's "I" is a universal subject, drawing on but not co-incident with a historical individual, the representation of a poetic first person remained a delicate aesthetic problem for the filmmaker, as he struggled to define the limitations of autobiographical details permissible in articulating and giving authenticity to that "I." In *Sculpting in Time* he wrote:

> Generally people's memories are precious to them. It is no accident that they are colored by poetry…It occurred to me then, that from these prop-erties of memory a new working principle could be developed, on which an extraordinarily interesting film could be built…It would be the story of his thoughts, his memories and dreams. And then, without his appear-ing at all—at least in the accepted sense of the traditionally written film—it would be possible to achieve something highly significant: the expression, the portrayal, of the hero's individual personality, and the revelation of his interior world. Somewhere here there is an echo of the lyrical hero incar-nate in literature, and of course in poetry; he is absent from view, but what he thinks, how he thinks, and what he thinks about built up a graphic and clearly-defined picture of him. This subsequently became the starting point of *Mirror*.[15]

Trauma, death, desertion, and conflagration become the nodal points for fo-cusing memory, just as later in the film the recollection of newsreels helps the narrator to give a chronology to his memories. When Alexei's mother tells him that Liza, with whom she worked in a publishing house during Stalin's terror, has died, a flashback in black and white appears, ambiguously her memory or his recollection of her account—here Pasolini's theoretization of a "free in-direct point of view" would be apt—of her frightened trip to the printer to correct a typographical error she thought she might have let slip through. This is one of two "urban legends" in the film. The first is what Synessios refers to as "a reputed incident" in which Stalin's name was erroneously typeset as "stralin" ["to shit"].[16] The other would be the story of the drill instructor who throws himself on top of a dummy grenade.[17] Like many urban legends, these incidents may have some veracious origins, but Tarkovsky exhibits the telltale characteristic of the genre by transforming the story into one in which he or an intimate was a participant.

The second of Arseny Tarkovsky's four recitations occurs during the printing house flashback. As Maria walks down a long corridor with the camera tracking ahead of her, we hear "I waited for you since yesterday morning." The poem contrasts a missed rendezvous "yesterday," when the weather was beautiful, with "today['s] dismal…raining," ending in a single-line stanza: "No word of comfort, tears undried." The episode crystallizes the anxieties and after-effects of the years of terror by coun-terpointing the elliptical mood swing of the poem to the narratively elabo-rated emotional outbursts of the memory. The editing rhythms dramatize the outcome of Maria's anxious rush to the printer in a drenching rain by first showing her relief and laughter when she finds she has not made the error and then her tears when Liza, heaping insults on her, accuses her of resembling Maria Timofeyvna in Dostoyevsky's *The Devils* (*Besy*): a deluded (even mentally disturbed), self-absorbed misfit. Maria runs from Liza to the factory shower but laughs at herself when the water runs out.[18] Liza, who rushed after her to apologize, in vain, walks back down a corridor, reversing the perspective of the long shot that accompanied the poem and incongruously takes a leap, clicking her heels, as she recites the opening lines of Dante's *Commedia*. The placement of Arseny Tarkovsky's poem over the one emotionally neutral shot in the episode interiorizes and concentrates the symbolically charged weather with erotic expectation and disappointment, before Liza viciously expresses Maria's repressed self-accusation: "If something doesn't suit you, you pretend it doesn't exist. I'm amazed at your ex-husband's patience. He should have bolted ages ago. You created the whole situation!... You can say he escaped in the nick of time before you managed to make him like you. I swear you'll make your children miserable." Although Synessios and Johnson and Petrie are quite justified in reading this outburst as a symptom of the anxiety of the period of terror, Liza is also the vehicle for unraveling the "poetic logic" of the sequence, which posits the imagined typo as Maria's self-destructive wish, in punishment for her failed marriage.

Yet since this entire psychic agon occurs in the consciousness of the narrator, the mother's self-accusation may be taken as the son's indictment of her as well. The following episode makes that clear. It is the first time the viewer is confronted with the shock or confusion of seeing Margarita Terekhova as Natalia, Alexei's wife, after so many scenes in which she plays his mother. She is looking at herself in a wall mirror as Alexei, offscreen, bickers with her. When he tells her she looks like his mother, she retorts, saying "Perhaps that's why we broke up," adding in a variant on Liza's speech, "I shrink to see Ignat becoming like you... You won't be happy with anyone. You seem to think that your very presence should make everyone happy." Ironically, she says this in an orgy of narcissism, never taking her gaze from an array of mirrors.

Of course, "perhaps that's why we broke up" also means its opposite: it was the imaginary identity that initially attracted him to Natalie. In one compressed moment, we learn the overall history of the narrator's adult life; before this we did not know he had ever married. Now we realize that he has already divorced and has a teenaged son. In the course of the dialogue the comparison of his former wife to his mother becomes both an indictment and an excuse. Indirectly admitting his self-absorption, he blames his mother for never remarrying and accuses Natalia of making Ignat like him by remaining single. Yet when she later asks his advice about marrying a writer, he denigrates the man as a talentless failure without even knowing his name. By claiming that the lack of a paternal presence conditioned him to act as he does, Alexei is attempting to assuage his profound guilt for leaving his family. In an interview with *Le Monde,* the filmmaker was quite explicit on this point:

> Relationships have been broken and the storyteller has to renew them, in order to find his moral equilibrium, but he is unable to do so. He lives with the hope that he will be able to pay his love debt back, but that debt is one which nobody can get rid of… *The Mirror* is not a casual title. The storyteller perceives his wife as the continuation of his mother, because wives resemble mothers, and errors repeat themselves—as strange reflection. Repetition is a law, experience does not get transmitted, everyone has to live it.[19]

Furthermore, in defensively identifying his mother with the cynical and narcissistic Natalia, the narrator implies previously unrepresented flaws in her character. Yet at the same time, he acknowledges that she sacrificed herself for him and his sister. Evidently his treatment of his divorced wife and their son repeats his own childhood trauma as an act of unconscious revenge. Psychoanalytic theory posits that such revenge motives can be a reaction to primal scene experiences, which would be consistent with the structure of the film and with works by two of Tarkovsky's most revered directors, Ingmar Bergman and Michelangelo Antonioni.[20]

The role of Natalia emerged and evolved as the film was being shot. Tarkovsky and the Mosfilm executives were so impressed with Terekhova's screen presence as Maria that they wanted to expand her participation. At the same time, the filmmaker was skeptical that his original plan to center the film around a long, hidden-camera interview with his mother would work. In effect, the psychic eruption of translating his memories and dreams onto film issued in the unanticipated incorporation of a version of his own failed first marriage, with Natalia and Ignat as thinly veiled representations of Irma Raush and their son, Arseny Tarkovsky. Although, according to Synessios, he "took issue with psychoanalysis… and especially criticized the way art is oversimplified by using this approach,"[21] his double casting of both mother and wife and young narrator and son encourages a psychoanalytical reading as perhaps no other film of comparable stature does.

Just before the first image in "present" time, there is a shot I have not mentioned of a hand, glowing red, between a fire and the camera, in the manner of Georges de la Tour's paintings. Eventually this image will be grounded as a reference to the red-haired girl the adolescent Alexei loved and for whom he thought his military instructor was a rival. Similarly, there is a roaring fire in a field between the episode of the printing works and the introduction of Natalia. It recalls the burning shed without actually representing it. Johnson and Petrie offer the following commentary on this imagery: Fire "is associated with… the uncontrollable force of nature or of sex," and in *Zerkalo* "the leaping flames from the gas burner contribute to the eeriness of the scene and also perhaps to its sexual subtext, and in Alyosha's later fantasy of the teenage redhead, the burning stick that she holds and the fiery stove behind her have clearly erotic significance."[22] Concurring with this reading of the fires, I would note that brief images of this order connect the opening primal scene memories and dreams to the narrator's telephone call to his mother, just as the imagined view of the mother in the shower links up to the scene of hair washing and to the image of his former wife preening before a mirror.

Recalling that poetry compels its audience "to build the separate parts into a whole," we have to pay close attention to such transitions and to the sequencing of episodes in this film, particularly because the filmmaker reorganized it several times as he was editing it. The median image of the fire marks the two moments it joins together as vectors of the psychosexual profile of the lyrical "I" of the film. Similarly, the frequently employed false countershots bind the separate parts of the film into a whole while maintaining their autonomy. Thus the introduction of Natalia at this point provides a new perspective on Liza's accusations of Maria. They become projections of Alexei's criticism of his mother and his first wife.

The use of false countershots is also the overriding method in which Tarkovsky incorporates newsreel footage in his film. In themselves, the newsreels establish a chronology and frame the events of the film within Soviet history. However, the shot-countershot syntax inflects the newsreels with poetic resonances that enlarge on the psychological undersong of the lyrical persona. The first of these interruptions—of the spatial and temporal logic of the scene with the narrator and Natalia—is so ambiguous that it may not be a false countershot at all. When Ignat looks offscreen at the sound of Spanish speech, there is an image of a middle-aged Spaniard heatedly talking to his family, apparently within the same apartment. Perhaps the notorious housing deficiency in Soviet cities accounts for this; for decades two or more families were forced to share a single apartment. Alexei and Natalia treat the sudden appearance of the Spanish family as if it were normal. He urges her to intervene to prevent a row. Then, unexpectedly, we see a torero kill a bull, followed first by the Spanish man passionately reenacting the bullfight to the continuing sound of the arena, as Natalia and others watch him in countershot. But his enthusiasm for the skill of Palomo Linares, a contemporary matador when the film was made, triggers a series of newsreel images from the Spanish Civil War. Over the second of these flashbacks—significantly of a woman attempting to save a cracked full-length mirror—the narrator resumes the voice-over mode we have not heard since the start of the film, telling us of the Spaniard's emigration during evacuation of the children of Spanish Communists to the Soviet Union in the late 1930s. The account refracts the theme of broken families—"his mother was ill...his father stood sadly on the sidelines"—and ends with the sound of flamenco music as the Spaniard's daughter begins to dance. At that point, the row Alexei has anticipated erupts. The father slaps the young woman for mocking him by showing she can perform flamenco, although she always resisted his teaching her. His wife, speaking Russian to Natalia, explains that his fury comes from the fact that they cannot return to Spain: their children are Russian. Then she storms out of the apartment, followed by Natalia in an echo of the scene between Liza and Maria.

With the return of flamenco music we see a documentary montage nineteen shots long of the bombing of Spanish cities, people rushing for shelter, and heartbreaking images of weeping parents and children (now with apparently synchronous sound) heading for the evacuation ship. The last of those shots is a crucial pivot. A girl, cradling a doll, loses her smile as she turns toward the camera and looks off in horror while we hear the whistle of a ship. Tarkovsky has placed in countershot to her stare a transitional, silent image of an immense weather balloon, lifted aloft on either side of it by smaller balloons, carrying two men. This shot in turn introduces a short sequence of Soviet aerial balloons and the parade celebrating Valeri Chkalov's flight over the North Pole, to the accompaniment of the end of Pergolesi's *Stabat Mater*.

On the one hand, the newsreel montage is a demonstration of pure, poetic cinema. Through the eyeline match of the young refugee it suddenly shifts from pathos to the sublime. It is a tragic sublime insofar as the balloonists died in the 1934 ascent and Chkalov's airplane crashed in 1938, as Soviet audiences would have known.[23] The musical quotation from Pergolesi, "Quando corpus morietur..." (When my body dies let the glory of heaven be given to my soul), accents the brief montage as a poem of heavenly ascent. The ambiguity of the construction allows us to see simultaneously the misery and strangeness of the Spaniards' translation into Soviet society, the power and mystery of cinema embodied initially in the narrator's experience of newsreels in his childhood, and an abstract audiovisual poem of temporal suffering and spiritual salvation (which will resonate with the last of the poems of Arseny Tarkovsky quoted later in the film).

The *Stabat Mater* can still be heard as the newsreel sequence ends with a return to color: we see an engraved self-portrait by Leonardo da Vinci in an old book, as Ignat indelicately peruses it. The symbolic equation between newsreels and a reproduction of a Renaissance engraving sets up an episode sketching the uncanny aspects of the boy's imagination (again as it occupies the narrator's thought). More than in any other part of the film, the music composed for the film by Eduard Artemyev plays a major role here in underlining the ghostly occurrences in the present-day apartment. The first, quite realistic sign of a disturbance in the psychic atmosphere occurs just after the boy feels a shock of static electricity while helping his mother pick up coins she spilled from her purse in her haste to meet an appointment. He tells her he has a feeling of déjà-vu, which she dismisses—"stop imagining things"—before leaving him alone to await his paternal grandmother (Maria). As soon as she leaves, he sees two elderly women in the apartment, as if they too lived there. Several commentators note the physical resemblance of one of the women to the poet Anna Akhmatova, who was the most ardent of Arseny Tarkovsky's supporters before her death in 1966.[24] As she sips her tea, she commands the boy to read aloud, from a handwritten notebook, a letter from Pushkin to the philosopher Pyotr Chaadayev, defending the uniqueness of Russia's isolation and her historic fate in repressing the mongul invasions: "We did not take part in a single one of [western Europe's] great events. But we had our own special predestination...Not for anything in the world would I change my country or choose another history than the history of our forefathers as God ordained it." Then she tells the boy to open the door, as if she sensed the presence of a person outside it. It is the aged Maria, who departs immediately, thinking she came to the wrong apartment because she does not recognize her grandson, nor he her. When Ignat turns back, the women are gone, as if they had been ghosts, but he sees the heat mark from the teacup slowly evaporating on the table, accented by a crescendo of the eerie music. Even if the casting was not an effort to evoke the persona of Akhmatova,[25] the apparition of the elderly, authoritative figure and the citing of the Pushkin letter awakens Ignat's and the viewer's consciousness of the historic destiny of Russia.

No sooner does the trace of heat evaporate than the telephone rings, bringing back Alexei's voice. When he asks Ignat if his mother came, Ignat tells him an old woman appeared at the door but she had the wrong address. In next suggesting that the boy invite a friend to keep him company, his father takes the opportunity of telling him about a redheaded girl with perpetually chapped lips with whom he was in love, at his son's age, during the Second World War. Then a flashback of the girl, followed by a countershot of the adolescent Alexei, introduces the period of the war. Included in the temporal shift are two new figures, the wounded and shell-shocked military instructor who was Alexei's rival for the girl's affections and Asafiev, an orphan Alexei's age from the Leningrad blockade, whose defiance of the instructor enacts the narrator's fantasies of revenge against his rival and father-substitute.

The flashback culminates in Asafiev's rolling the dummy grenade at the man. After the instructor falls on the grenade and realizes it is not live, he sits by himself. The image of the red-haired girl that ensues might be seen as a figure of his imagination, but when she turns, the countershot is neither he, nor Alexei, who was one of his students, nor Asafiev. Instead, there is a false countershot to an extraordinary newsreel of soldiers at Lake Sivash. One, completely nude, skirts the water shouldering a large wooden box, while at the same time dressed soldiers, trying to move a loaded wagon onto a pontoon ramp, lose control of it as it tumbles into the lake. This shot is framed by a return to Asafiev, who looks back at the place where the instructor sits as if he, like the red-haired girl, were watching the soldiers cross Lake Sivash, and then slowly makes his way offscreen. There follow seventeen shots of the fording of Sivash. Tarkovsky was very proud of having discovered this unknown archival footage and wrote of it rapturously; "When, on the screen before me, there appeared, as if coming out of nothing, these people shattered by the fearful, inhuman effort of that tragic moment of history, I knew that this episode had to become the centre, the very essence, heart, nerve of this picture that had started off merely as my intimate lyrical memories."[26]

As the heart and nerve of his film, the long Lake Sivash passage not only crystallizes the moment of Alexei's first love and the documentary truth of the sacrificial patriotism fictively exemplified by the urban legend of the dummy grenade, but it also, more crucially, grants a historical dimension to the sublimations of Arseny Tarkovsky's poetry. With great reluctance the filmmaker eventually came to recognize that a reading of the poem "Life, Life" was needed to underline this moment as "the very essence" of *Zerkalo*.[27] The poem does not come in until the tenth shot of the sequence, and it continues over the return to Asafiev as he climbs a snow-covered hill alone. The delay allows the newsreel sequence to acquire a solemn and autonomous presence, accompanied first by the sound of feet sloshing through water and later by music composed by Artimiev for the scene but muted almost to inaudibility by Tarkovsky. When the voice enters, the juxtaposition transposes the poem (written in the 1960s in defiance of forebodings of the poet's death) into an ode on the heroic sacrifices of what Russians call The Great Patriotic War, during which the poet himself lost a leg. The poem's maritime imagery coincides with shots of soldiers slogging across mud and dragging munitions through the shallow lake. The lines, "We're all already on the seashore;/ I'm one of those who'll be hauling the nets/ When a shoal of immortality swims by…" correspond with a slow pan of the lake to a raft loaded with cannon being pushed through the water by about twenty soldiers. In fact, one jumps down from the raft to assist in the pushing, as if incarnating the poet "who'll be hauling the nets." In the minds of Soviet viewers, some of these anonymous men would be among the nearly seven million who died fighting Hitler. Furthermore, the prophetic power of the poet, asserting "I'll summon any of the centuries, / Then enter one and build a house in it," heard in the same shot, evokes as well the filmmaker's summoning this documentary footage to be the heart and nerve of his film.

As he climbs the hill toward the camera while children are sledding down it behind him, Asafiev slips and gets up just as the poet chants: "And even now, in these coming times,/ I stand up in the stirrups like a child." There is a shift of tone from the celebration of immortality to the pathos of lost security in the final stanza, as the boy, quietly whistling, stops before the camera in close-up:

> I'm satisfied with deathlessness,
> For my blood to flow from age to age.
> Yet for a corner whose warmth I could rely on
> I'd willingly have given all my life,
> Wherever her flying needle
> Tugged me, like a thread, around the globe.[28]

Asafiev, too, is an allegorical emblem of the "essence, heart, nerve" of *Zerkalo*. He is the hyperbolic embodiment of the family romance at play in the film. As an evacuee from the blockage of Leningrad, where his parents were presumably among the thousands who starved to death daily, he occupies the imaginative position first staked out by the children taken to Russia from the Spanish Civil War; he is at once the emblem of orphanhood and homelessness. Lake Sivash and Leningrad had been metonymies for the reversal of the tide of war in late 1943 and early 1944, when the Red Army pushed the Germans back through the Crimea in the south and broke the Leningrad siege in the north. As Asafiev stands on the top of the hill, another montage announces the end of the war: we glimpse the taking of Prague, the corpse of Hitler in Berlin—a look-alike, it turned out—victory fireworks, a still photograph of a man with a crutch—evoking but not depicting the fate of the filmmaker's wounded father, and then, more ominously, with electronic underscoring, the Hiroshima explosion and another atomic test, perhaps the Soviet Union's first.

The perspective of the hill overlooking a pale green river with a large tree to the left of the frame is sufficient to evoke Pieter Brueghel's *Hunters in Winter* for most of the commentators on the film, even though the cinematic recreation lacks the returning hunters and their pack of dogs, who anchor the left side of the masterpiece. Missing, too, are the houses of the village and a blazing fire at the left of the canvas. The tiny skaters on Brueghel's double pond have been replaced by equally small figures playing in the snow. Above all, the bird in full flight, whose wingspan marks the point at which the distant imaginary mountainscape touches the green-gray sky, has its dramatic equivalent in the film in the image of a bird flying from the tree to land on the boy's head. Within Tarkovsky's scheme, Asafiev's place in Russian history and his role in the family romance makes him a prime candidate for poetic election, symbolically enacted in the arena of Brueghel's winter. In his previous film, *Solaris* (1972), he had evidenced his love of Brueghel by decorating the library of the space station with reproductions of his art. There Hari hears the sounds of the birds and of the dogs as she contemplates *Hunters in Winter*.

In *Zerkalo* the allusion to Brueghel operates with a significant deviation. Whereas the painting depicts a homecoming of the hunters from someplace outside the frame of the picture to the warmth and domestic familiarity of the village, where presumably some of the women and the children are members of the hunters' families, the film shows the boy distancing himself from the playing children; he is climbing away from their activities. Once the bird alights on his head, Asafiev reaches up to take hold of it. A rich literary and visual tradition uses birds to represent the Holy Spirit and the inspiration of poetry. Synessios adds that Tarkovsky's favorite Soviet filmmaker, Alexander Dovzhenko, once wrote that birds would sit in his hair and that both his screenwriter, Alexander Misharin, and the filmmaker's second wife claimed wild birds flew to their hands.[29]

As soon as Asafiev grabs the bird, a cut to young Chinese Maoists dramatizes the threat to Russia from the East with a series of some twenty shots centering on the efforts of young Soviet soldiers to restrain demonstrators on the disputed Damansky Island in 1969. The montage includes a series of dissolves on still images of a crowd made up of many pictures of Mao, a hand turning the pages of the Little Red Book, and a pan of an immense May Day crowd in China, loudly cheering (in contrast to the percussion music that gave an ominous tone to the other documentary shots). This final excursus on Russia's place in twentieth-century international affairs brings to mind Pushkin's letter about the spiritual and strategic position of the homeland in European history: "It was Russia who contained the Mongol conquest within her vast expanses.... [W]e were obliged to lead a completely separate existence which, while it left us Christian, also made us complete strangers in the Christian world, so that our martyrdom never impinged upon the energetic development of Catholic Europe."[30] In Tarkovsky's conception, the recollection of the poet's voice and the allegory of poetic election reveal the spiritual meaning of Russia's historical martyrdom between 1935 and 1969, the time span of *Mirror*.

Drawing on untranslated Russian sources, Robert Bird comments helpfully on the filmmaker's feeling for the authenticity of the documentary material of the evacuation of the Spanish children. He observes:

> These shots are all carefully edited, but Tarkovsky insisted that their inward tension bespoke their authenticity. In the original edit there was another shot of a child bidding his father farewell, which stuck out conspicuously wherever it was placed; Tarkovsky traced its origin and saw that it was one of three identical takes, meaning that "at the very moment that the child was flowing with tears the cameraman asked him to repeat what he had just done; to bid farewell once more, to embrace and to kiss [his father] once more." As a result, this shot "had been invaded by the devil and he [i.e. the devil] could not reconcile himself to the atmosphere [*streda*] [...] of sincerity." Thus, in addition to their resonance in the social imaginary and individual memory, these shots possess a kind of innate poignancy that resists being reduced to a mere function in the film.[31]

Such a commitment to transcendental authenticity contrasts markedly with the stagey appearance of the bird landing on Asafiev. Not only is the re-creation of the Brueghel scene contrived but also getting the bird to alight on the boy's head evidently took such elaborate trickery that two jump cuts remain in the scene, betraying its artifice. It would be disingenuous to argue that Tarkovsky composed the scene with deliberate awkwardness. Working with unnatural animal behavior and a child actor, he probably could do no better. The important point is that he not only left the rather transparent trick in the film but framed it with powerful archival footage that highlights its contrivance by contrast. The juxtaposition of the two styles evokes the ontological dichotomy at the origin of cinema, the realistic direction of the Lumières and the magical or "formative" direction of Méliès (as Siegfried Kracauer first formulated those alternatives). Of course, the iconic bird was crucial to the filmmaker's conception of the film: it reappears in the penultimate episode, that of the narrator's death. In a sense, the "essence, heart, nerve" of the film is not so much the Lake Sivash document itself, as *Sculpting in Time* claims, but the meaning of those shots in the context of both the chanted poetry and the demonstration of the oscillation between magic and documentation as the essence of cinema itself.

The last shot from Damansky Island shows the face of one of the young Soviet soldiers in the human wall holding back the book-waving Maoists. His eyes shift from right to head-on so that a cut across time and space to Maria crouching with her back to us constitutes another false countershot. Only the style of her hair, fixed in a bun, cues that it is indeed Maria rather than Natalia. The room in which she is crouching is so littered with ice and wood that it is unrecognizable. (It seems to be a different dacha in subsequent shots of the episode.) She is cutting pieces of wood when a man calls her. The reverse shot reveals her husband, in uniform, on leave from the war front, but the coolness of their reunion indicates that the decisive rift in their relationship had already occurred. We see the children outside quibbling about a book Marina, Alexei's sister, says her brother has stolen.[32] When they hear their father calling Marina's name, they both run to him. In his rush, Alexei trips, establishing a visual rhyme with the earlier image of Asafiev faltering as he climbs the hill. The crucial shot of the episode records Maria's look of alienation as the children embrace their father. As if commenting on her expression, the scene returns to the "stolen" book, previously established as the volume of Leonardo's works we saw Ignat perusing in his father's apartment.

A tracking shot with a bright highlight caressing a reproduction of Leonardo's portrait of Ginevra di Benci bridges this scene and the next, a parallel episode between Natalia and Alexei. In this context the painting looks like a visual synthesis of Maria and Natalia. On the soundtrack, the *recitativo accompagnato*, "Und siehe da, der Vorhang im Tempel zeriss in zwei Stück" (And behold, the veil of the Temple was rent in twain) from Bach's *St. John's Passion* puts considerable stress on the transition. In *Sculpting in Time* Tarkovsky commented on the painting, which he initially thought would be a leitmotif woven throughout his film:

> There are two things about Leonardo's images that are arresting. One is the artist's amazing capacity to examine the object from outside, standing back, looking from above the world—a characteristic of artists like Bach or Tolstoy. And the other, the fact that the picture affects us simultaneously in two opposite ways. It is not possible to say what impression the portrait finally makes on us. It is not even possible to say definitely whether we like the woman or not, whether she is appealing or unpleasant. She is at once

attractive and repellent. There is something inexpressibly beautiful about her and at the same time repulsive, fiendish…In *Mirror* we needed the portrait to introduce a timeless element into the moments that are succeeding each other before our eyes, and at the same time to juxtapose the portrait with the heroine, to emphasize in her and in the actress, Margarita Terekhova, the same capacity at once to enchant and to repel.[33]

The startling synchronization of the children embracing their father with the moment of Jesus's death in the oratorio seems to represent the filmmaker's attempt at "standing back, looking from above the world" by combining the reenactment of a dramatic memory with allusions to important achievements in the histories of art and music, and with a turning point in Salvation history. The complex, even contradictory, vectors that Tarkovsky dissects in his discussion of the portrait and its place in the film exemplify his theory of *poetic linkages* in cinema.

The parallel episode that follows throws some light on this nexus of poetic thought, although it depicts, in contrast, a deliberately mundane reunion in a long, complex sequence shot. In a tour-de-force of Terekhova's ability to "enchant and repel," we see and hear Natalia addressing the unseen narrator: "Come more often. You know how he misses you." The earlier dramatic epiphany of the father in the midst of The Great Patriotic War has now devolved into the son's infrequent meetings with his own son under the pressures of his daily routines. He proposes instead that the boy come to live with him, an invitation Ignat turns down as he walks into the shot. When the camera pans back to Natalia, she is examining large glossy photographs of herself and the aged Maria. Her belated acknowledgment of the similarity between them is met, this time, by the offscreen Alexei's denial of his earlier assertion—"Not at all." His contrariness prompts her to revenge; she analyzes the difficulty he has with his mother as a function of the guilt he feels for her sacrificing herself. Conversely, when she admits she is "meddling, as always," he recognizes in her somewhat sadistic focus on his relationship with his mother an unstated disturbance in her thought, making the relentless, fluid close-up of Natalia the most psychologically astute in the film and a vestige of the influence of Bergman. The only interruption in the sequence shot occurs when we see Ignat pass out of the apartment through a room piled with books. When the long take resumes, with the couple alone, Alexei prods Natalia to confess her dilemma regarding whether or not she should marry a writer she has been seeing. He mercilessly insults the suitor, without knowing who he is, as a talentless mediocrity and then disparages Ignat—"our dear dunce"—for his poor grades at school. During this exchange the camera follows Natalia as she wanders, clearly in pain, past two mirrors to a window through which we can see Ignat in the courtyard, tending a blazing fire in the rain. It is just at this point that Alexei, criticizing an acquaintance who writes for a newspaper—and by implication Natalia's lover—says, as if ventriloquizing Tarkovsky, "he doesn't understand that a book is a deed, not a paycheck. A poet must stir the soul, not nurture idolaters."

The sight of Ignat at the fire induces Natalia to ask, "Do you remember who the angel appeared to in the burning bush?" Alexei cannot resist answering, "No. Not Ignat at any rate," before recalling it was Moses. The shot and episode ends with the exhausted Natalia asking "Why didn't anything like that ever appear to me?" Here Tarkovsky's variation of "scenes from a marriage" gives the cruel manner of Bergman's most recent film at the time a biblical and poetic turn. Prophecy and the poetic vocation coincide in Tarkovsky's view, as his frequent invocation of Pushkin's poem "The Prophet" attests. He even quotes it in *Sculpting in Time*, at the place where he calls himself a poet: "Thus Alexander Pushkin considered that every poet, every true artist (and I consider myself as a poet rather than a cinematographer)—regardless of whether he wants to be or not—is a prophet."[34] Pushkin's poet extends the election of Isaiah, on whose lips a Seraph placed a burning coal, into an angelic renovation of eyes, ears, and tongue, culminating in the replacement of the prophet's heart with "a coal alive with flame." In definitively denying the epiphany to Ignat, Alexei is suggesting that his son will not have an experience like that of the burning shed, which was his own prophetic initiation. But the angel of Poetry sometimes sneaks up on Tarkovsky's protagonists less spectacularly, bestowing the poetic mantle in dreams and fantasies, through birds, fire, and even television; for despite Alexei's disclaimer, the pretitle sequence in which Ignat watched the television show on hypnotism is yet another displaced allusion to the event of the burning bush, when Jahveh revealed his prophetic mission to the tongue-tied Moses. When Natalia laments that she never had a prophetic-poetic epiphany, she is voicing her unhappiness with the gender mission Tarkovsky believed was divinely assigned to women: to sacrifice themselves utterly for their children.

The invocation of the Sinai revelation triggers another dream memory. It is an enigmatic evocation, mixing color and black-and-white shots, of Alexei's grandfather's house, where he was born. The voice-over narrator tells us that it is a recurring dream in which he is both compelled to return and "always prevented from entering," but we see him already inside the dacha. Shortly after that, it is a shed that he cannot enter, where his mother squats, sorting potatoes, in the dream's concluding shot. Just as he called out "papa" in the first dream, he calls "mama" in this one. In what appears to be yet another primal scene image,[35] a rooster breaks through a pane of glass just as the powerful Apollonian wind returns, knocking a lamp off an outdoor table and tossing about a loaf of bread. It frightens the boy back into the house.

The dream is followed by a memory, or perhaps another dream, of the adolescent Alexei accompanying his mother to the house of a wealthy doctor's wife to sell her turquoise earrings. As the boy sits in a room of the woman's dacha waiting for his mother to transact the sale, he examines his image in a mirror, while milk mysteriously drips from above onto a table and two raw potatoes. Irritated by his mother's embarrassing poverty and the condescending manner of the doctor's wife, he seems very uncomfortable as he waits. The coals of the fireplace turn his thoughts to the red-haired girl, who appears in his imagination or as a memory warming herself beside a furnace. A very quick elliptical shot of a hand closing the door suggests she may have been there with the drill instructor. It is only now that we see that the previous Georges de la Tour-like image of the hand before flaming twigs was a metonymy for her and a screen for her relationship with the teacher. When the women reappear, the patroness asks first Alexei, and then Maria, to kill a chicken for her. Her advanced pregnancy makes her squeamish, she tells them. Very reluctantly Maria chops off the bird's head and then leaves without concluding the sale.

In this episode the doctor's wife is the inverse of the seducer seen at the opening of the film. He is a doctor flirting with a woman with children whose husband is absent; she is the wife of an absent doctor. Within the symbolic economy of the film the broken fence corresponds to the house dripping with milk and, later, the decapitated rooster. Here yet again poetics and psychodynamics illuminate each other. The fusion of revenge and guilt cannot be overlooked in Tarkovsky's casting of his second wife, Larissa Pavlovna Yegorkina, as the odiously wasteful doctor's wife, just as he had used his first wife, Irma Raush, in *Solaris* (after he had left her for Yegorkina) as Hari, the replicant of Kris's suicidal wife, who returns lovingly to him on the spacecraft. An incident from Tarkovsky's childhood, recounted by Natasha Synessios, further illuminates the connections between this memory and the preceding dream. Maria Tarkovskaia swapped her own turquoise earrings, "family heirlooms that her husband loved,"[36] for a bushel of potatoes during the war.

The elements of dream and memory interpenetrate one another in a tight network of associations. The rooster that breaks through the window becomes the decapitated rooster in a symbolic equation of sexual penetration followed by castration. The sexual rivalry for the red-haired girl screens the primal scene complex of Maria with both Alexei's father and the doctor. Johnson and Petrie initiated a similar reading of this episode when they wrote: "The milk-semen parallel common in dreams can perhaps be seen in *Mirror* in connection with the hero's budding sexuality: In the earring scene images of dripping milk are followed closely by Alyosha's jealous speculations on the sexual encounter between the redhead and his competitor…"[37] Yet they do not connect Ignat's adolescent sexual awakening with the primal scene scenario that organizes the entire film from within.

The return of mother and son to their dacha reconnects the psychodynamics to the mythos of poetry. The process begins before they depart. After Maria chops off the bird's head, she opens her eyes and turns to stare into the camera. Her gaze links to the false countershot, in black and white, of her husband, shirtless, turning to caress her hand as she levitates before him above their brass bed. The false countershot ambiguously fuses the violence of the slaughter with the erotic tone of the imaginary image. The camera tracks into a close-up of Maria as she declares her love for him, in a dialogue detached from the visuals, and then tracks back to show her floating in the room all alone, except for a dove that quickly flies offscreen. Once she and Alexei leave for home, a long tracking shot of them walking apart beside a stream becomes the occasion for the last of Arseny Tarkovsky's poems to be heard in the film. It is "Eurydice." At this point the voice represents the Orphic poet who sings of the breakdown of the body and the release of the soul (represented by the dove we have just seen) which "flies through the eye/ Into the heavenly brook,/ On to an icy cogwheel/ Of a bird's chariot."

The mythic originary poet may be speaking in his own persona of the wife he was forced to abandon when, automatically succumbing to her cry, he looked back at her—and her soul flew through her eye, or his, back to Hades— or he may be ventriloquizing Eurydice herself, when he chants of a transcendence of the body in terms that move from apocalyptic to mundane: "I dream, of another/ Soul differently clothed/...It encircles the earth,/ In liquid fire, without shadow,/ Like the cluster of lilac/ Left on the table." In either case, by the time the Orphic voice identifies itself in the final stanza, the poem's focus rests upon "my child":

> Run, my child, don't lament
> Over poor Eurydice;
> Drive your copper hoop
> With a stick round the world,
> While in answer to each step—
> Even though you don't hear it—
> Both happy and dry
> The earth sounds in your ears.

I have been arguing that in *Zerkalo* both cinematic and verbal poetry ground the relationship between the individual and history. From this argument it is appropriate that the film eventually finds its path back to Orpheus, the founding figure of poesis. "Eurydice" accompanies three elaborate shots. The first matches the start of the poem to the entrance of Alexei into the frame. He is soon followed by his mother, who walks at the same pace, several feet closer to the camera. She keeps looking over to him without his returning her gaze, but eventually he passes out of the frame, and the object of her glance becomes the stream. Retrospectively, once the name of Eurydice is uttered, this shot echoes the mythic couple's ascent from Hades, with the boy usurping (or inheriting) the role his father assigns himself in his poem.

By the time we hear the middle of the second stanza the images have shifted from the richly saturated color of the first shot to a somewhat slow-motion black-and-white shot tracking through woods in the opposite direction. It follows the direction of a powerful wind until it comes upon the familiar table, now overturning the lamp and bread again, along with a potato and a table setting. Some of the phrases of the poem correspond to what we see—specifically, "The rattle of forests...," and more indirectly the reappearance of the table, with "Here's a riddle without a solution:/ Who will return/ Having danced on the platform/ Where nobody dances?" Other phrases in the poem relate to earlier film images, such as the bare-chested father and the flung shirt: "The soul is sinful without the body,/ Like the body without a night-shirt." Finally, a third shot, black and white and in slow motion as well, follows the five-year-old Alexei into the dacha, just when the stanza shifts to address the child and to name Eurydice. Finally, the camera pans away from the boy penetrating the depths of the house as the poem ends: Orpheus's voice dissolves in the Apollonian wind whipping the lace curtains hung to dry within the house. Alexei's somnambulistic exploration of the dacha is, accordingly, his Orphic *katabasis*.

Without cutting, the camera swings back to where the boy had disappeared in darkness, and it tracks into a mirror in which we now see the boy holding a beaker of milk—half his size, in fact, just like one situated behind the adolescent Alexei in the doctor's dacha. When he brings the beaker to his lips, the long shot finally cuts to a silent, color image of him swimming nude in a pond while his mother does laundry at its bank. The gradual introduction of muted sounds—a distant dog barking, birds, the susurration of a mild breeze—represent the auditory response of the Earth that the Orphic voice had promised in compensation for forgoing mourning for the mother.

Synessios rather optimistically glosses the sequence thus:

> The poem's last verse urges the child not to lament Eurydice, now beyond reach, but to keep moving through the world as long as the earth responds even with the slightest sound to his every step. It returns us to the realm of childhood where everything is still in the future and there is abundant hope, resonating with the film's final sequence and the boy Alexei's buoyant cry. Like the other poems, it takes us to an associative space which lies beyond the film but which simultaneously links up with images from it: the notion of Maria as Eurydice; a spirituous and shadowless soul—like the wind/father roaming through the film—that leaves lilac on the table to be remembered by. *Mirror* is pitched between two distinct, yet complementary, artistic sensibilities. Tarkovsky is in creative dialogue with the resonant world bequeathed to him by the absent father.[38]

The construction of the film localizes this "creative dialogue" immediately after or within its only fictive and dramatic scenes: the failed seduction of the doctor, the misremembered typographical error, the failure to humiliate the drill instructor with the dummy grenade, and the failed sale of the earrings. Arseny Tarkovsky's poems perform multiple roles in the film, but one of those is to redeem these invented episodes from their purely dramatic or illustrative functions. The conventional grammar of those fictional parts of the film sets up the situations in which the oneiric power of the subsequent images can bear the weight of inspired poetry.

From the recital of "Eurydice" to the end of the film, the filmmaker offers a sustained paean to the Russian landscape and to the image of the mother as a presence within uniquely cinematic time. He follows the swimming shot with a wonderfully constructed dolly through an empty room of the dacha in color. The camera pushes past a lace curtain into the sunlit room, where the only movement besides that of the camera dolly is a puppy playing atop a bureau. As if representing the point of view of Alexei—his free indirect discourse—the tracking shot turns in the room toward a window. On the sill a volume of poetry is open, its pages moved by a breeze. But as soon as the image tracks beyond the book, we see the boy outside; he appears as if materialized from the volume of poetry walking toward his mother, now the old woman played by Maria Tarkovskaia. He carries a feather as an emblem of his poetic vocation. If this detached perspective constitutes Pasolini's "free indirect point of view," it is in the service of a cinema of poetry of a lyrical intensity beyond what Pasolini would allow for the poetics of filmmaking.

In the magnificent conclusion of the film, the mother appears at once as the young and the aged Maria while we hear the opening of the *St. John Passion*: "Herr, under Herscher, dessen Ruhm in allem Landen Herrlich ist!" The verse Bach set to music begins Psalm 8. The film evokes the spirit of the Psalm itself:

> Out of the mouth of babes and sucklings hast thou ordained strength because of thine enemies, that thou mightest still the enemy and the avenger.
>
> When I consider thy heavens, the work of thy fingers, the moon and the stars, which thou hast ordained;
>
> What is man, that thou art mindful of him? and the son of man, that thou visitest him?
>
> For thou hast made him a little lower than the angels, and hast crowned him with glory and honour.
>
> Thou madest him to have dominion over the works of thy hands; thou hast put all things under his feet:
>
> All sheep and oxen, yea, and the beasts of the field;
>
> The fowl of the air, and the fish of the sea, and whatsoever passeth through the paths of the seas.
>
> O LORD our Lord, how excellent is thy name in all the earth!

But before we hear the Bach, there is a final, brief return to the narrator's apartment in the present, where he lies dying, attended by a doctor and the two mysterious women Ignat encountered. This episode is the only exception to the pattern of fictional scenes followed by a poem. It fulfills the need the film-maker perceived to bring closure to the flimsy narrative framework of the film, and—what is perhaps more important—to cast the final shots as a postmortem vision, as he will do again at the end of *Nostalghia*. Robert Bird understands this awkward moment as a crucial acknowledgment of the nature of narrative:

> The bounds of the director's conception extend far beyond the autobio-graphical screenplay...beyond even the specific memories and associa-tions on which Tarkovsky based *Mirror*; the conception includes also the implicit and perhaps unconscious scaffolding that supports any narrative, indeed which supports narrativity itself, and which reveals itself only when it collapses under its own weight...In this light Tarkovsky's entrance into the frame (as the bed-ridden patient behind the screen at the end of the film) is merely an acknowledgement of the fragile embodiment of the imaginary and of the violence with which time consumes not only the subject's concep-tion, but also his body.[39]

I take Bird to mean much more than that the disembodied voice of the nar-rator heard at the start of the film is finally visualized just as he expires and the film is about to end. This embodiment on the verge of disintegration becomes an allegory for narration, which he cautiously does not ascribe to Tarkovsky's intention. In making this point he alludes, too elliptically I fear, to statements by the filmmaker Bird culled from Russian sources: "Tarkovsky contrasted his presence within the frame to that of Fellini's *8 ½* and Bergman's *Wild Strawberries*, which 'fail by introducing the author as a regular character [which] makes the film a plot-based narration'...by contrast *Mirror* is 'the process of the maturation of the film and its conception, meaning that it won't contain a film as such.'"[40] In this context, Bird seems to be saying that rather than leave out the narrating voice and body, Tarkovsky includes this minimal scene to evoke and acknowledge their virtual absence from the film. This is a strong point and the most sophisticated apology for *Mirror's* framing devices I have read. Still, the inclusion of so clumsy a scene and its integral connec-tion to the awkward inclusion of Asafiev—confirmed by the reappearance of a bird—points to the tenaciousness with which the filmmaker clung to these two moments. They have to have been central to his conception of the film; for the narrator's final gesture is to release the bird that Asafiev grasped when it landed on his head. In the film it looks more dead than alive. Alexei has to heave it upward out of the frame because it appears barely capable of taking flight. The transference of the bird from the orphan of Leningrad to the fictive Alexei indicates, as Bird implies, a symbolic equation of these two personae "beyond the bounds" of the autobiographical chain of associations.

The epilogue is not only implicitly postmortem but prenatal as well: a slow pan of the landscape around the dacha zooms back and down to see the father and Maria lying in the grass. In a reaffirmation of the primal scene scenario underlying the narrator's quest, his father asks whether Maria would prefer to have a boy or a girl, but she only smiles and looks thoughtful as the camera zooms back from the close-up of her face this sequence shot had momentarily become. As she looks into the woods, the shots that follow articulate her scanning of both space and time; for she sees herself as a old woman walking with her young children, interrupted further by two probing shots recalling the burning shed; one looks into the well, now full of rubbish and overgrown with luscious moss and weeds, and the other glides around the insect-ridden ruins of the shed. Even though we return to her in the same position, as if the previous shots were from her point of view, the fluid movements of the camera here in the epilogue attain an autonomy that resists such grounding. Their unraveling of the point-of-view perspective is explicit when she looks back for the final shot of the film. We follow the older mother and the children again only to see her standing alone in the depths of the landscape as they pass. The Bach chorus suddenly stops so that we can hear a loud ululation from Alexei before the camera tracks away, recording the falling light of dusk and the sounds of an answering owl.

Zerkalo's ending owes something to Bergman's *Smultronstället* (*Wild Strawberries*) (1957), which also concludes with benign and valetudinarian images of the protagonist's parents. All of Tarkovsky's films end with impressive codas; in every instance it is as if the whole film were a prelude to the final epiphany. In the final dream of *Ivan's Childhood*, the return of the oneiric moment carries an extra power because we know Ivan, his mother, and his sister are all dead. The black–and-white epic *Andrey Rublev* withholds any picturing of the artist's work until the magnificent epilogue in color documents his "Trinity." Kelvin, a prodigal son, in the posture in which Rembrandt painted the subject—Tarkovsky would have seen the original hanging in The Hermitage galleries—embraces his father at the end of *Solaris* in the dacha mysteriously transplanted to an island in the cosmic sea of Solaris. The surprising telekinetic powers of the Stalker's daughter gives *Stalker* its strangely wonderful conclusion. Yet no image in all of Tarkovsky's work is as spectacular as the last shot of *Nostalghia*, in which, after the protagonist's death, he appears outside his dacha, itself within the massive ruins of a Gothic church. *Offret* (*Sacrifice*) (1986), too, has a powerful coda: the previously mute boy, Little Man, faithfully watering a dead tree, speaks the opening of the Gospel of John.

Generally, the films of Andrey Tarkovsky bear out the claim of Nicolas Berdyaev: "the Russian people in accordance with their metaphysical nature and vocation are a people of the End. Apocalypse has always played a great part both among the masses of our people and at the highest cultural level…In our thought the eschatological problem takes an immeasurably greater place than in the thinking of the West.…"[41] *Solaris* and *Stalker* use science fiction premises to explore religious, eschatological perspectives; *Offret* is overtly apocalyptic—a miraculous postponement of The End—and even *Andrey Rublev*, like

Bergman's *Det sjunde inseglet* (*The Seventh Seal*) (1957) to which it is hugely indebted, evokes a medieval aura of Last Days as an allegory of contemporary spiritual blight.

Nostalghia is a variation on the apocalyptic theme, or rather tribal obsession. Its plot is simple: a Russian writer, Andrey Gorchakov, in Italy to research the life of a serf musician of the eighteenth century, travels with his translator, Eugenia. They encounter Domenico, an Italian who had locked up himself and his family for years in anticipation of the end of the world. He convinces Andrey to fulfill a mission he himself had failed to execute: to carry a lighted candle the length of the pool of St. Catherine in Bagno Vignoni. Andrey dies just as he completes the task on the day that Domenico immolates himself astride the statue of Marcus Aurelius in Rome. Domenico's fanatical behavior translates that of the Old Believers in seventeenth- and eighteenth-century Russia, who resisted liturgical reform by taking to the forests and often committing suicide in the conviction that the Last Days had come. Thousands of them burned themselves to death, convinced that the cleansing fire was the holiest form of salvation in the face of the Antichrist.

Fire, in *Nostalghia*, is linked to the theology of light and of pneumatic inspiration, just as the superabundance of water (including fog and snow) points to baptismal purification. At a crucial moment we see a book burning as if struck by the tongues of fire described as falling on the apostles at Pentecost. The project initiated by Domenico and completed by Andrey echoes the injunction not to hide one's light under a basket (Matthew 5:15, Luke 8:16, 11:33) and the parable of the lamps of the ten virgins (Matthew 25). While five foolish virgins used up their oil keeping their lamps burning in anticipation of the coming Bridegroom, the five wise ones carried additional fuel so that they were ready and alert when the delayed Bridegroom finally appeared. Traditionally, this parable has been read as an admonition against recklessly acting as if the Day of Judgment were imminent. One must hold back reserves and patiently await the Parousia.

Tarkovsky's relationship to the eschatology of the Russian Orthodox Church was mediated by the great Russian novelists of the nineteenth century. This is most apparent in *Nostalghia*, for it summarizes the filmmaker's initial experience of Western Europe (and the consequent intense longing for his homeland) as it coincided with that of the novelists. *Nostos* is the Greek root word for "the return home"; Tarkovsky frequently stressed this to foreign interviewers. Fyodor Dostoyevsky, in particular, was a major inspiration in the making of *Nostalghia*. Before and after filming it, Tarkovsky tried to get permission from soviet film authorities to do a two-part version of *The Idiot*. For the highly social German spa in that novel, Tarkovsky gives us the nearly deserted Bagno Vignoli; for the persistent discussion of "The Woman Question," he dissects Eugenia's feminism; for Dostoyevsky's fascination with Holbein's *Dead Christ*, he fixes his camera on Piero della Francesca's *Madonna del Parto.* This is nothing new for the filmmaker, for, in addition to the reproductions of Brueghel's paintings in *Solaris,* other Brueghel compositions are reenacted in *Andrey Rublev* and, as we have seen, in *Zerkalo,* which also widely utilizes images from Leonardo, as does *Offret.* There is a Van Eyck fragment in a stream in *Stalker.* Finally, *Nostalghia* culminates in an homage to Caspar David Friedrich.

Tarkovsky seems to have had less interest in the West as it is than as a vehicle for bringing Holy Russia into cinematic focus. Thus Piero's great painting becomes a portable icon, carried in procession by devout women who enact a dreamlike fertility rite in which dozens of birds—the emblem of the Holy Ghost—are released inside the church of Santa Maria di Momentana as if out of the Virgin's womb. Two paintings by Friedrich, *The Ruins of Eldena* and *Hutten's Grave,* seem to be the inspiration for the spectacular final shot of the film, in which the camera slowly zooms back from a nearly still shot of Gorchakov—presumably he died the last time we saw him—and Domenico's dog sitting before a reflecting pool of water; we come to see his Russian dacha behind him, and finally the entire site is enclosed within the monumental ruins of a cathedral, as large snowflakes fall. Earlier we had seen Gorchakov walking through the ruined shell of the church of San Galgano in Tuscany, so this image of his posthumous Paradise is a distinctively Russified fusion of those Gothic walls and his frequently glimpsed country home, by way of Friedrich's paintings.

In *Hutten's Grave* (1823–1824), Friedrich depicted an aged mourner paying his respects to an imaginary tomb of the patriot and defender of Luther, who actually has no known burial site. Friedrich located the grave where the sanctuary would have been in the overgrown ruins of a great roofless Gothic church. Even more directly, *The Ruins of Elderna* (ca. 1825) shows a humble cottage within the ruins of a massive church, surrounded by trees, some as tall as the walls of the ruins surrounding it in turn. Two tiny male figures, one sitting, one standing, are conversing before the cottage. The implication, in both paintings, of the decay of the official church, redeemed by the reclamation of nature in a version of the romantic Sublime, corresponds to the fusion of natural piety and traditional religious awe characteristic of most of Tarkovsky's cinema. Significantly, the filmmaker concluded this spectacular evocation of "Gonchakov's grave" by dedicating the film to his mother, who died just before *Nostalghia* was shot.

The opening sequence shot of the film establishes the Byzantine inflection of the Italian landscape: Eugenia and Andrey emerge from a car that has stopped on a hillside. A thick mist inhibits a perspectival view, flattening the image. Gradually a path appears, rising to the top of the frame as if it were a road to heaven. Eventually we discern that the road leads to a church, at the top of the frame. Although Andrey rejects the chance to see Piero's *Madonna del Parto*—he is sick of the beauties of Italy—its power symbolically graces him. Eugenia enters the church as the sole tourist amid a group of pious women. There she meets with the reproof of the sacristan, who lectures her on the sacrificial role of women. As if falling from one of paraclitic birds released in the church, a feather lands—impossibly—on the head of Andrey, now seen in sepia, back in Russia, amid unidentified women beside his dacha. The feather and a white streak in his hair are signs of his poetic election, just as the feather in the hand of the five-year-old Alexei had been at the conclusion of *Zerkalo*.

The relationship between the Russian and his Italian translator grows progressively more tense. Early on they have the following exchange concerning the book of poetry she is reading: "What are you reading?" "Arseny Tarkovsky's poems." "In Russian?" "No, it's a translation. Quite a good one." "Throw it away immediately." "Why? The translator is a good one; he is a fine poet." "Poetry is untranslatable, like the whole of art."

Later, after she fails to seduce him and reacts with a hysterical outburst, she leaves for Rome. At this point he dreams of his wife (another Maria) and child in the Russian countryside. His sepia dream leads into a color shot of a statue of an angel under flowing water. The camera slowly pans up to Andrey, drunk, wading through a flooded foundation of a Renaissance church, reciting Arseny Tarkovsky's "In childhood I fell ill" in Russian—with memory lapses. It is a poem of fevered consciousness incorporating quasi-apocalyptic images: "Now trumpets start to blare, light strikes/ My eyelids, horses gallop by, my mother/ Flies above the road…" The submerged marble angel corresponds to the flying mother; an earlier simile, "like following/ The Pied Piper into the river…," even more concretely rhymes with the man wading through the water, while his inebriation reflects the "illness" that set the poem in motion.

After the recitation, Andrey throws down a book beside a fire and pours more vodka into a plastic cup. In his rambling monologue he says, "I must go and see Dad," as if Arseny Tarkovsky's poem had reminded Andrey of his filial duty. (The filmmaker could hardly be signaling his identification with his protagonist more blatantly.) Then he sights a girl sitting like a Carpaccio angel—an association strengthened when she tells him her name is Angela. A slow tracking shot toward the girl as she throws a pebble in the water is the occasion for the beginning of another of Arseny Tarkovsky's poems, "My sight—my strength—grows dim." This time Andrey recites it in an Italian translation. In this episode the filmmaker uses the poems to abet Andrey's fatal decision to carry out Domenico's request and, in so doing, die. The shift between languages, from Russian to Italian, with its implicit repudiation of his rude and absolutist response to Eugenia, already signals the transition from his rigidity to an acceptance of his apocalyptic self-sacrifice.

It is effected cinematically, as the episode unfolds, in its fusion of poetry and oneiric imagery: another shot moves toward the water and the detritus under it. The poem proleptically provides a scenario for the end of the film. We might infer from the final couplet of the first stanza that its speaker may be a dying angel, or Icarus: "And the two wings at my shoulders/ No longer shine." In the second of the two stanzas, the poet declares:

> I am a candle burnt out at the feast.
> Collect my wax in the morning
> And you'll find this page will tell you
> How you might cry and what to be proud of,
> How to give away the final third
> Of happiness, how to die easy,
> Beneath a fortuitous roof
> To blaze after death, like the word.

As the poem ends, we see Andrey, supine, apparently sleeping beside the pool. The pan from his head reveals the open book on fire: the archetypical volume of poetry is consumed with Pentecostal flames. This shot of the protagonist asleep opens the frame of a dream in which he finds himself on a deserted street littered with discarded clothes. There he encounters Domenico as his double. Thus the voice-over of Domenico can be heard as if speaking Andrey's thoughts, and when Andrey opens the mirrored door of a wardrobe abandoned on the street, Domenico's reflection replaces his own. Then he wanders through the ruins of the roofless church of San Galgano while a woman's voice converses with God, against the background of a chorus chanting a litany: "Lord, look at how he questions? Why don't you say something to him." "But what would happen if he heard my voice?" "Let him feel Your Presence." "I do, always, but he is not aware of it." The sounds of a bird's wings, repeated from the earlier dream of his wife, bring us back to the pool. Angela is gone, the volume of poetry consumed in ashes. The panning movement, in reverse of the previous one, finds Andrey still supine but with eyes open, closing the dream frame.

How does a filmmaker "let [his] light shine before men"? How does he use his light wisely in the uncertain anticipation of the Last Days? To the extent that carrying the lighted candle across St. Catherine's pool allegorizes the making of films in general, and of this film in particular, it is the absurdly "wise" gesture in contrast to the "foolish" protest of the self-destroying Domenico. Tarkovsky may be answering these questions when he ends *Sculpting in Time* with a gesture toward the fusion of poetics and theology: ". . . the one thing that mankind has ever created in the spirit of self-surrender is the artistic image. . . . Perhaps our capacity to create is evidence that we ourselves were created in the image and likeness of God?"[42]

Just as *Nostalghia* mines its sources in the Bible and in Russian literature (with a prominent place for the poetry of Arseny Tarkovsky), it argues with the films and filmmakers that have meant the most to Tarkovsky. Bergman's

Persona influenced its mood and some of the images: Domenico's suicide owes something to the documentary footage of a Buddhist bonze burning himself in Vietnam, which one of Bergman's protagonists watches in horror on a television. More directly, the dreamlike encounter of Eugenia with Gorchakov's wife in Russia reflects the caresses of *Persona*'s two female figures. Above all, the fusion of Domenico and Andrey when the latter sees the former as his mirror image comes from the core of Bergman's film. Eschewing Italian actors to play Domenico, Tarkovsky even chose Erland Josephson, the dominant male actor of Bergman's later films. In this way, he assimilates Bergman's middle style of the 1960s into the genre of his earlier religious films, the spiritual biography.

If Bergman is a distant but potent source for *Nostalghia*, Tarkovsky's friend, Michelangelo Antonioni, is his ever-present agonist. He took Antonioni's screenwriter, Tonino Guerra, as his collaborator on the script and complained in his diary when Antonioni's own needs kept him from using the set designer Schiaccianoci and the cameraman Tovoli. The character of Eugenia looks back to another beautiful translator in *L'eclisse*. Whereas Antonioni sympathetically poised Vittoria's (Monica Vitti) need for economic and sexual independence against the stock jobber Piero's (Alain Delon) narcissistic acquisition of the love of women so that he could reject them, Tarkovsky's antifeminist polemic portrays Eugenia as confused and lost without knowing the nature of her longing. She is Vittoria and Piero in one: a self-alienated dilettante who assumes that all attractive men desire her, she hence reacts hysterically to her failure to seduce Andrey and to the implicit challenge of his spiritual magnitude. Although she abandons him in anger, only to telephone to announce that she is traveling to India with a rich boyfriend, she rushes in the end to Domenico's death as if to Andrey's, which the film's editing presents as parallel and perhaps simultaneous events.

In *L'avventura* Antonioni depicted the beginning and the betrayal of an affair within the landscape of the Eolic islands and Sicily, often locating the passions of his protagonists at the sites of major Baroque buildings. All of Tarkovsky's films likewise make symbolic use of natural landscapes, but in *Nostalghia* he follows Antonioni's example closely, moving Gorchakov and Eugenia through Renaissance and Gothic locations in Tuscany and locating Domenico's end on the Campodoglio in Rome. But even if he subscribes to Antonioni's diagnosis of failure of contemporary relationships (and Bergman's existential anguish), he sees a Dostoyevskian antithesis to their despair in Russian spirituality, the sacrificial character of motherhood, and the immortality revealed in artistic creation. Tarkovsky's cosmological vision in *Nostalghia*—that is to say, the interplay of the sacredness of natural beauty, his eschatological obsession, religious nationalism, and his evocations of the cult of divine motherhood—embraces as a whole the central points of Orthodox spirituality.[43]

In the final paragraphs of the eighth chapter of *Sculpting in Time*, the filmmaker makes an important statement about both metaphor and the nature of his theoretical enterprise. I would like to conclude this discussion of poetry in his cinema by looking carefully at that passage (pp. 212–216), into which he inserts into the book his father's poem, "My sight—my strength—grows dim." After discussing *Hamlet*, which he staged in the Soviet Union, as the tragedy of a man who had to renounce his ideals, he writes of fidelity to nature as the mark of his "sincerity" as a filmmaker: "Nature exists in cinema as the naturalistic fidelity with which it is recorded." He is at pains to convince his readers, as he admits he has had difficulty doing with live audiences, that the images of the natural elements in his films "are no symbols or metaphors." Instead, he is "recreating [his] world in those details which seem to [him] most fully and exactly to express the elusive meaning of our existence." The concentration on water, fire, or wind shows "the audience, the world as it actually is, so it can be seen in depth and from all sides, evoking its very 'smell', allowing audiences to feel on their skin its moisture or dryness." The details he isolates, he asserts, would be those that "seem to [him] most fully and exactly to express the elusive meaning of our existence." The adjective *elusive* here functions as an index of poesis, just as does the phrase "in depth and from all sides." If we recall that the artistic image, for Tarkovsky, is always metonymic and consequently that through the poetic logic of association "an inner power which is concentrated within the image…comes across to the audience in the form of feelings," then even the "smell" his natural images conjure up is a metonymy for the depth and multisided but elusive poetry of pure cinema.

The filmmaker provides a fascinating example of this metonymy of natural imagery:

> Let me clarify what I mean with a reference to Bergman: in *The Virgin Spring* I have always been stunned by one shot of the dying heroine, the girl who has been monstrously raped. The spring sun is shining through the trees, and through the branches we see her face—she may be dying or she may be already dead, but in any case she clearly no longer feels pain…Our foreboding seems to hang in the air, suspended like a sound…All seems clear enough and yet we feel a hiatus…There's something missing…Snow starts to fall, freak spring snow…which is the piercing scintilla we needed to bring our feelings to a kind of consummation: we gasp transfixed. The snow catches on her eyelashes and stays there: again, time is leaving its tracks in the shot…But how, by what right, could one talk about the meaning of that falling snow, even though within the span and rhythm of the shot it is the thing that brings our emotional awareness to a climax? Of course one can't. All we know is that this scene is the form the artist found to convey precisely what happened. On no account must artistic purpose be confused with ideology, or we shall lose the means of perceiving art immediately and exactly with the whole of our being…[44]

I have quoted this passage at length—including the ellipses, which are the author's rather than my abbreviation—because this remarkable analysis seems to be Tarkovsky's invention. I have found no print of Bergman's film that contains such a shot. Of course, Tarkovsky did not have our advantage of digital copies of films in which we can easily check such details. But he claims to have seen the film more than once and to have been overwhelmed by the snowflake on the eyelid every time. There is indeed a freak snowfall in the sunny scenes. The flakes fall not on the dead girl, however, but on the face (not eyelashes) of the boy who has been forced by his older brothers, the rapists, to guard the corpse. Tarkovsky's error (unless he has seen a different version of the film) undermines one aspect of his example, but it reinforces another, more important, dimension of his polemic. The transference, in his recollection of the film, from the boy's cheeks to the girl's eyelids, deflates his argument for the accuracy of recording natural phenomena, but it strengthens the case of the power of association. The snow on the boy's cheek is indeed a metonymy for the flakes falling on all the objects in the scene. The poetic association "in depth and from all sides" even includes an unconscious "correction" of Bergman's film in his fellow filmmaker's oneiric imagination.

For Tarkovsky, as for Pasolini, Bergman's work is an ineluctable touchstone for a discussion of poetry in cinema. *Sculpting in Time* offers a theoretical framework in which to consider the complex and highly associative films Bergman made after Pasolini wrote "Il 'cinema di poesia.'" Even though the "free indirect point of view" offers a powerful tool for comprehending the structures of *Tystnaden, Persona,* and many of the films Bergman made after them, Tarkovsky's exploration of the relationship of poetry to cinema provides a more comprehensive account of Bergman's achievement, with its insistent emphasis on the linkages through which "the poetic design of being" can be glimpsed "beyond the limitations of coherent logic, and conveying the deep complexity and truth of impalpable connections and hidden phenomena of life" (p. 21). Pasolini's ontology of cinema as an oneiric, irrational sign system points the way to Bergman's and even Tarkovsky's art, but his version of narrative poetry is circumscribed insofar as it makes the manifest protagonist of a film the clear ground of the "free indirect point of view." It is central to Pasolini's thesis that these protagonists of "the 'cinema of poetry'" are neurotic representatives of the bourgeoisie. In *Sculpting in Time*, however, there is no place for neurosis or class considerations. If cinematic poetry "lay[s] open the logic of person's thought" (p. 20), it does not do so in order to delineate a psychology but to "record the very *movement* of reality" (p. 94). In its commitment to the model of poetic observation, Tarkovsky's theoretical position occupies a position between the narrative poetry expounded by Pasolini and Stan Brakhage's polemics for a cinema of visionary poetry.

As he concludes his chapter and his discussion of unnecessary symbolism, Tarkovsky moves immediately from the poetic elaboration of the snowflake in Bergman's film to an admission that "the final shot of *Nostalghia* has an element of metaphor." He confesses, "It is a constructed image which smacks of literariness: a model of the hero's state, of the division within him which prevents him from living as he has up till now." He then elaborates a reading of the scene that contradicts his disparagement of "the so-called 'poetic cinema' where everything is deliberately made incomprehensible and the director has to think up explanations for what he has done."[45] His reading of his own film is quite elaborate:

> Or perhaps, on the contrary, it is his new wholeness in which the Tuscan hills and the Russian countryside come together indissolubly; he is conscious of them as inherently his own, merged into his being and his blood, but at the same time reality is enjoining him to separate these things by returning to Russia. And so Gorchakov dies in this new world where those things come together naturally and of themselves which in our strange and relatively earthy existence have for some reason, or by someone, been divided once and for all. All the same, even if the scene lacks cinematic purity, I trust that it is free of vulgar symbolism; the conclusion seems to me fairly complex in form and meaning, and to be a figurative expression of what is happening to the hero, not of something outside him which has to be deciphered.[46]

Here, yet again, Tarkovsky's position on cinematic figuration is nearly identical to Brakhage's, who often used William Carlos Williams's dictum "No ideas, but in things" as a shorthand reference to his elevation of the poetic immanence of the cinematic image. It is not surprising, then, that Tarkovsky incorporates in the excuse for his contradictions a declaration about the filmmaker's use of theory that rhymes with Brakhage's assertion that all his writing on film is "of use as useless"; that is, as a catharsis of ideas which must be cleared away to make room for the unpredictable cinematic imagination. Tarkovsky is more discursive in his excuse: "It's unlikely that there are many works of art that embody precisely the aesthetic doctrine preached by the artist. As a rule a work of art develops in complex interaction with the artist's theoretical ideas, which cannot encompass it completely; artistic texture is always richer than anything that can be fitted into a theoretical schema."[47]

Cinema 16 Symposium:
Dylan Thomas, Arthur Miller, Willard Maas, Parker Tyler, Amos Vogel, Maya Deren.

Jonas Mekas, *Travel Songs* (2003): Pier Paolo Pasolini, flowers of Assisi [shot June 1967]
Image courtesy of Jonas and Sebastian Mekas

Poetry and the American Avant-Garde Cinema

In 1967 Pasolini's theory of the cinema of poetry took a significant turn toward accommodating his ideas on temporality. He opposed the imaginative notion of a camera endlessly running to record the life of a person to the shaping power of editing. The former he identified, somewhat fancifully, with the "sequence shot," the latter with the totalization of death. He still clung to the fiction that he was working within the domain of semiology when he wrote his four complex, ambiguous, and provocative essays that year: "Osservazioni sul piano-sequenza," "Essere è naturale?," "La paura del naturalismo," and "I segni viventi e i poeti morti."

Gilles Deleuze, the most astute and productive reader of Pasolini's film theory, took up the gist of Pasolini's reflections on time in the cinema and ignored the question of its relation to poetry. In transposing Pasolini's theory from its original context, he defanged its polemical thrust and its absolutist tone to adapt it to his more catholic view of the range and power of what he calls *L'Image-temps* in cinema. His goal was a new taxonomy of the spatial and temporal structures filmmakers have invented. Deleuze was particularly sensitive to Pasolini's insights into the general nature of cinema and the historical argument of "Il 'cinema di poesia.'" Pasolini's four later essays supported his observation that the most decisive event in the history of cinema was the shift from what he called "the image-movement" to "the time-movement." However, like all film theoreticians who see themselves primarily as filmmakers, Pasolini was really providing the theoretical bases for his own films, although he disguised that more than others: the examples he cites were from film history and the work of his contemporaries; rarely did he even mention his own films in *Empirismo eretico*. Deleuze capitalized on those critical insights, and he was quick to dismiss those aspects of Pasolini's argument that implied the centrality of the filmmaker's own practice. In *Cinéma 2: L'image-temps* he wrote:

> The image-movement has two sides, one in relation to the objects whose relative position it varies, the other in relation to a whole of which it expresses an absolute change. The positions are in space but the whole that changes is in time. If one assimilates the image-movement to the shot, one calls the framing the first side of the shot turned toward the objects, and editing the side turned toward the whole. The first thesis follows: it is editing (montage) itself that constitutes the whole, and therefore it gives us the image *of* time.... That the present would be the only direct time of the filmic image even seems self-evident. Pasolini, once again, calls upon it to support a very classical idea of editing: precisely because it chooses and coordinates "meaningful moments" editing has the property of "rendering the present past," of transforming our unstable and uncertain present into "a clear, stable, and describable past," in short, it manifests time. He even adds, in vain, that this is the work of death, not a fully accomplished death, but a death in life or being unto death ("death renders a lightning-flash montage of our life"). This black note reinforces the classical and grandiose idea of editing as king: time as the indirect representation springing from the synthesis of images.
>
> But this thesis has another aspect, which seems to contradict the first: it seems that the synthesis of the image-movements must rely on the intrinsic characters of each of them.... Therefore the shot needs to be a potential montage in advance, and the image-movement a matrix or cell of time.... According to Pasolini "the present transforms itself into the past" by virtue of editing, but this past "always appears as the present" by virtue of the nature of the image. Philosophy had already noted a similar opposition in the notion of "the number of movement," since the number appeared sometimes as an independent instance, and sometimes as a simple function of what it measures.[1]

Deleuze dismissed Pasolini's repeated employment of the metaphor of death, while at the same time he was the first to note that Jean Epstein had preceded him in using this metaphor in "Le cinématographe dans l'Archipel" (*Les Arts mécaniques*, Décembre 1928; *Écrits sur le cinema* 1, p. 199). Above all, he rejected Pasolini's semiology, not as Barthes, Eco, and others did, because it was gerry-rigged and amateur, but more fundamentally because the principle that "Cinema is not a universal or primitive language system [*langue*], nor a language [*language*]" is central to his argument. In his formulation, cinema "brings to light an intelligible content, which is like a presupposition, a condition, a necessary correlate through which language constructs its own 'objects'" (*Cinéma* 2, p. 262). Here readers of Pasolini might recognize his radical idea of a language of natural objects, denuded of its semiological attire, restated in more rational terms.

The metaphor of death as a marker of semiological closure first appeared in "Osservazioni sul piano-sequenza," the text Pasolini prepared for the Pesaro Festival of 1967. At that festival Jonas Mekas presented a number of programs devoted to recent works of the New American Cinema. Pasolini was unable to see those programs at Pesaro, but he assiduously attended when they were screened subsequently at the Cinema Studio in Rome. In reaction to the challenge they presented to his concept of a cinema of poetry, he wrote, "I segni viventi e i poeti morti" as an appendix to the text for Pesaro. There Pasolini reiterated and expanded upon the thesis of the festival paper that "*so long as we live, we have no meaning*, and the language of our lives is...untranslatable...*Death effects an instantaneous montage of our lives*" (HE, p. 236). He insisted that the final moments of a man's life can transform the meaning of his previous acts. In fact, he cites the "little tear" of Manfred that saved his soul in *Purgatorio* 3.114, adding that he was not interested in the afterlife of the soul but in the "secular...uncertain and continuous search...for expressive perfection." (He had previously quoted this passage in the epigraph following the titles of *Accatone*.) His poetic model for the "cinema of [narrative] 'poetry'" was Dante and the spiritual biographies embedded in the *Commedia*.

Whereas Deleuze would come to allegorize cinema as a "spiritual automation" obsessed with images and stories of automata, Pasolini here proposed a dying man as the emblematic figure of film form; the meaning of his life can be known only in his death. Thus the fiction films he made up until 1967 reenact sacrificial deaths: *Accatone* (1961), *Mama Roma* (1962), *La ricotta* (1963), *Il Vangelo secondo Matteo* (1964), *Uccellacci e uccellini* (1966), *Edipo Re* (1967). In cinematic terms, according to the filmmaker, the ambiguous continuity of life as it is lived corresponds to the "sequence shot" and the totalization of death to editing. So, in Pasolini's schema, there was no place for the varieties of filmic temporality later elaborated in Deleuze's taxonomy. It was precisely in terms of its temporality that Pasolini rejected the works he saw (and those he did not see) of the American avant-garde cinema. Careful attention to the terms of that rejection will nevertheless uncover further dimensions of his idea of a cinema of poetry, relevant to a productive discussion of many of the very filmmakers he dismissed (and Deleuze extolled). At stake is fundamentally the possibility for cinema of what Pasolini called "poesia-poesia," or a lyric as distinguished from narrative film poetry. Therefore, I propose to take up briefly the aspect of Pasolini's 1967 essays that Deleuze could not use. His repudiation of the poetic claims of the American avant-garde cinema may help us to focus on the opposite; that is, on what that cinema has contributed to a discussion of poetry in film.

After expounding and qualifying the Dantean idea of the crucial moment of death in "I segni viventi e i poeti morti," Pasolini turns to his critique of the New American Cinema. Excepting only "Burkage" (evidently he meant Stan Brakhage), he condemned the entire Exposition as "a cinema for convent schoolgirls" because its filmmakers imagined they were "destroying conventional time." This polemic against "the illusion of the passing of time," which recurs throughout the 1967 essays, is one of the most obscure points in Pasolini's film theory. It seems to stand in opposition to the narrative temporality of the meaningfulness of a life understood from its endpoint. In "I segni viventi…" he elliptically makes three arguments against the way in which the American avant-garde filmmakers conceive of cinematic time: (1) they reduce all narrative cinema to Hollywood commercialism, (2) as petit bourgeois artists they assume that their sense of time is that of all humanity, and (3) led by Allen Ginsberg, they "amateurishly" adapt the temporality of Indian philosophies. The chief example of these offenses seems to have been Jonas Mekas's *Diaries, Notes, and Sketches*, a film-in-progress, shown in an excerpt in Rome, although Pasolini names neither the film nor the maker.[2]

Yet again, without naming the film or the filmmaker, he cites an American avant-garde film as the paradigm of "the cult of reality pushed too far in its interminable sequence shots" in "Essere è naturale?"[3] He informs his Italian readers that "in the basements of the New York of the New Cinema, sequence shots which last for hours are shown (for example, a man sleeping)" (p. 241). The film he means must be Andy Warhol's *Sleep* (1965). It was not shown at Pesaro or anywhere in Italy in 1967. In fact, it is unlikely that Pasolini ever saw even one minute of the six-hour-long film (which contains no sequence shots, strictly speaking, although it is composed of several long takes, often loop printed, and frozen frames). Yet the idea of such a film conveniently fits his notion of the misguided temporality of the American avant-garde cinema in which "the long, foolish, inordinate, unnatural, mute sequence shot…generates in us a horror of reality…"

At the end of "I segni vivanti…," when rapid editing, rather than long takes, becomes the focus of his dismissal, he returns to the question of cinema and poetry (for the last time):

> As for me, I continue to believe in a cinema which narrates, that is, in the convention through which editing chooses the meaningful and valid pieces from the infinite sequence shots which can be shot. But I have even been the first to speak explicitly of a cinema of poetry. However, speaking of a cinema of poetry, I always meant to speak of narrative poetry (HE, p. 251)…Now, what I ask myself, after the failed experiments of the avant-garde, is if *a cinema of nonnarrative poetry* isn't possible—poetry-poetry, or, as it's usually called, of lyric poetry. Is it possible?

On this question I close my note, but not without first having tried to define the real terms of the problem. It is not possible to make a cinema of poetry (alas, let's call it thus) lyrical simply by *pushing too far* [*esasperando*] the techniques of the cinema of narrative poetry. Pushing Cassavetes or Godard too far, one makes bad Cassavetes or slapdash Godard...At times reality itself is poetic. The other evening we were talking about these things in an open-air restaurant, with Moravia and other friends, when a musician arrived (not seen, on the sly) and began to play his mandolin. That's it! It was such a poetic thing that everyone felt lost in his heart and had to forcibly restrain the emotion, to intellectualize it and express it. In that moment reality as non-symbolic language—that is, a mandolin player as a figural symbol of himself—that is, once again, a mandolin tune as living syntagma—was poetic. Would capturing moments such as this, by reproducing them, be the lyric poetry of cinema? But in this case, once again, how would the Semiology of Reality be indentified with that of Cinema (in fact, as we have seen, Cinema insofar as it is Langue is nothing but reality itself), so is the poetry of reality the same thing as that reproduced by cinema? But wasn't the mandolin player in time—in the time of an open-air dinner—and therefore in real time, in the illusion of real time, in a life that already had the characteristics of a story?...But I don't believe in a cinema of lyric poetry obtained through editing and pushing technique too far. (p. 252, Ben Lawton and Louise Barnett translation altered)

The three questions Pasolini poses here are not rhetorical. He feels that nothing he has seen of the American avant-garde cinema achieves the poetic power of the sudden appearance of the mandolin player while he was dining with literary friends; he is uncertain whether or not a recording or a recreation of that event would constitute a cinema of lyric poetry. He also asks if that would mean that cinematic lyric poetry is nothing more than the poetic dimension of reality. And finally, and most crucially, he wonders if such a fragment, in cinema, would have meaning without the biographical (i.e., mortal) framework of narrative cinema, as he recognized it, under the aegis of death. His resistance to the possibility of a nonnarrative poetry of cinema is so primal that he cannot bother to name the American filmmakers or their films, or in the case of Brakhage, get the name right. His disappointment that the films shown in Rome did not correspond to his enthusiastic appreciation of the American New Left also colored his reception of them.[4]

Although Pasolini would not have been familiar with the Cinema 16 symposium on "Poetry and Film" held October 28, 1953, and published ten years later in *Film Culture*, no. 29, his paradigm of the juxtaposition of the mandolin

player with the writers' conversation as a scenario for the cinema of lyrical poetry has a remarkable affinity to the imaginary film Maya Deren proposed as a
paradigm of cinematic poetry at the symposium:

> … [W]ords are not necessary when they come, as in the theater, from what
> you see.… However, if they were brought in on a different level, not issuing
> from the image, which should be complete in itself, but as another dimen-
> sion relating to it, then it is the two things together that make the poem. It is
> almost as if you were standing at a window and looking out into the street,
> and there are children playing hopscotch. Well, that's your visual experi-
> ence. Behind you, in the room, are women discussing hats or something,
> and that's your auditory experience. You stand at the place where these two
> come together by virtue of your presence. What relates these two moments
> is your position in relation to the two of them. They don't know about each
> other, and so you stand by the window and have a sense of afternoon, which
> is neither the children in the street nor the women talking behind you but a
> curious combination of both, and that is your resultant image, do you see?
> (*Film Culture Reader*, p. 179)

The moderator, Willard Maas, attempted to guide the discussion by calling
first on the poet and critic Parker Tyler, who distinguished between "the *theory*
of poetry, its possibilities as such in the film medium, and on the other hand
the *practice* of poetry, as concentrated in the avant-garde film" (pp. 171–172).
Deren took him up on this tack. She postulated two axes of temporality in
cinema: the *horizontal* as the development of plot over sequential time and
the *vertical*, or the exploration of the associations of a moment. "Poetry, to my
mind, is an approach to experience…" she claimed (p. 173). It is "a 'vertical'
investigation of a situation, in that it probes the ramifications of the moment,
and is concerned with its qualities and its depth, so that you have poetry concerned, in a sense, not with what is occurring but with what it feels like or
what it means. A poem, to my mind, creates visible and auditory forms for
something that is invisible, which is the feeling, the emotion, or the metaphysical content of the movement" (p. 174). The other panelists, Arthur Miller and
Dylan Thomas, were scornful of the bluestocking filmmaker-theoretician and
uninterested in Tyler's proposal to discuss the practice of film poetry in the
avant-garde cinema. Nevertheless, the panel evidences the importance poetry
had for the American avant-garde filmmakers of the 1950s. Yet it makes no
mention of the influence of poets on the filmmakers, although Maas, in his
repeated and vain efforts to bring the discussion around to the fusion of poetic language and cinematic imagery, does quote Ezra Pound's dictum that the
image "is an emotional and intellectual complex caught in an instant of time."

Maas's first film, *The Geography of the Body* (1943), is exemplary of the aspiration to fuse spoken poetry with filmic images. He made it with his wife, the
filmmaker and painter Marie Menken, and the poet George Barker. They posed

nude for the camera, recording in close-up bodily details of each other, often with a magnifying glass attached to the lens. Maas edited the film into some thirty-four shots, and Barker wrote and read a surrealistic prose poem on the soundtrack.

Its primitive sonic quality can cause a range of auditory ambiguities. The film's best critic, Bruce Elder, who wrote a thorough and brilliant analysis of the film in his *Body of Vision: Representations of the Body in Recent Film and Poetry,* heard several crucial words that diverge from the script as George Barker wrote it.[5] The prose poem immediately asserts its Alexandrian and oneiric qualities. It purports to be an admonitory address by an explorer steeped in poetic and painterly lore. So it begins, "I warn you that every move you make, O far from innocent criminals, is observed by Gautama Buddha under his Indian tree. Hitherto the foundations of nothing have not been possible, but with the introduction of the hydro-cephalous Rodin, all combinations appear to be feasible." The exotic geographical allusions extend from India to Africa, Hawaii, the Arctic Ocean, the Bahamas, Arabia, Mexico, Colorado, and even the moon and Eden. The names of Andrew Marvell, Sappho, Mozart, Sir Francis Shackleton, Machiavelli, Savonarola, Napoleon, Circe, Sirens, Achilles, and Astarte are threaded through the poem.

From the start Maas carefully avoids any identification of the "I" or "we" of the poem with figures on the screen. By the time the third image appears—the close-up of an ear—the phrase we hear, "At the entrance to the Hyderbadean temple no acolytes await us," identifies the aural canal with the temple "entrance." Later, the image of toes rhyme with "these rare Choric shells in which the Sirens have been imprisoned," and "[t]he idealized landscape of the floriculturist" corresponds to a screen filled with hair. In short, the text has turned the rhythmic array of body parts into imaginary terrains through which the verbal personae move. The cascade of allusions, with their persistent sadomasochistic and homoerotic suggestions, invoke an atmosphere of sexual excess despite the static or gently moving state of the images.

Sixty years later, Jonas Mekas proved, with his *Out-takes from the Life of a Happy Man* (2012), the continuing vitality of the lyrical voice in a cinema of poetry. His emphatic and ruminative voice-over identifies what Deren called the "vertical" dimension of cinema with the power of song. Over a cascade of some 170 images, for a stretch of seven minutes, while we see shots of New York's Central Park; Cassis, France; and parts of New England and glimpse children performing music and ballet, scenes of cooking and dining with friends, picking flowers, and numerous fragmentary self-portraits, we hear the filmmaker tracing his passion for filming and editing to the joy of singing to his father the events of his day when he was five years old:

Images! Images! It started...I think it began long, long ago, when I was sitting on the bed next to my father. I think I was maybe five...maybe five,
and telling him, singing, in this kind of singing voice...(I remember it very,
very clearly, like it was today) telling, singing about what happened that
day: what we did, what we did in the field; we went to the mill. Every detail
of that day I sang to my father, with such intensity, such involvement in it,
I was completely transported into this kind of recreation of the day, to the
very, like, essential details of the day. I remember it so clearly and I know
that all I am doing now, all I have been doing since, trying to regain that
kind of intensity, that kind of closeness to reality; when you see, you sing,
and it's there in front of you, right there! Every detail, every detail of the day,
and it's happiness! happiness! When I can come close to it, and then I look
at it I record it, I sing, and then it's all there and I look at it and it's there!
And I am happy that it's there and did it: I managed to capture some of the
beauty, some of the happiness, some of the beauty. That's all I care, to catch
some of the beauty around the daily, daily, daily beauty that is there. Ever
since age five and I'm still trying, trying to be as then at age five, the age of
innocence. So, but here, so many years later, trying to do the same. And it's
also a late, late evening—night, deep into the night. A late evening like then,
many many years ago, age five, sitting on the bed next to my father and, singing singing, singing, singing...

The ninety-year-old poet and filmmaker here declares that his signature
staccato style of filming raises the images of his daily life to the intensity of
song.

In the following section of this book, I shall examine some of the forms
that the aspiration to make what Pasolini called "poetry-poetry" took among
the American avant-garde filmmakers. In doing so, I shall have recourse
to discuss the relationship of the work of poets to the filmmakers to whom
I devote chapters: Dickinson and Garcia Lorca to Joseph Cornell; H.D. and
Robert Duncan to Lawrence Jordan; a wide range of poets, including Pound,
Stein, Duncan again, Charles Olson, Kenneth Patchen, and Ronald Johnson
to Stan Brakhage's oeuvre, especially his Vancouver series; John Ashbery to
Nathaniel Dorsky and Jerome Hiler; and ancient Greek poets and their diction
to Gregory Markopoulos. Like Deren, Tyler, and Maas at the 1953 symposium,
these filmmakers all thought that it was incumbent on filmmakers to discover
the poetic forms of their medium, rather than imitate the structures of the
poets that inspired them. Therefore, for the most part, I shall be following
Parker Tyler's suggestion, that we analyze "the *practice* of poetry, as concentrated in the avant-garde film." At one point in the discussion, he attempted
to reconcile Thomas's enthusiasm for the poetic moments he found in feature
films with Deren's theoretical formulation of the vertical and horizon axes and

Miller's claim that cinema was essentially montage and the magnification of life on the screen. He pointed out: "As a matter of fact, the surrealists started out by excerpting parts of commercial films, jumbling them up, and making little poems out of them...[P]oetic film means using film as a conscious and exclusive means of creating ideas through images (*Film Culture Reader*, p. 182). He might have cited the films of Joseph Cornell as a primary example of this process, but he may have been the only person in the auditorium who had seen Cornell's collage films at that time. They did not become available for public screenings until the foundation of Anthology Film Archives in 1969. So it is with those films that I shall begin.

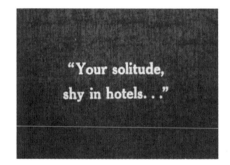

Joseph Cornell: *The Children's Party* (ca. 1938)
A Legend for Fountains (ca. 1955–1965):
Image and title from Garcia Lorca's "Your Childhood in Menton"
Rose Hobart (ca. 1940)
Bookstalls (date unknown)

The Dialectic of Experience in
Joseph Cornell's Films

Although nothing could be further from the raw violence, the explicit eros, and the social milieu of Pasolini's films than the subtle, witty, and delicate cinema of Joseph Cornell, his work constitutes a persuasive test case for the viability of a cinema of lyrical poetry. Pasolini's description of the "irrational, oneiric, elementary, and barbaric elements" at the core of filmic poetry might apply to both the films Cornell made by collaging 16mm films he had collected and those he directed by hiring cinematographer friends. But even more than Tarkovsky in his employment of newsreel footage in *Mirror*, Cornell sought to "heighten...feeling" through "poetic connections" in his films. He repudiated plot in his imagined scenarios, in his description of the films and actresses he loved, in his reediting of narrative, documentary, and children's films, and in every film he directed. The achievement of heightened feeling through poetic connections was the primary function of cinema for him.

All of Cornell's work speaks of the aesthetic mediation of experience. To encounter anything in its fullness was to come into nearly tangible contact with its absolute absence, its unrecoverable pastness, its evanescence. Contemporary New York, which he loved with passion and with a rare attention to its uniquenesses and peculiarities, both fused with and refused to coincide with his fantasy of nineteenth-century Paris, which he knew through novels, memoirs, and poems without ever traveling to France. If we think of Cornell as fundamentally a dreamer who walked the streets exploring shops and arcades, fantasizing that he was a *flâneur* out of the pages of Baudelaire and Gérard de Nerval, we lose more of him than we gain. In the resonant complexity of his art, the frailty, and even the absurdity, of such a fantasy declares itself. Yet the art, especially the shadow boxes, is so seductive that its magic too often blinds us to its ironic tensions. Cornell was not a nostalgist, a recluse, or a *naif*, even though he knew how to play those three roles expertly and knew their defensive strength. He was a dialectician of experience. A serious consideration of his filmmaking will lead us toward a clarification of his aesthetic mediations.

Joseph Cornell made his way toward filmmaking hesitantly and guardedly. We have scripts he wrote and published, montages he made out of bits of films he had collected, and films he actually directed, photographed by distinguished filmmakers. In 1936 the Museum of Modern Art published his artistic profile in the catalogue of "Fantastic Art, Dada, Surrealism":

> American constructivist. Born in New York, 1904 [sic]. Self-taught. Author of two Surrealist scenarios. Lives in Flushing, Long Island.[1]

The film scenario "Monsieur Phot (Seen through the Stereoscope)"[2] can be dated definitively as 1933, but what is the second surrealist scenario? Howard Hussey has suggested that it is "Theatre of Hans Christian Andersen," which appeared in a special number of *Dance Index* (published in 1945) celebrating the story writer as a balletomane.[3] "Monsieur Phot" is the more fully developed of the two. It has four detailed scenes and an epilogue. One can readily see in it the influence of contemporary French avant-garde cinema. The oneiric condensations and displacements of the two films of Salvador Dalí and Luis Buñuel, *Un chien andalou* (1929) and *L'age d'or* (1930), echo through his intricate repetitions and transformations of the central images, which include a photographer and his apparatus, nine urchins, a harp player, a pianist, a basket of laundry, falling snow that blends with images of shattered glass and a fountain, and, finally, "a pheasant of gorgeous plumage."

The violence of Dalí and Buñuel has no place in his script, nor does their overwhelming eros. Cornell knew French literature well enough to have no illusions about the novelty of surrealism. The serendipitous correspondences that Mallarmé describes in his prose poem "Le Démon d'analogie" define a poetic psychology to which he subscribed. The "revolution" of surrealism was largely its insistence that this psychology constitutes a fundamental epistemology. The surrealists often achieved this shift of emphasis by removing the organizing sensibility of the poet as the poem's center of experience. The reader is thrust directly into the world of irreconcilable incongruities. Yet Cornell saw an advantage to preserving symbolism's poetic mediator, although he consistently stripped him of a biography that might render his emotions rational. In his first scenario that mediator is Monsieur Phot, a man very like a camera, yet so sensitive that he is regularly overwhelmed by events in the world outside him (the world before his camera), especially when those events behave as if they were superior manifestations of the mind.

The pheasant, which appears in every episode of the imaginary film, represents the superabundant plenitude that motivates and yet escapes art. Its every appearance would be in color in this otherwise black-and-white film. We must remember that "Monsieur Phot" was written before the release of Reuben Mamoulian's *Becky Sharp* (the first commercial feature film in color) in 1935. Cornell was an authority on cinema; he read technical histories, as well as fan magazines. He knew that there had been experiments in color cinematography ever since the invention of the medium. He must have seen many hand-painted films from before the First World War, as well as works of the 1920s in various artificial coloring processes. But at the same time, he must have been aware of the extravagance of proposing an avant-garde film to be made with four sections in color. Of course, "Monsieur Phot" was written not to be made but to be imagined. Its extraordinary alternation of black and white and color indicates the superiority of imaginary cinema over products found in theaters. It points as well to the limitations of the medium in a scenario about the affective power of experience to exceed its sensory stimuli. Thus, M. Phot cries when he has confronted the power of his own imagination. It is not the carefully composed images but rather their ultimate relationship to each other that generates the poetic connections at which Cornell hints when he describes the photographer sorting the still images he shot.

Cornell himself gathered and sorted still images in creating the scenario. When in 1936 Julien Levy published "Monsieur Phot" for the first time in his book, *Surrealism,* he printed only the text. Yet there are five stereopticon images that Cornell used in typed copies of the scenario.[4] They not only illustrate the five locations of the film, but they indicate Cornell's creative process, which is reflected in that of Phot himself. The first image shows nine Victorian men standing at the base of an equestrian statue in a civic plaza. Obviously this image, like the other four, preceded the writing of the script. Just as obviously these pictures were the foundation, the static image ground, upon which Cornell's cinematic imagination played. He transposed the men into urchins. A harp and a basket of something covered with a white cloth also appear in the first image. Cornell seized on these elements as the props for his repetitions and displacements.

In the epilogue of "Monsieur Phot," the photographer comically approaches the condition of a filmmaker. The action is to be "carried out as in a ballet."[5] With those words, Cornell dramatizes the difference between the illusion of natural movement in a conventional film and the stylization of dance. Cornell's other published scenario, "Theatre of Hans Christian Andersen," is much more schematic than "Monsieur Phot." Its eleven episodes are printed on just two pages of *Dance Index.* The scenario is presented as a ballet. It contains, nevertheless, distinctive cinematic elements, just as "Monsieur Phot" contains a ballet. Before presenting his elliptical description of the scenes—ten of which represent Andersen stories and the eleventh simply a "Tableau-finale of all the characters"—Cornell describes the blending of stage and cinema that would give this scenario its imaginary form:

> Sometimes the footlights yield to the silver screen in animated cartoon, black and white or Technicolor, this latter tempered by the mellow charm of the colors of the magic lantern. Again, the stage is sometimes a colored transparency of the stereoscope come to life. There is nothing old fashioned about the mounting of these effects—it is the original "handmade" charm of the Romantic theatre.[6]

"Monsieur Phot" was written in 1933, the year the first Disney cartoons appeared in Technicolor. Cornell's association of the trade name for color film with the idea of an animated cartoon reinforces Howard Hussey's supposition that the Andersen scenario, although published in 1945, may have been written at the same time as "Monsieur Phot," or shortly after it. Cornell specifically refers to the cinema in three of the eleven ballets in the scenario: of the second, "Thumbelina," he writes: "Additional effects of cinema fantasy as the little heroine is pulled along the water on a leaf by a butterfly, the homeward flight of the swallow, etc."; the seventh, "The Wild Swans," has only the following description: "Cinema treatment. The countryside seen from above by Eliza"; finally, the ninth cites a specific cinematic style dear to Cornell: "The Court Cards: A pack of cards comes to life for a frolic reminiscent of the many charming things of this kind done in the earliest French trick and magic films, notably by Méliès."[7] In the extensive collection of films Cornell had assembled for his own amusement and that of his invalid brother Robert was *Hanky Panky Card Tricks*, an early French film, which he misattributed to Méliès—an error he made repeatedly. In it the royal cards come to life: the Jack performs acrobatics, the King and Queen dance.

Cornell often associated dance with film, especially when his model for cinematic structure was the style of the French trick film in the first decade of twentieth century. Among the films in his collection from this period were *Unusual Cooking*, in which giant knives and forks take on human arms and legs to dance together; *The Automatic Moving Company*, in which an entire apartment is stripped of its furniture, moved, and elaborately replaced in a new house without human intervention, all through stop-motion photography, which can turn an inanimate object into a graceful ballerina; and *The Danaif Sisters*, a film about a family of acrobats who spectacularly leapfrog over one another and form hilarious and complex shapes by linking their contorted bodies, in the manner of the dwarfs in Bergman's *Tystnaden*.

When Cornell, in his capacity as editor of the Andersen issue of *Dance Index*, described in an introduction the characteristics shared by Andersen's tales and the Romantic ballet, he unwittingly catalogued the qualities he also admired in the French trick films of the formative period: "their release, their escape, their flight, their defiance of the limitations of the physical world: their amiability; the subtler sense of light and air...."[8] In the draft of a letter to a French art historian, Claude Serbanne, dated March 26, 1946, he brings together his impressions of primitive and surrealist films: "I like certain parts of *L'age d'or* as I remember it I think as well as anything that I could ever see in Méliès."[9] Of Méliès's near contemporary, Zecca, he adds a further observation that enlarges our understanding of his interest in that aspect of cinema:

> Still I think we owe him a debt for doing what MELIES seldom did—
> working en plein air, leaving a record Atget-like of so many of the Parisian

fin-de-siècle landmarks (the unpretentious ones like the boutique of a char-cutier such as I have in my "The Man with the Calf's Head" which Dalí liked so much and in which he [*sic*] a quality of Gérard de Nerval. And then again this type of work influenced René Clair in his early work.[10]

Throughout the letter to Serbanne, despite its fragmentary, unfinished form, Cornell reveals his sensitivity and originality as a viewer of films. At one point, where the letter switches from English to French, he extols Jennifer Jones in *Love Letters* (1945) with an encomium that almost repeats his homage to Hedy Lamarr, printed in *View* in 1941–1942. Compare the two passages. Of Jones he wrote:

> Son visage quelquefois est quelque chose de rare sur l'ecran d'aujourd'hui. Au premier il y a quelque passages ou elle doue les close-ups d'un eloquence a rappeler l'age heroique du silence. Ici des eclats fugitives de [undecipherable] lyrique de Falconetti, pourtant sans le profondeur. A moi-meme, au moins.[11]

The homage to Lamarr, entitled "Enchanted Wanderer," yields the following passage:

> Among the barren wastes of the talking films there occasionally occur pas-sages to remind one again of the profound and suggestive power of the si-lent film to evoke an ideal world of beauty, to release unsuspected floods of music from the gaze of a human countenance in its prison of silver light. But aside from evanescent fragments unexpectedly encountered, how often is there created a superb and magnificent imagery such as brought to life the portraits of Falconetti in "Joan of Arc," Lillian Gish in "Broken Blossoms," Sibirskaya in "Ménilmontant" and Carola Nehrer in "Dreigroschenoper."
>
> And so we are grateful to Hedy Lamarr, the enchanted wanderer, who again speaks the poetic and evocative language of the silent film, if only in whispers at times, beside the empty roar of the sound track....
>
> Who has not observed in her magnified visage qualities of a gracious humility and spirituality that with circumstance of costume, scene, and plot conspire to identify her with realms of wonder, more absorbing than the artificial ones, and where we have already been invited by the gaze that she knew as a child!?[12]

The coincidence of these two texts points to a way of viewing the "poetic con-nections" that "heighten...feelings" in films that supersedes the particular fas-cination with Hedy Lamarr, Jennifer Jones, or any other actress. From that perspective, two principles of cinema emerge: that facial expression and ges-ture are its essential language and, more crucially, that the coming of sound has destroyed the immanent spiritual music of films. In some "profound" sense—his term—cinema was over before Joseph Cornell wrote his first sce-nario or made his first films. In this difficult time for cinema, the era of the

sound film—the "poetic and evocative language"—can appear only in "evanescent fragments," and their "realms of wonder" are necessarily mediated by
the memory of silent films. Cornell's odd rhetorical question in "Enchanted
Wanderer," "Who has not observed...?" defies sense and teases us with its
hints of meaning more than it can say. If the "artificial" realms are the scenes
and plots of the films in which the actress has appeared, then the "more absorbing...realms of wonder" must be the imaginary reflections that the
tawdry movie scenes initiate but necessarily fail to realize. That is fully consistent with Cornell's theory of the imagination: a collapse and failure of the
present that brings with it a poignant and powerful compensation. But what
could be meant by "the gaze she knew as a child"?

Here the syntactical contortions disguise a complex play of eros and time.
On first reading, one might conclude that Hedy Lamarr's "gracious humility
and spirituality" consist in her ability to sustain the concentrated and wonderful stare of a child in front of the tacky sets in which she performed as an
adult. But if that was all that Cornell meant, he could easily have said it with
less ambiguity; he was a very good writer.

The formula "the gaze *she knew* as a child" (my emphasis) continues to tease
me. As a child she would have gazed at silent films, as indeed Cornell did as a
child. The impossibility of sustaining childhood's vision is a persistent topos
of Romantic poetry, where it is linked to the equally dreadful impossibility of
forgetting its loss. In these terms Cornell's Lamarr is a metaphor for the mediation of the broken and fragmented sound cinema. Identification with her
dramatizes the cinephile's eagerness for and distance from what is attracting
him or her. Yet there is another sense to "the gaze she knew as a child" that the
following paragraph begins to reveal:

> Her least successful roles will reveal something unique and intriguing a dis-
> arming candor, a naivete, an innocence, a desire to please, touching in its
> sincerity. In implicit trust she would follow in whatever direction the least
> humble of her audience would desire.[13]

"The gaze she knew as a child" may not be her own after all. It is, to some extent,
the gaze of a grown man, "the least humble of her audience," focused on the little girl. These "realms of wonder" veer perilously close to the Wonderland toward which Lewis Carroll steered and then stared at the child he called Alice.

In a process of sublimation, then, the cinema preserves and distances the
erotic encounter of the adult and child, just as it incorporates the loss of innocent vision by the adult and the paradoxical thrill of that loss. Along parallel
lines the Romantic ballet is not aesthetically superior to the contemporary, but
it is inescapably conjoined with the lives of imaginative balletomanes and their
unfulfilled erotic fascinations. The illusionary intimacy and the actual imper-
sonality of cinema necessarily fuse the aspirations and failures of the Romantic
balletomane.

Cornell's first and most impressive film, *Rose Hobart* (c. 1936), illustrates many of the ideas he later expressed about Hedy Lamarr and Jennifer Jones. The film is essentially a reediting of *East of Borneo*, a 1931 jungle drama from Universal Pictures, with Rose Hobart and Charles Bickford. Apparently Cornell thought that George Melford's talking picture contained "passages to remind one…of the suggestive power of the silent film to evoke an ideal world of beauty."

Today *East of Borneo* seems an undistinguished period piece. In it, the brave and boyish Linda (Rose Hobart) undertakes a dangerous journey to the fictional Indonesian principality of Marudu to find her husband (Charles Bickford), who has become the drunken court physician to the suave and sinister prince (Georges Renavent). The doctor had abandoned serious medical research upon falling victim to the erroneous obsession that his wife was conducting an affair with a friend of his. In Marudu, Linda proves her fidelity by repelling the advances of the prince, despite her husband's cruel rejection of a reconciliation. The prince, a Sorbonne graduate with urbane notions of the superior sophistication of his culture and religion to that of the West, is mystically tied to the fate of the active volcano that looms over his realm. At the end of the film Linda shoots and wounds him just as the volcano is about to erupt. The doctor, after performing his moral duty as royal physician, comes to his senses and escapes with his wife just as the eruption destroys Marudu.

It is cheaply made film with a drolly concocted volcano and an assortment of jungle terrors, including a python, a panther, and a large number of crocodiles. Not very promising material. Nor is Rose Hobart's performance comparable to the achievements elicited from the chief actresses in the great silent films catalogued in "Enchanted Wanderer." Hobart can do little more than make quick, nervous gestures with her hands and quickly shift her expression from terror to laughter at herself whenever she sees that her fright is unfounded.

For the most part, Cornell has isolated these transitional moments and reorganized them in his montage. He included nothing of the final volcanic destruction and almost nothing of the lengthy and perilous voyage upriver to Marudu, which opens the original film. Yet his montage is startlingly original. Nothing like it occurs in the history of the cinema until thirty years later. The deliberate mismatching of shots, the reduction of conversations to images of the actress without corresponding counter-shots of her interlocutor, and the sudden shifts of location were so daring in 1936 that even the most sophisticated viewers tended to see the film as inept rather than brilliant. Yet Cornell carried this roughness several steps further. He incorporated some continuous passages from the original film—sequences containing as many as eight shots in a row—which serve to remind us of the obligatory fluidity of Hollywood editing during that period. They make Cornell's reconstruction look all the cruder. His retention of a connective shot here and there (say, the corresponding figure in a conversation with the heroine) underlines his eccentric ellipses. Finally, he displays a fondness for using some shots just as they were fading out or just as a door was closing, omitting the main action.

Only a collector of films could have made this kind of montage. When one owns a print of a film and shows it repeatedly, accidents happen in the projection and rewinding; passages are damaged and strange ellipses occur in their repair. Whereas most collectors regard these with horror and would prefer to ignore them, Cornell apparently made these accidents of deterioration the formal model for his first film. The editing of *Rose Hobart* creates a double impression: it presents the aspect of a randomly broken, oddly scrambled, and hastily repaired feature film that no longer makes sense; yet at the same time, each of its curiously reset fractures astonishes us with new meaning. In this first film, Cornell did what he would do with many of his boxes: he made the marvelous look easy, almost automatic. Yet nothing is more difficult than to sustain the illusion of an "accidental" overflowing of meaning.

I have been dwelling on the superficial roughness of *Rose Hobart*. However, Cornell simultaneously made a number of changes in the original film that give a new unity and lend dignity to its montage. First, he projected the sound film silently. By stripping it of its dialogue and mood music, he transformed its banality into an oneiric mystery. He not only showed it without the talk, but he also projected it at silent speed. With the coming of sound in the late 1920s, projectors were set at a uniform mechanical speed in order to reproduce the sound without the wavering pitch experienced when something touches and changes the speed of a record on a turntable. Until then, the projection and shooting speeds of films varied; often they were shot and projected by hand-cranking. By and large, the films of the silent era were shot at about two-thirds the pace of standard sound recording and projection. Therefore, a gear was added to most sound projectors to slow the standard 24-frames-persecond movement to 16 or 18 frames when silent films were shown on them, thus sustaining their illusion of realistic movement. By projecting *Rose Hobart* at silent speed, Cornell slightly retarded the gestures and action of *East of Borneo*, not enough to make them look like slow motion but to lend them a nuance of elegance and protraction. Then he filtered the light of the black-andwhite beam through a deep-blue glass plate.[14] While the now blue-and-white montage unrolled, he repeated, almost hypnotically, a passage of Brazilian music on a record player. The silencing, slowing, tinting, and musical accompaniment provide a unity and a fluidity that the montage style contradicts.

Despite its illusion of crudity, the editing is never haphazard. Cornell meticulously created a new plot by introducing a few shots from other films, probably scientific studies, and by radically rearranging the events of *East of Borneo*. In his letter to Serbanne, he expanded on his enthusiasm for *Love Letters* (1945), describing the film itself as conspiring "to produce an effect such as seizes one with disturbing emotions."[15]

Rose Hobart deliberately creates a labyrinth out of the banal plot of *East of Borneo*. It generates a seizure of disturbing emotions by reversing the dramatic coincidence of psychological resolution and natural disaster in the original film. The crucial natural event of *Rose Hobart* is an eclipse that Cornell introduced from another film. The entire montage is organized around it. The eclipse, in fact, is a skillful and startling montage of two very different elements: first, we see the total eclipse of the tiny disk of the sun, which lasts only a few seconds; as soon as the shadow passes over and the radiance of the disk returns, Cornell cuts to an image of a glass sphere falling through the air (the sphere is approximately the size the sun had been on the screen and suggests that the eclipse has actually dislodged it from the heavens); the sphere falls into a pool and sends slow-motion ripples through the water. Neither of these shots is from *East of Borneo*.

Cornell prepares us for this solar disaster by starting off his film with a shot (not in the original film) of people staring into the sky. Throughout the nineteen minutes of *Rose Hobart*, he has spaced forebodings of the climactic event. Early on, the heroine and the prince appear to be watching the imminent eclipse from a balcony. A fragmentary premonition of the splash occurs in this early episode. Hobart, in response to this premonition, is at first fearful, but she quickly overcomes her anxiety and shakes her head, laughing at herself for her overreaction. Most of the tension in this scene comes from Cornell's transformation of a sequence in the original film, in which Hobart rushes toward the camera along an arabesque corridor and looks down anxiously upon a pool filled with crocodiles. When she sees that they pose no threat to her, she becomes momentarily amused at her own anxiety in this strange new environment. Cornell substituted the reverberating pool for the crocodile pit so that we cannot empathize with her fear. The sequence has to recur at the end of the film, with the extraordinary collapse of the sun represented through montage, for the event to seize us with "disturbing emotions." When it does recur, and we see that the reverberations in the water have been caused by the fall of the sun, Hobart does not laugh but somberly fixes her gaze at the pool in which the star has drowned.

The thrill of that final montage, toward which the whole film points, comes from the filmmaker's poetic invention of a sun that is literally no bigger than it appears to be when seen from the earth. This shift from figurative to literal scale hyperbolically enlarges the catastrophe that terminated *East of Borneo*. Just as the volcano there had been a patently artificial one, cheaply concocted for the movie, the sun of *Rose Hobart* is nothing more than a simple prop. Yet the power of the montage derives from what is left to our imagination. In Cornell's reconstruction, the volcano has lost its destructive force because it causes merely a natural disaster. For the conventional audience of *East of Borneo* the destruction of Marudu was a good riddance. Only a cataclysm that occurs within the junctures of collage association can poetically induce truly "disturbing emotions" for this artist. The sublimely dreadful intimations of a world which has lost its sun is such a cataclysm.

In Cornell's collage-cinema, images are ironic. He shows the smoldering and exploding volcano, but in a context that makes it comic; as part of the seduction of Linda, the prince opens a curtain to reveal the belching crater. Cornell exquisitely times its appearance to suggest a displaced act of sexual exhibitionism: the suddenly uncovered nightscape seems to ejaculate to impress her. Cornell's "world of ideal beauty" is invisible and closer to music than to concrete imagery. The eclipsed sun, the falling sphere, and the spreading rings of water are not compelling in themselves. They are the points around which the viewer can order his imaginary film of the sun poked out of the sky. Furthermore, it is only that extraordinary and "invisible" event that gives meaning to the otherwise unfocused fears, anxieties, and intimations silently mimed by the heroine throughout the film.

Cornell once told me he was considering changing the title of the film from *Rose Hobart* to *Tristes Tropiques*. When I asked if he had been reading Lévi-Strauss, he told me he hadn't. He encountered the title in Susan Sontag's *Against Interpretation*, which attracted his attention after she wrote a review of a newly reissued book on surrealism in the *New York Herald Tribune*. The words themselves seemed peculiarly appropriate. They had the charming distance of French, a language he loved; they were alliterative and, perhaps most important, they pointed to the fundamental sadness underlying the humor and pleasures of his first collage film.

Cornell was very sensitive to the reaction to his work. Salvador Dalí became vicious and violent at the Julien Levy Gallery when he saw *Rose Hobart*. Gala Dalí later apologized to Cornell for her husband, explaining that Dalí believed Cornell had stolen ideas he had thought about but never executed. Dalí's reaction made Cornell wary of showing the film. In 1957, Cornell projected some of his own films and others from his collection at the New York Public Library to entertain the staff of the Picture Collection at Christmastime. He invited the filmmaker Stan Brakhage and the critic Parker Tyler to his screening. When Tyler expressed some reservations about the films after the projection was over, Cornell broke off relations with him for a long time. A few years later, in 1963, Cornell was very reluctant to allow the films to be shown by the Film-makers Cinematheque. Eventually he consented, with consequences that I shall come to shortly.

In the summer of 1965, the filmmaker Lawrence Jordan made a trip from San Francisco to Queens to work as an assistant to the artist. His help seems to have reassured Cornell about the value of his films and to have inspired him, briefly at least, to consider making more. Before Jordan returned to San Francisco, Cornell gave him three cinematic collages he had been working on, with instructions for their completion. He also gave him several other works-in-progress that he wanted Jordan to expand on however he saw fit.

The three nearly complete films were *Cotillion*, *The Children's Party*, and *The Midnight Party* (as named by Cornell). They are three versions of approximately the same material. Cornell had made several prints of a film about an elaborate party for children. At many points this material looks like the "Little Rascals" comedies. Into scenes of apple-dunking, streamer throwing, dancing in couples and in a chorus line, the artist inserts bits of films about stellar constellations, acrobatic acts, and mythological tableaux, perhaps intended to depict his imaginary entertainments for the overstuffed, gleeful children.

The construction of these three films is even more eccentric than *Rose Hobart*'s. Some shots are inserted upside down and backward. Brief bits of silent titles flash by on the screen much too quickly to be read. Often they, too, are upside down. In his discussions with Jordan about how to complete the films—which meant, essentially, the prolongation of certain shots by freezing the images into still pictures—Cornell explicitly stated that he wanted to keep the strange titles as he had edited them.

Here we see another transformation of a film collector's phobia into an aesthetic advantage. The 16mm silent film has sprocket holes on both sides of the film ribbon. A mistake in rewinding film or in threading it through the projector can lead to reversing the left and right sides of the image, or even to running the whole film upside down and backward. When the film is simply reversed, the image looks normal until a title appears or a word is seen somewhere in the field of vision. One can often watch a film for several minutes before such an occurrence indicates that the image has been viewed in reverse. Of course, when the image is upside down, it runs backward from end to beginning, and the error is immediately visible. Cornell incorporated such accidents in his collage films after *Rose Hobart*.

An untitled collage film found in the collection of films Cornell donated to Anthology Film Archives has been designated by them as *Bookstalls*; for, after a brief exposition of the Paris skyline, it opens with shots of browsers at the tiny bookstalls along the Seine. The period seems to be the 1920s, and the young men leafing through the books look like they might be the "urchins" of "Monsieur Phot." Paris was the center of Cornell's imaginary voyages, and the *flâneur*, who wandered the streets in search of idle amusement, was one of the important mediators of his mysterious encounters, as the same figure had been for Baudelaire. In *Bookstalls*, a double mediation occurs: the urchin-*flâneur* of the film makes an imaginary voyage as he peruses a book while Cornell uses serious and comic travelogues to illustrate that mental voyage. On one of the stalls the young man opens a volume, which through a sleight of montage shows pictures of a Spanish site, apparently the Escurial. One of the still images suddenly comes to life as a flock of pigeons bursts into flight. This transition from stasis to motion is something Cornell found rather than constructed with his own cinematic techniques, but it is so intimately linked to his themes of imaginary travel and the magic of birds that it seems to have been made especially for him. He cuts from the views of Spain into a sequence on the Caledonian channel in Scotland, where a title prepares us for a swift boat ride. Yet the impossible speed of stop-motion photography hilariously outstrips our most extravagant expectations of natural rapidity. The boat brings us through rough seas with geographical abandon to the island of Marken in the Zuider Zee, where we encounter children resembling the young revelers of the trilogy Jordan had completed. The harvesting labors of the adults of the island blend through collage into similar activities somewhere in Southeast Asia without any preparation for the transition. But that is as far as the travel goes. The young *flâneur* puts away the book and wanders toward another stall.

There is little that is rough in the montage of *Bookstalls*. The pieces are so carefully selected, the timing so acute, and the symmetry so balanced that there can be no doubt that the filmmaker meticulously constructed it. The Anthology Film Archives realized that if one of the unidentified reels in his collection could turn out to be a "finished" collage of this order, there was at least the possibility that others might be. Although none of them has the clear-cut elegance of *Bookstalls*, several are remarkable.

One of the most impressive of them has been called *By Night with Torch and Spear*, because that is the very prominent title that introduces us to the film's concluding shot. In this construction the filmmaker gets a powerful effect from the intercutting of tinted film stocks. Yellow images of an iron foundry, scarlet shots of the molten metal in furnaces, and a deep blue image of clouds clash with one another. For a long time the film seems to be projected the wrong way. Everything is upside down and moves backward. But in the middle of the film it shifts to normal orientation: a truck deposits steaming slag down the hill of an industrial dump; then billows of red-tinted smoke bridge a quick transition to American Indians dancing before a rhyming bonfire, tinted pale yellow. Negative images of a camel caravan and donkeys in a desert lead into more negative shots of the development of caterpillars from larvae. The titles throughout the film are mere flashes or run upside down until the end, when "By Night with Torch and Spear" appears right side up in bold letters and precedes a black-and-white shot of aborigines fishing at night.

After seeing the film once, one can project it without rewinding, so that the night fishing, caterpillars, camels, Indians, and the truck are upside down and backward at the start but the refinery appears to operate normally. This eccentric procedure is sanctioned by the precedent of Cornell's own reediting of the outtakes from Stan Brakhage's *Wonder Ring*. Cornell commissioned the film in 1955 to record New York's Third Avenue El before it was torn down. He recognized the beauty of Brakhage's film, but he was not completely satisfied with it, for Brakhage's kinetic experiences of light patterns and bodily movements on the train were far different from the thrill Cornell received from the momentary glimpses into strangers' apartments as the train rushed past the glass-enclosed frames (the shadow boxes) of their windows. In reediting

Brakhage's materials, Cornell slightly altered the montage, adding more images of people, but he transformed the film by flipping it from left to right and projecting it upside down and backward. At the end he added the title "The end is the beginning," which could be read normally.

Cornell's reconstruction of Brakhage's *Wonder Ring* provided a valuable tool for determining the status of some of the unidentified collage films. One of them is simply two halves of a documentary print about the development of butterflies and moths from larvae. It begins upside down and backward, then shifts to a normal orientation. Without the example of "The end is the beginning," or *Gnir RednoW*, as it is sometimes called, this collage might have looked like nothing more than a broken print haphazardly spliced and rewound. Of these palindromic films, only *By Night with Torch and Spear* has an elaborate internal structure that parallels the reversed directions of the imagery, where the thematic shift from contemporary steelmaking to primitive rituals and exotic scenes occurs immediately after the change of orientation.

The Midnight Party, one of the collage films that Jordan worked on, opens with the title "The End" appearing on the screen upside down. But as soon as the first image follows the title, the reversal is corrected. We see a shade rise on a window at night and bits of a documentary about stellar constellations; then the montage begins to alternate between vaudeville acts and segments of the very same party that is the basis of *Cotillion*. In this version, the imaginary relationship between the acts and the reactions of the children, which the editing invents, becomes much more explicit. A related film, which Anthology Film Archives called *Vaudeville De-Luxe* on the basis of an internal title, includes many of the same animal and acrobatic acts, but without the children. There is in that one, however, a jolting insertion of a shot from *East of Borneo* in which Rose Hobart hides a pistol in her purse and some images from the documentary on steel refining used in *By Night with Torch and Spear*. These repetitions indicate that the economy of images among Cornell's films is almost as great as in his boxes and collages.

The Children's Party, the shortest film in the trilogy and the one with the most varied materials, contains almost nothing of the children who dominate the other two similar collages. In the middle of this work, the frozen image of a sleeping girl with her doll suggests that it is a dream in which elements from the imaginary parties reappear in new and stranger contexts. The microscopic enlargement of an amoeba and the slow-motion study of birds in flight join with acrobatic and balletic images to suggest a principle of gracefulness and order of which the entertainments are merely one part. An "End" title divides this short film in half. The second part introduces several new images: the sleeping girl, a comet, and what appears to be a representation of Thor from a pre-World War I film; each time he flourishes his hammer, jagged lightning bolts cross the screen. In the dreamlike montage of the film, his bolts seem to threaten a house, perhaps the very one in which the girl dreams, for firemen are attempting to repair high-voltage wires near a second-story window.

Cornell used the dream structure most clearly in *Jack's Dream*, a film he gave to Jordan, who completed it and released it after Cornell died. It is a marvelously doctored puppet animation of a version of "Little Red Riding Hood." Again a book opens, identifying the story, before a page of text gives way to the puppet castle in which a dog dozes before a fire as servants wash dishes. In the dog's dream a princess comes upon a fire-breathing dragon eating food laid out on a dining table sideboard in a variant of "Goldilocks and the Three Bears." When the dragon catches sight of the girl, he pursues her, followed by the dog attempting to protect her, until he wakes to find himself still before the fire. Cornell transformed the charming children's film into something uncanny by first inserting shots of a sinking clipper ship as the dog dozes, wakes, and falls back to sleep. Then, after the ship disappears in the sea, he cut to shots from a documentary on seahorses, as if they were proximate to the sunken ship. At that point he returned to the puppet film and the first image of the dragon, which looks remarkably like a giant seahorse. Finally, just before the film ends, when the sleeping dog reappears, he cut in another clipper ship firing its cannon, apparently from a swashbuckler narrative. By separating and reversing the cause and effect sequence for the clipper ship battle, he suggests that the terrors of the dream work emerge from the psychic montage of images. Jack's dream is a wish fulfillment to the extent that the dog fantasizes himself as an epic hero.

Central to *The Children's Party* is a repetition of the concluding image of *The Midnight Party*, a girl with long hair riding a horse. This child seems naked, a tableau of Lady Godiva. Her long tresses discreetly cover her body. This playful image has stunning erotic reverberation, recalling the complexities of the phrase "the gaze she knew as a child." In *The Midnight Party* the appearance of this Godiva figure becomes the climactic revelation; in *The Children's Party*, it immediately precedes the repeated gestures of Thor. Yet there is no correlation in the montage of *The Midnight Party* between the reactions of the children and the entrance of this child on horseback. However, the scene that precedes it may provide a clue to its meaning: a court of children sits in judgment on two young dancers performing to the playing of trumpets. If a narrative is to be found in the associations of these films, then the horse ride of the naked Godiva might be a sentence of the court. Perhaps we can read the anger of Thor as a different response to the same event when it appears as a child's dream fantasy in *The Children's Party*. The film might even be said to evoke the myth of Semele, a young Theban woman seduced by Zeus and destroyed in a blaze of lightning when she demanded to see him in all his glory.

What kinds of dreams are depicted in *The Children's Party* and *Jack's Dream*? The emergence of repressed associations and images, such as the surrealists cultivated, made Cornell uncomfortable. In 1936, when preparations were under way for the exhibition "Fantastic Art, Dada, Surrealism," Cornell wrote to Alfred H. Barr, Jr., of the Museum of Modern Art:

> In the event that you are saying a word or two about my work in the catalogue I would appreciate your saying that I do not share in the subconscious and dream theories of the surrealists. While fervently admiring much of their work I have never been an official surrealist, and I believe that surrealism has healthier possibilities than have been developed. The constructions of Marcel Duchamp who the surrealists themselves acknowledge bear out this thought, I believe.[16]

We cannot be confident of Cornell's meaning when he writes of Duchamp's constructions as a guide to the "healthier possibilities" of surrealism. As a convert to Christian Science and reader of Mary Baker Eddy, he would have known the concept of "health" as an ontological rather than just a medical category. In the section of Eddy's *Science and Health* called "Science of Being," Eddy repeatedly couples dreams with physical phenomena as erroneous images of the Divine. For instance, she speaks of the intuition of the senses as "inverted images":

> A picture in the camera or a face reflected in the mirror is not the original, though resembling it. Man, in the likeness of his Maker, reflects the central light of being, the invisible God. As there is no corporeality in the mirrored form, which is but a reflection, so man, like all things real, reflects God, his divine Principle, not in mortal body.... The inverted images presented by the sense, the deflections of matter as opposed to the Science of spiritual reflection, are all unlike Spirit, God.... Because man is the reflection of his Maker, he is not subject to birth, growth, maturity, decay. These mortal dreams are of human origin, not divine.... That which material sense calls intangible, is found to be substance. What to material sense seems substance, becomes nothingness, as the sense-dream vanishes and reality appears.[17]

When he uses the unexpected comparative "healthier" to characterize Duchamp's erotic wit, Cornell imputes a "spiritual" dimension no one else would have been likely to find in the maker of "The Great Glass" or *Anémic Cinéma*. Perhaps this merely acknowledges the abstract surface of Duchamp's rebuses, his punning transformations of libidinal energies. The wit and even more devious eros of Cornell's films are matters of nuance. He did not photograph or direct the erupting volcano in *Rose Hobart* or the child Godiva in *The Midnight Party* and *The Children's Party*. He merely found them. Nor did he unambivalently emphasize their erotic exhibitionism. In a way, Cornell's wit is like that of his beloved Hans Christian Andersen, who was able tell a story about an Emperor who exposes himself to a whole city, and especially to a little girl, without the reader's noticing what is happening in the story. Successive generations of parents unwittingly have proven the moral of "The Emperor's

New Clothes" by seeing only the moral and blinding themselves to the exhibitionism. The children to whom they read it tend to titter; they understand what it is about. The child Godiva is, in fact, an inversion of the unclothed Emperor. If his exhibitionism is the perversion of an implicit pact not to notice the exposure of nudity, then the naked child on the horse would be the fulfillment of the exhibitionistic Emperor's fantasy. The little girl in Andersen's tale sees, judges, and accuses the Emperor. In Cornell's two films, child judges and an enraged Thor (or a phallically overpowering Zeus), juxtaposed with the image of the rider, play that role.

The dragon of *Jack's Dream* is an amusing and charming creature in his puppet form, even as he chases the virgin princess. By rhyming him with seahorses, Cornell further undermines his terror. Similarly, the reversal and separation of cause and effect in the sea battle turns the aggressive sinking of the clipper ship into an unexplained natural disaster while postponing and transforming the violence of the cannonade. Thus isolated, like the volcano of Marudu, the firing of cannon slyly suggests an orgasmic conclusion to the dog's nocturnal fantasy. In such moments the sexuality of Cornell's art emerges despite the severe evasions and repressions exerted by the persistently idealizing artist. The evocation of child play and fairy tales is the principal arena of that idealization.

In *The Uses of Enchantment* Bettelheim writes:

> Fairy-tale animals come in two forms: dangerous and destructive animals, such as the wolf in "Little Red Riding Hood," or the dragon that devastates an entire country unless each year a virgin is sacrificed to it…and wise and helpful animals which guide and rescue the hero…Both dangerous and helpful animals stand for our animal nature, our instinctual drives. The dangerous ones symbolize the untamed id, not yet subjected to ego and superego control, in all its dangerous energy. The helpful animals represent our natural energy—again the id—but now made to serve the best interests of the total personality.[18]

The surrealists, by contrast, sought the liberation of unconscious energies in the juxtaposition of disparate images. They cultivated the disruption of erotic and moral taboos and linked their art to political revolution. Cornell, instead, aspired after "the intangible." If the surrealists practiced free association to uncover the repressed schemata of the mind, Cornell utilized some of the same principles of association to emphasize the false corporeality of images and to help nudge substances toward nothingness in order to make the reflection of "the central light of being" the focus of his art.

The synthetic image, created as a sculptural or cinematic collage, necessarily points to the ephemerality of the images culled to make it up. As an ironic illusionist, the maker of collages always exposes all his tricks. The synthesis he creates is an ad hoc illusion for the viewer who wants to experience the transfiguration of substance into something less tangible. Similarly, the very origin of cinema has been in machines, one could almost say toys, with which the viewer could trick himself into seeing still things move. In his essay "La Morale du joujou," Charles Baudelaire extolled the protocinematic device called a phenakisto-scope precisely because whoever used it would experience the illusion of movement even though he understood the principle by which it worked. Another nineteenth-century machine for generating the illusion of movement is the praxinoscope, a drum with slots through which the viewer peeks at images reflected in a circle of tiny mirrors. The revolution of the drum makes the reflected clowns tumble and ballerinas dance. Cornell paid homage to this machine in his "Thimble Forests." They do not move, but when one looks through the drum, the thimbles perched on needles are vastly multiplied by the tiny mirrors. Even the gentlest handling of the object makes the thimbles wobble, and that wobbling too is magnified by the mirrors into a storm of shaking thimbles. The charm of the object, like that of the phenakistoscope and praxinoscope, comes from the difference between looking at it as a simple machine and peeking through its slots to experience the transfiguration of its props.

In his vision of cinema as an ontological toy, Cornell differs fundamentally from Pasolini. They both recognize that the poetry of cinema derives "as much [from] gesture and brute reality as [from] dreams and the mechanisms of memory..." in Pasolini's formulation. But the social environment Pasolini calls "brute reality" is a mere shimmering reflection of the reality or "corpo-reality" to which the tangible illusions of the world of representation point, according to Cornell's Christian Science of poetic "health."

There is no definitive chronology for Joseph Cornell's filmmaking. It would seem that he wrote his two scenarios before he edited *Rose Hobart* and the other collage films. Most of the films he directed were made in the middle and late 1950s, but as late as 1965 he was still working on the films Stan Brakhage, Rudy Burckhardt, and Lawrence Jordan photographed for him.

There is a consistency of style in all of the films Cornell directed: *Centuries of June, A Legend for Fountains, The Aviary, Nymphlight, Angel*, and *Seraphina's Garden*. Brakhage, who photographed *Centuries of June*, insists that he was merely a living machine for Cornell. Everything in the film resulted from the instructions he was given. Burckhardt tells a different story. Their work was a collaboration, "sixty percent Cornell and forty percent" Burckhardt. Cornell always maintained that Burckhardt should share the credit for the films he worked on. In all of these films the static compositions are very carefully composed, like the elements in the shadow boxes. The camera movements tend to be slow and very deliberate, panning from one dominant point of interest to another of equal weight. They are edited in a leisurely rhythm, except when the cutting jumps to catch the flight of a bird or a butterfly.

An unanticipated glimpse I had of Cornell's working methods and their relation to poetry occurred when I visited him, by appointment, in 1968. He told me he was working on a collage and could not stop. So he invited me to sit in the kitchen with him as he worked. I could not have been more intrigued and delighted. He had already pasted a parabola of light, more intense at the base than the arms, on a sheet of cardboard. He then carefully cut the signature of a young girl from a letter she had sent him. He glued it near the bottom of the parabola. I do not recall all of the other operations he performed, but when he felt he had finished that stage of his work, he held it up for me to see, asking, "Do you get it? Do you get the poem?" I saw the parabola, the name "Chase," and a letter "t." Decidedly, I did not get it. He offered a hint, which I readily accepted: the poem was in French. I still did not get it. It was "a hard one," he admitted, and quoted and identified a line from Jules Laforgue's "Complainte de Lord Pierrot": "J'ai le coeur chaste et vrai comme une bonne lampe." The rebus collage juxtaposed the image of a lamp—for the parabola of light resembled the shape cast by a shaded lamp—with the word "chaste." Cornell knew the poetry he loved so intimately that he assumed other readers would share his command of the texts. I had read Laforgue with interest, but I never would have remembered that line. Even if I had, I would not have solved the puzzle.

There is perhaps a reason for Cornell's absorption in that metaphor which extends beyond the obvious attractions of the poem: the Pierrot theme, the lament for lost love, even the early death of Laforgue himself would have interested Cornell. Yet when we note the context of the line, something else appears. Laforgue wrote:

> J'ai le coeur chaste et vrai comme une bonne lampe;
> Oui, je suis en taille-douce, comme une estampe.
> [I have a heart as chaste and true as a lamp;
> Yes, I am in gravure like a print.]

The identification with the engraving plate is at once a strikingly original metaphor and one with which the collage maker would have been particularly intrigued, since so much of Cornell's time had been spent collecting engravings to use in his boxes and collages. It was a fortunate accident that I arrived while he was working that morning. It provided me with an unanticipated glimpse at the transformation of poetry into imagery at play in Cornell's work. Yet I do not think that the rebus he was making is particularly crucial to understanding his achievement. What is important, rather, is the intensity of his interiorization of poems that the episode reveals. When I compared the version of the film inspired by Lorca that he gave me that day with what had been shown five years before, I discovered yet another aspect of his involvement with poetic texts.

In 1963 the Film-Makers Cinematheque showed it as *A Fable for Fountains*. The version Cornell gave to Anthology Film Archives in 1969 was almost twice as long and had been retitled *A Legend for Fountains*. The alteration reflects the difference between two translations of the line "si, tu niñez ya fábula de fuentes" in the poem "Tu Infancia en Menton." In his translation of the whole of *The Poet in New York*, Ben Belitt rendered it, "Yes, your childhood, a fable for fountains now." But in the *Selected Poems* Edwin Honig translated the line: "Yes, your childhood now a legend of fountains."[19]

The long version of the film itself is remarkable for the introduction of intertitles after the point where the first version ended. All of the intertitles are translations of lines from the poem, but Cornell selected phrases from both translations. His reading of Lorca's poem had been so personal and intense that he carefully examined both renderings for words that fitted his experience of it. From Belitt came the lines "Your solitude, shy in hotels, and your pure mask, in another sign" and "it is mine to seek out the scorpion's stone," while from Honig he quotes "tokens and traces of chance."[20] The other forty-odd lines of the poem are uncited. The subtitle he added to the film ("Fragments") acknowledges this ellipsis.

Lorca wrote "Tu Infancia en Menton" while he was in New York as a special student at Columbia University. It is a vivid cry against the loss or betrayal of love. I imagine that Cornell was intrigued by the idea of Lorca walking the streets of New York while suffering loneliness and the sense of erotic loss for someone in Spain (perhaps Salvador Dalí)—seeing many of the same sights that the artist saw in the late 1920s and could even continue to see in certain neighborhoods in the 1950s.

Cornell's black-and-white film follows a young woman through New York's Little Italy and parts of the Lower East Side, where little had been done to disturb the look of shops since the time Lorca lived in New York. She seems timid, lonely, perhaps poor, and alternately appears breathless in the winter chill, as if running somewhere, or without anything to do but gaze in store windows, as if they were composed as shadow boxes. In the film she represents both the poet and the beloved. The aesthetic experience for Cornell is the experience of others. It entails the voyeurist's desire to be invisible, so absent that the solitude of whomever he observes is not disturbed. Cinema generally effects an illusion of intimacy, and the camera, as an inflexible mechanical observer, reinforces the counterthrust of distance to that intimacy. In the films Cornell directed, the camera often organizes its sights as if it were the eye of a lonely wandering consciousness. In fact, Cornell was an important influence on the development of a crucial phase of the American avant-garde cinema that I have elsewhere called the *lyrical film*.

In lyric poetry the poet's language mediates between the raw and often aggressive presence of the natural world and the moral consciousness of the poet. The words bear the burden of simultaneously representing the environment or situation in which the poet finds himself and his precarious autonomy in relationship to it. In the great lyrics that Cornell loved passionately, the poems of Mallarmé, Keats, Dickinson, Laforgue, and Lorca, the poetic text emerges from a crisis that it somehow both prolongs and attempts to resolve.

The Romantic dialectic of self and nature in these poetic forms uncovers a disturbance caused by superimposition of two contradictory dimensions of language itself. The exteriority of words, as objects and names of objects, does not coincide with the intimacy of those very words as emblems of the self. This tension molds from within the imagery of Romantic lyrics; the complexity of the imagery derives from its innate inadequacy to totalize or to resolve the tension. Therefore the Romantic lyric takes the shape of an obsessive series of images qualifying and finally surrendering a hope of reconciling mind and nature.

Poets turn repeatedly to a fixed point of reference—a season, a time of day, a specific location—to find a ground for the encounter in language of an exterior world and a consciousness that seeks to organize it or to make it somehow sufficient. By denying the convenience of a fictional protagonist, someone invented to weather or at least to contain the crisis from which the poem originates, the lyric poet puts the reader in the position of reconstructing the encounter from the logic of the image sequences and from the rhythms and connotations of the words.

The lyrical poem is so familiar a literary form that we often ignore the complexity of its premises. The lyrical film, however, posed an enormous challenge to both filmmakers and viewers as it emerged as a vital cinematic form in the 1950s. Its success owes much to the genius of Stan Brakhage, whose orchestration of imagery, camera movement, and editing brought to maturity the film-without-a-protagonist—or one whose protagonist is the fiction of the filmmaker behind the camera. In this development Brakhage was exposed to two significant influences: Marie Menken and Joseph Cornell. When Cornell commissioned Brakhage to make a film of the Third Avenue El in 1955, he provided the funds and, indeed, the first opportunity for the young filmmaker to make a film without a protagonist. Later that same year, Cornell engaged Brakhage as the cameraman for the film that eventually became *Centuries of June*. It was the young artist's first lesson in organizing a film of silent images to evoke the poignancy of the loss of those very sights that the film preserves. Thus, working with Cornell provided Brakhage with his first practical experience in the dialectical organization of filmic images.

In the films Cornell directed, the occasional protagonist plays an ambiguous role. The young woman of *A Legend for Fountains* and the little girl of *Nymphlight* stand for, and therefore mediate, the artist's experience of the world they encounter. Yet they are the center of *his* encounter. This ambivalence generated alternate versions of the films. *Cloches à travers les feuilles/ Claude Debussy* is a print of *Nymphlight* without the girl and her broken parasol. The reel called *Mulberry Street* is a montage of material from and related to *A Legend for Fountains* without the young woman. In *Centuries of June, Angel,* and *The Aviary*, the subjectivity of the films is not mediated by a protagonist at all; they describe the encounters of the camera with special places.

Even in *A Legend for Fountains*, the ambivalent status of the woman in relation to the organizing sensibility structures the two parts of the film. As soon as the titles appear in the second half, the use of the second person in "Your solitude, shy in hotels..." surreptitiously reflects an unnamed "I" who does not appear but nevertheless controls the lyric. Cornell's selection of translations and elliptical fragmentations of Lorca's cry against the loss of love reduces the poem to these lines:: "Your solitude, shy in hotels.../...pure mask in another sign...I ...tokens and traces of chance...I ...to seek out the scorpion's stone..." Lorca's often repeated word "love" does not appear in the titles. Instead of translating the line

> ¡Amor de siempre, amor, amor de nunca!
> ¡Oh, si! Yo quiero. ¡Amor, amor! Dejadme,[21]

the artist finds the inscription of "Love" in the graffiti on a wall in Little Italy. The camera sweeps again and again past a chalked heart in which only the words "I love" remain visible. The name of the loved one has disappeared. Eventually the panning discloses that this vestigial expression of love had been written on the wall of the apparently defunct "Monarch Doll Company." The filmmaker thus brings together the themes of lost childhood and eradicated love by rhythmically dwelling on the graffiti and postponing the revelation of the poignant site of its inscription.

These signs are the "tokens and traces of chance," in Lorca's translated words. They take on meaning when the camera, and by implication the wandering woman, reads them and returns to them. Even the shop windows can be read as compositions of meaningfully juxtaposed items, as if they were there to indicate what the solitary woman, and the errant camera, lacked and sought. In one window the beaming graphic sun of "Il Sole" antipasto evokes a cheerful, hopelessly foreign dawn, imported into the winter cityscape. Cornell often used those very antipasto labels in his constructions.

Near the end of the film, he shoots the street from inside a shop. Frozen in the window display and peering out with us is a mannequin in a wedding dress, eternally poised in anticipation of emotional and erotic union like the figures Keats found on a Grecian urn. The camera focuses beyond the static bride at the street, at what she would see if she could. The pane of glass catches reflections of passersby and records them as translucent ghosts. The dummy is more real, weightier than the people who look at her and at her dress from outside.

In his version of their collaboration in Little Italy, Rudy Burckhardt has made a film called by the very Cornelllike title *What Mozart Saw on Mulberry Street*. Mozart here is a bust of the composer posed in the window of a designer's shop. The title and the montage reverse the relationship of seer to seen. The statue stands for the controlling consciousness of the film. Such a reversal plays an important role in *A Legend for Fountains*. The film stands enmeshed in an exchange of impossible glances: what Lorca would have seen in New York in

1929, effaced by the passage of twenty-five years; what the wanderer sees when, like Lorca, she goes "to seek out the scorpion's stone" or, as the alternative translation makes less ambiguous:

> I'll search the stones for scorpions
> and your childlike mother's clothes,
> midnight lament and ragged cloth
> that tore the moon out of the dead man's bow.
> Yes, your childhood now a legend of fountains.[22]

It is also what the antipasto sun, the eternal bride, and a boxed doll would see every day. Through this labyrinth of sightlines, Cornell passes unseen, as Burckhardt's camera records a present moment, an often repeated walk, in which everything seen (and metaphorically seeing) reflects the tension between duration and change. Even the structure of the film itself, first edited by Burckhardt, with the second part edited a decade later by Jordan according to the artist's instructions, attests to the ambiguity of the cinematic process, which begins with a pure affirmation of here and now in the moment of shooting the film and allows for endless reconstruction in the acts of editing.

The organization around the glance of an eye, the interplay between seer and seen, is the common thread that unites the very different style of filmmaking encountered in *Rose Hobart, Bookstalls,* and *A Legend for Fountains.* The most perfect example of the mediation of Cornell's glance is the use of the beautiful little girl in *Nymphlight.* Dressed in a frilly white party dress, carrying a broken parasol, she rushes to Bryant Park behind the New York Public Library. We watch her watching the parades of pigeons, the rhythms of a water fountain, old men on benches, and finally another little girl. This is the most clearly narrative of Cornell's films. As our attention is directed from the presence of the girl to what she sees, she gradually withdraws from the film. She is the spirit of the place, and once the film has heightened our attention to its orders, making her way of seeing ours, she vanishes. In the mystic hint of the title, there is a clue that like a figure from Ovid she has returned to the fountain which dominates the park. Only her discarded parasol remains, in a wastebasket missed by a sanitation man in his rounds.

Therefore the story of *Nymphlight* is a version of metamorphosis. In *Centuries of June, The Aviary, Angel,* and *Seraphina's Garden,* the cinematic occasion is an act of invocation to the spirits of places consecrated in Cornell's experience. Those spirits do not appear in the flesh and carry parasols, but in each of those films, the Inanimate gestures toward the observer and offers up an image of mediation or a series of such images. In the vacuum created by the withdrawal of a protagonist, another image is drawn out of the flux and comes to stand, if only momentarily, for the tenuous situation of the observer in the film. Nowhere is this clearer than in *Cloches à travers les feuilles/Claude Debussy.* There Cornell has edited the human "nymph" out of *Nymphlight.*

Suddenly a second little girl, who in the other version had been observed by the girl with the parasol, looms up. The numerous acts of attention that compose the film now center on her and through her.

In 1955 Cornell had asked Brakhage to photograph an old house that was about to be torn down. He called the film *Tower House* for at least eight years. A public screening of his films at the Film-Makers Cinematheque in 1963 inspired Cornell to reconsider his cinematic achievement. His sister, Elizabeth Cornell Benton, found the following note among his papers. It is dated November 15, 1963: "digression—not realizing until reviewing 'Tower House' film how beautifully—how fully the spirit of Emily Dickinson was caught."[23] The same note to himself suggests an editing change in *Angel* and a collective title, *The Lonesome Glory* (from Dickinson's poem, "Gathered into the Earth" [no. 1370]), for both it and *Seraphina's Garden*. Subsequently he gave *Tower House* its final title, *Centuries of June*. This, too, comes from Dickinson: "There is a Zone whose even Years" (no. 1056).

In the film, piles of fresh dirt and bare-chested workers intimate the coming destruction of the house, to which the camera repeatedly pans, even haltingly approaches, as the cameraman takes a few steps toward the porch. In the insistence on recording the house, filming the view from its windows, even through the slats under its porch as if seen by a hiding child, there is an urgency that forebodes its loss.

Cornell never set out to illustrate Dickinson's text. The association of the poem with the film was an afterthought. Nevertheless, when Cornell retitled his film with it, he left us with a valuable clue to the dialectical structure of his imagery. As the presence of the old house ceases to dominate the film, it becomes a backdrop first to the incessant movements of butterflies and moths and later children. They in turn become signs of the prolongation of a moment that, in Dickinson's words, "constructs perpetual Noon." The children are as indifferent as the insects to the temporal destiny of the house: the house appears as the static center of a world in which everything else is in flux; but the structure of the film insists on the uniqueness of the house and its coming destruction, whereas the insects and children will be repeatedly replaced. The recognition of that reversal marks the moment when the center shifts to what Dickinson calls "Consciousness," the force through which "The Centuries of June/And Centuries of August cease."

The sublime in Dickinson's poetry flashes out from mundane particulars of the New England environment. The climate of her poems is the everyday weather of sun, shadows, a "slant of light," birds, butterflies, flowers, and grass, but rarely the high Romantic mountain peaks, torrents, and storms. From the intensity of her self-consciousness as she evokes the commonplace sights she gathers intimations of the great negative abstractions of death, time, and eternity. Cornell's cinema—at least those films he directed rather than collaged—is in close accord with Dickinson's poetic project. He employed cinematographers to accompany him on his ruminative walks and guided them to capture the moods evanescent things provoked in him. The delicacy and exquisite timing of the films evoke nuances of anguish, loss and mortality in contrast to the mildness of their imagery.

In *The Aviary*, Cornell filmed a statue of a mother with two children and edited it into a film of bird movements and playing boys, as if the statue watched over and protected their activities in Union Square. But the statue and the children are foils for the congregation of birds, who seem to endow the barren trees and other statues of the park with a meaning by settling on them. The transformation, in this case, is simply identified by the film's title. We see a park, its human scale defined by statues, trees, and buildings that tower above our eyes; but for the birds, the ruling spirits of the place, it is a contained arena of tranquility, an aviary and a sanctuary.

Thus each of the films Cornell directed involves some shift of perspective, which the film invites us to make without insisting upon it. In the cemetery film *Angel*, Cornell has organized a series of shots that dramatize the presence of the statue of an angel, as if the stone were responsive to the moods of its viewer. The film is a masterpiece of tonal nuance. The statue appears at first in a brilliant autumnal light. Filmed beside a fountain in a graveyard, it seems at first a stone prop, a simple marker to denote the place where the film occurs. But when the montage returns to it after showing the pool of a fountain, on which float orange leaves, disturbed by a light rain, the angel seems to brood upon the seasonal change and mourn the passing of a Persephone. So long as the camera frames the statue head-on, it appears diminutive and tied to the earth, as if it grew up from the ground like the flowers beside the pool. At the end of the short film, Cornell frames it from below without the trees to dwarf it. In shadow, the stone wings fill the bottom of the image, leaving only the turbulent cloudy sky visible above. Suddenly, thus filmed, the statue becomes a massive creature of the sky, descended onto earth.

The shifting aspect of the angel gathers winter into fall and sky into earth and links gravity and flight. The angel is merely stone, a conventional funereal statue, but the composition and rhythm of the shots animate it without ever letting us forget its dumb heaviness. The images of water prepare for the transformation of the angel; the pool reflects the sky, thereby making one image of the two. Within the frame joining sky to earth, dead leaves float beside the living flowers. The iconography is simple. Yet Cornell makes this natural specularity the visible icon of the power of cinema to show what can and what cannot be shown, of another reflection in which the reassurance of seasonal alternation is matched by its contrary, "the lonesome glory" of mortality. In Dickinson's poem, "awe" defines the inadequacy of imagery. When she writes that the lonesome glory has "no omen here but Awe." Cornell worked in awe of the power of cinema to show what can and cannot be shown.

Joseph Cornell's cinema remains the central enigma of his work. His films have a roughness and an insidiousness that the constructions and collages never exhibit. A convenient attitude to take toward them would be to undervalue them, as many have done, including the artist himself.

For all of his privacy, despite his reluctance to show his films publicly until decades after they were made, he exerted a powerful influence on other filmmakers. The "accidents" of personal encounters with him and his films significantly affected the filmmaking of Stan Brakhage, Lawrence Jordan, Ken Jacobs, Jack Smith, and Jonas Mekas. Just as Cornell himself was an intuitively brilliant reader of the poets he admired, seeing complexities and tensions in their expressions that could inform his visual dialectics, so these filmmakers quickly apprehended hints and directions in Cornell's films that they could explore on their own.

 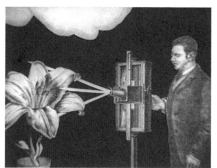

Lawrence Jordan:
Sophie's Place (1986):
In Hagia Sophia; the projector; the two Magi or instructors; a third instructor; Balloon face
[Bottom Right] *Duo Concertantes—Centennial Exposition* (1964):
Projector

Lawrence Jordan's Magical Instructions

Lawrence Jordan (b. 1934) has produced a massive body of work that encompasses several overlapping genres and includes many of the most inventive films ever made by means of cutout collage animation, a range of lyric films that capture the spirit of his life and the lives of other California artists in the late 1950s and early 1960s, and films directly inspired by and incorporating poetry. At seventy-four, he completed his longest film by far, *Circus Savage* (1961/2007–2009), a twelve-hour "visual autobiography."

Over his long career Jordan has essayed a number of strategies for avant-garde filmmakers to survive economically from their work. With Stan Brakhage he made a naïve attempt to travel around America in the mid-1950s and earn a living by showing their first works from town to town. After an initial effort to which not one person came, they gave up. But Jordan was undaunted: he founded two important showcases in San Francisco and was among the original organizers of the Canyon Cinema Cooperative, which still distributes avant-garde films after almost fifty years in operation. He drew up a plan to interest galleries in selling original 16mm prints to collectors, and he was one of the first avant-garde filmmakers to explore video sales. After selling VHS tapes of Jordan's films for many years, Facets Multimedia released a four-disc *Lawrence Jordan Album*. Its twenty-five films represent a little more than half the titles in his oeuvre.

Jordan came to his mature styles slowly. His earliest films—*The Child's Hand* (1953–1954) and *Morningame* (1953–1954), for example—show the influence of Brakhage, with whom he attended Denver's South High School in the late 1940s, and aspects of their careers continued to overlap and coincide until Brakhage's death in 2003. At the start, apparently, Jordan followed Brakhage's lead. Later Brakhage returned the compliment, giving his unique inflection to techniques and strategies Jordan pioneered. Brakhage spent one disastrous semester at Dartmouth and dropped out the year before Jordan went to Harvard, which he too quit after a year. Together with friends from high school, they put on plays in Central City, Colorado, and then explored life among the poets and filmmakers of San Francisco and New York, until Jordan settled by himself in the Bay Area in 1955. In fact, Brakhage acted in two of Jordan's earliest works—*The One Romantic Venture of Edward* (1952–1956/1964) and *Trumpit* (1954–1956)—and Jordan showed up in Brakhage's psychodramas from the same period: *Unglassed Windows Cast a Terrible Reflection* (1953) and *Desistfilm* (1954). Marriage and family life, however, soon distanced them. Brakhage settled in Colorado and eventually moved to Canada, where he died. Jordan remained in the Bay Area but for a few long voyages as a Merchant Marine in the late 1950s, a brief stay in Mexico, and a summer spent assisting Joseph Cornell in Queens, New York, in 1965.

From very early on we can see interwoven traces of the three funda-mental temporal articulations of Jordan's art: a foregrounding of cinematic time in the rhythms of montage and camera movement, an evocation of timelessness, and an obsession with transfiguration. Even before Jordan abandoned Brakhage's initial fusion of neorealism with the oneiric mode of Maya Deren and Kenneth Anger to forge a more contemplative style, the poet Robert Duncan saw something in the young filmmaker that was not yet evident to most viewers of his work, and he enlisted him to read the role of the magician Faust in the 1955 performance of his masque *Faust Foutu* at the Six Gallery in San Francisco. Around that time Duncan's partner, the painter and collagist Jess, introduced Jordan to Max Ernst's collage novels *La femme 100 têtes* (1929) and *Une semaine de bonté* (1934), which eventu-ally became the decisive influences on his animated films. Jess, Duncan, and the company of artists the young filmmaker kept in San Francisco nurtured his work and abetted his nascent interest in mysticism. During those tran-sitional years, Jordan taught Bruce Conner to edit film, and together they founded the Camera Obscura film society (in 1957), which grew into The Movie, a theater devoted to showing experimental work (in 1958). He as-sisted the veteran filmmaker Christopher Maclaine with cinematography on *The Man Who Invented Gold* (ca. 1957) and helped collage artist Wallace Berman make his only film, *Aleph* (1956–1966). Taking one of his first films, a subjective play of the filmmaker's hand gestures (the camera held with his other hand), Jordan recorded a poem by Philip Lamantia on the sound-track, transforming the hitherto silent work into *Man Is in Pain* (1954–1955). He shot *Visions of a City* (1956–1957, reedited 1979[1]), an eight-minute film composed of images of his close friend, the poet Michael McClure, reflected in windows and off distorting metallic surfaces as he wandered around San Francisco. McClure and his wife, Joanna, along with the poet Kenneth Rexroth and his daughter Mary, were the models in the play of light and shadow that constitutes *Spectre Mystagogic* (1957). Later, Lamantia and McClure would appear with Berman and graphic artist John Reed in Jordan's visual hymn in quest of peyote, *Triptych in Four Parts* (1959), which the filmmaker called "a spiritual drug odyssey seeking religious epiphany" (as quoted in the Canyon Cinema catalogue). Aspects of Duncan's theos-ophy, Berman's Cabala, Reed's mystical Christianity, and Lamantia's fusion of surrealism and Catholicism can be seen in Jordan's later films, although he never elected a sectarian religious discipline for himself. Seemingly, the closest he has come to such an attachment would be to the Tibetan Buddhism of his film, *The Sacred Art of Tibet* (1970–1972).

Like Duncan, Jordan came to look upon the artist as a shaman whose inspiration entails the reception of modes of knowledge and language beyond his experience. In "The Truth and Life of Myth: An Essay in Essential Autobiography" (1968), Duncan wrote:

> The poetic imagination faces the challenge of finding a structure that will be the complex story of all the stories felt to be true, a myth in which something like the variety of man's experience of what is real may be contained.... Where Philosophy raised a dialectic, a debate, toward what it calls Truth; Poetry raised a theater, a drama of Truth.... We have been converted by and have now taken our faith in a truth that has been patently made-up.[2]

The fundamental truth of the fictive, poetic imagination is a vital principle of Jordan's cinema, in which filmmaking is a continual act of revelation. Even though he does not believe in a life after death,[3] the evocation of the Underworld has been a primary goal of his imaginative work.[4] His masterpiece *Sophie's Place* (1986), subtitled "An Alchemical Autobiography: Transformation and Again Transformation," presents the complexities of the filmmaker's life story as a truth patently made up, enacted in a theater of transformations. It conjures the magical truth of an unforeseen poetic engagement with the process of cutout animation.

In fact, cutout animation was the technical means through which Jordan reached his artistic maturity and at the same time mastered an area of filmmaking utterly distinct from Brakhage's ambitions. As early as 1959, in *The Soccer Game* and *Minerva Looks Out into the Zodiac*, he began experimenting with animation. His homage to Jess, *The 40 and 1 Nights (or Jess's Didactic Nickelodeon)*, followed the next year. Although these initial experiments in animation gave intimations of an experience of timelessness—through the play of the moving camera or foreground figures in motion against static lithographic backdrops—they were primitive exercises, unequal in depth to the rhythmic exuberance the filmmaker had already achieved in *Man Is in Pain, Triptych in Four Parts*, and *Hymn in Praise of the Sun* (1960). The latter, a celebration of the birth of Jordan's daughter, Lorna, as a manifestation of ancient Egyptian cosmology, represents the lactating fecundity of his wife, Patricia, as a source of floral abundance. Brakhage concurrently transformed the elements of this modest, diaristic lyric into the epic cosmogony of his *Prelude: Dog Star Man* (1961). Just as three years later, when he temporarily switched from 16mm to the more economical 8mm in his series *Songs* (1964–1969), he took Jordan's *humilis* modes as his models.

In so rapid an account of Jordan's early development, I would have passed over *The Seasons' Change: To Contemplate* (1960) were it not for the following, astonishing letter the filmmaker sent me in November 2008:[5]

> I have to my own knowledge made only one truly profound film: *The Seasons' Change: To Contemplate*. In it is the discovery that the so-called "Present Moment" is existentially always the *same* moment.
>
> This little movie has never been taken up by anyone. (It has hardly ever been shown, yet it vividly remains whole in my mind.) The one time in the '60s it was shown in a theatre, the person behind me exclaimed in derision, "action" when the plum dropped from the tree.
>
> A profound work almost by definition is a subtle one. Even to its author. There are resonances undiminished by time. Significances seep out only years after completion. A diamond is never impatient to be discovered, nor does it ever lose its integrity.
>
> There is nothing in *The Seasons' Change* that fights with itself. Struggle is a falsification of reality and of natural processes. There is time. There is the Moment (timelessness). And there is change or outcome. That is what the film is about.

The triad "time/Moment/change" and the elimination of anything that "fights with itself" would be fundamental principles of Jordan's aesthetic. His intensive concentration on the simple objects before him, unhindered by "a falsification of reality," unfolds the complex manifold of temporality at the core of his cinema. The opening shot of *The Seasons' Change* shows a window with a Japanese candleholder in the form of a thin, bare-breasted woman, her head turned as if she were gazing into the yard beyond with its plum tree swaying in a lively breeze. The evocation of a woman at the window suggests a dominant motif in the American avant-garde film, originating with the image of Maya Deren pressing her hands against the glass in *Meshes of the Afternoon* (1943). But whereas Deren built her film around the play of psychic forces in which everything "fights with itself" (to the extent that the figure of the protagonist multiplies, culminating in suicide), Jordan contemplates the window and the vegetation outside it for seven minutes, in some twenty silent shots, gently panning the camera to caress the bibelots on the windowsill or to study the play of shadows on leaves and fruit moving in the wind. Devoid of drama, *the film keeps time*.

Jordan kept returning to the imagery of *The Seasons' Change* in some of his best films: *Hymn in Praise of the Sun* replaces the statue with living flesh and moves entirely into the garden; likewise, his exuberant *Big Sur: The Ladies* (1963–1964) uses rapid, in-camera editing to show two women sunbathing on a veranda overlooking the Pacific. The most striking return to the frozen gazer at the window, however, is the animation *Patricia Gives Birth to a Dream by the Doorway*, the second of the two-part *Duo Concertantes* (1961–1964).

The animation methods with which the filmmaker created most of his best work for the next five decades were largely in place with *Duo Concertantes*. He moved cutout figures along the surface of some twenty-five nineteenth-century engravings for the first segment, *The Centential Exhibition*, while operating with a single backdrop for *Patricia Gives Birth to a Dream by the Doorway*. The former intermittently follows the movements of a man absorbed in looking at a birdcage on a printed card as he wanders across different locations. Around him a ball bounces, shifting scale from backdrop to backdrop, while birds and butterflies suddenly appear and disappear. The alchemical machinations of archaic paraphernalia set off an eruption of shooting stars. At one crucial moment a man, hand-cranking a projector, makes a planet or moon rotate, clockwise and then counterclockwise, before winged creatures shoot out of the projector. This is the first of many avatars for the filmmaker as a magician of the cosmos to appear in Jordan's cinema.

In the exquisite *Patricia Gives Birth to a Dream by the Doorway*, the backdrop plate shows a woman looking through the open door of a cabin onto a lakefront. There is a dog with her. Her posture duplicates that of the candleholder in *The Seasons' Change*. The animated cutouts descending from above or manifesting on the watery horizon make visible her reverie. When a screen appears with flashing images that either fly off or fall into the water, Jordan acknowledges the mystery of gravity in the cinema. With the interplay of frozen vistas and ephemeral images, most poignant at the instant of transformation, the filmmaker found an ideal medium for the fragile synthesis of time/Moment/change.

Collage animation has been a very fecund medium for Jordan. *Duo Concertantes* is in black and white. He followed it with the monochromatic blue of *Gymnopédies* (1966) and *Carabosse* (1980), the interplay and occasional superimpositions of monochromatic fields in *Our Lady of the Sphere* (1969) and *Moonlight Sonata* (1979), the richly dissolving colors of *Once Upon a Time* (1974), and the hand-colored images of *Orb* (1973) and *Masquerade* (1981)—the latter again using a single backdrop. The pattern of progressively introducing new formal elements and then returning, refreshed, to an earlier mode recurs throughout his career.

Jordan spent five years animating the eighty-six-minute *Sophie's Place*, working every morning without a plan, from a storehouse of images he had previously collected, colored, and cut out. He told an interviewer that "One rule was 'no planning ahead.' When you finish one idea, you go into the next. You simply go in the next morning and look at your layout and the first idea that pops into your head you have to do, whether it takes two days or two months. You cannot equivocate and say, 'Oh, I should have a better idea.' Equivocation short circuits your entry into the Underworld."[6] In this statement, equivocation and the Underworld correspond to "anything that fights with itself" and the "Moment," respectively. In Jordan's thinking there is an affinity, perhaps a symbolic equation, between the timelessness of the Moment and the unconscious, or the imagination. For him alchemy is the spiritual vehicle for change or transformation. In the same interview, Jordan remarked, "You know Harry [Smith] and Kenneth Anger were both practicing magicians, but I'm not a practicing magician. I'm a practicing alchemist.... I don't think the practicing alchemists ever had a codified system. Every one of them were off on their own kick. They had imagery that was like a common language and I use that language.... Alchemy and constructionism are two ways of saying that you take the things laying [*sic*] around you as detritus, as litter, and you make something that is formal art out of it.... I've been manipulating old imagery with new technology as part of my alchemy."[7]

The unexpected and puzzling term in the subtitle of *Sophie's Place* is "autobiography." Insofar as autobiography is a narrative in which the author delineates his or her development, the film's genre seems to be mislabeled. The overflowing phantasmagoria of winged creatures, exploding eggs, giants, floating body parts, and geometric figures in continual transformation on top of some forty backdrops stymies any reasonable correlation of the filmmaker's life to the imagery he drew from his unconscious over the course of five years. However, if we understand an "alchemical autobiography" as a version of what Duncan called "essential autobiography," we can see how the poet's discovery of an "enduring design" in what one would take to be free association shapes Jordan's film, in which the sequence of backdrops provides allusive hints at an autobiographical schema underlying the work. In a letter dated January 26, 1987, to Howard Guttenplan of the Millennium Film Workshop discussing the newly completed film, Jordan virtually repeated Duncan's subtitle:

> I call it *Sophie's Place*, because it evolved from and revolves around the mosque (both interior and exterior) of Saint Sophia in Constantinople. *Essentially* it is *an autobiography* in animated form (as once suggested by Stan Brakhage many years ago), but a spiritual one, an "alchemical" one. It is interesting in that the film took place in a *timeless* working atmosphere, where no limits or restrictions were ever placed on how long it took to complete an idea or a sequence. No pre-plans were made; it all took place under the camera—that is, it is the reality of what happened there not a "re-enactment." [my italics]

Here the "timelessness" fundamental to the filmmaker's aesthetic occurs within the working process, and the danger of a falsification of reality is called "re-enactment."

Jordan's emphasis on the image of the Hagia Sophia proffers an invitation to interpret the film. The sacred interior provides the backdrop for two early sequences. I take them, somewhat tentatively, to correspond to moments of formal instruction in the development of the filmmaker's sensibility. The second of them might be related to his year at Harvard, where screenings of

Eisenstein and Cocteau at the film club awakened his excitement for his future métier. In *Sophie's Place*, the first projection device and screen (recalling those within *Duo Concertantes* and subsequent animations) appear within the ecclesial interior. That the Hagia Sophia never recurs in the film would support its identification with the theater of formal instruction, which ended for Jordan, as we noted, after his freshman year at college.

In thus correlating some of the backdrops to critical moments in the filmmaker's history, I am tempted to read certain other series, which seem to derive from Old Testament illustrations of the valley of prophetic vision and the Exodus as aspects of Jordan's life among the artists of the Bay Area. Particularly, the exterior view of a mosque, followed by a visionary city, coming soon after the Hagia Sophia interior fits the biographical pattern of the filmmaker's first move to San Francisco. Eventually we see the interior of a tent, located within a temporary Exodus tabernacle,[8] in which two priests preside over a magical altar. If I might pursue the admittedly tenuous logic of this hermetic path, I would identify these priests as formative influences on the spiritual growth of the autobiographical subject, perhaps even fixing the pair as Robert Duncan and Jess. The emblematic signs of their influence are the mesmerizing stares with which they fix the ever-transforming male representatives of the filmmaker.

There is yet another, parallel, figure who emerges later in the film, in a different region, whose prolonged stare may be even more efficacious. By the same principles of chronology and influence, that figure might be said to correspond to Joseph Cornell, whose collage boxes struck Jordan as "the best work I'd seen in any of the arts, and so I was completely devoted."[9] Working backward to the brief sequence separating the Hagia Sophia from the visionary city, we would expect to find some allusion to the often tumultuous time Jordan spent with his friends mounting plays in Central City, Colorado. Thus the boxing match of that animated scene might reflect his sometimes violent rivalry with Brakhage.

In surmising that the mesmerizing figures reflect the central mentors[10] of Jordan's artistic incarnation, I am operating from the conviction that the film centrally explores the growth of the artist's imagination. At its rhythmic apogee, an apocalyptic vision occurring five minutes before the end of the film, background images from William Blake's *Glad Day* (ca. 1796) and *The Great Red Dragon and the Woman Clothed with Sun* (ca. 1803–1805) precede several from Gustave Doré's illustrations of Dante's *Inferno* (1857). With representations of Dante swooning in the arms of Virgil, his poetic mentor, the latent theme of the film momentarily becomes manifest. The scene returns to the opening plate, depicting a mother and child in what the filmmaker described as "a paradisiacal garden." Thus *Sophie's Place* moves from an origin in biological childhood through the education of a sensibility to a fully achieved, creative use of childhood. Significantly, Jordan told Paul Karlstrom in an interview for the Smithsonian's oral history archives, that "few artists have captured [childhood]: Cornell is one.... And, of course, Robert [Duncan] and Jess...had their fingers on that one."

All through the film a red-striped hot air balloon floats across the static plates. It has human features, almost a "Mr. Balloon Face." It surveys the settings and transformations, often dropping large tears, as if it were the manifestation of the autobiographical consciousness reviewing and weaving together the scenes of poetic incarnation. Unbeknownst to Jordan, he had virtually illustrated a passage from Ralph Waldo Emerson's "Nature" (1836)—the very passage I would take, in *Eyes Upside Down*, to be central to the aesthetics of the American avant-garde cinema. Emerson wrote:

> Nature is made to conspire with spirit to emancipate us. Certain mechanical changes, a small alteration in our local position apprizes us of a dualism. We are strangely affected by seeing the shore from a moving ship, from a balloon, or through the tints of an unusual sky. The least change in our point of view, gives the whole world a pictorial air.... Nay, the most wonted objects, (make a very slight change in the point of vision,) please us most.... Turn the eyes upside down, by looking at the landscape through your legs, and how agreeable the picture, though you have seen it any time these twenty years![11]

In rotating the eyes of the Balloon Face as the final gesture of his alchemical autobiography, Jordan asserts the power of the autobiographical imagination to give a pictorial air with the eyes upside down to the most wonted objects.

Another aspect of the filmmaker's lifelong engagement with poetry can be seen in the "H. D. Trilogy" (1990–1993): *The Black Oud, The Grove*, and *Star of Day*. In all three parts, Jordan follows Joanna McClure, first in Rome and Greece, then in England (with recollections of Greece), and finally to her home in San Francisco (with interludes in Italy). Like Anger, Menken, Hugo, and Brakhage, Jordan dares to revisit typical European tourist sites (the Pantheon, Delphi, the Tower of London), testing the power of the cinematic imagination to revitalize such ruins by making them the theater of a confrontation between the poetic self and time. In the case of Brakhage's *The Dead* (1959; shot in Paris's Père Lachaise cemetery) and Hugo's *Gondola Eye* (1963; shot in Venice), the subjective camera conjures images of mortality. In *Eaux d'artifice* (1953; made in the Tivoli gardens), Anger follows a fleeting figure, mediating the filmmaker's double sense of precarious identity and ecstatic dissolution. Jordan's ambition here is even more complex than his antecedents. On the one hand, he is celebrating his relationship with McClure, even ironically echoing at the start of the sequence the reflected urban images he had recorded of her former husband three decades earlier in *Visions of a City*. At the same time, they are both paying homage to H.D., whose magnificent three-part *Hermetic Definition* (1960–1961, published posthumously 1972) McClure reads on the sound track. The fiction of the film represents McClure alone (and with a younger male companion in the middle section) as a stand-in for the septuagenarian poet, reflecting on magic, the fragility of her identity, and the painfully awkward attraction she has for a much younger man. Usually the poetry and cinematic images evoke separate, autonomous realms, but at times the images almost coincide with the text: for instance, when we see McClure drinking at a sidewalk café, we hear, "I keep remembering/ my glass of red wine"; when she is reading and lighting candles at home, we hear McClure's voice-over intone: "until I turned over these pages,/ and read *I want to light candles.*" Furthermore, the camera movements through the European sites are edited to suggest both the subjective perspective of the solitary woman tourist and the view of the filmmaker, strolling with his companion, both of them appreciating together H.D.'s response to similar places three decades earlier. As such, the "H.D. Trilogy" is yet another variation on Lawrence Jordan's earlier discovery that "the so-called 'Present Moment' is existentially always the *same* moment."

Stan Brakhage:
[Left] *The Mammals of Victoria* (1994)
[Right] *The God of Day Had Gone Down upon Him* (2000)
Stills courtesy of Fred Camper and Marilyn Brakhage

Stan Brakhage's Poetics

Stan Brakhage began to make films in 1952 as a precocious teenager. His encounter with modernist poetry was immediate and eccentric. But it made so forceful an impression on him that the modernism of the American avant-garde cinema has been largely defined and molded by his achievements. He quickly assimilated the modernist dimensions of the avant-garde filmmakers who were at work when he entered the field. His passion for poetry and his eagerness to incorporate the advanced work in both practice and theory, of the composers and painters of his time as well, accelerated his meteoric development and influence.

Brakhage's immediate predecessors had all commenced filmmaking in the 1940s; he was a generation younger and began his career just after dropping out of Dartmouth College as an alienated freshman. He thought to enroll in Sidney Peterson's filmmaking workshop at the California School of Fine Arts, but Peterson had left off teaching in 1950. For a while Brakhage lived in New York, at times as the guest of Maya Deren, where he became a close friend of the poet-filmmaker Willard Maas and his wife, the painter-filmmaker Marie Menken. Later he lived and worked in Princeton, New Jersey, where he met and befriended James Davis, a sculptor turned filmmaker. Maya Deren, Peterson, Davis, and especially Menken were crucial influences on Brakhage's concepts of cinema and his several styles. Crudely synopsized, the shape of Brakhage's career moved from an initial embrace of the psychodramatic trance film to the adaptation of Menken's somatic camera in the invention of the crisis lyric. It was the crisis lyric that established his preeminence among avant-garde filmmakers by the end of the 1950s. He supplemented the lifelong production of crisis lyrics with the mythopoeic serial film *Dog Star Man* (1961–1964), the 8mm series *Songs* (1964–1969), several autobiographical series, and what he called "imagnostic" films—articulations of colored light in Davis's mode: the long film *The Text of Light* (1974), and then *The Roman Numeral Series* (1979–1980), *Arabics* (1980–1982), *The Egyptian Series* (1984), *Babylon Series* (1989–1990), and *The Persian Series* (1999–2000), He had been painting on film intermittently since the 1960s, but after 1988 it became his dominant mode of production.

Before he came to cinema, Brakhage thought of himself as a poet. His modernism grew out of a passionate reading of twentieth-century poetry, as Bruce Elder has demonstrated in his book *The Films of Stan Brakhage in the American Tradition of Ezra Pound, Gertrude Stein, and Charles Olson*. In Brakhage's 1977 lecture "Poetry and Film," he recounts how his friends presented him with Ezra Pound's *The Cantos*—"the most important single book in my life"—on his sixteenth birthday as a joke. Although he could hardly understand it, he said: "I hear his song, and I heard it even when I was utterly baffled by a book that obviously had been given to me as a joke. . . . It became the great book for going over and over."[1]

For a brief period in the early 1950s, he rented the San Francisco apartment of the poet-filmmaker James Broughton (who was making a film in England) in the house of the poet Robert Duncan, whose powerful influence on him was immediate and lasting. Duncan convinced Brakhage that he was not gifted as a poet, but he nevertheless strengthened his adolescent attraction to the work of Ezra Pound. Pound's learned manner and his cranky and assertive compression of history and culture clearly influenced Brakhage's polemical writings, although they owe as much to the Poundian poet Charles Olson, another of Brakhage's elective mentors and Duncan's enthusiasms, as to Pound himself. But ultimately the more radical poet Gertrude Stein would prove to have had the greater influence on his films. During the period of Brakhage's residence, Duncan had put himself under a regimen of writing in the manner of Stein on a regular basis, ultimately producing his book of "derivations," *Writing Writing*. Thus it was Brakhage's peculiar fate to come under the influence of one of the very rare poets of that generation who actively assimilated the lessons of both Stein and Pound at a time when their followers were as opposed as the two poets had been to each other.

Olson was clearly an aspirant to the mantle of Pound. His manifesto, "Projective Verse" (1950), affirming the centrality of breath and the poet's body in the rhythmic infrastructure of poetry, became the clarion for Duncan, Brakhage, and a group of poets associated with Black Mountain College, where Olson reigned as Rector through most of the 1950s. Following Pound, Olson maintained the centrality of history to poetic inspiration, but whereas Pound looked to classical Greece, Renaissance Italy, and ancient China for material, Olson explored the Maya, Pleistocene man, and the history, particularly pre-Colonial history, of his hometown, Gloucester, Massachusetts. For Olson, as for all Poundians, poetry was an archaeology of origins.

Stein's version of modernism entailed a repudiation of the past, a disavowal that entailed a deep suspicion of the role memory might play in the creative process. Writing, for her, at times, meant a derailing of even the role of syntax so that the unstudied parts of speech—the conjunctions, articles, adverbs, participles, prepositions—would suddenly loom into the foreground, revealed and unmasked as the hidden architects of meaning. The full impact of Stein's work would not affect American poetry until the 1970s with, simultaneously, the advent of the "Language poets," the feminist critique of patriarchal language, and the academic fascination with "deconstruction."

When Brakhage was making his first films, Pound was incarcerated in St. Elizabeth's Hospital in Washington and Stein was dead. But, in a sense, their work was both contemporary and as oppositional (to each other and to everything else) as it had been when they were rivals in the 1920s. Between 1951 and 1958 the Yale University Press issued eight large volumes of Stein's previously unpublished and most difficult work. This included most of her poetry and particularly the very long serial poem *Stanzas in Meditation* (1956) that continued to obsess Brakhage until his death in 2003. Just when Stein became posthumously a contemporary poet, Pound followed the dazzling publication of *The Pisan Cantos* (1948) with two more installments of *The Cantos, Section: Rock Drill 85-95 De Los Cantares* (1955) and *Thrones* (1959). The birthday present Brakhage received in 1949 would have been the 1948 edition, which included *The Pisan Cantos*.

Reading the newly published texts of these poets in the mid-1950s, the young filmmaker might ponder the opening lines of Pound's "Canto 90":

> "From the colour the nature
> > & by the nature the sign!"
> Beatific spirits welding together
> > as in one ash-tree in Ygdrasail.
> > > Baucis, Philemon.
> Castalia is the name of that fount in the hill's fold,
> > the sea below,
> narrow beach.
> Templum aedificans, not yet marble,
> > "Amphion!"

Twenty-two lines later he would find:

> Castalia like the moonlight
> > and the waves rise and fall...[2]

Then he could read in Stein's *Stanzas in Meditation*:

> It is not easy to turn away from delight in moon-light.
> Nor indeed to deny that some heat comes
> But only now they know that in each way
> Not whether better or either to like
> Or plan whichever whether they will plan to share
> Theirs which indeed which can they care
> Or rather whether well and whether.
> May it not be after all their share.

> This which is why they will be better than before
> Makes it most readily more than readily mine.
> I wish not only when they went. [Part V, Stanza XXVII][3]

Thus Pound opens his ninetieth canto invoking the Castalian fountain, the Delphic source of poetic inspiration, with his typically elliptical compression of Neoplatonic philosophy (John Heydon's doctrine of signatures), Greek and Norse mythology, and an untranslated Latin phrase. Poetry, he implies, reveals the beatific stamp of sacred patterns in the welter of metamorphoses.

Early in his career Pound had distinguished three factors in the poetic composition:

> Melopoeia, wherein the words are charged, over and above their plain meaning, with some musical property, which directs the bearing or trend of that meaning.
>
> Phanopoeia, which is a casting of images upon the visual imagination.
>
> Logopoeia, "the dance of the intellect among words," that is to say, it employs words not only for their direct meaning, but it takes count in a special way of the habits of usage, of the context we *expect* to find with the word, its usual concomitant, of its known acceptances, and of ironical play.[4]

In a different essay he concisely defined the program of modernist art:

> The function of an art is to strengthen the perceptive faculties and free them from encumbrance, such encumbrances, for instance, as set moods, set ideas, conventions: from the results of experience which is common but unnecessary, experience induced by the stupidity of the experience and not by inevitable laws of nature.[5]

In his "Canto 90," the rhythm, the play of names and languages, and the honed attention to detail should "heighten the perceptive faculties" and free the reader from the encumbrances of conventional verse. Pound invites such a reader to a lifework in poetry and hermetic philosophy. His allusions are learned but ultimately accessible to the adept and the scholar.

But for Stein such poetry as Pound writes is "moon-light." For moonlight is both something and nothing: it is not the light of the moon, but the reflected, diminished, metaphorically displaced, light of the sun after the turning of the earth has made its direct rays invisible. Thus moonlight is her icon of enigma of representation itself. She admits that it has its illusionary seductions (*some heat*) and implies that its imaginative charm is matched with verbal assonance (*delight... moon-light*) but she turns away from it to a poetry indifferent to mythology and ancient languages, which does not share classical allusions, a radically modern poetry divested of phanopoeia. Its startling melopoeia (*which... why, better... before*) reveals the hidden music of the unstressed words of ordinary language. She seems to be asserting that such a reorientation of poetic consciousness "makes it most readily more than readily mine" even though its signature is manifestly hers. This poetry does not entice us to philosophical and poetic learning but to an unaccustomed state of attention to the moiling forces of language heard in a line such as "Or rather whether well and whether," where the unexpected use of "and" is even more striking than the puzzling rhyme "rather whether." If this is logopoeia, it is not what Pound meant by the term.

How Brakhage utilized his reading of Pound and Stein in forging his cinematic style is a tricky question. It was not until 1958 that he had put in place the elements that allowed him to enter his first major phase as a modernist filmmaker. The thirteen films he made between 1952 and 1957 fall into two not utterly discrete categories. The eight black-and-white films are for the most part variants of the trance film which he inherited from Deren, Anger, Markopoulos, and Peterson (and one comedy—*The Extraordinary Child*, 1954, in Broughton's manner). The five color films range from his most fanciful trance film, *In Between* (1955), to a portrait of New York's elevated subway in *Wonder Ring* (1955), a study of cats in *Nightcats* (1956), and a portrait of a couple making love in *Loving* (1957). His radical breakthrough occurred when he found a convincing manner of fusing both modes in *Anticipation of the Night* (1958).

Brakhage was at once more prolific than his immediate predecessors and more inclined to persist with his unique version of trance film mode.[6] The surrealist tradition and the symbolist cinema of Jean Cocteau had a greater influence on the first Americans to work in the trance film mode than on him. They tended to create dreamscapes with symbolic objects: Deren's *Meshes of the Afternoon* (1943) begins with a draped figure whose face is a mirror; Anger's *Fireworks* (1947) takes its title from the substitution of a Roman candle for an ejaculating penis. But Brakhage's earliest trance films remained committed to realism in their evocations of heterosexual erotic anguish. It is not until his fifth film, *The Way to Shadow Garden* (1954), that he depicts a purely symbolical event: when the isolated protagonist Oedipally puts out his own eyes, the film plunges into negative as he gropes through a garden. It is significant that in this film and in the subsequent *Reflections on Black* (1955), in which another Oedipal blind man has his eyes scratched off the emulsion of the filmstrip, the violation of realism entails a "metaphor of vision."

At the core of Brakhage's trance films there is a primal scene fantasy, explicit for the first time in his impressive third film, *Desistfilm* (1954). There he made a great stylistic leap without abandoning realism: dynamic swish pans, sudden jump cuts, a musique-concrète soundtrack of instruments and voice sounds mark this psychodrama of five young men and one woman. Their solipsistic games—one makes a house of books, another strums a mandolin, another cleans his navel, another plays with matches—terminate when the woman and one of the men begin to embrace, riveting the mocking attention of the others.

As if to substitute the abuse of a victim for their erotic frustration, they toss the smallest of the company in a blanket until he flees to the woods chased by his tormenters. At the end of the film the four males leeringly surprise the embracing couple.

Loving is a reprise of *Desistfilm* in a celebratory register. The constantly moving camera swoops across the bodies of a clothed couple as they embrace, lying in the woods. The freewheeling camera movement gives this silent film its rhythmic structure and rhetorically represents the unseen presence of the filmmaker as the voyeur of the scene. The camera dynamics, apparently intended to evoke the free indirect point of view of the lovers, is so hyperbolical it cannot fail to inscribe the voyeur-filmmaker in the film.

His encounter with Joseph Cornell had been a crucial factor in the evolution of Brakhage's mastery of the moving camera and his invention of a lyrical form in which the interaction of the filmmaker and the visible world becomes the subject of the film. On a recommendation from poet and critic Parker Tyler, Cornell telephoned Brakhage to commission him to make a film of New York's Third Avenue El, the elevated rapid transit train that was to be torn down. It seems that what Cornell loved most about the train was its fleeting glimpses into the lives of people whose windows opened onto the tracks, but they play no part in Brakhage's *Wonder Ring*. Instead he captures the rocking rhythms of the train, its accelerations and arrests, and the movement of light within the cars.

He tested the lyric mode of *Wonder Ring* in *Nightcats* and *Loving* while continuing to make psychodramas. With his first masterpiece, *Anticipation of the Night*, he retained a vestige of his trance films: it ends in suicide by hanging. The temporal development of the film describes the melancholy visual experience of a figure represented by his shadow, occasionally his hands, and primarily the camera movements that reflect his somatic navigation of the world. The style is a decided development of the three preceding lyrics. But unlike *Wonder Ring, Nightcats*, and *Loving*, the film is not anchored in a single, unified object of observation. Instead, it proceeds through a linked series of situations—the exiting of a door, observation of children at an amusement park, the dance of the moon choreographed by the moving camera, a baby on the grass, children sleeping, animals in a zoo, the dawn seen from a moving car and, of course, the final hanging. The diffusion of subjects draws further attention to the unifying presence of the unseen filmmaker and reinforces the identity between the suicidal shadow man and the camera operator, as the episodes bleed into one another. In the initial presentation of the movement from indoors to outside there are proleptic glimpses of the trees at night filmed from a moving automobile; amid the sweeps of the crawling baby we will see echoes of the earlier passage through the door.

The primary lesson Brakhage had learned from Stein was that there is no such thing as repetition. Every recurrence has a new meaning. The fugal mesh of repeating images and movements in *Anticipation of the Night* owes more to Stein's prose narratives than to her poetry. When we read her story "Miss Furr and Miss Skeene," we encounter a similar gradual elaboration of new material in a rhythmically reiterating and contrapuntal matrix:

> The voice Helen Furr was cultivating was quite a pleasant one. The voice Georgine Skeene was cultivating was, some said, a better one. The voice Helen Furr was cultivating she cultivated and it was quite completely a pleasant enough one then, a cultivated enough one then. The voice Georgine Skeene was cultivating she did not cultivate too much. She cultivated it quite some. She cultivated and she would some time go on cultivating it and it was not then an unpleasant one, it would not be then an unpleasant one, it would be a quite richly enough cultivated one, it would be quite richly enough to be a pleasant enough one.[7]

Stein's repetition was the basis of her rhythmic invention. The transposition of this principle into filmmaking was Brakhage's first and most powerful modernist gesture. Although *Anticipation of the Night* draws largely on the permutating sentences of Stein's early prose, Brakhage soon found equivalents to the more complex rhythms of her middle period. Here is an example of that style:

> Having divided the difference between wheat and white between calf skin and doe skin and does it shine. After a choice of birds.
> > After a choice of birds. Having said that after having said that.
> > Astonishingly a rain-bow.
> > Pass and pass it.[8]

Absorbing the lesson of Stein's astounding sensitivity to language, the young Brakhage quickly made himself the most subtle and the most comprehensive master of cinematic rhythms. In the late 1950s and early 1960s, he demonstrated this mastery as he perfected the form of the crisis lyric; his rhythmic organization extended from his editing and camera movement to every aspect of his recording of the nuances of stillness and motion. The crisis lyric draws upon the filmmaker's mood and personal experience at the time he is making his film; it presents an intense emotional situation without the representation of a protagonist within the film. The images and the way they are filmed and combined point to the thoughts and feelings of the unseen subject (filmmaker) of the film.

Brakhage's move from the psychodramas of the trance films to the invention of the crisis lyric has a biographical foundation. He married Jane Collom just before completing *Anticipation of the Night*. In the next eight years they had five children and moved into a cabin in the Rocky Mountains that would remain their home until the dissolution of the marriage in the late 1980s. The first step in Brakhage's subsequent evolution of the crisis film was his renunciation of the melodramatic fiction he used to organize *Anticipation of the*

Night—that is, the suicide. His wife and growing family became his principal subjects. He resolved to concentrate his work on what he could see in his daily life. In the introduction to *Metaphors on Vision*, he called this Emersonian principle "soul-in-action" and attributed its inspiration to Charles Olson's essay "Proprioception":

> I would say I grew very quickly as a film artist once I got rid of drama as prime source of inspiration. I began to feel that all history, all life, all that I would have as material with which to work, would have to come from the inside of me out rather than as some form imposed from the outside in. I had the concept of everything radiating out of me, and that the more personal or egocentric I would become, the deeper I would reach and the more I could touch those universal concerns which would involve all man.[9]

Underlying Brakhage's emphasis on interiority and subjectivity there has always been a sense of art as mimesis, the imitation or representation of perceptual and mental processes *in motion*. The filmmaker insisted that the abstract expressionists "were the first to paint closed-eye vision. They painted it without knowing it, without being conscious of it...Of course in Turner you can find the 'Ur' of this whole sense of vision, the paideuma, the gristly roots (as poet Ezra Pound put it) of this need that flowers into the picturing of the unnameable"[10] Similarly, in his 1982 radio program, "The Test of Time" (no. 9), he declared "I do deeply believe that music is not abstract, that it's just another way of thinking. And that there are patterns which are expressed through music, which do reflect directly the most blunt political troubles or world crises we're either trying to survive or are perhaps trapped in."

By interpreting abstract expressionist painting as the representation of phosphene phenomena on closed eyes and all music, including aleatoric works, as the charting of metalinguistic thought in process, Brakhage denied the formalist approach to modernism and recuperated his original tendency toward realism. Such a peculiar empiricism may have motivated his early impulse toward theoretical elaboration. The period of his powerful invention of the crisis film was also the time in which he wrote *Metaphors on Vision*.

That writing was clearly influenced by Pound, Stein, Olson, and Duncan. He cites them all frequently in the book. His polemics were densely encrusted with puns and cryptic allusions: the book opens as a prose poem on vision and the possibilities of cinema as a vehicle for overcoming primal fears. A chapter of scripts and script fragments leads to another in which conventional typography had to be supplemented by handwritten words that eventually gave way to arrows, circles, and squiggles. The book's only precedent in the American avant-garde cinema was Maya Deren's *An Anagram of Ideas on Art, Form and Film* (1946). The negative frontispiece might even be a remote allusion to the negative image of Deren on the cover of her book. But her argument was formal and classically reasoned, addressed to intellectuals; Brakhage's was a poetic exorcism of his theoretical preoccupations. Whereas Deren had accepted the filmic apparatus as a given and extolled its objective rendering of reality, Brakhage decried its ideological manipulations and urged filmmakers to wrestle with optical and mechanical norms in order to approximate individual visual experience.

In the initial chapters Brakhage addresses himself to the status of iconography in a polemic against fear ("Metaphors on Vision"), the constrictions of the filmic apparatus ("The Camera Eye"), the individuality of seeing ("My Eye"), and the complexities of movement in general, of his own moving from home to home, and of meaning ("Move Meant"). Behind these early chapters are an implied set of convictions: (1) The eyes are always moving, scanning in response to all visual stimuli. (2) Vision never stops; the eyes see phosphenes when closed, dreams when asleep. (3) The names for things and for sensible qualities blunt our visional receptivity to nuances and varieties in the visible world. (4) Normative religion hypostatizes the power of language over sight ("In the beginning was the word") in order to legislate behavior through fear. (5) The self-conscious and responsible use of language is poetry. (6) There can be no naïve, untutored vision. Therefore, only through an educated and comprehensive encounter with literature can a visual artist hope to gain release from the dominance of language over seeing. (7) The artist is repeatedly challenged to sacrifice the gratifications of the ego and the will to the unpredictable demands of his or her art. The cardinal principles of these initial theoretical essays sustained his whole prodigiously prolific career.

During the period when Brakhage had been in daily contact with Robert Duncan, the poet wrote "Poetry before Language," in which we read:

> I want to describe Poetry as it was before words, or signs, before beauty, or eternity, or meaning, were. Poetry would not allow the brain to falsify what it was in giving it a word or a "meaning".... The organs of the body not only communicated but all the organs made things. The act was dancing, the product of the act was the dance, poetry. In one kind of dancing the hand and eye danced together. Thus the hand "saw" the stones and sticks, and the eye "felt" them.... There were dumb perceptions. A mountain came into view. The eye saw the mountain happen...There is an earlier reality even today when Poetry takes over what we had thought was language and we find ourselves confronted by such a mountain in view.[11]

Brakhage massively assimilated this Vician "revelation" of poetry before language, even if he encountered Vico only filtered through Duncan. *Metaphors on Vision* is a young filmmaker's attempt to situate cinema as a "dance" in the fields of "dumb perception." Brakhage's version of modernism might be summarized as the pursuit of cinematic poetry as the means not to "allow the brain to falsify" the "earlier reality" of what his eyes see.

The crisis films of 1959–1964 utilized a range of techniques that were new to Brakhage: superimposition (*Sirius Remembered*, 1959; *The Dead*, 1960), hand painting over images (*Thigh Line Lyre Triangular*, 1961), collage of fragments on Mylar film strips (*Mothlight*, 1963). He redeployed these same techniques in his most Poundian film, the cosmological epic *Dog Star Man* (1961–1964), a sequence of films including a prelude and parts 1–4, corresponding to the seasons from winter through fall. *Dog Star Man*, in turn, provided the basis for *The Art of Vision*, which extended its seventy-five minutes to a four-and-one-half-hour systemic work, unfolding all the permutations of its various superimpositions—two for the prelude and part 2, three for part 3, and four for the final part.

One result of superimposition, collage, painting, negative imagery, fast cutting, anamorphic photography, and swish panning was the flattening of the visual field. In demoting photographic depth from the norm to the exceptional instance, Brakhage pushed the filmic image in the direction of the most ambitious painting of his older contemporaries, Jackson Pollock, Willem de Kooning, Clyfford Still, and others. In the late 1960s his discovery of Robert Rauschenberg's Dante series, first as illustrated in *Life* magazine—later he borrowed a set of the lithographs from the sculptor, John Chamberlain—had a strong influence on his work of the 1970s and 1980s; for Rauschenberg was fusing the gestural painting of abstract expressionism with photographic images, as Brakhage himself had done in *Thigh Line Lyre Triangular*.

In *The Horseman, the Woman and the Moth* (1968), Brakhage attempted for the first time to sustain an autonomous work purely by painting clear film stock. Subsequently, in the early 1970s, he painted on a plate of glass while he filmed scenes through the glass in stop motion: *Sexual Meditations* (1970–1972) and *The Wold Shadow* (1972). However, in the 1980s painting became a major factor in his work; from the 1990s until his death it became his dominant practice. The development of Brakhage's cinematic painting had technical and aesthetic ramifications. His earliest painting over film images was printed directly on a master filmstrip by contact printing. This method was both dangerous for the laboratory's printers and limited in the thickness and texture of the paints the filmmaker could apply to the film. The consequence of the process was a vibrant gestural skein that formed a frontal plane behind which the photography receded slightly. The stop-motion glass method allowed him freedom in using all textures and densities of color, but it prohibited the recording of continuous natural movement and restricted his painting gestures to minute daubs. The loss of gestural dynamism concomitant with this method was compensated for by a new degree of control and a subtlety of pastel tones. Here Brakhage seems to have drawn on his previous experience filming through windows affected by fog, frost, or rain. In *The Wold Shadow* he found a subject well suited to this method: he set up his glass plate before a forest landscape. The resulting film combines shimmering variations of light intensity with hovering regions of hues to capture his "vision of the god of the forest," a theme central to Ezra Pound's poetry from "The Tree" (1906) to the late *Cantos*. Brakhage made *The Wold Shadow* during a period in which he was expanding his interest in American painting from postwar modernism to the study of the major landscape painters of the nineteenth century, particularly Frederick Church. This line of investigation quickly took him from painting on glass back to photographic cinema, culminating in *Creation* (1979), an investigation of the dramatic imagery of Genesis influenced by Church's masterpieces of the 1860s, "The Icebergs" and "Rainy Season in the Tropics."

The breakthrough film in Brakhage's hand-painting was *The Dante Quartet* (1987). Here he used an optical printer, a machine for printing films of any thickness one frame at a time. With it, the filmmaker can create new rhythms by repeating, reversing, superimposing, or masking a single frame or a sequence of them. In this film Brakhage returned to the inspiration of Rauschenberg's Dante lithographs for his own interpretation of *The Divine Comedy*.

The flourishing of Brakhage's hand painting of the 1990s occurred when the filmmaker Phil Solomon joined him on the faculty of the University of Colorado. Solomon was adept in the use of the optical printer. He guided Brakhage through the printing process and collaborated with him on a few of the dozens of hand-painted films Brakhage made in his last decade. The practice of making so many films wholly from marking raw film stock with color renewed and extended Brakhage's appreciation of the second-generation abstract expressionist, Joan Mitchell.

A parallel version of abstraction flourished in his work in the 1980s but was rooted in his early encounter with James Davis. *The Roman Numeral Series, Arabics, The Egyptian Series*, and *Babylon Series* are photographed films of light and color without reference to recognizable objects. These very short films, extended to serial sequences, explore the nuances and ramifications of his 1974 exercise in the abstract sublime, *The Text of Light*, a seventy-minute film of dramatic bursts and splays of light, which he shot entirely through a large crystal ashtray, fulfilling at long last an adolescent boast that he could make a feature film in a waste receptacle.

If one line of development in Brakhage's work leads from the great crisis films of the 1960s through abstraction, first mainly photographic, and later mainly marking raw film with dyes, paints, and scratching tools, another was more explicitly autobiographical than his earlier work in the sense that he studied his process of memory and the nature of temporal change on his visual experiences in many of the films he made between 1967 and 1984. In the course of making the four-part *Scenes from Under Childhood* (1967–1970) he envisioned *The Book of the Film*, which he imagined to be a twenty-four-hour-long film of his (and his wife's) life. Sometime in the 1990s, after his marriage ended, he came to call the long sequence *The Book of the Family*, beginning it now with *Songs* (1964–1969). It is thirteen hours long. He recycled *The Book of the*

Film as the title for a projected sequence of his more abstract films, including *The Art of Vision,* as well as the imagnostic and hand-painted works.

It is significant that Brakhage conceived his autobiographical project from its inception as an ontology of film itself. The films that he has at times designated as chapters of *The Book of the Film* were usually serial works themselves, including *The Weir-Falcon Saga* (three films, 1970), *Sincerity* (five films, 1973–1980), *Duplicity* (three films, 1978–1980), and *Tortured Dust* (1984). From the beginning the filmmaker grounded this monumental enterprise on the observation of his five children with Jane Collom. But the degree to which it would explore the temporal growth of the children manifested itself very gradually. The shift of title is the final acknowledgement of this reorientation.

A resistance to chronology is inherent in his autobiographical work. Brakhage recognized at the start that his memories were more associative than sequential. The five children constituted a synchronic arena for the observation of diachronic change. Looking at them, filming them, he sometimes gained access to the automatic memories that he took to be the core of the autobiographical quest. He respected and preserved this process in the finished films; at the same time, he was at pains to delineate the noncongruence between the actions of his children before his camera and the lost events of his own life. In doing so, he ran counter to the conventional autobiographical strategy of assembling memories and impressions in accordance with the external grid of successive years. Yet as a filmmaker he knew that in every film the ordering of shots entails the rhetorical disposition of illusions of simultaneity or succession despite the relentless diachrony of frames and shots. So for him a rigorous and critical examination of his memory coincides with the fundamental experience of making films.

In several of these films the examination of still photographs plays a distinctive role. The photograph is both a representation of a past presence and the visible acknowledgement of an unrepresentable past. Brakhage probably nurtured his iconic use of photographs on the model of Jerome Hill's autobiographical *Film Portrait* (1970) and the photographs in Gertrude Stein's *The Autobiography of Alice B. Toklas.* From Stein, also, he may have derived the binary focus: she told her life by ventriloquizing Alice telling her life with Stein and followed this with the generic *Everybody's Autobiography.* Brakhage organized *Scenes from Under Childhood* as the autobiography of himself and Jane. (Jane, more literally Steinian, was writing *The Autobiography of Stan Brakhage* at that time.) Just as the observation and optical identification with the five children substitutes intersubjective synchrony for first-person diachrony, the dual focus inscribes an intersubjective dimension to the implied authorship of many of the films in *The Book of the Family.*

Crudely schematized, one could say that *Scenes from Under Childhood* scrutinizes the relationship of seeing to affects; *The Weir-Falcon Saga* turns on the nature of metaphor and its conventionalization in language; *Sincerity,* in turn, addresses the relationship of simultaneity to diachrony; *Duplicity* looks at human gesture as inextricable from performance or acting. *Tortured Dust* forms the palinode to this ontology of cinema: the breakdown of the dual focus, foreshadowed again and again in the earlier films, now lends a dark mood to the whole work as the filmmaker is repeatedly alienated from the action he depicts—the lives of his grown children and grandchildren.

Bruce Elder argues that its "construction has a strikingly Steinian/Cubist character...Brakhage radically fragments...actions and repeats them...just as Stein rearranged clusters of words...Brakhage uses many long fade-ins and fade outs. [This technique] evokes a sense of sadness, as it makes what we see seem so very evanescent."[12] The alienation and its effect of sadness introduces the most severe crisis of Brakhage's career, which coincided with the breakup of his marriage to Jane Collom and his remarriage to Marilyn Jull in the late 1980s. The last phase of Brakhage's filmmaking spanned the years from 1989, the year he married Marilyn Jull and published *Film at Wit's End*, until his death in 2003. In that 1989 book, his most lucid and coherent since *Metaphors on Vision*, Brakhage offered his analysis of the sensibilities of eight of his contemporaries in the avant-garde cinema.

The filmmaker's often repeated tendency to elaborate on an isolated experiment or an idea from an earlier moment of his career, producing much later an extended series of films, makes demarcation of periods frustratingly complex. Such is the unexpected production of eleven films with soundtracks out of the total of thirty films he made between 1987 and 1992. Although seven of his first twelve films (1952–1957) had soundtracks, only four (*Blue Moses*, 1962; *Fire of Waters*, 1965; *Scenes from Under Childhood: Section No. 1*, 1967; and *The Stars are Beautiful*, 1974) of the some 200 films of the intervening years were not silent. Similarly, painting on film had been one of Brakhage's privileged strategies since 1961, but it did not assume a dominant place in his filmography until the 1980s. Not only did he call on earlier options from his filmmaking for further exploration, but he measured and questioned his development and its modes of consistency by returning to previously fecund themes, locations, and image associations.

Brakhage's *The Riddle of Lumen* (1972) had been a response to the systemic modernism of Hollis Frampton's *Zorns Lemma* (1970), especially to its central section in which cycles of twenty-four shots, each one second long, of signs in alphabetical order are gradually replaced by wordless images. More than any other of the filmmakers of the American avant-garde cinema, Frampton shared Brakhage's commitment to modernist poetry. When Brakhage was making his first films, the young Frampton was one of the daily visitors to Pound's cell at St. Elizabeth's, seeking the path of his own poetic vocation. For him it entailed a passage through still photography and the company of painters and sculptors—Frank Stella, Carl Andre, Michael Snow—before he found in cinema a fusion of Pound's neoplatonic theology of light and Duchamp's ironies. So it was particularly important for Brakhage and Frampton to engage each other in a somewhat competitive dialogue about the place of cinema in modernism. Their aesthetic differences emanated from the question of the centrality of language in art and consciousness. For Frampton, Brakhage was the victim of "the syndrome of logophobia…pandemic throughout recent practice in the visual arts." He claimed that "every artistic dialogue that concludes in a decision to ostracize the word is disingenuous to the degree that it succeeds in concealing from itself its fear of the word…and the source of that fear; that language, in every culture, and before it can become an arena of discourse, is, above all, an expanding arena of power, claiming for itself and its wielders all it can seize, and relinquishing nothing." [13] Yet despite their fundamental disagreement, their modernism was grounded in the conviction that their work participated in a heated conversation with their masters and each other. Brakhage was disappointed that Frampton did not feel the need to "answer" *The Riddle of Lumen* with yet another film.

Most of Brakhage's energetic output of films in the 1980s refracted the prolonged crisis culminating in the end of the marriage in which he had been so invested as an artist and polemicist since the late 1950s. The key documents representing aspects of that agony would be *Tortured Dust*, a four-part film of sexual tensions surrounding life at home with his two teenage sons; *Confession* (1986), depicting a love affair near the end of his marriage (1987); and the *Faust* series (1987–1989), four autonomous sound films reinterpreting the legend that obsessed Brakhage throughout his career.

Apparently the filmmaker did not have a series in mind when he made the first part, *Faustfilm: An Opera* (1987), in collaboration with the composer Rick Corrigan. Joel Haertling, himself a composer and filmmaker, played Faust. The narrative action is carried largely by Brakhage's voice-over, almost unique in the immense corpus of his films, while human action is nearly reduced to silhouetted figures in dark interiors. In the schematic episodes of the film we see Faust drinking, masturbating, and playing the French horn. At the instigation of his Mephistophelean "friend," his imaginary female companion materializes as Gretchen. The film concludes with Faust and Gretchen on a bed blowing bubbles while the naked friend whispers in Faust's ear. Brakhage quickly followed that film with a further meditation of Faust's erotic imagination, *Faust's Other: An Idyll* (1988). Haertling composed the music for this work. In it we see Heartling and his girlfriend, Emily Ripley (also listed as a collaborator for the use of her paintings in the film), alternating domestic chores with scenes of him playing music and her painting. The cinematic style is more typical of Brakhage at this period than the static, nearly monochromatic imagery of the first Faust film had been: it has a rather rapid change of richly colored shots with regular shifts of focus, giving elaborate attention to details within the unfolding daily events. The next section, *Faust 3: Candida Albacore* (1988) seems to be a dramatic rehearsal for a performance in which Ripley and Haertling are joined by other masked and gaudily costumed musicians and actors in a "*walpurgisnacht* to Faust."[14] The series concludes with an extended, somber periegeton, or travel poem, *Faust 4* (1989), with minimalist, often rasping music, once again by Corrigan. Occasionally the editing reminds us that Faust (Haertling) is the subject of this episode, but otherwise it constructs its rhythmic force from nonstop moving camera shots, usually from an automobile, of a trip that includes the oppressive modernist architecture of Oral Roberts University in Tulsa, the decaying house in Winfield, Kansas, where Brakhage was born, and the monumental ruins of Mesa Verde.

Brakhage told Suranjan Ganguly in an interview celebrating the artist's sixtieth birthday: "Faust, for me, is *the* major legend of Western man."[15] Permutations on the Faust story had been central to his education as an artist. In 1947, when he was fourteen and entering high school, three of the most influential authors in the world published versions of Faust. The eventual translation of two of them and the assimilation of all three would have occurred during the formative period of the precocious filmmaker. One of these, Thomas Mann's *Doctor Faustus*, was probably the most prestigious novel published in Brakhage's adolescence. He quotes elliptically from its climax in *The 23rd Psalm Branch* (1966–1967): "'Then, take back Beethoven's Ninth,' he said."[16] As a would-be dramatist with modernist convictions, Brakhage may have known that Gertrude Stein wrote *Doctor Faustus Lights the Lights* in 1938 and that Paul Valéry had written *Mon Faust* in 1940; both were published in 1947. Furthermore, from the time of its publication, William Gaddis's *The Recognitions* (1955) was acknowledged as a major literary achievement within some of the avant-garde circles of Brakhage's contemporaries; Gaddis repeatedly incorporates allusions to Faust in his narrative of forgery, disillusionment, and eventual redemption. However, Brakhage would have been less favorably disposed to Jack Kerouac's Faust, *Dr. Sax* (1959).

Yet above all other versions, Robert Duncan's *Faust Foutu* (1956) seems to have challenged the filmmaker's imagination during his formative period. Duncan's masque, "an entertainment in four parts" depicts the anguish of Faust as an abstract expressionist artist in a witty, plotless phantasmagoria: as he marks his canvases, he compulsively narrates to himself the personal associations his colors and shapes call to mind. It is apparent from his mention of Duncan's masque in *Metaphors on Vision* (1963) that Brakhage considered it to be a crucial statement of the limitations of "affection" and an instrument for understanding (and thereby overcoming) the first crisis of his marriage to Jane Collom. A year before that marriage, he had begun to write his own *Faustfilm* (1957) but never finished or filmed it.[17]

There may even have been a psychodramatic element in the association with Duncan's play at the time Brakhage returned to the theme of Faust. Duncan himself had been a mentor, teacher, and at times a tormenter of Brakhage from the time he moved to San Francisco, in the early 1950s. Duncan became his first model for the serious Artist, his poetic father, with whom he had an unresolved agon; for the poet never disguised his disappointment in the films Brakhage made after 1957. This judgment of his work was exceptionally painful for Brakhage, and it brought about a deterioration of their relationship. Yet Brakhage perpetuated to the end of his life Duncan's fascination with Gertrude Stein. Her *Doctor Faustus Lights the Lights* may have inspired Duncan's early play; certainly it inspired Brakhage, who had his collaborators and cast study it during the making of *Faust's Other: An Idyll*.[18]

When *Faust Foutu* was first performed at the Six Gallery in San Francisco in January 1955, Brakhage's high school friends, Lawrence Jordan and Yvonne Fair, played the chief roles; Jordan was Faust, and Fair played Helen, the film actress Faustina, and other roles. Earlier, in Colorado, Brakhage had competed for Fair's affection, but ultimately Jordan prevailed in their erotic triangle. Therefore, if Duncan's inflection of the legend of Faust had once been interfused, for Brakhage, with his potentially traumatic displacement by Jordan, certainly as Fair's lover and more remotely as the subject of Duncan's benign recognition, his surprising return to the *Faustfilm*, at least in title and theme, after thirty years might be seen as a reengagement with the sexual and psychic tensions that immediately preceded his first marriage; for he started the Faust series during the severe crisis of the failure of his marriage to Jane and continued the series of four films through the period of his divorce, living in isolation in rented rooms in Boulder, Colorado, and he was still working on the series during his subsequent courtship of Marilyn Jull. That period was also marked by Robert Duncan death (1988).

Whereas Goethe's Faust contracted with Mephistopheles for youthful vitality, in *Faustfilm: An Opera* Brakhage's Faust asks for the advantages of age: the filmmaker, speaking in voice-over, identifies "his absolute wish that he, Faust, suddenly could have fulfilled his every last task without having to live through the intervening years of tedious accomplishment." Yet nothing we see confirms this chiasmus. The initial *Faustfilm: An Opera* shows us a young man, sometimes accompanied by a boy, in his house. He plays the French horn, drinks wine, talks to another man, masturbates, and seems to make love to a woman with the friend watching, naked. It is the voice-over that informs us Faust is a divorced, solitary drinker, "... estranged from the ways of God and men," raising his son in his father's house and desperately seeking a confidant. Many of these details reflected Haertling's domestic situation. In the culminating erotic scene, Brakhage confirms the woman's passage from imagination to reality as, the voice-over continues, she "finally becomes flesh to his imagination ... is real then as she always was somewhere ..."

Duncan had preceded Brakhage in dismissing Faust's will to be young again: his Faust proclaims near the end of the third act: "It was the tradition that Faust sold his soul to regain his youth. But *my* youth has lasted so long it is like a world-burden, a straightjacket of guilelessness."[19] But Brakhage's invention provides a double perspective to the psychology of his collaboration with the musicians and actors of his serial film: literally, he projects onto his protagonist the desire to be like Brakhage himself, a senior and accomplished artist, but without the long and often painful labor required for such accomplishment; and in this way he points to his artistic achievement and its costs by indirection, elliptically attempting to reassure himself of the value of his life's work in the midst of his crisis. At the same time, he defends himself in the narrative fantasy against the very quest for renewal that he is blatantly putting into practice, both in associating—"collaborating"—with young artists and in returning to a psychodramatic mode of cinema he had abandoned at their age or younger. Therefore, his return to psychodrama at the end of his thirty-year marriage combined elements of regression, desperation, and the weight of the experience of a life of staggeringly prolific filmmaking.

Thus the double perspective of *Faustfilm: An Opera* may be projected into the film through a double identification; for just as the filmmaker is obviously exploring his long dormant empathy with the figure of Faust, he cannot have forgotten the motor principle of his entire mature oeuvre—explicitly stated by the actor of *Blue Moses*: "We're not alone! There's the cameraman...There's a filmmaker in back of *every scene*..." If, indeed, the man behind the camera is necessarily a primary character in every film, then Brakhage is also representing himself, tacitly and sinisterly, as Mephistopheles, or "Faust's friend," the voyeur and almost participant in his amours.

In fact, in casting Joel Haertling, a composer and filmmaker, as "the contemporary Faust I was looking for,"[20] Brakhage happened upon a psychodrama with parallels to the legend: the shift from Gretchen of the first film to Emily of the second records the change of Haertling's paramours; by the third part Haertling was feuding with Brakhage and consequently suffering from a sense of artistic and erotic betrayal by another friend and collaborator. In these young artists and their overlapping music and theater companies, Architects Office and Doll Parts, Brakhage seems to have found a situation similar to the society he knew in his late adolescence with Jordan and Fair.

Sidney Peterson's film, *Mr. Frenhofer and the Minotaur* (1949), the preeminent allegory within the American avant-garde cinema of artistic aspiration and its erotic consequences, preceded Brakhage's indirect evocation of the mature accomplished artist. In the collapsing of the fictional Frenhofer and the historical Picasso, Peterson invented an ironic model for the artist Brakhage's Faust desires to be, and in his reimagining Poussin as an art student he created something of a precursor for Faust himself. In filming the young "Gretchen," the sometimes naked object of Faust's masturbational fantasy, Brakhage nearly reenacts Frenhofer's pact with the artist: Frenhofer will let Poussin see his "unknown masterpiece" if he offers him his mistress, Gilette, as a nude model, to compare his imaginary portrait with a supremely beautiful woman. Poussin's

older friend, Porbus, plays a role similar to Brakhage's Mephistopheles, symbolically dancing with Gilette on a mattress before encouraging and witnessing her modeling for Frenhofer. Therefore it is not surprising that the first
three parts of the Faust series are indebted and pay homage to the films of
Peterson, with whom Brakhage had intended to study when he moved to San
Francisco in the early 1950s. *Faustfilm: An Opera* may also derive from *Mr.
Frenhofer and the Minotaur* its use of voice-over, mise-en-scène (action limited to a few interior sets and emphasis on the gestures of unheard figures in
conversation). There is even a comparable focus of visual excitement: an isolated circular disk—in *Mr. Frenhofer and the Minotaur* the interior mechanism
of a music box, in *Faustfilm* a prismatic mobile in the shape of a wheel. Yet the
most revealing allusions to Peterson's masterpiece[21] are deferred to the second
part, *Faust's Other: An Idyll*, in which the overall tone suggests Brakhage's early
Cat's Cradle (1959) and even Anger's *Inauguration of a Pleasure Dome* (1958)
more than *Mr. Frenhofer and the Minotaur*: the copresence of a female fencer
and a cat, Peterson's uncanny displacements of Theseus and the minotaur.
Finally, anamorphic cinematography, the dominant stylistic feature of *Mr.
Frenhofer and the Minotaur,* does not enter the Faust series until the third film,
Candida Albacore, which owes much more to Peterson's (and Broughton's) *The
Potted Psalm* (1947), a film without anamorphosis, than to *Mr. Frenhofer and
the Minotaur.*

   In his chapter on Peterson in *Film at Wit's End* Brakhage praised his ability
to "assume a woman's viewpoint," comparing him to D. H. Lawrence.[22] One of
several elaborate ironies Peterson marshals in *Mr. Frenhofer and the Minotaur*
gives the organizing voice-over to a female art student and model who,
moving across the threshold of sleep, imagines herself as Picasso's Ariadne and
as Gilette, the heroine of Balzac's *Le chef-d'oeuvre inconnu*, Poussin's mistress,
and the model for Frenhofer's almost Galatean portrait of the ideal woman.
Brakhage's recognition of the perspectivism Peterson gained by creating a female protagonist may account for his curious note for *Candida Albacore*: "...it
is the modern Walpurgisnacht to Faust, but the daydream of 'his' Emily: it
exists that a woman have, finally, something of her ritual included in the myth
of Faustus...and that 'muthos' /'mouth' become a vision."[23]

   If, as Brakhage's catalogue notes indicate, *Candida Albacore* corresponds
to the Walpurgisnacht (there is one in each of the two parts of Goethe's
drama), *Faust's Other: An Idyll* would be his version of the Helena drama.
Thus "Emily," who replaces "Gretchen" of *Faustfilm*, would function as
Helena, even though the narrative evaporates after the first film of the series.
Brakhage does not repeat the death of Helena's child (Euphorion in Goethe
and Duncan, Echo in Mann); the role of Faust's son simply withers away as
the series goes on. Mephistopheles (called "Faust's friend"), too, disappears
after the initial film, unless the title *Faust's Other: An Idyll* derives from
the preface "To the Wary but Not Unwilling Reader" of Paul Valéry's *Mon

Faust: "The personality of Faust, like that of his fearful partner, has an indefinite right to fresh incarnations.... The creator of Faust, and of the Other, brought them to birth so that they might, through him, become instruments of the world's imagination..."[24] In that case, we might say the Other moves behind the camera, or recedes within Faust, or both. Without this questionable clue, the "other" in the title would seem to be "Emily," Faust's [other] companion.[25]

Faust's Other combines glimpses of domestic life with preparations for a stage drama—painting sets, making props, composing music—which presumably becomes the focus of *Candida Albacore*. It ends with Emily caressing Faust as he holds a cocktail. In a 1955 scenario published in *Metaphors on Vision*, Brakhage had written: "The legend of Everest is Faust in reverse.... [His] flights of fancy are interfered with by...a young woman who loves him. The scene between them realizes that she has more claim to his body than he has.... Once the young woman has left him for a time, that time becomes a trial in torment. He is confronted with his own selfishness."[26] It remains a credible gloss on the connection between the second and fourth parts.

Faust 4 explores the landscape of the Rockies and the Southwest in a rhythmic mesh of images shot from moving vehicles with periodic reference to shots of Faust and Emily, now familiar from the second part. The fourth act of *Faust Foutu* may be the model for this conclusion, but Duncan goes even further in discarding his dramatis personae, replacing them with five independent voices. The whole series schematically suggests that the mastery Faust gains is a masturbatory self-deception; he gets the power to attract women seriatim, but his brief idyll of energy and connubial harmony only results in an artistic failure, from which he flees or attempts to flee.[27]

Much more than a narrative sequence, the Faust films are occasions for the filmmaker to return to the scenes of his aesthetic origins and his artistic growth. The editing rhythm and colors of *Faust's Other* recall *Cat's Cradle*, one of his breakthrough lyric films. In it he refracts the tensions he and Jane, then newly married, brought into the home of his friends, James Tenney and Carolee Schneemann—like "Faust" and "Emily" a composer-painter couple who had performed together in his *Loving*. Brakhage is speaking:

> By part 4 I had to work my way out because I knew by then that I had to free myself from psychodrama, and from the dramatics of *Faust* itself, and inherit the landscape again. *Part 4* is the obliteration by single frame of the memories of the past in the swell of the earth and in the desert. Also, by this time, I had met and fallen in love with Marilyn, and the film resulted from a road trip we took during which I photographed the landscapes of the west and the midwest. So in Part 4 there is no story really—but a going to the desert to rid myself of these "pictures" and encompass the whole spectrum of sky and earth and what lies between the two.[28]

This statement echoes remarkably the interview-introduction of *Metaphors on Vision* conducted thirty years earlier, in which the young filmmaker described his growth as an artist as a function of ridding himself of psychodrama at the time he met and married Jane, although now intensified by the allusion to John the Baptist and the desert Fathers. The Faust series, as such, schematizes the movement of Brakhage's much earlier career: a narrative psychodrama provides the basis for a more complex, subjectively filmed, "free indirect" psychodrama, and a commissioned film precedes and spurs on a liberation from both narrative and psychodramatic conventions in a new crisis film of expressive camera movements. This crude outline would make *Faustfilm: An Opera* the counterpart of his first film, *Interim* (1952), and *Faust's Other: An Idyll* the equivalent of the more intricate and subjectively photographed psychodramas of 1955 to 1957 with elements from the early transitional lyrics *In Between*, *Nightcats*, and *Loving*. *Candida Albacore* can be called a commissioned film only insofar as it centers on the work of the company Doll Parts and may have benefited from a grant to support regional arts. In his artistic development, the commission from Joseph Cornell to film the 3rd Avenue El in New York was a crucial spur to Brakhage's origination of his lyrical mode, even though the resulting film, *Wonder Ring*, lacks the power of his subsequent, more personal lyrics. Finally, with *Faust 4* he ended the series with a work parallel to his breakthrough film, *Anticipation of the Night* (1958), in which there are traces of a psychodramatic frame story—the shadow protagonist hangs himself at the end—but the originality of the work lies in his exquisite articulation of camera movement and contrapuntal montage.

The Faust films are not just an exorcism of the ghosts of Brakhage's earlier career. They reflect the themes and modes of the strongest films he made just before them and immediately after. The texts of their soundtracks are even the nuclei of Brakhage's theoretical writing in the 1990s. Let me take the latter point first. The use of voice-over in the first, second, and fourth films in the series is a radical departure for Brakhage; the only previous instance of voice-over in his filmography had been the aberrant film *The Stars Are Beautiful* (1974), in which the filmmaker recited a series of fanciful cosmologies. In *Faustfilm: An Opera* the spoken narrative controls the film's plot, providing us with Faust's history, motivations, and thoughts. But from the start of *Faust's Other: An Idyll*, the voice-over enters a new, and a startlingly original mode. Without mentioning Faust once or even alluding to the legend, the spoken text elaborates in dense poetic language a theory of auratic vision and its relation to affects. This prose poem on the process of isolating pictures from the field of vision eventually leads to a visionary analysis of love:

> All is a'tremble, the waves of light, the eye itself enpulsed and continuously triggering its moods, the jelly of its vitreous humor (the first bent of light), the wet electrical synapse of each transmission, the sparking brain; but then

comes the imagination of stillness midst the meeting of incoming light and discrete sparks of nerve feed-back, the pecking-order of memory which permits cognizance of only such and thus such, and imposes-on each incoming illumination an exactitude of shape and separates each such with a thus/distancing in the imagination: it thereby creates, of the dance of the inner and incoming light, imaginary tensions. These tensions, then, in taut network containment of these shapes constitute warp/woof of memories "pick" of shapes acceptable to the imagination. The entire fretwork of these picked shapes at "taught" distance from each other are/therefore, in the mind's eye, the composition of image. The moves-of-shapes within the elasticity of such networking is/are the gestalt of acceptably sparked picturing; and the whole-of-the-process is the domain of picture.

....The very air trembles with the electric possibilities of this dance. The vapors round the cells stance-dance. The synapse is arrested, or as-if arrested which stops all known-dance. Leaps of an as-if imagnosis opts for aura. Little threads-of-color are warp to the woof of shadow-aura-gateway then. The eyes in drowse-of-love be fit to blur these weaves to an as-if-enlargement, vibrant as plucked strings seen slow-motional as unwinded fog or psychological haze. Magic!

My punctuation of these passages and even the accuracy of some clipped or slurred words has been abetted by access to the typescript of *The Dominion of Picture*, a long theoretical text unpublished at the time of this writing.[29] If, as we may reasonably conclude, *The Dominion of Picture* was written during the period of the making of *Faust's Other*, the context in the book of such passages may illuminate the perspective of the voice-over of the film. *The Dominion of Picture* is a long love letter incorporating the author's experience of love-making and masturbational fantasies into an explication of the nuances of his optical epiphenomena. It is addressed to "Dear Reader," although its tone forcefully suggests it was written initially for a particular lover, probably his future wife, Marilyn.

Unlike the voice-over of *Faustfilm*, there is no irony or authorial distance in these elaborations of aesthetic psychology. They become the free indirect discourse of Faust's thought. Yet the structural irony of the four-part whole indicates that this collapsing of filmmaker and protagonist, vividly represented in the fusion of words and image, is the paradigmatic moment of error, a dangerous seduction. "Sound is crucial for psychodrama principally because there is a lack of, what I would call, vision," Brakhage said to Ganguly. "What is psychodrama after all but the drama that's in the mind, and the extent to which you approach dramas, even in the oblique way that I did in *Faust*, involves engaging with picture and continuity as well as a whole hierarchy of symbols. In the absence of vision sound becomes necessary to stitch the loose threads together and make it all bearable."[30]

Six minutes before the end of the series a short monologue suggests Faust's redemption in terms of death and rebirth, darkness and sight, being and knowing, with echoing reverberations of the syllable *own*, and an un-heard anagrammatic play on *now*: "...and all that was kn*own* is *now* newly known.... Multitudinous montane shapes vie with inner clouds' geometries so that 'that,' that was, is *now* reborn one. To wear/ the curve/ of earth itself, be weave, bear black's intrusion on one's closed, kn*own*, old illusional buzz of being; what one was is *now* one's end-z*one*. Gone to ground being then the very saw-teeth of the comb s*own* between sky and mind. The wild mountains of eyes' irregularities and all that was kn*own* be *now* then one's *own*."

The catalogue note for the film reflects this language, while providing a synopsis much more explicit than the film itself: "This is the imaged thought process of the young Faust escaping the unbearable pictures of his broken romantic idyll, mentally fleeing the particulars of his dramatized 'love,' Faust's mind ranging the geography of his upbringing and its structures of cultural hubris—the whole nervous system 'going to ground' and finally 'becoming one' with the hypnogogically visible cells of his receptive sight and inner cog-nition... and all that I could give him of Heaven in this current visualization of these ancient themes."[31] Actually, there is a concentration of images from *Faust's Other* during the speech near the opening, but visual echoes of it recur infrequently and separated by long intervals; they have disappeared totally by the time the second text is heard. Instead, the film is an elaborate mesh of shots from a moving automobile, often in superimposition. Synchronized to the phrase "symbols of human hubris," the image of a monumental sculpture of praying hands appears for the first time. The montage suggests the vanity of aspirations to permanence by associating this bronze inflation of piety with the mysterious ruins of Mesa Verde and the mournful look of the weathered house where Brakhage lived as a baby. The superimpositions of the ruins of Mesa Verde and the wooden house in near-dilapidation suggest that these (and other modernistic structures from the campus of Oral Roberts University) are icons of the "error of envisioned meaning," from which Faust flees through the desert and past a body of water to a neutral, flat, rural landscape. But since the weathered house is, in fact, Brakhage's first home in Winfield, Kansas, the oscillation between filmmaker-narrator and the film's ostensible protagonist continues at least in this obscure personal reference to the "geography of his upbringing." From this opening a melancholy tone dominates the film.

Ironically allegorizing the breakdown of their collaboration, Haertling told me: "Brakhage sent me to Hell, while he went off on a trip with Marilyn." The film, however, suggests that a more accurate description might be that Brakhage was extricating himself from the problematic psychodrama of his Faust project when he fell in love with the woman who would soon become his wife. It is as if he accented the melancholy—"Faustian"—dimension of the landscape at the very time that he was grasping a new, enlarged vision of it.

Thus *Faust 4* documents that extrication and sketches out his next project, the brilliant *Visions in Meditation*, a series of four films made in 1989 and 1990. It rekindled his confidence in the eloquence of the embodied moving camera and resolved the crisis that engendered the initial return to Faust.

In fact, the phrase "vision in meditation" first occurs in the opening commentary of *Faust 4*. However, the four periegeta that make up the *Visions in Meditation* lack the grimness of that film. Even the spectacular *Visions in Meditation 2: Mesa Verde*, which tries to articulate the horror Brakhage felt at the site, is an exuberantly beautiful, vibrant film. As he travels through Canada and New England (in the first) or studies a "dust devil" or miniature tornado in *Visions in Mediation 3: Plato's Cave* (1990) or makes a pilgrimage to D. H. Lawrence's home in Taos (in the fourth section, 1990), Brakhage films and edits with renewed energy and acuity. The melancholy that pervades the Faust series and clings to the periegeton of *Faust 4* dissipates in these films; in its place comes a vital engagement with the landscape and a depth of wonder and visual intelligence unsurpassed in all of Brakhage's cinema.

The sustained crises of the late 1980s that brought Brakhage to return to the psychodramatic form of his early career in making the Faust series coincided with his more fundamental shift away from cinematic mimesis. It is well known that Marilyn Jull did not want Brakhage to make her or their future children the subjects of his films, as Jane and the five children he had with her had been. However, this does not adequately account for the dominant change of style in Brakhage's cinema. He had been growing uneasy with pictorial representation throughout the 1980s. Subtle nuances of photographed light and color modulations had become the material of his *The Roman Numeral Series* and *Arabics*; it was a process he would sustain and extend by etching and painting directly onto film stock in his cinematic meditations on hieroglyphics and calligraphy in his *The Egyptian Series, Babylon Series, The Persian Series* and his final sequence, *Chinese Series* (2003). He linked this process to his considerations of poetic history and revelation in his masterful *The Dante Quartet*, which incorporated the hand-painted *Hell Spit Flexion* (1981).

In the 1990s and until Brakhage's death in 2002, hand-painted films would predominate. From the late 1950s on, all of his films had hand-etched titles. He painted over the photography of the birth of his third child, Neowyn, and associated the experience of viewing the birth with superimposed animal images in *Thigh Line Lyre Triangular*. He used the same technique sporadically all though *Dog Star Man*.

He wrote in "The Lost Films":

> ...I only became aware of what I sometimes call "visual ineffables" in my work when I first showed the film *Nodes* (1981), a four-minute hand-painted film...In my program description of the film I used the word "cathexis" for the first time in a film blurb. This whole Freudian psychological concept is

evoked in an attempt to elucidate the creative process that produced the film and resonate with the title word, "node," which *Webster's* defines as a "*point at which subsidiary parts originate or center*" (my italics).

The "subsidiary parts" seem to me a fair corollary of the previously mentioned peripheral visions, unacknowledged sights, which collect a host of associative memories and thus seed dreams. The Greek word "cathexis" (as Freud uses it) seems to suggest "holding" or "investment," at the moments of neurological synapse, but it also suggests "haunt." Are these little overlooked films, then, akin to ghosts—now you see them/now you don't? But isn't the notion intrinsic to cinema in general?

The capacity to remember *any* imagery from the flowing-river experience of motion pictures is exactly dependent upon one's capacity to *name* what one has seen. A picture is (as I define it) a collection of namable shapes framed (i.e., in interrelated composition). But it is almost impossible to name the motions of these shapes-as-things in other than the most general way.. .

Only a ghost film could possibly break thought-bonds of language and exist as, say, movement haunt, tone-texture haunt, ineffable-haunt...Such a film might eventually prompt whole new ways of recollection that are essentially free from language—indeed might prompt whole new definitions of what "language" might eventually come to be...an un-nouned, non-dichotomous series of light-glyphs available for arrangements of cathectic exchanges which directly reflect each person's synapsing inner nervous system.[32]

"Visual ineffables," then, include hand-painted films, etched films, photographed films that elude "namable" images, and the fusions of these techniques. Thus *Passage Through: A Ritual* (1990), his fifty-minute long minimalist response to Philip Corner's composition *Through the Mysterious Barricade, Lumen 1 (After F. Couperin)*, itself a musical homage to *The Riddle of Lumen*, would be an extension of this domain into the area of synchronized sound. Brakhage edited short bursts of frames from about two minutes of flashing lights into a matrix of black leader to make this film, the longest of the eighty films he made in the 1990s, excepting *A Child's Garden and the Serious Sea* (1991), which at seventy-four minutes is the longest work without subdivisions in Brakhage's enormous corpus of films.

Because virtually all of the work that the filmmaker made in the final thirteen years of his life would correspond to the definition he gives of "visible ineffables," it would seem useful to consider the Vancouver Island tetralogy—*A Child's Garden and the Serious Sea*, *The Mammals of Victoria* (1994), *The God of Day Had Gone Down upon Him* (2000), and *Panels for the Walls of Heaven* (2002)—under that rubric. Most of the eighty films he made in that period eschew photography; they are etched or hand painted. The rare exceptions to the "ineffable" mode include some films given to him that he reworked from Charles Boultenhouse and Joseph Cornell and the extraordinary four-minute-long *Christ Mass Sex Dance* (1991), a work in superimposition photographed at a performance of the *Nutcracker* ballet and edited to James Tenney's sound collage, *Blue Suede*, which harks back to the filmmaker's earlier critiques of mass culture, such as his *Oh Life—a Woe Story—The A-Test News* (1963), *Western History* (1971), and *Murder Psalm* (1980). Furthermore, even as he was returning to the psychodrama to make the Faust series, he was writing the longest theoretical text of his later years, *The Dominion of Picture* (which he retitled *The Domain of Aura*).

Although Bruce Elder has written of *A Child's Garden and the Serious Sea* as a revision of *Scenes from Under Childhood*, I take the film to be a palinode to *Anticipation of the Night* primarily and to the autobiographical films in which children predominate (including *Scenes from Under Childhood*) secondarily.[33] There is always a dialectical complexity when childhood is at stake in Brakhage's work. He is haunted by what Hart Crane called the promise of "an improved infancy" ("Passage"). In fact, Crane's "Passage" and "Voyages II," which Brakhage may not have known, might serve to guide us through *A Child's Garden and the Serious Sea* as effectively as the poems he explicitly cites in his catalog notes on the film, Ronald Johnson's *ARK* and Charles Olson's "Maximus, from Dogtown—I." This should not be surprising insofar as all three poems are variants of the fundamental American sea chant, established by Whitman and echoing through Eliot and Stevens, as well as Crane and Olson.

The filmmaker's own accounts of his childhood were "Dickensian": adopted as a baby by a couple in crisis (the father eventually moved away with his male lover), the asthmatic, obese child spent time in an orphanage and a foster home. Later, he was obsessed with imagining the growth of a child's perception, especially sight, from the prenatal stage to the acquisition of speech and concomitant socialization. In *Anticipation of the Night* the twenty-five-year-old filmmaker envisions a shadow protagonist who contemplates a baby crawling in grass, as well as children sleeping and on amusement park rides, before hanging himself. *Scenes from Under Childhood* examines the movements and activities of his own children in an effort to represent the ecstasies and terrors of infantile perception. In *Sincerity (Reel One)* (1973) he draws on photographs from his childhood and that of Jane to reconstruct a schematic meditation on the processes of memory focused on childhood experiences.

In these and in many other films based on observing the first five of his seven children, a melancholy countersong intimates the vanity of his efforts to recapture preverbal cognition. To paraphrase Brakhage's first theoretical book, *A Child's Garden and the Serious Sea* proposes further metaphors on childhood vision. The effort is metaphorical in that it can never be literal. Brakhage recognized, as early as *Anticipation of the Night*, that he could only invent cinematic figures that troped the visual experience of children; he could never reproduce it. So he acknowledges at the beginning of *Metaphors on Vision* that regression is impossible:

> But one can never go back, not even in imagination. After the loss of inno-cence, only the ultimate of knowledge can balance the wobbling pivot. Yet I suggest there is a pursuit of knowledge foreign to language and founded on visual communication, demanding a development of the optical mind, and dependent on perception in the original and deepest sense of the word.

Thus his version of Crane's "promise" of "an improved infancy," accessible through filmmaking, has to be a sublime fantasy. Furthermore, each of Brakhage's radical revisions of that project is a palinode of all the previous attempts. Yet fundamentally, the filmmaker's quest for a cinematic trope of childhood vision is a central manifestation of the core dilemma of his art—that even though of all the arts cinema offers the greatest possibility of repre-senting the visual process, yet it can never adequately mimic eyesight.

By the 1990s his very conception of eyesight had evolved into a dual process, as he succinctly summarized it in his creedal statement, "Having Declared a Belief in God" (1995):

> The twin aspects of seeing, (1) the sheer reception of the entire fiery illumi-nation of the world, its bounce-light, and (2) cathexis-of-such into visual thinking, *can* be guided (in imitation of language, perhaps) to co-exist at once and one, like the yes/no or then/now of unconscious process. It is as if that which sparks the meat-tongue and heaves the diaphragm into such shaping of air as we call "speech" can also cathect, haunt, *invest* light waves, sparked optics, and the electricity of thought into memorable coherency with*out* any loss of one's sense of chaos (i.e., chaos; "a state of things in which chance is supreme," as *Webster's* has it).[34]

The shift of theoretical focus from the duality of seeing with continual eye movements and closed-eye vision to this "twin aspects of seeing" is slight but important. As early as 1963 Brakhage had claimed in the introductory in-terview to *Metaphors on Vision* that during the shooting of *Thigh Line Lyre Triangular* he could see "brain movies" as he filmed the birth of Neowyn: "At moments like that, I get flashes of what I call 'brain movies.' I'm taking Michael McClure's term there; he said, 'When you get a solid structure image that you know is not out there, but is being recalled so intensely that you literally see it in a flash, that's a brain movie.' Most people only get them with their eyes closed...It was as if something had gotten backed up in my mind, so that it could release symbolic terms at me as soon as it had a crisis." By the 1990s the twin aspects of seeing implied that the epistemological priority had shifted from perception of the external world (with secondary, superimposed mem-ory images triggered by a crisis) to a primary rhythmic moiling of liminally visible electrostatic charges on which all recognizable imagery is organized—his own speculative "beyond the picture principle."

If the cathexis of "moving visual thinking" constitutes the theoretical foundation of Brakhage's hand-painted and scratched films in the final phase of his career, the "twin aspects of seeing" underlies most of his photographed films after 1987. Consequently, the first three films of the Vancouver Island series represent Brakhage's most elaborate attempt to refigure and reposition the natural world within the magma of "moving visual thinking," while the fourth is his longest and most ecstatic hymn to the "cathexis-of-such." Brakhage shot *A Child's Garden and the Serious Sea* in 1990 when he and Marilyn paid a visit to her family home. Their periodic returns to the island entailed further filming, so that the first film became the start of an unanticipated series that would eventually incorporate *The Mammals of Victoria* and *The God of Day Had Gone Down upon Him*. When, at last, the filmmaker retired from the University of Colorado to settle in Victoria, British Columbia, he extended the trilogy into a tetralogy with *Panels for the Walls of Heaven*. Brakhage's bladder cancer, diagnosed and operated on in 1996, and its recurrence in 2002 inflected the perspective and tone of the two final films of the series.

According to Fred Camper: "The Vancouver Island films represent Brakhage's imaginary biography of Marilyn: 'I wished that Marilyn and I could have grown up next door to each other and began a family. I missed her whole childhood and adolescence, so I'm trying to give my sense of such a thing.' Filmed in and around Victoria, British Columbia, where Marilyn grew up, they include snippets of her childhood home and garden and extensive footage of the sea—which Brakhage, who was raised in Kansas, didn't see until his early 20s."[35] The fiction of retracing his wife's optical biography was a fecund pretext for yet another quest for an improved infancy for Brakhage. He sustained that fiction through *The Mammals of Victoria*, but the shock of his cancer treatment may have dispelled it from the two later films of the series, in which he seems to trope his own mortality. This reflects a pattern he repeated throughout his career. He was never able to sustain a preconceived superstructure without making significant alterations as the series progressed. In fact, his pragmatic suspicion of such structures is one of his great strengths. *Scenes from Under Childhood*, the *Sincerity/Duplicity* films, the "Faust" series, and even *Dog Star Man* (though to a much lesser extent) dissolve their systemic structures and abandon their dialectical logic before they are completed. His catalogue note for *A Child's Garden and the Serious Sea* does not mention the imaginative biography, but it introduces another contemporary poet into the pantheon of his influences:

In poet Ronald Johnson's great epic *Ark*, in the first book *Foundations*, the poem "Beam 29" has this passage: "The seed is disseminated at the gated mosaic a hundred feet / below, above / long windrows of motion / connecting dilated arches undergoing transamplification: / 'seen in the water so clear as christiall' / (prairie tremblante)" which breaks into musical notation that, "presto," becomes a design of spatial tilts: This is where the film began; and I carried a xerox of the still unpublished *ARK* 50 through 66 all that trip with Marilyn and Anton [their first son] around Vancouver Island. As I wrote him, "The pun 'out on a limn' kept ringing through my mind as I caught the hairs of side-light off ephemera of objects tangent to Marilyn's childhood: She grew up in Victoria; and there I was in her childhood back-yard...": and then there was The Sea—not as counter-balance but as hidden generator of it all, of the The World to be discovered by the/any child...as poet Charles Olson has it: "Vast earth rejoices, / deep-swirling Okeanos steers all things through all things, / everything issues from the one, the soul is led from drunkenness / to dryness, the sleeper lights up from the dead, / the man awake lights up from the sleeping" (*Maximus, from Dogtown—I*).

Brakhage once had felt such a fierce commitment to reading his contempo-raries that he resisted owning the books of long-dead authors. By the time he began the Vancouver Island films, several of the poets whom he had read religiously were dead: Williams (d. 1963), Olson (d. 1970), Pound (d. 1972), Zukofsky (d. 1978), and Duncan (d. 1988). Michael McClure (b. 1932) con-tinued to inspire him, and the poetry of Ronald Johnson (1935–1998) gradually assumed a preeminent place in his reading; in *ARK* he believed he had found the modernist Paradiso he had long sought.[36]

His reading had always been selective and extraordinarily intense. Phrases he plucked from his contemporaries' poems became tools for his description of his own work and the world in general; some of these formulae recurred in his writings and speech for more than forty years. One such instance would be McClure's metaphor of "a solid moving through an inferno." His attention to detail and the assimilation of elements from the language of the poets he read faithfully may have made him somewhat resistant to the sort of typolog-ical commentary on poetry I frequently invoke in my writings on avant-garde cinema. Whereas I have emphasized the relationships between his films and types of poems he read obsessively, he would insist on the particularity of the poets' words and phrases as his source of inspiration.

I do not mean to dismiss the specific attraction of *ARK* to Brakhage.[37] In the first place, he believed he had deep affinities with Johnson: they were both born in Kansas and had felt passionate attachments as children to L. Frank Baum's Oz books; they traced their poetic lineages to Pound and Williams, took Zukofsky, Duncan, and Olson as their mentors, and shared at times a close friend in Guy Davenport. From the many recurring references in *ARK*, Brakhage found reflected his own attractions to Rilke, Simon Rodia, Blake, and Ives, making *ARK* more immediately accessible to him than *The Cantos, Patterson, A, Passages,* or *Maximus* had been. More significantly,

Johnson abjured the historical references and the political polemics characteristic of those other long poems, as Brakhage always had done in his films. Furthermore, the absence of autobiographical material in *ARK* should have attracted Brakhage as he was turning away from the autobiographical dimension of so much of his earlier work.[38] Yet far more striking than these affinities, I believe, would have been Johnson's attention to the nature of eyesight, his grounding of the poem in mineral, vegetable, and animal phenomena, and his use of puns as markers of the irreducible mediation of language. *ARK* begins its unending paean to light with a bird's-eye view of earth, sun, and sea, invoking angels (an obsessive metaphor for Brakhage) as units of the speed of light:

Over the rim
Body of earth   rays exit sun
Rest to full velocity to eastward pinwheeled in a sparrow's

eye
—Jupiter compressed west to the other—

wake waves on wave in wave stripped White Throat song

along the reversal of one
contra-
centrifugal
water to touch, all knowledge

as if a central silver
backlit in gust.

All night the golden fruit fell softly to the air,
pips ablaze, our eyes skinned back.
Clouds loom below. Pocket moon fills half the sky. Stars
Comb out its lumen
horizon
in a gone-to-seed dandelion
as of snowflakes hitting black water, time, and again,

the dot the plain
186,282 cooped up angels tall as appletrees

caryatid
one sudden tide of day
O
wide bloom the pathed earth yawn

on purpose porpoised pattern
this reeled world whistling joist its polished fields of sun
pulse race in a vase of beings, bearings
all root fold forms upon
to center eternity
or enter it
instruments of change.

And bareback as Pegasus guess us

The intricate web of images and the cascading rhythm of their enjambment might be said to correspond to the silent play of film shots in the first three of Brakhage's Vancouver Island films. The qualities they share with Johnson's poetry conform to the fundamentally American crisis lyric. However, Brakhage seems to have had little interest in the idea that both *ARK* and "*Maximus from Dogtown—I*" might be variants of Whitman's "A Word Out of the Sea" and "As I Ebbed with the Ebb of the Ocean of Life," and still less in modernist versions by poets outside of his usual reading, such as Crane's "Voyages," Eliot's "Dry Salvages" from *Four Quartets*, Stevens's "Ideas of Order at Key West" and "Like Decorations in a Nigger Cemetery," and Ashbery's *A Wave*. Yet, as I said above, locating the Vancouver films as an offshoot of that line of poetry may guide us to recognize in them confrontations with death and origins, beyond the trope of his imagining Marilyn Jull's schematic biography. The filmmaker, meditating on the rhythms of the sea, the alternations of day and night, and the vegetative cycle, takes stock of his circumstances: that he was remarried in his late fifties, with an infant son, thrust into the middle-class environs of his young wife's family. In making *A Child's Garden and the Serious Sea* he was deliberately divesting his art of "all melodramatic self-imagining."[39] That divestment meant eschewing, or at least radically reimagining, the imagery, symbolism, and structures of such earlier achievements as the suicide lyric, *Anticipation of the Night*, and the graveyard meditation, *The Dead*.

In his superlative essay on the initial three Vancouver films, Paul Arthur asserted: "...the three films ha[ve] as much to do with the filmmaker's own imagined states of development as those of his wife. Due to the manner in which they were shot and edited, these works are exceptionally difficult to describe..." Still, he makes a stunning effort at capturing their look succinctly:

Moreover, the repertoire of techniques employed in rendering aqueous states is relatively straight-forward: zooms and nonlinear camera movements of several types, contrasting color film stocks, different camera speeds, gradations of exposure and focal setting, several different lenses, and occasional hand-formed mattes. Transitions between adjacent shots tend to be fluid, matched on speed or direction of movement, often softened by intervening black frames; hence, there are few instances of montage collision or metric exchanges between clusters of images.... All three feature land-based vegetation, from bright flower gardens to dim overhead views of a forest. Dogs, waterfowl, and other birds make fleeting appearances. Several types of boats, buildings perched on a distant shore-line, hands, the exterior of a house, a tacky amusement park are motifs that bridge at least two of the films. The point of this rough inventory is to suggest that, when viewed in order, it is possible to establish common threads without ever intuiting an overall thematic trajectory or progressive formal development.[40]

The film may be seen as a long, sustained attempt to reduce the natural world (garden, ocean) to the core of "moving visual thinking," the source or matrix of all visualization according to Brakhage. The minimalization of human figures, rarely seen and always so ephemeral as to make individuals indistinguishable, reflects the idea that Marilyn Jull "senses falsification" in being photographed.[41] The divestment of "melodramatic self-imagining" entails the reduction of such "falsification." The first human image, of a young child sitting on grass in the upper portion of the frame, does not occur until some twenty-eight minutes have elapsed. Up until that fleeting moment there had rarely been a shot held long enough or with a sufficiently wide view to give a sense of where the film-maker stood in taking the image.

Initially, the interweaving of garden and ocean, which occurs throughout the film, was composed of fragments so brief and so close that for some seven minutes the recognizable imagery blended with the prevailing blackness from which points of light emerged and danced. The filmmaker makes much of the specular highlights or lens spots most professionals try to eliminate. The octagonal or dodecahedral spots clearly alert the viewer that the cinemato-graphic mechanism is generating its own imagery. Technically, the bright light of the reflected sun bounding off the blades of the lens diaphragm creates these geometric shapes. Brakhage seems to employ them as metaphors for the "firing of synapses" in "moving visual thinking." They might also be seen as crystallizations of light, mediating between the eye and the sun, in the terms of *ARK*'s "Beam 5," in which Johnson speculates: "After a long time of light, there began to be eyes, and the light began looking with itself. At the moment of death the pupils open full width."

In these early minutes the blackness repeatedly gives way to flash-frames interrupting the prevailing darkness that elides shifts of camera direction. Initially, the space of the film is primarily optical, without clear clues about the location of the filmmaker. Then, in the sixth minute, a full-frame image of the sea begins to define the geographical space, which alternates between the garden and the sea, but we never learn where the one spatial field stands in relation to the other. Correspondingly, we get a temporary sense of the filmmaker's position at this point in the film, when he shoots up at the branches of trees and the sky beyond them.

Early on he catches sight of a whale turning in the sea. There is a glimpse of a house at eleven minutes and upside-down lawn furniture at eighteen, when the child appears. This radical fragmentation precludes the development of any event in the film that would require two consecutive shots to elaborate or conclude it. In short, "nothing happens" in *A Child's Garden and the Serious Sea*, or in any of the Vancouver Island films, for that matter. The throbbing of the sea is the most stable action throughout the first three films of the series, but even the steady rhythm of breaking waves becomes subject to the altering speeds of Brakhage's filming and the manipulations of his montage. Such scattered images inevitably evoke the natural cycles of seasons, tides, flowering, and decay, but the structure of the film does not accentuate or even follow these cycles. Paul Arthur made the point eloquently when he wrote, "the twin spectorial tasks of ordering successive moments into coherent patterns and anticipating what might come next are, to a significant degree, confounded."[42]

A conversation between Brakhage and Ronald Johnson, originally filmed for Jim Shedden's documentary portrait *Brakhage* (1998), offers some interesting, if enigmatic, clues to how the filmmaker thought the argument of his film was structured:

> When we're sunk in all this adulthoodness, and the child's imagination is trying to make it leap into some semblance of flower, something fit to weave with the sea, Nick [Dorsky] saw that my hand starts becoming integral with the lens. You can see parts and bits and pieces and shadows of my hand blocking things out, so my hand comes in to shape, to struggle with and grapple literally with the environs. And Nick saw it come to this point where, and I agree, where Eden *does* get restored. But it's not as it was before, it's now more remembered. It's there amidst a series of emblematic pictures, like the child and the man and the boat and the crow. It's not as it was. It's remembered, and among a series of things.... I work with ephemera. I can take pictures of them but they remain forever representations. I did try very hard, and took the kinds of pictures that would be supportive or inspired by the concepts of [William Carlos] Williams' "No ideas but in things," but in fact it's not that applicable to film, whose nature is fleeting and moving on. It's a weave of light that's forever dissolving.... You can create inferences, since the eye is always roving. The eye is very open to the reverberating spread of what we would call metaphor, I guess, in language, open to a multiplicity of visual means, but not an endless multiplicity. There's a skein or net of great exactitude.[43]

Here Brakhage implies that within the film there is a movement from the Eden or ecstasy of childhood, in which the garden can "weave with the sea," to a painful period of "adulthoodness" that requires a poetic "leap" to recover a memory of that Eden. In this memory state, the images of "things" turn into metaphorical emblems. This scenario, then, corresponds to one Whitman employs in his "A Word Out of the Sea" (also known by its opening line: "Out of the cradle endlessly rocking"). As Whitman wanders the shores of Paumanok, he ventriloquizes the song of a lone bird. He makes the bird a key to both the origin of poetry and his own incarnation as a poet; against the droning background of the maternal sea, chanting death, death, death, the bird's cry becomes an Orphic song of lost love and loneliness.

Brakhage's film is so economical with its images that every manifestation of a new, recognizable sight takes on significance; therefore, when a bird appears flying in the sky forty-two minutes into the film, the "inference" of the image in this context "reverberates' with Whitman's poem. I take this to be exemplary of the functions of what the filmmaker calls the film's "emblematic pictures, like the child and the man and the boat and the crow." Just as his exploration of the environs of his new wife's childhood home opened up the fantasy of an "improved infancy," the ensuing return to origins brought within the horizon of his film (and the three subsequent Victoria Island films) considerations of the origin of art and of his own emergence as an artist. Although Whitman's great poem was probably not in Brakhage's mind when he made these films, it is nevertheless the prototype of American lyrics of poetic incarnation and a direct ancestor of Johnson's *ARK*.

Two minutes after the bird in flight we see for the first time a corny amusement park that will come to dominate the second half of the film. The first adults soon appear, playing miniature golf (54 minutes), then a car or two. The amusement area puts up a greater resistance to abstraction than the sea or garden. In one sense it is a pollutant to the sublime, Adamic vision Brakhage is crafting on Victoria Island. But it is also an ambivalent emblem of the middle-class normalcy which he despises and yet of which he feels deprived. He attempts to gauge that ambivalence here and to a lesser degree in the subsequent film of the series. One of the central tropes of *Anticipation of the Night* had been to participate mimetically, through camera movement and editing, with the children taking amusement park rides at night, in a rhythmic oscillation between elation and more profound deflation. Nearly forty years and more than 200 films later, Brakhage is considerably more subtle and restrained. He keeps an eloquent distance from the theme park, fascinated, disgusted, uncertain what to make of it, discovering instead what he can make with images of it.

In the amusement park there is a giant clock with moving figures. Its blatant commercial appeal to children encapsulates the abstract ordeals of primary education by evoking the idea of learning to "tell time." In fact, Brakhage was engaged in writing a series of articles for the Canadian journal *Musicworks* under the rubric of "temps... on dit," which he would collect in a volume he entitled *Telling Time: Essays of a Visionary Filmmaker* (2003). But it is the vibrant, existential temporality of cinema as constructed by its artists rather than the communal synchronization of the clock he had in mind in using that phrase. The park, in this respect, represents the banality of conventional adult ideas of childhood and its needs, commercially designed to lure parents and entice children. Similarly, a fountain in the park ostentatiously hurls globs of water into the air. It recalls the final image of Marie Menken's *Arabesque for Kenneth Anger*, itself an homage and parody of Brakhage's favorite film by Anger, *Eaux d'Artifice*. In all three films the fountains call up an ejaculating penis; for Anger it is a magical icon into which the moth queen dissolves; Menken, in turn, pokes fun at the phallic idolatry of the gay men with whom she surrounded herself. For Brakhage, this image too is ambivalent. Although he follows Menken, jibing at the iconography to which the Canadian parkgoers blind themselves, he does not shy away from the sexualized optics informing the entire Vancouver Island project.[44]

The most explicit clue to this would be his unpublished book, *The Dominion of Picture*, which might well be understood as the theoretical polemic on behalf of Brakhage's filmmaking during his second marriage. In it he sets out to defend the idea of seeing auras. In addressing the argument to a Reader with whom he postulates an intimate relationship, Brakhage evidently writes the book to and for Marilyn. Convinced that "Aura is most recognizable midst sensuality's measures of body rhythms…," his starting point is the optical phenomena occurring during sexual intercourse: "I want to write first then about sex, to trick flat language into some strum which at least trembles in realm-of-rhythming, exists tangent to the quake grounds of love—else this be but descript and worthless even to give you a picture." "Picture" is an irony here; for the entire book posits "the Domain of Picture" in opposition to aura. In the subsequent forty manuscript pages he meticulously analyzes the relationship among acts of seeing, remembering, and naming that occur as he makes love to her and then thinks about her in her absence:

> …some "us" divided then even midst your/my being around/into each the other, but separated too by each other's confusions and the separate thrwarted-seeming-shared-wishes, but ephemerality of such wishing whereat each of us must rely on different imaginations rather than differences of real flesh meeting/mating, the unreality of it…all of which came, as I came, to such intensity-of-feeling there inside you as I never felt before, as neither of us felt before, if you remember, as if ALL possible love I'm having, either of us are having…were concentrated then/instanter at the tip of my penis being given over to you inside you….
>
> I find the mind tries to hold details of your being, the exact roughage of your hand's life-lines, the bottoms of your feet, the irregular curl of every toe, the ankle mtn./mole-hill volleying into heel, its soft solidity, the ephemeral light ruddiness and reddening all round your foot pad formed from the

weight of life's walk. I'm hating the intrusion of my mind's wish to sense what this foot was when you were six, or three years old, then when fifteen, or in your future, because these imaginings become more real, as if solidified-to-touch inasmuch as they are newer than the last contact my hand has had with your actual flesh; but this enragement, mental also, grapples with the fictions of your childhood skin: the rage and kinder-images both are of MY flesh, not yours, are factors of the immediate meat of the brain; and they struggle with strength of immediacy, and are the thought-upness of *now* triumphing over all dimming memorium of what-once-was.... .

The purity of you remembered thus does not lend its image to masturbatory trickery or any release of flesh-loss-tension but rather is held aglow in the mind-heart's unmeasured timeless pleasure, whereas fingers as if vined spiraling around my penis...all the packed artifactual eruptions of memory process could,/would I willfully pursue, explode sperm from the dark erect slit tip-of-penis purpled with the desperation of my blood...and I'd be calm, be becalmed, in this exchange of (1) love's lit thought for (2) sperm-in-air, of living memory as carrier of your being within me for imagination's wit-end of me being in you.

Presumably, this theoretical essay derives from a love letter the filmmaker composed shortly after his intimacy with his future wife commenced. The middle passage of the three I have here quoted (with some condensations) represents, in somewhat negative terms, the scenario in which he later outlined the Vancouver Island films. Although the films themselves make no direct allusions to his or Marilyn's erotic life, the primacy of the erotic imagination in Brakhage's thought accounts for the frequent displacements of sexual references in these, as in most of his other films.

Although there is hardly an image in *A Child's Garden and the Serious Sea* that is stable—that is, without a shift of focus, camera movement, or intensity of exposure—we can consider the glimpses we get of the exterior world in the last minute as a symbolical finale. After several returns to a small bird pecking at a shard of flesh on the shore—this may be what Brakhage calls "the bird" in his catalog of emblems unless he refers to the one in flight, or both—we see two figures in a rowboat, either just putting out to the sea or about to land—the brevity of the image and the combination of minute zooms and shifts of exposure make the direction ambiguous. Then, in rapid camera sweeps, we rush past the house and garden and view trees from below. Placed thus at the end of the film, these trees recall those of *Anticipation of the Night* on which the shadow-protagonist hanged himself. The centrality of an amusement park in both films cements the association. The film not only divests itself of the earlier work's "melodramatic self-imagining" but even puts the notion of "self-imagining" into question.[45] In a cosmos made up of "bounce-light" and proprioceptive energies, the self becomes a dubious, intermittent construct.

The scavenger bird, the rowers, and the house and garden are simply there, and yet there are inevitable intimations that they are psychic projections. The filmmaker-subject is both the bird and its prey; the rowers can stand for Brakhage and his wife, in idle recreation or poised at the verge of oceanic mortality in a hopelessly flimsy vessel. Such, the film finally suggests, are the thoughts of a man at the threshold of old age, in the backyard of his in-laws' coastal home. Thus in *A Child's Garden* Brakhage seeks a version of Ronald Johnson's splendor of light despite the reflective melancholy that sometimes intrudes on his otherwise buoyant spirit of renewal. This is *Anticipation of the Night* without the overt loss and the suicidal despair. As he is reexamining the cinematic quest of his youth, with a new family, the film sublimates the echoes of his failed marriage and the inevitable disillusionments of child rearing.

The descriptive character of the catalogue notes to *The Mammals of Victoria* suggests that it may have been written in large part by Marilyn Jull:

> The film begins with a series of horizontally running ocean tide waves, some-times with mountains in the background, hand-painted patterns, sometimes step-printed hand-painting, abstractions composed of distorted (jammed) TV shapes in shades of blue with occasional red, refractions of light within the camera lens, sometimes mixed with reflections of water—this "weave" of imagery occasionally revealing recognizable shapes of birds and humans, humans as fleeting figures in the water, as distant shapes in a rowboat, as human shadows, so forth. Increasingly closer images of water, and of light reflected off water, as well as of bursts of fire, intersperse the long shots, the seascapes and all the other interwoven imagery. Eventually a distant volley-ball arcs across the sky filled with cumulus clouds: this is closely followed by, and interspersed with, silhouettes of a young man and woman in the sea, which leads to some extremely out-of-focus images from a front car win-dow, an opening between soft-focus trees, a clearing. Carved wooden teeth suddenly sweep across the frame. Then the film ends on some soft-focus horizon lines, foregrounded by ocean, slowly rising and falling and rising again in the frame. This film is a companion piece to *A Child's Garden and the Serious Sea.*

The stress here on a limited cycle of images and the gradual introduction of new elements corresponds to the structural uniqueness of *The Mammals of Victoria* within the Vancouver Island tetralogy; for unlike its companion films, and especially when seen immediately after *A Child's Garden and the Serious Sea*, it seems to be construed on a systemic principle, yet one sufficiently flex-ible to avoid the sense of mechanical organization (in addition to the tendency toward the full-frame, centered image Bart Testa observed[46]). The images ap-pear to be grouped in some thirty or more sets, largely but not wholly ar-ticulated by fades or brief passages of blackness.[47] Within most of these sets there will appear images of fire, passages of hand painting, distorted shots of a television screen, orange-tinted passages of negative film, colored octagonal lens spots, and many shots of the sea at different times and distances. The recurrence of variant configurations within these categories of shots endows the film with a cyclic architecture, while providing a backdrop against which new and unprecedented images, such as the wading couple or two appearances of the flying volleyball, stand out.

The texts collected in *Telling Time* provide a fascinating guide to Brakhage's thought during the years he was engaged in the Vancouver Island series, at least in its initial stages. He articulated in many different forms the consequences of his meditations on the origins of vision from the prenatal formation of an optical reflex in anticipation of the focused light that envisions an exterior world. He is continually at pains to accentuate the apperception of cellular, electrostatic molding of any subsequent image. In one central essay he distinguishes "geometric versus meat-ineffable" thought, positing the latter as primary, and claiming that language itself is a derivation from secondary, geometrical (and idealizing) thought, which in turn revises the optical synapses to see "a collection of nameable shapes within a frame" or a "picture," in his specialized use of the term. For cinema, this means that the otherwise overlooked granular texture of the film image should be an index of the origin of the art in its evocation of primary perception:

> [T]he process of the transmission of organic radiance finds, in Film, an almost corollary—except inasmuch as commercial filmmakers eschew what's natural in favor of traditional ideals...(for example, photography's "fine grain" drive to eliminate any visibility of the chemical constituent of film stock, the silver halides, etc. which compose image at scratch, the "graininess" of Film: these, a shift each frame, constitute a visual paradigm of cells themselves variably radiating light's lightning-like transmission of image.) [Brakhage's ellipses][48]

The structure of *The Mammals of Victoria* enlarges on the principle of the dominant "graininess" of its images: it generates recycling "weaves" of interiorized thoughts of sea, television, fire, painted phosphenes, and reflections as "corollaries" to what the filmmaker calls the "bio-logic" of meat-ineffable thinking. Thus some of the most striking "events" distinguish themselves through their conventional perspective as "perfectly photographed" images, such as the ruined sand castle and the volleyball. But the fact that the fleeting appearances of people are shadowy and grainy whereas many images of the sea are crystal clear should warn us against making too much of the distinction between these manifestly important occurrences and the mass of the film. Rather, the "events," as Testa calls them, offer one or more potential narratives in a swarming arena of "moving visual thinking" in which "finally each cell...can be intuited to be 'telling' its 'story' interactive with every other cell's story...overridden by some entirety of rhythming light."[49]

Early on, a few shots of mounds of sand, apparently a sand castle already disintegrating in the oncoming tide, get emphasis because of the crispness of focus amid a series of otherwise grainy, hand-painted, negative, or optically distorted shots. The sand mound (itself an allegory of the photographic emulsion) recalls an image from the previous film in the series, but by its insistent recurrence here it evokes as well Jerome Hill's *The Sand Castle* (1960), a Tati-like comedy built around Carl Jung's ideas of the formation of the pre-adolescent imagination. In *Film at Wit's End* Brakhage briefly synopsized the film, stressing the difference of adult reactions to the washing away of the sand castle ("disappointed and horrified") to that of the boy who built it ("He is not saddened at all; he is delighted").[50] Following Testa's observation that the collapse of the sand mound in *The Mammals of Victoria* is the first "event" to stand out from its repeating matrix, I would argue, contra Testa, that it is also the first trope of Marilyn's "biography" in the film; that is, that it marks the falling away of childhood, both as a disappointment and as a delight, in this supremely ambivalent lyric. In fact, all of the "events" that call attention to themselves configure that "biography," and they may be the only images that do so.

The formal innovation of *The Mammals of Victoria* accompanies a shift of mood and ambition on Brakhage's part. The excitement of a new life and a new place that enlivens *A Child's Garden and the Serious Sea* has waned. Whatever he imagined he was doing in regard to Marilyn's biography has apparently changed as well; he recognizes the epistemological gap inherent in contemplating another's past life, and he expresses that recognition through a series of self-conscious tropes. The language of the catalogue note, with its allusions to "humans as fleeting figures" and "human shadows," directs our attention to the ephemeral representation of persons. He told Suranjan Ganguly in 1993: "...*Garden* [has] been understood as an attempt to recreate Marilyn's childhood, of trying to see the garden through her eyes as she was growing up when I had no such intention. I have no illusions that people can see through somebody else's eyes via aesthetics."[51] He shot the film the summer after he made that statement, yet he was still speaking of it in terms of his wife's adolescence. After his death, she told an interviewer: "In 1993, on another summer vacation, Stan decided he would continue this theme with 'an imagination of my adolescence.' However, these ideas about 'me' were really just starting points, as it were, and the film is really 'about' anyone's adolescence, as evoked through physical and metaphorical presentation of the natural environment."[52] Brakhage had just turned sixty; he now had two sons with Marilyn. With the routines of family life and summer vacations on Vancouver Island, he achieved, at least temporarily, a contemplative, distanced sense of his own life and of human ephemerality.

In saying that "the film is really 'about' anyone's adolescence," Marilyn may be paraphrasing one of Gertrude Stein's ironies: after writing *The Autobiography of Alice B. Toklas*, in which she told her own life by ventriloquizing her lover, she continued the genre with *Everybody's Autobiography*. The parallel would not have escaped the filmmaker; for Jane Collom Brakhage (aka Jane Wodening) had written and published several chapters of *The Autobiography of Stan Brakhage* before their marriage ended. The typology of childhood and adolescence had been, of course, the theme of Hill's *The Sand Castle* and an important subject for its source, Carl G. Jung. Jung was on Brakhage's mind at this time: he refers to the muses as "manifestations of…Jung's 'collective unconscious'" in the Ganguly interview.[53] Jung's schema of adolescence illuminates many ambivalent "events" of *The Mammals of Victoria*. Take, for example, the volleyball image that appears twice late in the film. It is a witty surprise, suddenly floating before cumulous clouds, its bright clarity a contrast to the granular texture of most of the film. As a synecdoche of Sport itself, it alludes to collective activity, especially associated with youth. The ambivalence of the trope leaves open whether the filmmaker is positing himself merely as an elderly observer, left out of the game, or whether he is wondering if the teenaged Marilyn participated in or was alienated from such games. Similarly, the shadowy images of a boy's frolicking in the water and those of a couple wading may evoke the awakening erotic fantasies of an adolescent girl or the memories of a sixty-year-old man.

Jung's ideas of the fragility of adolescent identity and the complexity of separation from the parents may be projected onto these cinematic events. Even the penultimate montage of driving a car in the rain to what the catalogue note calls "a clearing" can be read as the exhilaration of the illusion of freedom an adolescent experiences with learning to drive (or perhaps merely on a family excursion); it links up with the first shots of the distant hills and mountains appearing in the film. In the distant hills a light, perhaps a car's headlight, beckons the phantasmal "subject" of the film out beyond the familiar cove. For the adolescent consciousness the island, and the world of the parents, has grown small and confining; the fantasies of escape match the filmmaker's growing familiarity with Vancouver Island and his sense of its limitations.

The note's echo of "horizontally running ocean tide waves" with "soft-focus horizon lines, foregrounded by ocean" points to the circularity of the film's structure. In the concluding two shots there is a Rothko-like band of light "falling and rising again in the frame." In the first of the two, a tiny dark speck, a distant bird in flight, holds our attention until it disappears out of the top of the frame shortly before the final, brighter and blanker floating horizon appears. The barely visible, disappearing bird is the visual analogue of Whitman's "A Word Out of the Sea":

> With angry moans the fierce old mother yet, as ever, incessantly moaning,
> On the sands of Paumanok's shore gray and rustling,
> The yellow half-moon, enlarged, sagging down, drooping, the face of the
>   sea almost touching,

The boy extatic—with his bare feet the waves, with his hair the
    atmosphere dallying,
The love in the heart pent, now loose, now at last tumultuously bursting,
The aria's meaning, the ears, the Soul, swiftly depositing,
The strange tears down the checks coursing,
The colloquy there—the trio—each uttering,
The undertone—the savage old mother, incessantly crying,
To the boy's Soul's questions sullenly timing—some drowned secret
    hissing,
To the outsetting bard of love…
Delaying not, hurrying not,
Whispered me through the night, and very plainly before daybreak,
    Lisped to me constantly the low and delicious word Death,
And again Death—ever Death, Death, Death,
Hissing melodious, neither like the bird, nor like my aroused child's heart,
But edging near, as privately for me, rustling at my feet,
And creeping thence steadily up to my ears,
Death, Death, Death, Death, Death.

Ironies abound. In his chapter on James Broughton in *Film at Wit's End*, Brakhage finds his older colleague's "symbolic rituals" before "the Great Mother, the Sea" foolish. He attributes the pretentiousness to a lifelong commitment to Jungian psychoanalysis. Elsewhere, the filmmaker speaks of Walt Whitman only in critical terms. Yet despite these reservations, I believe Whitman's great sea chants haunt the Vancouver Island films, even to the extent that I hear the "mama" in *Mammals* as a reverberation of the "fierce mother" in "A Word Out of the Sea." The curious title of this film might even be an example of what Brakhage has called "at wit's end." "Wit," he reminds us, "points out those things in life that are disturbing or incongruous."[54] Incongruously, *The Mammals of Victoria* is a film with no mammals, aside from the few shadowy human silhouettes, comparable to the comically speeded-up figures of Broughton and his wife as "humans reduced to some tiny creature-ness"[55] in *Nuptiae* (1969), the film Brakhage photographed for Broughton of the latter's wedding.

Brakhage might, perhaps, have borrowed the title of his second Vancouver Island film from the book by C. W. Brazemor, surveying the strange fauna of Victoria, Australia, including monotremes and marsupials. By contrast, the subjects of his film are the humans of Vancouver Island, primarily himself and his family (all unpictured); it is a contrast, too, to the numerous mammals that crowded earlier Brakhage films centering on his previous marriage. The uncanny glimpse of wooden teeth near the end of the film suggests that an imaginary mammal haunts the film. What are we to make of this image? symbol? "event"? Is a poet-prophet at the verge of the sea, the filmmaker, a would-be version of Jonah, coughed up from the belly of the whale? The brief flash of carved wooden teeth, perhaps from a totem pole, inscribes the threatening undertone of danger in such enticements, while at the same time it represents the lure of the exotic and the primitive as the goal of the automobile excursion.

The filmmaker's wit is more pointed in calling the subsequent film of the series *The God of Day Had Gone Down upon Him*. This is his note for the film in the expanded version he read at Bard College, March 1, 2000:

> This film of single-strand photography begins with the "fire" of reflective light on water and on the barest inferences of a ship. Throughout, the interwoven play of light and water tell the inferred "tale" of the film through rhythm and tempo, through visible textures and forms in gradual evolution, through resultant "moods" generated by these modes of making, and, then, by the increasingly distant boat images, birds, animals, fleeting silhouettes of people and their artifacts, flotsam and jetsam of the sea-dead, as well as (near end, and almost as at a funeral) flowers in bloom, swallowed by darkness midst the crumbling of the sand castles. These nameable objects (sometimes, at first, quite enigmatic) are the frets of Symbol; but always the symbolic content is swept back into the weave of sea and light and seen, as is the merry-go-round near the beginning of the film, or the horizontally photographed fountain mimicing incoming ocean waves, to be as if spawned in the mind during oceanic contemplation. In fact, the structure of the entire film might be characterized thus: meditation on ocean is interrupted continually by rapidly cut visual frets of (at first) irritated thought; but then gradually across the course of the film these fraughts of symbols and rapidly edited constructs become a calm 'kin to resignation, become more at-one with the diminishing light and incoming waves. The turning point of the film is near its midpoint where tall and relatively violent waves smash their cold and fearsome colors left to right across the screen, interwoven with an old man sitting in a dark blue room, followed by hints of backyard fences, grasses, distant ephemeral flowers and a hung whirling decoration. Reminders of this midpoint are accomplished through visual rhymes such as similarities of blue and a madly whirling kite against a bright sky, as well as by the (near end) entire sequence in which multiple garish flowers invade the (by then) almost fully meditative sea imagery. There are visual rhymes also connecting this work with its two previous "parts" (*A Child's Garden and the Serious Sea* and *The Mammals of Victoria*), such as an orange ball attached to a boat which "rhymes" with thrown orange balls in the previous film. As the whole film is stitched with red-orange-yellow flares (indicators of light-struck sections at beginning and ending of individual 100-foot rolls) making of the film a distinctive sequential evolution, so the end of the film has a slight flare-up (or fillip of hope?) after burgeoning dark.

The mention of "nameable objects" as "frets of Symbol" rhythmically reabsorbed "into the weave of sea and light and seen" virtually recapitulates the epistemological schema of "Geometric and Meat-Ineffable," while the film's title obliquely evokes the 1995 essay "Having Declared a Belief in God," in which Brakhage had argued a position very different from the Dickensian hyperbole "The God of Day Had Gone Down upon Him." There Brakhage's God is both a "cradling mother...an infinitely *moving* experience" and "a feeling of movement, of being so much at-one with an intricacy of cosmic rhythms, with felt radiant particle/waves...."[56] in what reads like a theological inflection of his theories of biofeedback. However, the title phrase of the film is an example of Wilkins Micawber's melodramatic, hypocritical rhetoric:

> At last Mr. Micawber's difficulties came to a crisis, and he was arrested early one morning, and carried over to the King's Bench Prison in the Borough. He told me, as he went out of the house, that the God of day had now gone down upon him—and I really thought his heart was broken and mine too. But I heard, afterwards, that he was seen to play a lively game at skittles, before noon. [Charles Dickens, *David Copperfield*, Chapter 11: "I Begin Life on my Own Account, and Don't Like It"]

The gesture of identifying with Dickens's Micawber, the melodramatic self-imaginer, a lovable, garrulous, irresponsible sponger and squanderer, is a remarkable instance of Brakhage's sense of humor at sixty-seven. Four years earlier he had been operated on for bladder cancer. Using Micawber's hyperbole to describe his reaction to his medical fate brings him to his "wit's end." The title pompously suggests that just one year after his public declaration of faith, God turned against him. But at the same time the title mocks that very pomposity. His prolific return to filmmaking following his operation is his "lively game of skittles."

Astonishingly, Brakhage appears to have been deaf to Dickens's humor when he first heard Micawber's complaint, if we are to trust his account at the Millennium Film Workshop: "[W]e were reading *David Copperfield* aloud as a family at the time, suddenly this sprang up out of the text: 'and the God of Day had gone down upon him.' And that raised the hairs on my neck sufficiently. I said that's the title..."[57] Although this may have been an unanticipated reaction to Dickens's wit, it is appropriate to the film that alternates its intensities from dejection and rage to resignation. Of course, despair had been a frequent dimension of Brakhage's cinema. It characterized the early works in which masturbation and suicide were paradigms: *The Way to Shadow Garden*, *Reflections on Black*, *Flesh of Morning* (1956), and *Whiteye*, and culminating in *Anticipation of the Night*. The films collaging newsreels and other found materials record profound anguish about the world at large: *Oh Life—a Woe Story—The A-Test News*, *23rd Psalm Branch*, and *Murder Psalm*. The autobiographical series *Duplicity*, the public exposition of an extramarital affair, *Confession*, and the first three films of the "Faust" series further catalogued the filmmaker's despondencies. The third of the Vancouver Island films differed from all of those in the range and rhythms of its fluctuations.

At the start of *The God of Day Had Gone Down upon Him,* Brakhage "began filming an envisionment of death, of what one could begin to imagine of death when it was in the bones... That stillness which pervades so much, and these were the great sources of inspiration of Rothko's last paintings, of Braque's old age paintings, of those of Joan Mitchell's final paintings and so on."[58] Earlier, when he began the Vancouver Island series, he had spoken of the Muse as a figure for the collective unconscious, as I mentioned. If he were now backing away from the pagan theology of his earlier discussions of inspiration and possession toward a personal version of Christianity, he might have found in the parable of Jonah a monotheistic version of the terrors of the Muse, as he had been used to portray her. Jonah vainly tries to escape the burden of prophecy, but neither a sea voyage nor being thrown overboard nor even the belly of the whale can keep him from his unwanted election. Then, even when he does submit and prophesies the destruction of Nineveh, God relents because of the city's contrition. The humiliated, pouting prophet takes refuge under the shade of a tree God provided for him, only to wither it and harass Jonah with sun and wind to teach him a lesson in divine mercy. In short, the vatic artist or prophet operates under ineluctable instructions and cannot dictate the terms or conditions of his revelations.

The "inferred 'tale' " in Brakhage's note posits a consciousness seeking a quiet end, plagued by the continual interruptions of "frets of symbols." That consciousness owes something to Jonah 4:8: "And it came to pass, when the sun did arise, that God prepared a vehement east wind; and the sun beat upon the head of Jonah, that he fainted, and wished in himself to die, and said, It is better for me to die than to live." Yet the difference between Jonah and the filmmaker wandering the beaches of Vancouver Island "at wit's end" is so vast that the comic figure of Wilkins Micawber has to mediate the gap.

The looming hull of a moored ship is more prominent at the opening of the film than Brakhage's exceptionally expansive note suggests. As one of the "frets of symbol," it might be Odysseus's ship (where Pound's *Cantos* begin) or an echo of the ship on which Jonah fled from the prophetic call of God that had come down upon him. Odysseus and Jonah appear among the welter of allusions in the final five Arches of *ARK* (including a segment dedicated to Brakhage).[59]

Close to the shore Brakhage filmed scum and seaweed rhyming visually with Whitman's cataloguing voice in "As I Ebbed with the Ebb of the Ocean of Life":

Fascinated, my eyes reverting from the south, dropt, to follow those
    slender windrows,
Chaff, straw, splinters of wood, weeds, and the sea-gluten,
Scum, scales from shining rocks, leaves of salt-lettuce, left by the tide,
Miles walking, the sound of breaking waves the other side of me,
Paumanok there and then as I thought the old thought of likenesses...

But even if he feels an identification with the broken ejectamenta that he sees (as Whitman did: "I too but signify at the utmost a little wash'd up drift,/ A few sands and dead leaves to gather,/ Gather, and merge myself as part of the sands and drift"), the filmmaker never enacts a comparable rejection of himself in this film. Early on, the divinity of light (his God of Day) has already begun to ebb away from him. Later, in a spurt of energy and brighter light, for the first time in the series, he turns his camera on rough waters, intercutting a shot of his recently deceased father-in-law (identified in the note as the elderly man of the "turning point"). The violence in nature is both a metaphor for his rage at his illness and an intimation of destruction, soon represented by the flotsam on the sea surface, suggestive of a shipwreck. Yet after the turbulent waves we see a sea lion, ducks, geese, birds, and a frolicking dog, as if Brakhage were reminding himself that the sea sustains life and that it can be the arena of play for the mammals of Victoria, displaced from the previous film in the series.

Nevertheless, the waning of the light progresses. The vegetative sexuality of the flowers and accompanying autumnal images, which the note calls "funereal," mock the renewed vitality with which the series opened, as the sequence bids adieu to the erotic life. Near the end, a shadowy couple, a final human emblem recalling *The Mammals of Victoria*, walking on the shore, suddenly disappear from the frame, troping the filmmaker's immanent disappearance.

Marilyn Brakhage signed the catalogue note for *Panels for the Walls of Heaven*:

> This film is an entirely hand-painted film composed of a combination of highly complex step-printed superimpositions of hand-painting (at variable speeds), and raw and highly textured strips of hand-painted original film run at speed (24 distinct frames every second). It can be considered the fourth part of what had been called the "Vancouver Island Trilogy"…making the entire work now the "Vancouver Island Quartet."
>
> Purple flashes are followed by a curtain of purple and blues, first seemingly static and then in motion. Close-ups of textures of paint evolve into flashes of jewel-like red, then more cascading blues and purples and white—"falling," seemingly, down from the top of the screen, at other times multi-directional bursts of rolling colors. Red, blue and yellow course through in an up-down motion, then blues and yellows enter from left and right in a complex medley of not solidly formed, but very vibrant pulsations of color, at times only slightly hinting at a solidity of "wallness" upon which the paint might exist. But it is a "wall" suffused with light. Suggestions of fire and water, textures of paint on wall, sparkling jewels, and chunks of blue-white ice arise, as the textures of paint at times become a riotous rainbow of tumbling hues flowing in a river of light, creating the paradoxical experience of a fully substantial insubstantiality.
>
> The film clearly echoes back to earlier Brakhage films, including "A Child's Garden" and the "seriousness" of the sea, as well as hand-painted

works such as *Spring Cycle* and *Stellar*. The image holds briefly on a vision of depth of black with jewel-colored edges, followed by a wash of yellow, more "panels" of color, then sheets of ice-like blues joined by red and finally turning to dark green. There is a seeming movement into the details of the paint itself. Curtains of black web-like lines explode once again into tumbling yellows and mauves, slowing, then becoming faster again, going into a step-like movement, frame to frame, of views of walls that are not walls, showing an increasing tactility, with occasional apparent "holes," and then resuming a multi-directional flow, and moving on into a recapitulation of some earlier forms: greens, reds, blues, red/black, greens and yellows, with sparkling blacks and swatches of red, loosening up once again on a whiter ground, with forms reminiscent of swimming spermatazoa and ending finally on a cumulative repetition of earlier visual themes.—Marilyn Brakhage

The title repeats that of a sixty-seven-page-long poem by Kenneth Patchen, divided into forty-four "Panels," published in an elegant single volume with the poet's drawings in 1947. Brakhage would have known the book, as he briefly knew Patchen himself, when he moved to San Francisco in 1954. However, I find nothing within the postsurrealist text, intensely misanthropic and apocalyptic, that bears a strong or clear relationship to the film. Even the refrain of the final panel—"Pleasing death O come pleasing death for I am tired of being alive"[60]—would fail to express adequately Brakhage's concession to his increasing pain, although it is important to note that the chronic pain from a back injury and subsequent operations that Patchen endured was at the center of Brakhage's memories of him.[61] Throughout the Vancouver Island films, up to the very end, the filmmaker clings to the life force that remains to him; his moments of resignation never seem to turn into a will to die.

Even in the barely discernible structure of *Panels for the Walls of Heaven* there is, or seems to be, a musically complex interweaving of a limited set of film strips, rather than one continuously changing field of color for thirty-one minutes; but the variations of superimposition, stop printing, and fading in and out make it impossible to distinguish the elements or even to gauge how long these elements are, even though the impression is distinct that later parts of the film recall directly earlier passages. The very structure indicates that the filmmaker is clinging to his waning vision, calling it back and exploring its riches with all of his psychic strength, until finally the film itself insists on terminating. Camper is the best critic so far of the film. He wrote:

> Brakhage said...in January [2003]...that his film does not aim to be "worthy of heavenliness"; rather, it's an "imagination of same." And the viewer might be hard-pressed to see any conventional heaven here—not only are there no recognizable pictures, there isn't even a single mood. Hating symmetry, avoiding all forms of predictability, Brakhage produces

compositions that are off center, weighted toward one area as if ready
to tip over. And each image does tip over, very rapidly, into the next,
yielding to its successor. . . .

Brakhage seeks not spectacular pictures—certainly not to the extent he
did in some earlier work—but constant change, making one question the
very nature of existence. Pushing his films almost to the point of chaos and
denying the viewer images from the world we know, he creates the sense of
teetering on a brink, of consciousness suspended over a void by the slender-
est of threads.[62]

Camper locates the resistance to symmetry within the film frame and within
the evolution of the hand-painted film. It can be extended, in a way, to the
series as a whole. There we find a rejection of triadic form anticipated by *The
Dante Quartet*. Inspired by the *Commedia*, but repelling its Trinitarian insistence on triads, in the rhyme scheme as well as the set of Cantice, he deliberately assembled *his* Dante in four parts. The addition of the hand-painted
finale to the Vancouver Island series repeats this gesture while inverting it; for
The Dante Quartet consisted of three largely hand-painted films and a fourth
incorporating photographic images.

There is a structural analogy between *ARK,* followed by *RADI OS,* and the
three photographed Vancouver Island films capped by *Panels for the Walls
of Heaven.* Brakhage knew that Ronald Johnson completed his long poem
in ninety-nine sections and published it as such. It was one part short of the
Commedia's hundred, but he often spoke of his earlier *RADI OS* as the cap-
stone to *ARK. RADI OS* is an abstraction or a creative act of subtraction from
John Milton's great epic. Johnson composed it by finding new words within
Milton's letters, just as he found his title within *[Pa]Radi[se L]os[t]*.

Vancouver Island was both a real place and an imaginary topos for Brakhage.
He made the first three films of the series as a visitor. When he finally came to
reside in Victoria, he made the final part without any photographic or index-
ical link to the landscape. One dimension of the imaginary status of the place
was his fiction of a schematic biography of the life of Marilyn Brakhage, a vita
nuova that "improved," in Hart Crane's ironic formulation, his earlier odes on
childhood, adolescence, middle age, and the intimations of heaven. Thus the
series grew into a palinode to his oeuvre as a whole. His last stance "at wit's
end" became the cinema of wisdom.

Nathaniel Dorsky:
Triste (1974–1996); *Variations* (1992–1998)
August and After (2012): George Kuchar's last day; flower
Stills courtesy of Nathaniel Dorsky and Nina Zurier
Jerome Hiler:
Words of Mercury (2011) Sunflowers; dogs swimming
Stills courtesy of Jerome Hiler and John Borruso

Nathaniel Dorsky, Jerome Hiler, and the Polyvalent Film

Light, seeking light, doth light of light beguile...
Varying in subjects as the eye doth roll
To every varied object in his glance:

Love's Labour's Lost, Act I, scene I; Act V, scene ii

In the first decade of the twenty-first century Nathaniel Dorsky reached the pinnacle of his powers and reputation as a filmmaker. But he took a long route to his prominence in the American avant-garde cinema. He had an early start making films, as did most of his strongest peers of the generation who came to cinema in the 1960s. The first films he exhibited, *Ingreen* (1964), *A Fall Trip Home* (1964), and *Summerwind* (1965), established him as a creditable filmmaker at a time when many young aspirants were trying to launch careers. Most of them disappeared quickly, and, in the late 1960s, that seemed to have been Dorsky's fate as well.

Within the large, unruly flock of filmmakers shepherded by Jonas Mekas in those years, there were several coteries. Andy Warhol's was the most famous, of course, and one that branded its adherents the most indelibly. Another was led by Gregory Markopoulos who generously championed the early work of Warren Sonbert, George Landow, and Robert Beavers (with whom Markopoulos lived in Europe from the late 1960s until his death in 1992). Dorsky and Jerome Hiler, another filmmaker, as well as an artisan of stained glass, who has been Dorsky's partner for more than forty years, were mentored by Markopoulos. In 1966 they moved from New York to rural Lake Owassa in New Jersey, where they stayed until relocating to San Francisco in 1971. From the time he left New York until 1982, Dorsky ceased completing and releasing films, although he continued to shoot and to show his footage to gatherings of friends. This had always been Hiler's practice until 2012. Before then he rarely exhibited any of his work in public. Within the avant-garde film community, the private evenings of film appreciation hosted by Hiler and Dorsky attained cult status.

Filmmaker Warren Sonbert was a major beneficiary of those screenings. When Dorsky finally edited, from 1980 to 1982, the material he had shot between 1967 and 1970 into *Hours for Jerome*, Sonbert wrote: "*Hours for Jerome* is simply the most beautifully photographed film that I've ever seen; here we enter the realm of the compassionate and the full achievement of what film can do cinemagraphically…is achieved…It is a privilege to experience the thoughtful unfolding of these images." By that time, Sonbert himself had attained a major reputation within the field. His career parallels Dorsky's in inverse: after making apprentice films in the late 1960s, he found his mature style and relentlessly sought venues of exhibition just as Dorsky was withdrawing from the public arena. Sonbert's style incorporated some of the principles Dorsky and Hiler had extolled and exemplified in their private screenings—most notably an eschewing of the soundtrack. But unlike Stan Brakhage, who had loudly affirmed the superiority of silent film, Sonbert, Dorsky, and Hiler shared a deep appreciation of several Hollywood auteurs (Sirk, Hitchcock, and Ford) and European filmmakers (Rossellini and Antonioni) who influenced their compositions, tempi, and montage. In fact, it was this orientation that gave Sonbert first and Dorsky later sufficient distance to evade the overwhelming influence of Brakhage for whom their respect and affection grew the more films they produced.

By withdrawing for fifteen years, Dorsky sat out the most contentious period in the history of the avant-garde film. Fierce aesthetic battles over the prominence of minimal forms ("structural film") and the status of video art were supplanted by even more acrimonious political disputes over sexism, imperialism, idealism, the importance of theory (especially French), and canon formation. Brakhage was the largest and most battered target in these academic skirmishes. When Dorsky reemerged, there was a new audience, wary of the political factionalism, eager for the contemplative beauty and the cultic appreciation of cinematic genius he quietly preached. That audience was small at first, but it grew considerably in the 1990s at the very time that his filmmaking was attaining its full maturity. The growing appreciation of his films over the next ten years, in turn, paved the way for Hiler's much-delayed debut.

Dorsky told Mary Kite, "We spent our youth speculating on an open form of film…The montage I'm talking about moves from shot to shot outside of any other necessities, except of course the accumulation of being. It has no external obligations. It is the place of film."[1] Dorsky, Hiler, Sonbert, and their friends, among whom were the poets Michael Brownstein, Anne Waldman, and Ted Greenwald, nurtured ideas of films that would have no narrative or thematic organization, none of the Aristotelian unities of time, place, or action beyond the immanent rhythms binding one cinematic image to another. Such films could not be interpreted by what Pasolini came to call "free indirect point of view." Encouraged by his poet friends, Dorsky found the inspiration for this concept of cinema in his reading of John Ashbery's early books and spoke of editing his work in "stanzas." However, his failure to achieve to his satisfaction the open form he envisioned contributed to his blockage of a decade and a half.

Hours for Jerome (1982), at forty-five minutes, remains Dorsky's longest film. He divided it into two parts and organized it to follow the seasons. It breaks down into a series of spectacular montage fragments, some of them edited in the camera. For the first time he abjured a soundtrack and took advantage of the silence to project the film at 18 frames per second, giving its movements a slight retardation. He never returned subsequently to soundtracks or sound speed (24 frames per second). This two-part lyric was his first serious effort to create "a place where film itself can be, can dream." (Here, and throughout this chapter, I am quoting from conversations with Dorsky.) But Sonbert convinced him that the editing was "too descriptive." He meant, apparently, that the filmmaker was too loyal to his memories of life in New York City and on Lake Owassa, at the expense of the organic form of the film itself. According to Dorsky: "When you go into polyvalent editing, as Warren usually did, . . . the *place* is the *film*."[2] By polyvalent editing, the filmmaker means organizing the shots and rhythms of a film so that associations will "resonate" [his word] several shots later. Because it was important to Dorsky not to overstate such associations, he eschewed parallel editing, classically practiced by D. W. Griffith and the masters of silent Soviet cinema. Yet, like Eisenstein, he found a model for his film form in classical Japanese poetry and in Dorsky's case, Chinese poetry as well.

Before assembling *Hours for Jerome*, the filmmaker continued to photograph fragments of his daily life in San Francisco and attempted to make a film by severely restricting his image material to grasses. During this period he also began a film built exclusively on gradations of blackness, but he admits he lacked the courage to complete and exhibit it. Although Dorsky abandoned these projects, the aesthetic satisfaction of editing *Hours for Jerome* and the consequent feeling of rejuvenation encouraged him to complete a series of ostensibly simpler films displaying his love of the basic cinematic material: color, grain, texture, the flickering light of the screen. It was as if he felt he had to discipline himself for another decade to a new and rigorous apprenticeship to his art. In *Pneuma* (1977–1983) he used a wide variety of outdated film stocks to assemble unphotographed bits of color and light flares, whereas *Ariel* (1983) achieves similar but bolder effects through home processing unexposed rolls of defunct Anscochrome. In temporarily renouncing the photographic talent that made *Hours for Jerome* a gorgeous but unwieldy chain of spectacular epiphanies—nearly a catalogue of effects—he forced himself to shape the most elemental visual magma into films that might sustain attention and orchestrate the inherent music of cinematic movement for between twenty and thirty minutes, which was to become roughly the time scale of his works until now. Then he slowly reintegrated photography into his art, under severe restraint. *Alaya* (1976–1987) concentrates on patterns of sand as hyperboles of film grain. In *17 Reasons Why* (1985–1987) he made a 16mm film from unslit 8mm rolls, which produce four small frames for each image in two pairs of sequential frames. The side-by-side sets of doubled images deflect attention from the free camera movements and frequent superimpositions within those frames to the generalized impression of filmic representation—that is, sets of nearly identical rectangles—an impression which Dorsky enhances by some-times sweeping the etched scratches and marks of chemical processing across all four frames at once. These techniques and similar constrictions had played a prominent role in the structural film phenomenon of the 1970s. But Dorsky had no interest in the aggressive use of duration or epistemological parables; instead, he emphasized the sensuality immanent in such minimal imagery. His reductive films proclaim the sheer beauty of filmic light, an approach particu-larly effective for the small cult of aficionados for whom he would project the edited originals in his home.

By 1996 he was ready to make another attempt at the open form, or pol-yvalent film, of which he had dreamed. He turned to the material he had gathered from random shooting and aborted projects since 1974 to compose *Triste* (1996), thereby initiating his mature style. After thirty years, he finally achieved the mode of lyric he had theorized. Later Dorsky would quote the acknowledgement of fellow filmmaker Phil Solomon: "You found a way around [Brakhage]." However, Brakhage had made his own version of a purely poly-valent film in 1972 when he edited his extraordinary *The Riddle of Lumen*, also from scraps of film he had saved from earlier projects, in polemical response to Hollis Frampton's *Zorns Lemma* (1970). The "riddle" of the title refers to the question of what holds the shots together, that is, what they have to do with one another; and the answer, too, is in the title: light (lumen). Within Brakhage's vast corpus of films *The Riddle of Lumen* represents one of the many attempts to still the power of the "egotistical sublime": that is, to transcend the intense subjectivity at the core of his art. Dorsky, in his major phase, did not so much find a way around Brakhage as find a way to make the most serene of Brakhage's protean lyric modes wholly his own.

Triste established the model for Dorsky's version of the polyvalent lyric: the shots are leisurely paced, usually between ten and thirty seconds long, without superimposition or rapid camera movement—when there is camera move-ment, it usually follows a figure in the image. There is no intercutting; very rarely does a camera setup or even an image recur. Consequently, the rare repetitions or recurrences acquire particular emphasis. For instance, two se-quential shots of a snake in *Triste* link them to two earlier shots of a horse. A brief sequence near the end, of Hiler in his kitchen, in which the only gen-uine repetition in the film is a shot of his face, makes him the central presence of the work and associates his image with a brief set of variations on a stone votive angel, in positive and negative.

The prevailing autonomy of the shots evokes monadic worlds, while the montage teases out the preestablished harmony among them (if I may impose unintended Leibnizian concepts on the filmmaker). This is a remarkably delicate process entailing subtle shifts of mood through which an overall psychological tone tentatively emerges and "evaporates" (Dorsky's term). Framing, chiaroscuro, and proximics inscribe the filmmaker's presence in the worlds he reveals. In *Triste* he is a dejected wanderer, barely able to enter into a crowded baseball arena but drawn close to an isolated cigarette butt, one submerged shoe, or a slithering snake. But in the next film he made—*Variations* (1998), using freshly photographed images for the first time in decades—image after image absorbs the rapturous filmmaker, as if the long-awaited achievement of *Triste* renewed the glory of the world for him. In his brilliant short book *Devotional Cinema* (Tuumba Press, 2003), he wrote:

> When cinema can make the internalized medieval and externalized Renaissance ways of seeing unite and transcend themselves, it can achieve a transcendental balance. This balance point unveils the transparency of our earthly experience. We are afloat. It is neither our vision nor the belief in exterior objectivity. It belongs to no one and, strangely enough, exists nowhere. It is within the balance that the potential for profound cinema takes place. (pp. 27–28)

At times Dorsky has discussed this "balance" as a resistance to both the first-person and the third-person evocations of a filmic voice or persona.

The polyvalent or open-form films Dorsky has made since the early 1990s register what the filmmaker once called "the mystery of seeing and being" in different psychic temperaments. *Triste* and *Variations*, along with the subsequent *Arbor Vitae* (2000) and *Love's Refrain* (2001), constitute a set of "Four Cinematic Songs," whereas he calls *The Visitation* (2002) and *Threnody* (2004) "Two Devotional Songs." *Song and Solitude* (2006) seems to form a triad with the previous two.

Not since Bruce Baillie made his strongest films in the 1960s, has a filmmaker so crammed beauty upon beauty into his work with Keatsian lushness. *Arbor Vitae*, his envoi to the millennium, pushes the banality of natural beauty—butterflies, flowers, birds—to extremes. More than ever before, the filmmaker's characteristic urban landscape borders on architectural promotion, but he ultimately overcomes the decorative elegance pervading the film by evoking intimations of the power of gravity that circumscribes the flights of birds and butterflies and holds the skyscrapers rooted to the earth like crystalline excrescences. More powerfully, *Love's Refrain* accumulates images of veils, subtle foreground-background discriminations, reflections, and layered shadows as if to manifest the capability of cinema to "unveil the transparency of our earthly experience." The very tactility of the imagery dialectically suggests its evanescence until the culminating portrait of the poet Philip Whalen on his deathbed anchors the lyric just this side of the threshold of eternity.

When Dorsky titled *The Visitation*, he had in mind medieval illuminated books of "the hours of the Virgin Mary," in which the Visitation of the pregnant Mary to her cousin Elizabeth, herself pregnant with John the Baptist, illustrates Lauds, the ritual service for dawn. The emergence of light and its subsequent sweep over the surface of the world is the true subject of the film, which seems to have nothing to do with the meeting of Mary and Elizabeth. It opens with the only instance of reverse-angle cutting I have found in Dorsky's mature films: we see Hiler from behind, wiping a large sheet of glass (which he will use for a stained-glass work) followed by a shot, through the glass, of his face mottled by the filtered light as he inspects the pane. This unique opening reminds us that the film camera is a chamber with a glass screen constructed to preserve the moving stains of light that pass through it. Hiler has been the central influence on his partner's films since they met at the first New York screening of *Ingreen*. *The Visitation* reflects Hiler's conceit of stained glass as the cinema of the Middle Ages, the one subject on which he has lectured in public. Many of the monadic shots that follow the introductory motif show light penetrating fog, the edges of clouds, display windows, and water. Numerous grids, including shots of chain-link fences, extend the permeable barrier of glass into the realm of other objects. As the film builds to its climax, the lyric seems to be proposing or testing a series of culminating images: the sun moving behind and out of a cloud formation shaped like a heart or angel wings, an androgynous young woman fresh from an outdoor pool, the half-moon gliding in the night sky, a bright yellow fish circulating in a tank in a store window, and finally layers of flat waves in a dazzlingly reflective sea sweeping vertically over the screen.

As Brakhage intuited, the polyvalent lyric is a riddle in light. Whereas in most lyrical cinema the accumulation of images narrows and defines its subject, establishing a thematic and sometimes dramatic field in which the viewer's anticipation can be confirmed or frustrated, the polyvalent lyric constitutionally resists the definition of its subject and abolishes the expectation of a thematic development. This results in the suppression of a future tense within the film. Each image founds a new present moment. With Dorsky's cultivation of the monadic shot, the feeling of an amassing present, reverberating with the echoes of the earlier image-worlds, is particularly strong. As the film unpredictably proceeds, each new shot sets in play a minor, or sometimes even major, revision of the fragile interior relations of the images and rhythms that preceded it. The revision is naturally most intense at the very instant of the shot change, but it is by no means limited to that transition. Dorsky has compared "the energy at the moment of the cut" to the "kabbalistic tradition of the Spark of Goodness or sparks of openness" that Jewish theologians argued constitute the holiness imprisoned in corporeal nature. Thus each cut would draw one of the tiny sparks toward the fire associated with divinity and which the filmmaker, I believe, thinks of in terms of the ineffable coherence of a polyvalent film. For it is essential to him that the coherence remains mysterious. Although Dorsky, who is consistently helpful and good-natured, can easily be led to offer ad hoc accounts of how shot combinations work for him, he is very wary of his own "reductive analysis," lest a film be misread as "a slightly difficult map of a symbolic road that could be understood, or an obscuration of a symbolism that might be defined."

By the time he made *The Visitation*, Dorsky felt he had sufficient mastery of the open-ended lyric form to inflect his photography with intimations of the pervading tone of the film while he was shooting it. That was the case in the two elegies of 2004 and 2006. From the start he knew he was making *Threnody* as "an offering" to the recently dead Stan Brakhage. In fact, he filmed his shots as if Brakhage were gathering his last glimpses "of earthly phenomena" as he ascended into the Empyrean. Of course, Dorsky didn't actually signal a mediation of the images as if through a Brakhage persona. The cinematography and editing are manifestly Dorsky's. There is not a hint of "free indirect point of view" in the whole film; in fact, there is nothing within the film to associate it explicitly with Brakhage or his works; for, within Brakhage's montage the shot has an atomic function. The incessant fluxions of the handheld camera and the intricate plays of light bind often very short shots together in complex molecular units so that the autonomy of individual shots disappears. Even in *The Riddle of Lumen*, in which Brakhage seems to be examining the polyvalent power of the shots, the units never have the monadic self-sufficiency of Dorsky's, and the rhythm Brakhage orchestrates is not immanent.

The "devotional" mode that links *Threnody* to its predecessor elicits an engrossment in the individual shot that would draw the viewer "to participate in its presence" so that the subsequent cut might induce a "visceral" shift in the most "tender" manner. Mystery, suggestiveness, intriguing indiscernibility, or even sheer beauty might be marshaled to invest the monadic image with sufficient "presence" to give a delicate "poignancy" (Dorsky's terms) to the instant in which the image changes through montage. So a shot of Hiler's hand as he writes meticulously in a journal, or of a shop window in which we can make out a metallic hand and a pseudo-Hellenic bust scattered willy-nilly among other curios (while passing cars are reflected in the window), engages us for several seconds until the encapsulated world of the writing hand gives way to another realm, say, one in which the camera slowly pans down vertical cords with signage in the background or the foliage of a fir tree replaces the disordered window display. The viewer would not know that Hiler is copying out notes he took at a seminar on the *Tibetan Book of the Dead* or that the shop is that of a palm reader in transition or that a striking shot of trees weighted down with snow late in the film was photographed when a blizzard coincided with the memorial service for Brakhage in Boulder, Colorado, yet such meta-physical associations seem to have influenced Dorsky's absorption so that he could use these images effectively as nodal points in the film. The poignancy the filmmaker sought may be a function of the timing of the editing; again and again he turns from a shot, almost sacrificing it, just an instant before we can be sated in our scrutiny.

In contrast to *Threnody*, a prevailing darkness at center of most of its images marks the mourning of *Song and Solitude*. Dorsky made the film during the year his friend Susan Vigil was dying of ovarian cancer. A beloved pillar of the San Francisco avant-garde film community, she had housed, fed, and befriended local and visiting filmmakers for more than thirty years. Her acceptance of her imminent death was heartbreakingly heroic. During her last year she visited Dorsky weekly to look at the unedited rolls of the film as they came directly from the laboratory. Yet she is not the overt subject of the film. The only image of her in it is a close-up of her hands as she reads a poem (T. S. Eliot's "Ash Wednesday"). As in *Threnody*, the elegiac tone emerges from nuances. For instance, early in the film there is a wonderously timed shot of a figure in an orange sweater in a restaurant. The fluctuations of offscreen sunlight bring into prominence and then nearly erase two thin metal shade cords in the center of the composition. Such rhythmic coming and going of light, oscillating through the whole film regularly, put the central darkness on the verge of illumination. If the delirious beauty typical of Dorsky's cinema is muted in *Song and Solitude*, it is because, one feels, he has exercised an extraordinary effort of his will not to be distracted from the intensity of sharing his friend's last days.

The next decade of filmmaking, between 1997 and 2007, was one of extraordinary success for Dorsky, aesthetically and with his audiences. He quickly became one of the most prominent avant-garde filmmakers in the world. His new films were regularly shown in the annual "Views for the Avant-Garde" sessions of the New York Film Festival. One measure of his success was his ability to command a separate session for his films (or for his and Hiler's) to avoid the exhausting omnibus screenings favored by the curators of the "Views." He also began to tour Europe regularly, participating in the London and Rotterdam festivals and showing in the venues which had arisen to both excite and satisfy an interest in American avant-garde films in England, France, Spain, Austria, and the Czech Republic.

Yet this success had its price. In the 1980s and early 1990s both Dorsky and Hiler had frequently expressed good-humored criticism of their friend, Warren Sonbert, for the eagerness with which he worked to complete a new film each year in time for the New York Film Festival and then made the rounds of European venues with it. In 1996, a year after Sonbert died, Dorsky moved into a similar rhythm of production and exhibition. Just as Sonbert had, he consistently thrilled his audiences with the beauty of his work, but also like Sonbert he fecundly produced new films that struck many of his viewers as nearly indistinguishable from his previous ones. Dorsky never publicly addressed this problem as far as I know. Instead, he was at pains, in his introductions and interviews, to point up the differences that individuated each new film.

Often he spoke of the crisis into which the discontinuation of Kodachrome film stock had pushed his work after 2006. He had been shooting Kodachrome since he was a child. As a cinematic colorist, the termination of the film stock posed a serious problem for him. Yet I believe his focus on this aspect of his poetics also entailed as well a displacement of a more acute crisis, compounded of his desire to appeal to an audience and to film curators, his anxiety about economic survival as he approached seventy, and the disruptions of his previously ritualized life in San Francisco, where he alternated his time between making his own films and earning a living as a film doctor—reediting otherwise unsuccessful documentaries. Above all, the discussion of the end of Kodachrome masked the vital question of whether or not he had exhausted the polyvalent open form itself.

In an interview with Max Goldberg, he commented on the new film stock:

> When you have Kodachrome in your camera, you feel like a jeweller working with gold. You're working with this very hot and precious transmutable substance. With the colour negative, it feels like a lesser metal. The new film will be a combination of the Fuji negative and the Eastman negative. I shot all Fuji negative in Rotterdam, which was interesting. Every day I was going to look at Dutch paintings. There are two famous Dutch painters, Jan van Goyen and Salomon van Ruysdael, and they always have a windy seascape, a landmass, a castle, and they're painted in these tones of yellow, brown, and gray. The Fuji can't comprehend colours as the sun goes down; it collapses into this reddish-brown. And so I saw the rolls yesterday—I said to myself, "Oh my God! It's like a Dutch painting! The Fuji went Dutch."[3]

The filmmaker spoke of a color stock as a lover. He had been thoroughly familiar with Kodachrome; it was the companion of a lifetime. The metaphor of the disoriented lover is latent in the titles of his first three films using Ektachrome and Fuji negative: *Aubade* (2010), *Pastourelle* (2010), and *The Return* (2011). The first two name troubadour genres of erotic poetry; the song of the lover departing at dawn and the witty exchange between a seduced shepherdess and her lover, respectively, whereas *The Return*, more remotely and ambiguously, might be taken as a return to the familiar lover, or to the poetics of the films he made before 2010. By contrast, the last of his Kodachrome films, his envoi to the tonalities of the stock, takes its title from religious devotions: *Compline* (2009), the last of the canonical hours.

Dorsky himself groups the films of the transition into a "late quartet"— sometimes subtitled "Variations and Theme"—suggesting that they be screened out of chronological order: *Sarabande* (2008), *Compline, Aubade*, and *Winter* (2007). These works are largely purged of human figures and particularly of the eloquent hand gestures and affectionate portraits that punctuate the earlier films. Of course, they are replete with the gorgeous images that the filmmaker obsessively crafts, but they are also his least accessible, most reticent films. Although the iconography changed little, the imagery takes on a greater density and complexity. Goldberg enthusiastically wrote:

> [T]he films of the "Quartet," [are] committed...to dissolving the hierarchy of background and foreground. One is struck straightaway by the opening shot of *Sarabande*—a shot of the sky (or: the moon through layer-cake clouds through winter tree branches through a gauzy black fabric)—that Dorsky is now able to accomplish with a single image what took several in *Alaya* (1987)....What's remarkable about Dorsky's cuts is their freedom from juxtaposition. There is great wit to some of the threads, but in general they're aimed at retraining our mind's eye not to read an image too quickly, so that we might first be absorbed by its graphic forms. The advancement in *Sarabande* is that with the play of textures now so assuredly nested within the image, the montage is free to enjoy itself—the sweet sensations of buoyancy and balance follow.[4]

To the contrary, I found a fragility in the montage of the Quartet, as if the filmmaker were evasively apprehensive of a truth he did not want to emerge—about his theme, or the sequence of his moods, or exhaustion of his lyrical mode, or even accumulating a fusion of all these anxieties at the threshold of old age. One might also approach the fragility in terms of poetics and ontology, seeing the Quartet as a radical questioning of the polyvalent form and an inquiry into the sources of his creative influx. That would not be a surprising consequence of the intense study of poetry in which Dorsky has been engaged since making *Winter*. With Nick Hoff, the editor of Dorsky's *Devotional Cinema*, and a small company of friends, he has been part of a poetry study group that meets every three or four weeks. Aside from Whitman, they have concentrated on poets of the twentieth century and their poetic theories: Pound, Eliot, Crane, Olson, Toomer, Niedecker, H. D., Spicer. It was the last, along with George Oppen (on whom the group spent eighteen months), who meant the most to Dorsky. In an email message to me on January 6, 2013, he wrote:

> In the last five or so years, coincident with the time of making *Pastourelle*, I began to study the poetry of George Oppen and Jack Spicer. These two poets work in a highly condensed and compacted form. Their concreteness as language, both in terms of how language sounds and how it means, creates an intense reality that is experientially present. But like a diamond, they are multi-faceted. Their fractured surface breaks open as sudden birth and revelation.

Oppen's prime mantra was "clarity." The ease with which he moved from picturing concrete particulars to delicately posed abstractions may be what Dorsky perceives when he speaks of the fractured surface breaking open. Consider Oppen's "A Theological Definition":

> A small room, the varnished floor
> Making an L around the bed,
>
> What is or is true as
> Happiness
>
> Windows opening on the sea,
> The green painted railings of the balcony
> Against the rock, the bushes and the sea running

Wedged between the detailed images of the first and third stanzas, the seven words of the middle stanza transforms Keats's culminating equation of truth and beauty in his "Ode on a Grecian Urn" to a terse interrogation of happiness and a comparative modality of truth. Oppen gets the maximal charge from the tiny conjunction "or." This might be a paradigm for the "breaking open" for which Dorsky strives in the editing of the Quartet, although the pressure is never as localized in those films as it is in the middle stanza of "A Theological Definition." Rather, it is diffused throughout each of the films, as abstract speculation is woven amid the images of the following untitled poem by Oppen from his *Discrete Series* (1934)

> Closed car—closed in glass—
> At the curb,
> Unapplied and empty:
> A thing among others
> Over which clouds pass and the
>   alteration of lightning
> An overstatement
> Hardly an exterior.
> Moving in traffic
> This thing is less strange—
> Tho the face, still within it,
> Between glasses—place, over which,
>   time passes—a false light.

Here the poet's attention to matter and light defining an urban "thing among others" closely resembles not only the cars but also the buildings, café doors and windows, crockery and utensils of Dorsky's cityscapes; for he too would make the inclosed things and shifts of illumination "overstatement[s]"— emblems or types in which truth and falsehood are at stake.

When we turn to Spicer, we see that in writing a letter to the dead poet Federico Garcia Lorca in his early book *After Lorca*, he articulates his longing to capture the sense of real things in space and time that the open-form, poly-valent cinema makes its vocabulary:

> Dear Lorca,
>
> I would like to make poems out of real objects. The lemon to be a lemon that the reader could cut or squeeze or taste—as real lemon like a newspaper in a collage is a real newspaper. I would like the moon in my poems to be a real moon, one which could be suddenly covered with a cloud that has nothing to do with the poem—a moon utterly independent of images. The imagination pictures the real. I would like to point to the real, to disclose it, to make a poem that has no sound in it but the pointing of a finger.
>
> . . .
>
> Things do not connect; they correspond. That is what makes it possible for the poet to translate real objects, to bring them across language as easily as he can bring them across time.... (pp. 33–34)

The disclosure of real objects is particularly ephemeral in *Aubade*, Dorsky's most abstract film since *Pneuma* (1983). Points of light, wandering sparkles, the play of shadows, and flowers touched by a gentle breeze predominate among the images. The film begins slowly, suggesting, without actually representing, the coming of dawn (as hinted by its title). It ends even more quietly with an unanticipated shot of shadow figures passing through a door.

Spicer, too, followed Lorca's example in writing an "Alba." It is a medieval genre, expressing the feelings of a poet leaving his lover at dawn. In his short Alba the fourth line (which I have italicized) is a striking elliptical apposition, grammatically ambiguous in buffering the initial conditional and the final imperative sentences.

> If your hand had been meaningless
> Not a single blade of grass
> Would spring from the earth's surface
> *Easy to write, to kiss—*
> No, I said, read your paper
> Be there
> Like the earth
> When shadow covers the wet grass. (p. 27)

Dorsky's *Aubade* suppresses any explicitly erotic marker that might function like Spicer's infinitive "to kiss." Yet there are two shots, taken in France, that stick out for their simplicity and vividness: one from an apartment window of a nearby building and moving clouds; the other of a bridge over the Canal de l'Ourcq. Distant figures on the bridge, with what seems to be a baby carriage, are the only human presences in the whole film. The filmmaker seems to be drawing attention and holding back at once. He has glossed the image of the canal by pointing out that Jean Vigo shot his *L'Atalante* there, as if that troubled epithalamium of 1933 haunted his film three-quarters of a century later.

With *August and After* (2011) and *April* (2012), Dorsky recovered the strength he had in the polyvalent films up through *Song and Solitude*. Here yet again the elegiac mode quickened his cinematic imagination. He spent all of August 2011 visiting his friend, the filmmaker George Kuchar, in the hospice where he was dying of cancer. That summer his friend of even longer standing, Carla Liss, who would die in January 2012, began her decline. *August and After* opens somberly with the obscure image of the stained-glass door of the hospice and a shot of a flapping flag as the sun breaks through an overcast sky. As if following the path of light into the hospice, Dorsky introduces the dying filmmaker with an image of sunlight on his frail arm and hand. In the dimly lit room we then see Kuchar's face and the strains of his gesture as he wipes his head. Before showing him wheeled out of the room, Dorsky inserts a dark image of Carla Liss, rhyming with the previous melancholy shot, as if she too were visiting on the filmmaker's last day alive. The sequence is capped by a brighter, profoundly pathetic shot of Mike Kuchar, the brother of George and himself a filmmaker, staring off. Only his beard distinguishes his looks from his shaven twin. As he awaits the death of the person closest to him throughout his life, he might be looking at his own mortality, just as Dorsky, entering his seventh decade, tropes his own mortality in this astonishing opening "stanza." The elegiac tonality pervades the rest of the film, not merely in the prevailing but by no means unremitting darkness of the exposures but also in the recurring images of mechanical men and mechanical ascents and descents. The temporal extension of *August and After*—poignantly in its *aftering*—evokes an effort to recover the devotional enthusiasm for the rhythms and textures of the daily world that distinguishes Dorsky's best work: eventually images of mechanization give way to the vibrancy of flowers and a vegetable market, a colorful stanza where first a blue, than a pink shopping bag set off a hand in a purple glove testing the ripeness of melons. Yet *August and After* never quite recovers from the shock of its initial stare at dying. Even in the gorgeous final shot of the sea and a freighter, the symbolic charge of a Stygian passage reverberates.

April, too, derives its power from exceeding the polyvalent form, however tentatively. At first it seems the film would return us to the familiar discretion of monadic images, bright colors, and vernal rejuvenation. But soon an unexpected subtheme emerges as Dorsky films his familiar terrain invaded by cell phones and plasma screens, as if he alone were left to savor the beauty of the city and the country while the inhabitants are checking their instant messages, calling each other from cafes, or falling prey to electronic advertising. The people he films without cell phones look bewildered, lost, or at a loss in the city. Among them one animated man, lunching with an unseen companion, good-humoredly gesticulates and shrugs. Whereas Dorsky tacitly admonishes us to turn off the cell phones and look about before ravenous death seizes us, this lively older man keeps conversation going despite the electronically anesthetized young with whom the filmmaker's montage symbolically surrounds him.

The New York Film Festival premiere of *The Return* was accompanied by that of Jerome Hiler's *Words of Mercury* (2012). Hiler had hitherto been one of the rare company of filmmakers of the American avant-garde cinema who hid their light under a bushel: for decades Joseph Cornell was reluctant to show his films, as I have mentioned; Wallace Berman would not exhibit his sublime *Aleph* (1966) which became available only after his death; Dean Stockwell still does not permit screenings of the films he has made. The very few people who managed to see any of the handful of films Hiler has made over the past fifty years have praised his cinema highly—most of all Dorsky, who has been Hiler's partner all those years. Filmmakers David Brooks and Warren Sonbert not only admired his work but evidently learned much from it. Critics Wheeler Dixon (also a filmmaker) and Scott MacDonald briefly discussed him in their books.[5]

Hiler, a New York-born autodidact, has worked for a music copyist, assisted the society photographer Frederick Eberstadt (who commissioned his film, *Target Rock* [2001]), projected films at the Filmmakers' Cinematheque—all when he was living in New York and on Lake Owassa in New Jersey. In Hollywood he and Dorsky made the exploitation film *Revenge of the Cheerleaders* (a cult classic from 1976), and he has lived in San Francisco as a carpenter, caretaker of a convent, and stained glass maker. He directed, with Owsley Brown III, *Music Makes a City* (2010).

The latter reflects Hiler's obsessive passion for obscure domains of music, in this case, the impressive international roster of composers commissioned to write work for the Louisville Orchestra in the 1950s. Even as a teenager he boasted an encyclopedic knowledge of medieval and Renaissance music; later, he devoted years to the study of French composers in the late nineteenth and early twentieth centuries. Similarly, he is a scholar of stained glass. He has lectured occasionally on it as the "Cinema before 1300." In 1997 the Hiler permitted the New York Film Festival to show the camera original of his then recently filmed *Gladly Given*, a ten-minute birthday present for Dorsky.

The structural principle of *Words of Mercury* reflects that of the Notre Dame composers of the twelfth- and thirteenth century, Leoninus and Perotinus, who alternated Latin verses sung in complex polyphony with verses in plainchant. Their polyphony highlighted the melodic purity of the plainchant, while the monophonic lines made the multiple voices sound all the richer. In a similar way, especially in the opening half of his twenty-five minute film, Hiler interlades lengthy superimpositions with one or two shorter shots in alternating rhythms that might be called polyoptic and monoptic. The superimpositions

almost always employ camera movement, and the monoptic shots are typically static. The effect parallels that of Notre Dame polyphony: following the
elaborate superimpositions, the still shots acquire a stressed intensity, giving
a distilled concentration to the unobscured movement of reeds in the wind,
the flight of birds, or the frolicking of a dog in the ocean. These, in turn, sen-
sitize the eye to the intricacy and wonder of the next set of superimpositions.
The turning point of the film is a monoptic panning movement around a
bronze-colored statue of Neptune, incongruously abandoned just outside the
fence of a truck lot.

This weathered head of this forsaken god separates the images of winter
from those of spring. Because the film was shot primarily in central California,
the seasonal distinctions are subtle. Although there is one monoptic shot of
snow in the mountains in the first part of the film, the patterns of hue and
tonal value play primary roles in distinguishing the film's two parts. In the
spring poem, the interludes of monopsis nearly disappear. Hiler told the
New York Film Festival audience that he sometimes forgot what he had filmed
on the underlayer of superimposition or even that he had already laid down
a track of shots, so that the developed rolls of film were a revelation to him.
The counterpuntal rhythm of the finished film transfers and sustains the excitement of the filmmaker's discovery of the in-camera polyopsis, as the long,
superimposed compositions slowly unfold. The monoptic shots, too, are carefully timed, with handmade fades that poignantly recur just before the polyoptic sequences have exhausted their charges.

Hiler provided the following note to his film:

> At the very end of *Love's Labour's Lost*, as the cast is frolicking around, a mes-
> senger comes in to announce a death which brings a sudden shift to the very
> end of the play. One of the most comical characters, now newly sober, ends
> the play with a quick dismissal of the audience: "The words of Mercury are
> harsh after the songs of Apollo. You that way—we this way."
>
> *Words of Mercury* is, if nothing else, economical. It was shot on reversal
> film and is being screened as original. Its layers of superimpositions were all
> shot in the camera. Half of the many fades in the film were made by submerg-
> ing the original film in a black liquid. The film is silent. The shooting ratio
> is low and there are areas which are unedited since taken from the camera.
> I generally shoot first and ask questions later, but I'm struck at the influences
> that I see in *Words of Mercury* because they reach back to the very first times
> that I saw great 16mm films in the early Sixties: Marie Menken, Gregory
> Markopolous, Stan Brakhage and my lifetime companion Nathaniel Dorsky.

Hiler's confession of influences is accurate. Menken pioneered the handheld
somatic camera, concentrating on and transforming everyday urban life. By
running the camera at a slow speed and sweeping over streetlights and neon
signs, she created "Night Writing" in her *Notebook* (1942–1970). The opening

superimposition of *Words of Mercury* similarly layers a dance of jittering lights over a crepuscular landscape, as if the pencil-thin white and colored lines of light were swarming midair before a barely discernible background of trees, as night falls. When the layer of "night writing" vanishes, the trees remain as soft-focused patches of light float through the foreground, suggestive of the camerawork of Stan Brakhage and his brilliant adaptation of Menken's cinematic rhetoric in *Anticipation of the Night*. In fact, the very play of the superimposition owes a debt to Brakhage, who used two layers, constructed largely by chance operations, in his *Prelude: Dog Star Man*. But unlike Brakhage, Hiler composed his superimpositions in the camera, spontaneously. In this respect he was preceded by Gregory Markopoulos, who made both *Lysis* and *Charmides* in the camera in 1948 and refined the technique in 1966, with rhythmically staccato superimpositions for *Ming Green* and the portraits of *Galaxie*. In-camera superimposition provides a more vivid palette than multi-track printing and perhaps the most obvious debt Hiler owes to Markopoulos is his color sense.

Viewers familiar with Dorsky's films seeing Hiler's work for the first time might conclude that his greatest influence has been Dorsky's mature cinema. For instance, the first monoptic shot—ten static seconds of a field of overgrown weeds before a bramble of brush—sustains the poetic charge of the previous three-minute-long polyopsis in the manner of Dorsky's stanzaic "open form." Yet one might, with equal justification, claim that Hiler has been the primary influence on Dorsky. For many years their filmmaking practice consisted largely of showing unedited footage to each other and to a small circle of friends. What Dorsky calls "open form" and "polyvalent editing" characterizes Hiler's films as well and evidently was as much his invention.

The structural or generic similarities between *Words of Mercury* and Dorsky's films bring into focus their fundamental differences. The rhythmical tension between polyoptic and monoptic images is unique to Hiler. He is also the more sophisticated colorist. Unlike Dorsky, who has a keen eye for human gestures, Hiler nearly eliminates people from his film. The distant figures of two men walking a dog on a beach in the winter half of the film minimally inscribe human presences almost to underline their absence from the rest of the film. The result is an undertone of gorgeous melancholy in which the power of cinema to wring sheer beauty from loneliness becomes a compensation for the mortal, solipsistic consciousness of the isolato behind the camera.

Shorty before editing *Words of Mercury*, Hiler saw *Love's Labour's Lost* three times. In Shakespeare's most word-intoxicated comedy, the "words of Mercury" bear the message of death. By extension, in the images of Hiler's silent film, the visual-rhythmic "songs of Apollo" are tinged with "words of Mercury." These images, as if delivered by the gods' messenger, Mercury/Hermes, are at once mercurial and hermetic. Their connotative penumbra is the most elusive and yet daunting aspect of the film for a critic daring to write about it. At the risk of putting too much weight on the title (and the filmmaker's note), one is tempted to read the conclusion of *Love's Labour's Lost* as a clue to the delicate moods of the film. In the play the "songs of Apollo" are the two performed just before the end, "Hiems" (winter) and "Ver" (spring), which neatly correspond, though in reverse order, to the two seasons of the film. For Shakespeare's frustrated, aristocratic lovers whose labors are lost because of the message of a death, the cuckoo in the song of spring heralds the specter of cuckoldry in the season's erotic frenzy, while the owl of winter wisely oversees the "merry" consolations of the humblest aspects of domestic life. Hiler's film proffers the wisdom, in turn, of a visually luscious acquiescence to time and nature's mortal and erotic betrayals.

The Markopoulos Temenos (June 28–July 1, 2012)
[Bottom] Robert Beavers and Lizzie Calligas speaking at the Temenos press conference
July, 1, 2012
Photographs by Linda Levinson

Markopoulos and the Temenos

*Recently I remembered an early conversation with Gregory while still
in New York in 1966. He said to me, "Brakhage thinks of himself as a
painter-filmmaker." I asked him, "And how do you think of yourself?" He
answered, "I am a poet-filmmaker."*
—ROBERT BEAVERS[1]

In the extraordinary case of Gregory J. Markopoulos (1928–1992), we encounter a revelatory concept of poesis and of pure cinema so powerful that it
brought the filmmaker, in the final decade of his life, to refashion in the most
radical manner all of his work, ensuring thereby that his oeuvre would be almost impossible to see. Consequently, he left one of the most ambitious and
unique projects of the cinema: *Eniaios*, an exceptionally long serial film, to be
projected at only one site, the Temenos, a modern version of a sacred Greek
precinct in central Peloponnese. This unique project represents a monument in
the history of the conjunction of cinema and poetry. Markopoulos was a prolific filmmaker and writer. He completed more than eighty films. Furthermore,
he published a book of *Poems* (1964), his journal for the production of the film
Serenity (*Quest for Serenity*, 1963), theoretical and critical essays on cinema in
four slim volumes (*Chaos Phaos*, 1971), followed in the same format by *Erb!*
(1975) and *ΗΡΑΚΛΗΣ: A Bibliography Containing the Marvellous Distortions of
My Films as Reviewed in Books, Programs, Periodicals, and Newspapers During
Thirty-Three Years 1945–1978* (1979), and numerous broadsides. He also left a
considerable body of unpublished writings, including a diary he kept all of his
adult life.

He was deeply concerned with his heritage. He preserved everything he
wrote, commissioning elegant bindings for his voluminous notebooks, film
scripts, correspondence, diaries, and even many of the meticulously annotated
books in his library. This material is housed in the Temenos archives currently
located in Zürich. Yet between 1986 and 1990, when he reedited almost all
of his films—those he had made before he immigrated to Europe in the late
1960s and dozens of films he made subsequently but had not exhibited—into

the twenty-two cycles of *Eniaios*, he threw away all the original films from which he had culled the briefest fragments. He did this with the unflinching conviction that *Eniaios*, which will run about eighty hours when it is finally printed and shown in the fastest viable form, would be the summa of his art and that eventually audiences would make pilgrimages to see it at the designated Temenos site.

The concept of "poetry" is not thematic in Markopoulos's writings or notebooks. Yet in his copy of Claude Samuel's *Entretiens avec Messiaen* he noted the passage "it is certain that my mother raised me in a climate of poetry [climat de poésie] and of fairy tales which, independent of my musical vocation, was the source of everything I did."[2] In the margin he wrote: "I too." He read with particular interest the poets of the homoerotic tradition: among others, Walt Whitman, Stefan George, Constantine Cavafy, Hart Crane, Federico Garcia Lorca, and Jean Cocteau.

At one point he writes: "I am enchanted with/by Santayana's 'Athletic Ode' and his dramatic poem, 'Lucifer.' Both I am photocopying to show [Robert Beavers],[3]" but otherwise such allusions to specific poems are very rare. More fundamentally, he identified poetry and poesis with the Greek language and ancient Greek literature in general. He read assiduously the works of Homer, Plato, and Pindar and the tragedies as well as philological studies of these works. His copiously annotated books and photocopied articles show that he consistently read these primary and critical texts with his filmmaking practice in mind. His marginalia frequently note "apply to film" and "as in film," unless he gives himself a more elaborate direction, for example, "use in analogy to hitting lens of camera + causing 'bouncing effect'" beside a page of G. S. Kirk's "The Structure of the Homeric Hexameter," in which he read of "the amphibrach word-type ($\breve{\ }-\breve{\ }$)" which causes "contiguous trochaic cuts with their famous 'bouncing' effect."[4] Even though we cannot determine precisely what Markopoulos intended to make of such intuitions, the frequency of notes relating to metrics suggests that his readings of Classical Greek prosody inspired some of the rhythmic principles of his film editing. We might tentatively suggest, then, that his sense of poetry involved a conception of an original and unitary power of rhythm at the source of all artistic expressions. His favored readings in philosophy, evidenced by the passages he copied into his notebooks from Plato, Schopenhauer, Nietzsche, Santayana, and to a lesser extent Heidegger, would tend to confirm that conception. The paucity of his own comments on poetry and poetics in the notebooks for *Eniaios* and the abundance of passages he copied out of his readings on the subject have led me to read those citations, with some critical reserve, as indices of the filmmaker's own conceptions.

Markopoulos identified filmmaking with poetry early in his career, but he tended to move away from the association after he moved to Europe in 1967.

An early letter (April 2, 1950) concerning his film *Lysis* (1948) is particularly interesting. He described the film as follows:

> Each 100' of the film are a whole. There are no cuts in the film. I tried to write a poem, by filming an idea, which was not on paper but in my mind—thus all cutting was done in the camera. We have the youthful Walt Whitman wandering through and he is at once all that is "Lysis." The various figures, reincarnations—each "whole" depict a mythological phase, but also imply several other ideas...

Here he identifies Whitman as the emblematic poet in a film that derives its title from Plato's dialogue on friendship. Above all, it is significant that he describes the act of transposing a Platonic concept to cinema as trying to "write a poem, by filming an idea." In "A Part of the Alphabet" (1961) he refers both to "poets of the Cinema" and "the poetry of cinema,"[5] while the same year he writes, "Motion pictures, say the New American Cinema filmmakers, have the beat of poetry; a poetry which is not an imitation of the written word"[6] ("Avant Garde Chronicle"). A similar preference for cinematic over written poetry can be found in "Jean Genet's Only Film: *Un chant d'amour*" (1961): "*Un chant d'amour* is the divine moment of inspiration before the poet has destroyed his idea by writing it on paper."[7] Yet the following year in "The Golden Poet" he places verbal and cinematic poetry on the same plane: "Ron Rice's images in *Senseless* become linked in a golden chain, and like the words of a poem they quarrel, dispute and seek their meaning through the joyous encounter of light upon imprisoned celluloid."[8] Such attempts to speak of cinema in terms of poetry disappear from his later writings until, changing his notion, he attacks the very idea in the 1986 essay, "The Amygdaline Grove," in which he would declare: "Not knowing what film was Parker Tyler spoke of the poetry of the film."[9] By this time his mantra "film as film" left no room for analogy to another art form.

Markopoulos's writings demonstrate that he distrusted systematic theoretical discourses and never intended to produce one. There is very little exposition or sustained argument in his essays, and what there is of it diminishes with the years. Early on, he writes of the filmmakers who impress and inspire him; he recounts his experiences as a filmmaker; he records his insights and sketches his plans. After meeting Robert Beavers in 1965, he seldom wrote of any other filmmakers. They lived together in a number of European countries until Markopoulos died in 1992. When he is not discussing his own work, he is expressing his enthusiasm for Beavers's films. This proceeds for a decade, film by film.

After 1976 almost all of Markopoulos's writing focuses on the exhibitions and plans of the Temenos, his Wagnerian project for a cinematic pilgrimage site devoted to his and Beavers's works. The notion of such a site seems to have struck the filmmaker sometime in the late 1960s. It evolved in purely theoretical terms for at least a decade, perhaps in dialectical opposition to the Anthology Film Archives, which initiated the utopian phase of its project in 1970. Markopoulos's writings on the Temenos focused somewhat more concretely once he had chosen a site for it.

Thus Markopoulos decided in 1980 that there was only one place in the world to show his films as they were intended. That was near Lyssaraia, a village high in the mountains of Arcadia in the Peloponnesus, from which his father had immigrated to Toledo, Ohio, where the filmmaker was born. Alluding to ancient Greek religious traditions, he called the place he had selected for his theater a *temenos*—a sacred precinct, literally a place "cut off" and dedicated to a divinity, where usually an altar, a temple, and a cult image would be erected. For seven years, he and Beavers held al fresco screenings there every summer.

His death prevented him from seeing any version of *Eniaios* printed or projected there. Under Beavers's guidance, the Temenos resumed its continuing exhibition in 2004, 2008, and 2012 with the initial cycles of *Eniaios* being shown there in three-day-long festivals. Beavers's intention is for this process to continue every four years as more reels are prepared for projection. Since no one, not even Beavers, has seen the entire *Eniaios* at this time (2013), I can only describe the first three manifestations and the notes for the project that I have read in the filmmaker's published essays and in the manuscripts held by the Temenos archives. Therefore, I shall largely reprint here and elaborate on reports I wrote for *Artforum* following the screenings of 2004, 2008, and 2012 before discussing Markopoulos's writings and their relation to poetry.

For three nights, from June 25 to 27, 2004, between 100 and 200 spectators gathered in the field outside the village of Lyssaraia in Greece to view the premiere of the first three of twenty-two cycles of *Eniaios*. If the whole work, whose title means both "Unity" and "Uniqueness," is consistent with the portion of it we saw then and subsequently, it will be the most demanding film ever made; it will also be one of the most rewarding. The pilgrims who visited the Temenos that first summer found a large screen, a powerful freestanding projector, and, of course, the filmic image. A few benches and remarkably comfortable beanbag cushions defined the freshly mowed theater. Nothing in the simplicity of the setup would prepare us for the splendor of the event, aside from the beauty of the surrounding landscape; for it was here in Arcadia that the urbane poets of the Greek and Roman world imagined shepherds inventing and refining poetic language. Markopoulos's vision of the Temenos encompassed the idea of cinema as the fulfillment of the spirit of poetry and a key to its origins.

The first two and a half cycles of *Eniaios* turned out to be an astonishing revelation of cinematic power.[10] Markopoulos stripped his films of their often complex soundtracks. Excluding the few black-and-white films he had made before 1960, he reedited almost everything else, from *Psyche* (1947) through *Sorrows* (1969); he embedded short fragments, sometimes just single frames, from these works in rhythmically organized stretches of black or clear film. He included some sixty-five previously unseen films (mostly portraits and films of places—many of the sacred places: Delphi, the Aesclepion of Kos, Chartres Cathedral, the Theater of Dionysus) in the twenty-two cycles. It wasn't until 1997, when Beavers printed the reediting of *Twice a Man* and permitted the New York Film Festival to screen it, that it was possible to get any sense of Markopoulos's new conception of his life's work. Yet that glimpse hardly prepared us for the Temenos exhibition. The isolation of the event, the sense that the serial film had been created in harmony with the natural environment in which it was shown, the amassing rhythms stretched over three nights of some ten hours of projections, and the internal intricacies of *Eniaios* gave it its extraordinary cumulative force. Both the scale and the internal dynamics of *Eniaios* belie the impression created by the reedited, silent *Twice a Man*, which will be divided into four parts and incorporated in cycles IV, VIII, XV, and XIX (see Appendix).

The dedication of *Eniaios* and the first cycle, which Beavers decided at the last minute to screen over the first two nights rather than in an initial five- or six-hour stretch, turned out to be among the most demanding film session imaginable. The first three-quarters of an hour of *Eniaios* introduced the whole work with scattered flashes of white frames and glimpses of ancient stones from the supposed funeral pyre of Herakles. By the 1980s Herakles had become the most fascinating mythological figure for Markopoulos. He even dated the entries in the set of his notebooks (called *Chiron*) that he devoted to researching the background of *Eniaios* by what he called the "homosexual year" or *days of Herakles*, beginning day 1 of his calendar: December 25.

Pyra Heracleos (the funeral pyre of Herakles) flashes its title in a code of white frames representing different letters of the Greek alphabet. Of course, viewers could not decipher the cryptogram, but the cinematic rhythms it produces tutor the eyes for the hours to follow.

In ἑνιαῖος *(The Divine Series)*, volume 9, begun January 2, 1988, Markopoulos first conceived of the idea of spelling out words with film frames. He tried the Roman alphabet before turning to Greek. Thus he noted that "fire" would be "6 9 18 5." He adds "Result: a visual script—but no one would know what the word or words were. What is the worth of all this?" On the opposite page he answers his own question: "of course, after numerous viewings, the Amor, spectator could be told what the line of frame variations represented. This would result with Skeptics and Enthusiasts." From this entry we can infer that the filmmaker envisions a community of committed viewers of his work in the future (called individually "the Amor") who would look at the eighty-hour film repeatedly and, further, that even among those viewers there would be two camps—those skeptical about the use of frame flashes as cryptograms and those enthusiastic about following the leads they provide. Apparently, he believed such a division of opinion was a productive response to the work. As an artist who spent years scouring libraries in his study of ancient and modern texts, he seems to be imagining future viewers of *Eniaios* tracking down the allusions, parallel to the critical reception of, say, Joyce's *Finnegans Wake* or Pound's *The Cantos*.

There are no titles or formal breaks in the *Pyra Heracleos*; so this "dedication" seamlessly shifts to an equally minimalist revision of *Psyche*—the film that had established the reputation of its nineteen-year-old maker, in which very short flashes, often just single frames, of the originally lush adaptation of a Pierre Louÿs novella, was now divested of its narrative logic and even of its illusions of movement: the fragmentation brought the imagery to the brink of stasis, so that after some hours hovering around that threshold, the image of a couple walking into a Japanese garden had the breathtaking effect of the reinvention of cinematic movement. As we all recalibrated our expectations and adjusted to the unfamiliar rhythms of *Eniaios*, it became apparent that Markopoulos was pacing the dedication and the first cycle for the long haul of the eighty-hour opus. Not even Warhol's most static films so firmly insisted on establishing an unexpected and expansive temporal scale. *Eniaios* both fascinated (with its elusive yet intricate rhythms) and severely resisted absorption. The minimalization and persistent interruption of the images permitted us to see the screen as an object, trembling with projected light, under the starry night as the moon rose and set and as the "septet" of Ursa Major, under which the screen stood, imperceptibly swung a giant arc. The tension between the rapidity of the montage and the slowness of its thematic or imagistic evolution encouraged the double consciousness of this unique film, meticulously articulating its own frame of reference, and of all films, or rather the cinema itself, hieratically declaring its fundamental elements, making the screen an altar at the edge of the night sky. Not until the second night would we know that Markopoulos did not extend the radical minimalism of the opening hours consistently throughout the cycle—or the whole work for that matter.

The next day, discussions of Markopoulos's work and attempts to make sense of the first screening fueled the camaraderie of the pilgrims during the daylight hours. A persistent question was whether or not it was an advantage to have seen *Psyche* (or any of the other elements of *Eniaios*) in its original version. Beavers believes it would be advantageous to encounter the work freshly in its final form. That was the case for the great majority of the spectators. It was a young audience. I don't think more than a handful of us had ever met the filmmaker; certainly no one there knew him longer than I had. I may have been the only one to have studied repeatedly and to have written on the films Markopoulos released before immigrating to Europe. We met and became close friends in 1961, although that friendship was troubled after his emigration from America to Europe. I mention this because my personal relationship to Markopoulos and to his early films was inextricable from the overwhelming charge I felt watching the end of the first cycle the second night.

For more than forty years I had seen his first trilogy, *Du sang, de la volupté et de la mort* (1947–1948) consisting of *Psyche, Lysis,* and *Charmides,* as a sequence with diminishing success. The first installment, a narrative of the troubled love affair between a man and a woman, struck me as a work of genius; the second, an autobiographical poem edited in the camera, was fascinating and often brilliant; but the third, also edited in the camera, merely left me puzzled. In those years, I had questioned the aptness of the titles of the latter two, taken from early, deliberately inconclusive dialogues of Plato—*Lysis,* on the nature of friendship between young men and *Charmides,* on temperance, inspired by the physical beauty of the eponymous adolescent. That the young Markopoulos was pointing to the homoerotic foundations of Platonic discourse was evident, and perhaps he even identified with the objects of Socrates's attention. Freighted with my memory of the earlier film versions and with periodic readings of Plato, my response to the second night turned out to be quite different from the puzzlement expressed by many of my fellow pilgrims, who did not recognize material from the earlier films or even know their original titles.

As at past Temenos events, there was an elegantly printed program—sixteen pages in a 16-by-11½" format—distributed free to the spectators. It contained two articles by Markopoulos with Greek titles—"Entheos"[11] ["Inspired", "Full of the God"] and "Eikones Auton"[12] ["Images of Selves"]. Like all of Markopoulos's essays, these are poetic texts: elliptical, sometimes baffling, seemingly hyperbolical in their claims. But it has been my experience in reading Markopoulos's essays that what might appear inflated at first turns out to have considerable cogency and originality on careful reexamination. I shall consider his writings in some detail further on.

In "Entheos," he wrote of the work of "Time, Patience, and most of all Reflection" in the Temenos experience, dismissing educators, historians, and polemicists of "the New." "Eikones Auton" claims that "The creative man seeks to give the Spectator those parts of himself which allow him, the creative man, to be creative." As he often did, he calls his goal "film as film." The essay culminates thus: "A pulse when the placement of a series of frames, independent of each other predominate, and, are cast towards each other; and against one another. Therein establishing the beat to the pulse. *This is the ultimate aspect of the film as film*" (Markopoulos's italics).[13] I took his encouragement of the spectator's reflection, his confidence in the pulse of microinstants to generate the matrices of meaning, to justify the ineluctably personal character of my thoughts and emotions throughout the long chilly second night's screening.

One of the tutelary deities of the Temenos is the physician-god Asclepius, whose cult was a special object of Markopoulos's study. The Temenos archive holds a copy of K. Kerényi's *Asklepios: Archetypal Image of the Physician's Existence,*[14] acquired by the filmmaker in 1969. He also collected photocopies of numerous articles on Greek medicine and the Asclepius cult, including Gregory Vlastos's impressive critique of the book *Asclepius* by Emma and

Ludwig Edelstein[15] in which he repudiated their attempt to treat the cult as a confraternity of physicians devoted to rational medical practices.[16] In pagan Greece, patients would make pilgrimages to the shrines of Asclepius as though to a sanitarium where they would sleep and have their dreams interpreted as part of their cure. Markopoulos conceived of the Temenos, and the pilgrimages necessary to benefit from it, as a cure of media pollution. The Temenos experience would reunite "film as film" to the landscape of ancient poetry as an essentially rhythm-induced therapy. It asserts its own time frame and requires the patience that makes creative reflection possible. He took the Asclepian tradition quite seriously. In the margins of Kerényi's book, next to the sentence "The presence of a well fits in with a 'temple secret' recorded by the Greek traveler Pausianias," he wrote: "in the Temenos there must be a secret—what secret?" Perhaps the code of flashing frames for letters of the Greek alphabet would be the temple secret he pondered while reading Kerényi. Further on, besides "Hippocratic writings bound everyone wishing to practice medicine to consider his teacher as his father…" he questioned: "apply to new filmmakers and who teaches them?" Once he completed the editing of *Eniaios*, he immediately embarked on what would have been an even longer film, *Asklepiades*, of which only unedited rolls of film remain, shot at Hölderlin's Tower, Alessandro Manzoni's house, a Goethe and Schiller monument, and a World War I memorial.

The fragments from *Lysis* seemed longer than those of the previous night, and the shots from *Charmides* were much longer still, although very quick by conventional standards. Somewhat adjusted to the temporal dynamics of *Eniaios*, marveling at the nuances of pulsation within the first cycle, I found myself wondering if it were possible that the nineteen-year-old Markopoulos had had a profound understanding of Plato's texts. The fragmentary images from *Lysis* seemed to resonate with new beauty. The reediting stripped the trilogy of its genres, investing individual images with new weight and dignity. In so draining the original films of their contextual meanings and associations, Markopoulos was enacting an aesthetic version of the apophatic theology of the Greek Orthodox Church in which he had been instructed as a child: a state of ecstasy and a process of deification accompany the denial of positive attributes to God. As manifested in *Eniaios*, "film as film" is a repudiation of the conventional attributes and genres of cinema.

Following trains of thought and stimulated by the isolated images drawn from *Lysis* and *Charmides,* I realized that the spectators gathered in the Temenos were joined in bonds of friendship abundantly manifested in various ways among the foreign pilgrims. Had the young Markopoulos noticed that, although the definition of friendship alludes to Socrates and his interlocutors in the dialogue, the discussion itself creates and reinforces friendships? How deeply had the filmmaker read in *Charmides* the tension between the physical appeal of a young man and the spiritual ambiguity of his acts, now brilliantly lucid in the reedited frames "cast toward each other, and against one another"? The isolated images of a college campus and a young man holding the small figure of a horse with a missing leg, clarified Markopoulos's polemic against university education and the moral damage it can cause adolescents that had always been implicit in the film. Its seriousness and depth hit me, as did an insight into the disappointment, bordering on a sense of betrayal, that my own career as a professor and the consequent academization of my critical prose in the 1970s may have caused Markopoulos and clouded our friendship. This train of thought ended when suddenly there appeared the kaleidoscopic rhythms of *The Illiac Passion* (1967), the filmmaker's intricate compendium of mythological themes inspired by Aeschylus's *Prometheus Bound*.

The third and final night of the Temenos was the longest. The whole second cycle and half of the third were screened, at which point Beavers decided it was necessary to halt the projections, under pressure from the Lyssaraia firemen, who had been on duty for seven hours that night to keep an eye on the gasoline-driven generator. It was also the most sensuous and spectacular of the projections. Opening with images from *Ming Green* (1966), an exquisite evocation of the filmmaker's New York apartment, the cycle featured a series of portraits: Parker Tyler (from *Galaxie* [1966]), Mark Turbyfill (from *Through a Lens Brightly: Mark Turbyfill* [1967]) and four previously unseen portraits from *Political Portraits* (1969, reedited ca. 1976). Markopoulos generally posed his subjects sitting or standing still, as if for a painting or a photograph. So the very brevity of the shots of these figures or of the rooms, when flashing on the otherwise blank screen, kept the second cycle at the threshold of stasis we had experienced in watching the first cycle of the film, even though images were apparently longer, richer in color, and more varied. In this context, the second manifestation of *The Illiac Passion* again marked the moment of maximal internal movement. Other incorporations were largely of films with little movement within the frame: *Eros, O Basileus* (1966); the first of half of his previously unseen film of Delphi, and *Sorrows*, a study of Wagner's house. This allusion to Wagner early in *Eniaios* implicitly acknowledged the debt of the film and the Temenos project itself to the Ring Cycle and to Bayreuth.

The remarkable visual style of *Eniaios* is a radicalization of the editing techniques the filmmaker had developed throughout his career. When he made *Psyche*, Markopoulos explored the dynamics of very quick editing. Two years later, he extended his initial discoveries into the extensive montage sequences of *Swain* (1950), rapidly recapitulating images from shots seen earlier in the film. In 1963 he gave his editing style a theoretical basis in the essay "Towards a New Narrative Film Form"[17] in which he argued for "the use of short film phrases which evoke thought-images." In *Twice a Man* (1963), these brief phrases could be as short as single frames—shots lasting only 1/24th of a second. Enthusiasm for this mode of editing, both in the camera and on the editing table, inspired an astonishingly fecund period of filmmaking for Markopoulos. He made his densest and most complex films between 1963 and 1968. Yet at the same time he began to make extraordinary works filmed in a single session or two—portraits (thirty of them are collected in *Galaxie*) and evocations of places, such as his apartment on West Eleventh Street in New York (*Ming Green*) and the Church of St. John on Hydra (*Bliss* [1967]).

From the start of his career, the filmmaker had liberally drawn on literary models: Plato, Aeschylus, Euripides, Pierre Louÿs, Hawthorne, and Balzac. After visiting Caresse Crosby's Italian castle Roccasinibalda in 1961, he wrote an adaptation of Julien Gracq's novel *Au château d'Argol* (1938), which he intended to film there. However, when he revisited the castle in 1967, he filmed just two one-hundred-foot rolls of film—approximately five minutes—recording only its interior details, and its environs, without a narrative or even people. Then he edited them into a fifty-five-minute-long film, *Gammelion* (1968), by placing very brief images amid a thousand fades to black or clear leader. I believe this transformation of five minutes of imagery into a nearly hour-long film was the germ of the style of *Eniaios*, in which brief glimpses of places, people, and actions appear amid passages of white and black. For hours in *Eniaios*, the screen flashes and winks with gorgeous vestiges of ancient ruins, mythic narratives, and figures from the art world. However, until Order XIII is restored and projected, we will not be able to compare *Gammelion* within the matrix of *Eniaios* with the version of the film he completely remade specifically for it.

Four years after the first unveiling of *Eniaios*, between June 27 and 29, 2008, the Temenos presented the second installment of the film to an international audience of about 200 spectators, with large contingents from the United States, Great Britain, Germany, and Greece. Some came from as far as Brazil and Australia. Robert Beavers screened Orders III, IV, and V, each running three to four hours. On the basis of the eight orders we have seen so far and the schematic outline of the whole film, it appears that Markopoulos reedited all of his films separately, embedding single frames and very short fragments in carefully constructed rhythmic patterns of black and white leader, without fades or dissolves. While reediting the individual films and apparently shooting several sections—predominately films of ancient sites—specifically for it, he assembled the monumental opus into twenty-two orders, dispersing the longer films throughout the work. There are two parts of *The Illiac Passion* (1964–1967) in all twenty-two orders, with four sections of it in the finale. *Eros, O Basileus* (1967) appears in eight orders, also with three segments alternating with the four of *The Illiac Passion* at the end. *Twice a Man* and *The Mysteries* (1968) each participate in four orders but never together, *Himself as Herself* (1967) is likewise in three. Five other films will appear in two parts each.

Temenos 2008 demonstrated the abiding power of *Eniaios*; the three evenings in which Orders III, IV, and V were screened revealed the continuity of the vast project and the aesthetic autonomy of its parts. Even the disappointment of a truncated Order IV, seen without the concluding three reels—the first segments of *Eros, O Basileus, Twice a Man*, and *Chronion* (a film of the Asclepian ruins on Kos made specifically for *Eniaios*), which could not be printed in time—failed to diminish the triumph of the event. *Eniaios* sustained its initial authority in exalting the purity and glory of the cinematic experience. A pattern of construction with the orders began to appear: each comprises between four and eight elements. Portraits tend to appear near the beginning of a cycle; segments of the mythic narratives appear in the second half. Depictions of places can appear in either half. The short fragmentary shots from the narratives are often longer than the rapid-fire flashes from the portraits and places. The combination of these genres sets in motion elaborate thematic reverberations that contribute, along with the rhythmic orchestrations, to the tonal identity of each order.

The screenings of the first night of Temenos 2008 overlapped with those of the third and final night four years earlier. In Order III, a complex series of portraits precedes two installments from the longer films—the third fragment of *The Illiac Passion* and the first glimpse of *The Mysteries*, originally a Huysmansesque psychodrama. The witty double portrait of the British artists, Gilbert and George as "living sculpture" opens the order. It is followed by *Genius* (1970), in which portraits of the artists David Hockney and Leonor Fini are intercut with one of art dealer Daniel-Henry Kahnweiler. Initially Markopoulos shot three autonomous portraits, but he quickly came to believe that he had been making a version of Faust without realizing it. He first called the film *The Illuminations of Faust* and later settled on *Genius*. In his essay "The Redeeming of the Contrary," published in the spring 1971 issue of *Film Culture*, Markopoulos stressed the ambiguity of his creation and the intuitive nature of his working processes: "I had no idea that these three figures of the art world…would become the very elements of my Faust. And yet they did. They evolved, once the decision was made, effortlessly."[18] The spontaneity of this evolution from autonomous portraits of figures "sitting in their own rooms" lies at the core of what Markopoulos took to be his gift to his future audience:

> Beloved spectators of my distant Temenos, what evolved was the ultimate concern for the medium of film. A continuous working decision not to betray you as film spectators; not to impose a message in your laps. But to deposit before you on a virile screen the very depths which concerned the present work in such a manner that you might one day at its presentation realize that I have been concerned always for you. I now repeat again the word, an effortless illusion and triumph with the legend of Faust; and, with the future film spectator of the Temenos supplying the very brilliance.[19]

I find it unlikely that any of us watching the film in Arcadia thought of Kahnweiler as a figure for Faust, Fini as Mephistopheles (despite the clue of her cat in her lap), or Hockney as the servant, Wagner. Rather, I would take the Whitmanian expression of affection and confidence in "the future film spectator" to suggest that the tonality of each of the orders frames and guides the range of associations stirred up as we watch the cycles and gauge the nuanced relationships of the filmic elements to one another. Thus in the first five orders, Markopoulos locates himself and his artistic ambitions amid distinguished artists, critics, and collectors and situates his work in the context of ancient art and religion. Within that schema, the third order, subtitled *Schemata tou stomatos* (Shapes of the Mouth), suggests undercurrents of an uncanny disturbance within Promethean creativity, for which the legend of Faust would be an appropriate analog, but not an allusion essential to catching the tone of the cycle. Beavers, offering a rare insight into the organization of the order during the conference that he offers the third afternoon of each Temenos festival, pointed out the predominance of Promethean fire in the cycle. It is particularly dominant in the segment from *The Illiac Passion*.

The cumulative effect of the portraits of Gilbert and George, the triad of *Genius*, and the subsequent portraits of ballerina Marcia Haydée, sculptor Barbara Hepworth, collector and restaurateur Hulda Zumsteg, and poet/critic Edouard Roditi introduce disturbing moments within the Asclepian dreamscape under the veneer of serenity. The ironic displacement of violence becomes most apparent when Roditi seems to kiss or lick a skull. Like the "unsuspecting figures" of *Genius*, who, Markopoulos asserted, "represent, in their own milieu, the crises of our times,"[20] in the context of this order, Roditi bridges the portrait series and the fragmentary narratives that follow it; his gesture anticipates the antics of Taylor Mead as the "Demon or Sprite" of *The Illiac Passion*, crystallizing the order's critique of homosexual postures in the art world.

Nephele photos (The Cloud of Light), as Markopoulos titled the fourth order, shifts the tone. A somber, regal portrait of Giorgio de Chirico precedes the religious imagery of the reedited *Bliss*, in which the play of light within a Byzantine church allows us to glimpse the iconic representations of the prophet Jonah, St. John the Baptist, and the Virgin Mary. Redemption and prophetic rejuvenation would seem to be the theme of the order, although without seeing the three concluding reels we can only speculate about its ultimate impression. The aged figures of De Chirico and Alberto Moravia (whose portrait occupies the fourth segment) would contrast with the youthful images of the teenage Beavers, whom Markopoulos filmed, nude, as the god of love in *Eros, O Basileus*. Furthermore, that is the theme of the final reel of that order: the opening of *Twice a Man*, which retells the myth of Hippolytus and his resurrection by Asclepius.

The most impressive revelation of Temenos 2008 occurred within the fourth order. The hitherto unseen *Cimabue! Cimabue!* (1971) followed the reel of *Bliss*. The original version was probably the most complex of all the films

Markopoulos completed but never printed before he began *Eniaios*. In its elaborate editing, with extensive use of upside-down shots, it interweaves images of several of the filmmaker's friends and supporters in Florence—the portrait painter Pietro Annigoni, poet Carlo Betocchi, painter Silvio Loffredo, and the art restorer Umberto Baldini, whom we glimpse restoring Cimabue's great Crucifix, damaged by the Florentine flood of 1966. Following the religious exultation of *Bliss*, the film celebrates both restoration and film editing as if they were modes of prayer, while it treats the new friends the filmmaker found in relocating to Europe as saints in a Byzantine mosaic. The Cloud of Light, from the subtitle of the order, simultaneously refers to traditional halos and to the emulsion of the colored frames of film embedded in the flashing passages of white and black leader. *Cimabue! Cimabue!* is clearly the companion piece to Robert Beavers's first masterpiece, *From the Notebook of...* (1971–1998), which he made in Florence during the same period. Both films rejoice in wonder at the artistic traditions of Florence and mark the period of their creation with enthusiasm for working within that city.

The title of the fifth order, *To mega chasma* (The Great Chasm), seems at first to refer to the gap of time between the present and the Grecian past; for two of the four elements of the cycle (*Hagiographia* [1973] and *Epidaurus*) depict the ruins of the Byzantine city of Mistra and the Asclepian clinic of Epidaurus. The fifth segment of *The Illiac Passion* and the second of *The Mysteries* constitute the other parts. Instead of reediting the original version of *Hagiographia* (1970) for *Eniaios*, Markopoulos returned to Mistra in 1973 to make a one-hundred-and-fifty minute version of the original sixty-minute film, which he completed in 1979. *The Great Chasm* continues the religious/ Byzantine strain of *Cloud of Light*, emphasizing the vestiges of religious and sexual agony amid evocations of transcendence and cure. Markopoulos uses the film screen as an iconostasis. For him, the temporal chasm was not a simple matter. At the very start of the 1970 essay, "Towards a Temenos," printed in the elegant brochure distributed to all the spectators of Temenos 2008, he posed the question "What is a vision?" and answered it: "A vision is always the future. The moment we consider the past or the present we are consumed by the constant future."[21]

Markopoulos would not have envisioned the labor and expense of restoration (after the original edited reels of film sat untouched for up to twenty years after he edited them) required to make any of the orders of *Eniaios* finally visible. Nor would he have conceived of the temporal scale of a commitment to see the work in ritualized intervals of up to four years per installment. (He imagined a continuous performance that a pilgrim could see in one extended visit.) Yet his film implicitly, and the accompanying text explicitly, dwell on the extraordinary structures of time at the heart of the Temenos experience. The film repeatedly invokes the monumental history of Greek civilization, showing at once the deterioration of its cultic centers and the survival of ruins.

It hammers home the mechanical limit of cinematic time—the single frame of 1/24th of a second, on the very threshold of visibility—against the nocturnal rotation of the fixed stars and wandering planets, perceptible only when the spectators, turning from the flickering screen to the surrounding sky, recall the positions of those celestial bodies the last time they looked away. Thus, this remarkable masterpiece of the cinematic sublime raises the question of whether any of us will live to see the work in its entirety.

Although the division of the film into sets of three orders every four years is an accident born of the economic impossibility of exhibiting all twenty-two orders in sequence, as Markopoulos would have wished, each of the three installments screened thus far has produced its own revelations. As exhibited in 2012, Orders VI, VII, and VIII highlight the importance of Christian religious sites and experiences for the filmmaker, as well as his ambivalence toward them. Furthermore, these orders play evocations of religious ecstasy off his love for Beavers. Uncharacteristically, all three orders have roughly the same shape: a portrait, a religious site, another portrait, followed by excerpts from *The Illiac Passion, Eros, O Basileus*, and either *Himself as Herself* [VI] or *Twice a Man* [VIII]. (Order VII substitutes the first of two explorations of the ruins of ancient Olympia for the final two film excerpts. The second Olympia film will appear in XVIII).

In reediting *Himself as Herself* for its first insertion into *Eniaios*, the filmmaker started at the conclusion of the film, selecting frames from the scene in which the anguished, narcissistic protagonist falls to his knees in Boston's Trinity Church. In this new context, Markopoulos has erased his original critique of what he called "black-tie Athenianism" (referring to the closeted clique of affluent American homosexuals) to resituate the film in a field of allusions to the aesthetic sublimation of eros in the Christian West. It marks the end of Order VI, whose argument begins by framing a lengthy vision of Chartres Cathedral with a portrait, first of the studio and work of the Léger-influenced painter Diamantis Diamantopoulos, then of the painter himself, before the first appearance of *The Illiac Passion*. Between that and *Himself as Herself* Markopoulos has placed what will probably be the longest of ten sections of *Eros, O Basileus* scheduled to appear in *Eniaios*. The schema for the whole work indicates that in the final order, three sections of that film will be interlaced with four of *The Illiac Passion*, underlining the centrality of these two works to the immense project.

The atomization of *The Illiac Passion* in Order VI divests Taylor Mead (in his role as the Sprite or fire-spirit) of his campy performance. In nearly still flashes his encounter with the Prometheus figure at the heart of the film takes on a prophetic intensity that Beavers in his quadrennial public conference, acknowledged was closer to Markopoulos's intention. In fact, in near proximity to the evocation of Olympia (Order VII), the Sprite's startled gestures suggest the role of the seer from the east pediment of the temple of Zeus, now in the Archaeological Musueum at Olympia. Thus the fire-spirit seems to have seen something ominous in the restrained beauties of Diamantopoulos and Chartres as the filmmaker conjured them. His Chartres Cathedral was all façade until a final tantalizing flash of the rose windows: images of the towers, the masonry, the pedimental statues, often upside down.[22] In dialectical opposition to the first half of the order, Markopoulos offers much more sustained images from *Eros, O Basileus.*

The role assigned to Chartres in Order VI is fulfilled by *Punschun* in VII. The title means "silver thistle" in Romansh, the language of Graubünden, Switzerland, where the film was shot and where Markopoulos and Beavers lived in the early 1970s. Its triadic structure, labeled "pathos, logos, phobos" in the program notes, moves from the gorgeous landscape surrounding the small Catholic chapels built in the late seventeenth century to their interior and exterior details and, at last, to a long passage of flashes of a St. Sebastian altarpiece. The Guido Reni-like image of the saint with his hands tied above his head rhymes with the subsequent glimpses of the Prometheus of *The Iliac Passion,* symbolically holding up his arms as if bound to a rock. Nested between portraits of Georges Auric, who composed the music for most of Jean Cocteau's films, and Alberto Cavalcanti, the filmmaker of *Dead of Night* (1945), a covertly gay horror film (for which Auric also composed the score), *Punschun's* St. Sebastian looms as an icon of the pathos and phobos of homosexual life in the Christian era. As *Eniaios* emerges, its grand themes seem to be the metamorphoses of luminous energy and the anatomy of homoerotic love.

Just as the reduction of *The Illiac Passion's* lush imagery and mannerisms to still or nearly still flashes transformed the Sprite's performance in Order VI, the rapid glimpses of Icarus's wings—a brightly colored celluloid construction—gives them a magical aura in VIII. In fact, Beavers, speaking in his conference to the audience of the 2012 Temenos, speculated that the mythology of the film as it appears in *Eniaios* was "closer to the filmmaker's intention" than in the leisurely shots of the 1967 version. Icarus and Daedalus are central to VIII, in which the excerpts from *Eros, O Basileus* and *Twice a Man* suggest the tragic or problematic relations of sons to their parents. The passages from the latter two films are the longest shots to appear (as of 2012) in *Eniaios.* They include Eros's contemplation of an egg—a reference to his birth from the "egg of Night"[23] according to Hesiod—and Hippolytus's visit to Phaedra's house as his Asclepian lover awaits and/or mourns him.

The first three elements of Order VIII have no apparent connection to the anxieties of filial relations. A portrait of the Greek poet, Odysseus Elytis, precedes a longer study of an ephebe posing inside and outside a Byzantine church in Thessoloniki. A portrait of the painter, Valerio Adami, in his studio follows that. Adami is a pop artist whose cloissonist serigraphs, clearly seen in the portrait, resemble stained glass windows. (There are frequent instances in his work of explicitly homosexual themes, although we do not see any in the film portrait.)

It may be an error to look for a rigorous thematic cohesion within each order. The Greek titles Markopoulos assigned to them are as elusive as they are suggestive. In the first place, his Greek is often a strange fusion of classical and modern diction and just as often thoroughly ambiguous; for example, the phrase chronō ouden ousa (his title for Order VI) is made up of the noun *time,* the pronoun *nothing* or *no one,* and a feminine form of the participle *being*; it has no clear sense in either modern or ancient Greek and no obvious relevance to any of the six films incorporated in the order. However, the expression he gave to VII, φωνη φωνων, can be translated "sound of sounds" or "voice of voices," so it would be appropriate for a cycle that begins with the portrait of a composer. He seems to have invented the compound ouranobatēs (VIII): "heaven-tread" or "sky-step" (or adapted it from the modern technical vocabulary of still photography, in which it might refer to shooting the sky). The aeronautic pair, Daedalus and Icarus, the winged god, Eros, and even the twice-born Hippolytus can be considered under this rubric. More remotely, it would encompass the Nobel-prize winning poet, Elytis, of "The Axion Esti" and the Byzantine church with its images defaced by iconoclasm. Yet, in the end, the Greek titles become another disconcerting element in the puzzle. Of course, it will be many years before the monumental mosaic of *Eniaios* can be viewed with clarity. Yet this much is certain: it is continually surprising in its inventions, ravishing in its details, and fecund in its elusive provocation of thought.

From the very first texts Markopoulos wrote, we can see that the young filmmaker had an extraordinary sense of mission and absolute faith in his instincts. The account of the abandoned 1951 film *L'Arbre aux champignons* begins discussing the inspiration of sorcery and speaks of the filmmaker's process as akin to dreaming. The even earlier diary of Robert C. Freeman Jr., quoted in "From Fanshawe to Swain," records with wonder the uncanny reliance of the young filmmaker on his muses: "When in a few instances I have protested obscurity of purpose and inconsistency, he (dictator as he admits himself to be) claims some sort of divine guardian (his achievements support him strongly) in his inconsistent consistency." The oxymoron "inconsistent consistency"[24] might well characterize Markopoulos's entire poetics. He is an Emersonian, like so many other major American avant-garde filmmakers, who took to heart the warning of "Self-Reliance": "A foolish consistency is the hobgoblin of little minds, adored by little statesman and philosophers and divines. With consistency a great soul has simply nothing to do."

As Markopoulos became a more experienced writer and filmmaker, his articulations of the divine guardianship of which Freeman wrote became more and more sophisticated, while many of the reversals of his polemical positions are startling. When he wrote "The Driving Rhythm" in 1966 he had already begun to use the automatic fade mechanism of his Bolex camera, yet he asserted that "from the very beginning of my interest with the medium of film I regarded the use of fade-ins, fade-outs, dissolves and other such effects with complete abhorrence."[25] In essays of the early 1970s, he states that the use of fades-in and -out are central structural principles of his work. "Stille Nacht" (1961) opens with the laudatory line: "For some twenty-one films, Stan Brakhage has been invading the motion picture screen, possessed with the majesty of silence."[26] Yet, four years later, in "Inherent Limitations," he cites Brakhage as an example of a filmmaker who ignores the essential function of sound and consequently "refuse[s] to understand the element invested in the human form."[27] Ironically, it would be another twenty or more years before Markopoulos would ultimately decide to divest his life's work of its soundtracks and present *Eniaios* silently at the Temenos. The only trace of that decision in his published writings, however, is a cryptic remark in "The Unification of the Frame" (1990): "for the Filmmaker Physicians, the stupendous act of belief is, even now, the return of the image in its entirety; the sound removed, the space of the image regained."[28] Markopoulos's astonishing confidence in the influx of the creative imagination always outweighs his previous strictures. To be a serious filmmaker, he implies, is to be free of all laws, even one's own.

His 1965 letter "Inherent Limitations," advising Robert Beavers to abjure specialized training and learn the craft of filmmaking by making his own films right away, is an elaborate and nuanced version of his rejection fifteen years earlier of Freeman's idea that they collaborate on a film project the latter had been nourishing. Do it yourself, Markopoulos told Freeman. The letter to Beavers is also the first written indication of what was to be a decisive shift in Markopoulos's allegiance to the filmmakers of the American avant-garde cinema. Two years earlier, in "Projection of Thoughts," he enthused over the community of artists who had founded the Film-Makers' Cooperative: "every one of them has that divine fire and confidence which the ancient Greeks called *thrasos*. That is to say insolence. But insolence of a divine nature."[29] In 1965, disillusioned with their collective energies, he envisions a subsequent phase of the migration of the "creative spirit…full of greater illumination."[30] He suggests that such a migration might entail abandoning New York, and perhaps leaving the United States, as he was to do two years after sending the letter.

In 1960 Markopoulos had been the only filmmaker with a genuine pedigree in the American avant-garde cinema to join the New American Cinema (NAC) Group when Jonas Mekas founded it. Mekas at that time envisioned an American equivalent to the contemporaneous emergence of the Nouvelle Vague in France and similar phenomena in Italy, Poland, and Great Britain. Like the other members of the NAC Group, Markopoulos had hopes of making and distributing 35mm feature films in America. Since the mid-1950s he had been engaged in the production of *Serenity*, which he shot silently on 35mm in Greece. He was editing the film and completing its soundtrack (in four languages) when he joined Mekas's group and participated in their first (and only) collective exhibition at Gian Carlo Menotti's Festival of Two Worlds in Spoleto, Italy, in 1960, where Markopoulos showed *Serenity* as a work in progress.

The difficulties Markopoulos endured in making *Serenity*—the dissolution of his promised funding, the disappearance of all copies of the film as he edited it—was the most dramatic, but not the only, disaster that befell the NAC Group. Within a year, it was clear that none of the 35mm films completed by its members would get adequate commercial distribution. Mekas turned his energies to founding the Film-Makers' Cooperative, in theory a vehicle for the distribution of all films submitted by their makers, but in practice an agency for avant-garde filmmakers largely working in 16mm. Markopoulos was the only member of the NAC Group to join Mekas in that venture when it began, although a few others allowed the Cooperative to forward requests for their films directly to them and would later make use of it after its success had been demonstrated. The largest contingent of filmmakers came over from Cinema 16, which had been selective about which filmmakers and which of their films they would promote. Of the first generation of members of the Film-Makers' Cooperative, Stan Brakhage, Stan Vanderbeek, Robert Breer, Marie Menken, and Kenneth Anger had released some of their films through Cinema 16; Ron Rice and Ken Jacobs were among the artists who had not distributed work previously. Markopoulos saw the eruption of creative energy and the enthusiasm of cinematic discoveries that attended the early manifestations of this foundational moment as a religious phenomenon. If, on the one hand, the filmmakers were possessed by *thrasos*, he saw the audience of the Film-Makers' Cinematheque (the exhibition vehicle of the early Film-Makers' Cooperative in New York) as a Dionysiac confraternity in "Institutions, Customs, Landscapes" (1967):

> Undergoing examination, holding firm, munching on sandwiches, drinking cognac from tiny flasks, motionless, entranced (like the initiates at Delphi) the New Cinema Spectators at the Film-Makers' Cinematheque became future spectators, i.e., actors, the real, the actual, existing in the present but involved thusly, in the Past and in the Future. Beginning by tolerating himself, tolerating the spectator next to him, tolerating the total assembly of spectators in the tradition of the ancient theatre of Greece, aloof and apart from the sense of boredom, of posing, of brooding (as is the case in the Broadway Palaces and even at Lincoln Centre), the New Cinema Spectator begins to reflect the Silver Screen, and many an emotion which has not glistened as truly as on Mediterranean or Chaldean mirrors returns with Joy incising the Light Years, Past, Present and Future, while mixing with the waves of Sound outside the body Face. Gradually, the New Cinema Spectator reconsiders time itself his own, his dearest possession from sunrise to sunset. To sit through [Warhol's] *Sleep*, [Brakhage's] *The Art of Vision*, or the proposed *The Last Homeric Laugh* [by Markopoulos](a total retelling of the "Iliad" by

Homer) becomes an inevitable religious act: containing all that the Sciences, various as they are, very often do not contain, and often as not do not communicate to the average spectator.[31]

Here we find, *in nuce*, the basis for the visionary exfoliation of the projection situation that will eventuate in the Temenos. That concept entails a special theory of the film spectator, which is one of Markopoulos's most fascinating contributions to film theory. Rejecting the sociological models of the film audience, as well as psychoanalytical accounts of spectatorship, he posits a viewer, new to the history of cinema but congruent to ancient notions of ritual theater. In this formulation the exceptionally long film seems initially an important ingredient, but it will not remain so in his writings on the film spectator, despite the fact that his ultimate project, *Eniaios*, will turn out to be one of the longest films ever made. Yet not only was *The Last Homeric Laugh* to be a film of exceptional length, but also it is even more significant that in preparing it Markopoulos began his explorations of Greek prosody and philology that would later characterize his work on *Eniaios*. In his copy of *Yale Classical Studies: 20—Homeric Studies*, edited by Geoffrey Kirk and Adam Parry, he copiously marked "LHL" to indicate passages and details relevant to his film project.

To satisfy thoroughly the religious dimension that he attributed to cinema would require what the filmmaker obscurely called "immediate visionary speculation" inherent in the films themselves. He used this expression to qualify his praise for Kenneth Anger's *Scorpio Rising*: "*Scorpio Rising* with all its brilliance lacks for me one of the great requirements of this greatest art, motion pictures: the need for immediate visionary speculation such as is found in the simplicity of Genet's *Un chant d'amour*, in the magnificence of Stan Brakhage's work, in the awakening art of Jack Smith."[32] I believe the closest Markopoulos ever comes to defining this quality is the peroration of "Inherent Limitations" in which, as perhaps elsewhere, he uses the term *Eternity*[33] as functionally the equivalent of "immediate visionary speculation."

Markopoulos was baptized and raised in the Greek Orthodox Church, but his concept of religion owes even more to his readings of the ancient Greek poets and Plato. One place in Markopoulos's writings in which pagan Greek religion and Orthodoxy converge is in the figure of the "artist-physician." In adapting the myth of Hippolytus in *Twice a Man*, he referred to the figure of Asclepius (whom he also made Hippolytus's lover) by that designation, although the mythological sources identified him as the god of healing whose "arts" are exclusively medicinal. The dual role of artist and physician is traditionally assigned to the Evangelist St. Luke in Christian iconography. In fact, the Orthodox churches attribute the origins of holy icons to him, and he is especially venerated as the first painter of images of Mary. The concept of the artist-physician becomes a central factor in Markopoulos's film writings beginning in the late 1960s. It quickly shifts to the formulation "filmmaker-physician," which he frequently uses as an honorific term for Robert Beavers. His only concrete reference to the healing power of cinema can be found in a footnote to "Innocent Revels" (1964), in which he writes: "I believe the motion picture is a sacred art. It is capable of healing. For instance, what would occur if in cases of cerebral palsy the patients were photographed re-enacting a puppet play (those who cannot from one moment to another re-call what has transpired) and then had the images returned to them, systematically through the medium of motion pictures, i.e. projection—double, triple, projection."[34] More frequently, the allusions to the therapeutic potential of cinema, and specifically of the Temenos screenings, suggest that Markopoulos generally conceived of his art, and especially of his great project, as a modern version of the Asclepian cult (whose sites such as those at Kos and Epidauros he filmed specifically for incorporation in *Eniaios*). The implication is that the Temenos pilgrimage would be a cure for the media pollution, false artistic values and fashions, psychological and sociological criticism, obtuseness of cinematheques and similar institutions to what he calls "film as film," and the other cultural and political deviations the filmmaker prophetically railed against in many of his later essays.

In 1963, while editing *Twice a Man*, Markopoulos published "Towards a New Narrative Film Form":

> I propose a new narrative form through the fusion of the classic montage technique with a more abstract system. This system involves the use of short film phrases which evoke thought-images. Each film phrase is composed of certain select frames that are similar to the harmonic units found in musical composition. The film phrases establish ulterior relationships among themselves; in classic montage technique there is a constant reference to the continuing shot: in my abstract system there is a complex of differing frames being repeated.[35]

Narrative is the key term in this central, although very brief, essay. The innovation he proposes depends, in its initial formulation, on the interruption of single-frame bursts into a passage of narrative continuity. In the case of *Twice a Man*, the film proceeds in a narrative sequence in which relatively long shots follow each other with the temporal logic the filmmaker had employed since making *Psyche*. However, at almost every moment of the juncture of two sustained shots, he inserted a flurry of single-frame images, some forecasting the shot to come, some recapitulating a point in the shot that was ending, and sometimes flashing other moments of the film, past and to come. Significantly, he conceived of this innovation first in psychological terms; they were "thought-images" of the characters depicted in the longer shots.

Soon Markopoulos's practice and theory of the single frame would renounce the psychological analogy. The narrative matrix would cease to be an essential dimension of his films and of his writing about them. Instead, the rhythmic and connotative forces of the film frame would become the center of his work. Although he was not the first filmmaker to make extensive use of very brief shots, including single frames, he was the first to give the matter theoretical expression. Breer, Brakhage, and Kubelka had made such editing strategies signature aspects of their filmmaking.[36] Breer never entered the domain of film theory, Brakhage never addressed the issue of single-frame editing directly, and Kubelka (whose theories often intersect with those of Markopoulos in fascinating ways) maintained a stubborn silence about his working methods and ideas on cinema until he was first welcomed by American audiences in 1966. The theoretical work for which he is known was largely formulated in the 1970s.

Rapid editing was not new to Markopoulos. He had used extended montage scenes in *Psyche* and *Swain*. But these were gestures of recapitulation that accented the psychological crises at the climax of those films. In *Twice a Man*, and theoretically in "Towards a New Narrative Film Form," the rapid montage became much faster and, more significantly, it was distributed over the entire film. He had even experimented with filming in short bursts as early as *Lysis*, when, driven by economic necessity, he had edited his film in the process of shooting it. In the late 1960s when he began to make cinematic portraits and evocations of places, he returned to this technique and gave it new theoretical articulation. This is what he refers to when he writes in "Correspondences of Smell and Visuals" (1967): "It is true that Eisenstein, Dovzhenko, Gance, and Griffith used short phrases. The difference, however, is that they cut into phrases. They did not begin with the premise of taking short phrases. Technically and psychologically, the difference should become apparent to anyone wishing to consider the problem..."[37] Composition in the camera makes the narrative deployment of single frames in the manner of *Twice a Man* impossible. Yet in "The Filmmaker as the Physician of the Future" (also 1967) he asserts that both strategies should be viewed from the same perspective:

> To those creative film spectators who would understand the two films, *Through a Lens Brightly: Mark Turbyfill*, and, *Himself as Herself* [...] I would suggest the following:
>
> A—Do not attempt to single out any one film frame or series of film frames passing across the screen, and thus neglect others. Such abstraction would lead to a total misunderstanding of either film.
>
> B—To view the film as image composed to image, regardless if it is only a single frame. It is the Invisible that the film spectator must seek. This Invisible will lead him forwards and backwards and ultimately towards the Future; the future in this case is the understanding of the films.[38]

This implies that the single frame editing of *Himself as Herself*, ostensibly the same system as *Twice a Man*, does not intend to evoke thought-images but instead forgoes narrative and with it the temporality that narratives articulate. In a mere three years of intensive practice and theorizing, the filmmaker had come to a vision of cinema as a metaphysical tool for revealing what he sometimes calls "True Reality" or "eternity":

> What it does to the film spectator is not so much to tell him who is this and who is that, but rather, because of the shortness or longness of the images, to reveal in *after images* what the film is about. An emotional illusion is created towards everyone's search for the True Reality. I say True Reality, for I have always felt very strongly that there is a very, very great element of "eternity" in each bit of film. The secret is absolutely there; especially in the use of the single frame, and of slow motion. I am convinced that, when aborigines talk of being photographed and fear the image captured, it is this awesome idea of "eternity."[39]

At the same time that he began to formulate his theory of the function of the single frame, Markopoulos speculated on a new function of film sound. Here he was calling on his current practice rather than a long-standing tendency of his cinema. His first sound films utilized musical compositions of which he was fond. In this respect he followed the practice of several other avant-garde filmmakers, such as Kenneth Anger, Oskar Fischinger, and Harry Smith. He put Ralph Vaughan Williams's *Serenade to Music* with *Psyche* and *Christmas U.S.A.*; Honegger's *La danse des morts* with *Lysis*, Milhaud's *Protée Suite* with *Charmides*, and for *Swain* he used Villa-Lobos. Yet from the start of his career he had written scripts and imagined that he would make films with synchronized dialogue once he found the economic means. That had been his plan for *Serenity* before the producer's sabotage of the film drove him to a new phase of inventiveness: he created and recorded a voice-over commentary in four languages. Likewise *Twice a Man* had been conceived first as a talking film, then as a combination of several voice-over monologues; but after he recorded the voice of Olympia Dukakis as his Phaedra, he hit upon one of his most startling innovations. He cut into her words, fragmenting sentences and even single words in a manner analogous to his single-frame editing of the visual track.

By the early 1960s the rather casual practice of providing an avant-garde film with a soundtrack excerpted from a single piece of recorded music was dying, along with the rarer practice of commissioning a musical score as Maas, Broughton, Menken, Hugo, and others had done. Markopoulos's focus on the potential complexities of the soundtrack was in keeping with the thought and practice of some of his most prominent fellow artists. His correspondence on the subject with Stan Brakhage was published in *Film Culture* No. 29 (1963), along with interventions from the composer James Tenney. Andy Warhol's acquisition in 1964 of an Auricon camera, with which he recorded sound directly on 16mm film without the intermediate step of a tape transfer, allowed him to make a feature-length talking film nearly every other week. In 1965 he made twenty-six sound films, some incorporating refilmed video images, which he occasionally exhibited on two screens simultaneously. Peter Kubelka came to the United States in 1966 and began to tour with his films, and thus began his theoretical work. On completing *Unsere Afrikareise*, the film became a model for his theory of the "synch event," in which he posits the unique power of cinema residing in the ability to synchronize visuals and sounds that do not occur together in nature.

Markopoulos began to articulate his thoughts on sound cinema in this environment, but, as with his theory of the single frame, he reflected more intensely on his own previous intuitive practice than on the contributions of his colleagues. However, he never proposed a unitary formal element for the soundtrack to function as the single frame does in his writings about visual representation. The argument of the important 1967 essay "Towards a New Sound Complement for Motion Pictures" turns on the implied principles that the auditory "complement" should be unique to each film and derived with spontaneous intuition from the process of composing the visual imagery of that film. Thus, for example, because of his practice throughout the 1960s, he came retrospectively to a new realization in 1971 about the sound-picture relationship of *Charmides*: "The music utilized for *Charmides* is Darius Milhaud's *Protée*. Psychological distance between image and sound, in this case music, *becomes* the film."[40] For *The Illiac Passion* he recorded his own voice reading from Thoreau's translation of *Prometheus Bound*; he repeated many words and phrases several times as he skipped through the play. In some of the late 1960s films he continued to quote from classical music, but never for the full length of a film. For instance, he carefully fragmented Poulenc's *Gloria* for *Himself as Herself*, Wagner's *Five Songs for Mathilde Wesendonk* in *Ming Green*, Roussel's *Serenade* in *Gammelion*, and Beethoven's *Fidelio* in *Sorrows*. He used Indian bells minimally in *Galaxie* and read brief passages from Rilke and Valéry in *Gammelion* and *Political Portraits*, respectively. He also contemplated using an Auricon and letting his actors say whatever came to their minds for his Byzantine-inspired but unrealized project *Ascension*. He intended to superimpose sound over the spontaneous track to create the auditory equivalent to his multilayered visual compositions such as *Galaxie*.

The notebooks of ένιαίος *(The Divine Series)* elaborate several different schemata for sound in the twenty-two cycles of *Eniaios*. At one point, he thought he would take passages or fragments from the texts that inspired sections of the film, producing the following outline (Vol. 4, begun December 25, 1986):

Idea of word recitation for film orders
Swain—Shakespeare's Sonnets
Illiac—Promethus Bound
Genius—Goethe's Faust
Cimabue! Cimabue!—Dante's Divine Comedy

Further word recitation
Psyche—Pierre Louys
Lysis, Charmides—Baudelaire or Plato
Balzac for Himself as Herself
Euripides Hippolytus for Twice a Man
Hawthorne Fanshawe, for Swain

A year later he lists a sequence of natural sounds to be used in the film series (Vol. 8, begun December 26, 1987):

The sound: eagle
Thunder
Rain
Rain/thunder
Wind—birds
Fire—birds
Waves—birds
Crickets—birds
Bees—birds\running brook—birds
Peacocks—birds
Grasshopper—birds
Tiger—birds
Elephant—birds (use in Lysis)

In 1972, while he was envisioning possibilities for the Temenos, he described his earlier meditations on even more radical options for sound ("The Complex Illusion"): "Once, I believe it was in 1958, I considered the projected area of film might be peered down into, rather than stared at; this was while at the theatre in Delphi. The question is how to subscribe to the sound; it must perforce emerge from some subterranean element; and the audience must experience a visual incubation such as in the ancient temenoi where the patient was visited by the illusions of his malady."[41] In these two sentences we find the remarkable continuity of Markopoulos's thought and the nucleus of his core ideas. Thus, in his visit to the oracular site of Delphi, while shooting *Serenity*, he considered the possible convergence of ancient ritual theatre with cinematic projection. The disjunctive use of sound remained problematic even thirteen years later, when he revisited the idea in terms of Asclepian medicine in which *incubation* is a key term, referring to the climax of the ritual, when a therapeutic dream permits the patient to enter the *temenos* for the period of healing sleep.

As Markopoulos envisioned him, the physician-god Asclepius was the lover of Hippolytus. That would be consistent with the view of homosexuality that underlies some of his essays and even inflects some of his theoretical positions. Markopoulos was proud of his homosexuality. He had contempt for those who attempted to repress homosexuals or deny their own homoerotic impulses. Following Plato, he posited an aristocratic ideal of male love (which he sometimes called "Athenianism") as an enlightened quest for beauty and spiritual value. In this way, his Athenianism linked him and his work to a great tradition that he considered crucial to his vocation.

The influence of Plato is profound and persistent in Markopoulos's films and writings. He begins his essay on the sound complement by citing the *Timaeus*: "Believing more and more in the truth inherent in Plato's dictum *that time is the moving image of eternity* I propose a new sound complement for motion pictures."[42] In "A Solemn Pause" (1971) he assigns to the alternation of fades a role comparable to that of the speakers in Plato: "One technical element is the use I have devised for fades—fade-ins and fade-outs—which depending on the length or duration, which depending on their placement in the film construction[,] carry the counter-part effect similar to the dialogues of Plato."[43] Consequently, in "Erb and Tree" (1975), he takes the unexpected appearance of a volume of the dialogues in the Piazza of San Marco in Venice as an auspicious augury for Beavers's film *Ruskin*: "There in front of us, the volume of the *Socratic Dialogues of Plato*, in Greek. The eventful sign. Athenianism is always the Beginning and the End."[44] All of these allusions to Plato are deeply personal and manifestly tangential to the contexts the filmmaker assigns them. Markopoulos was never a Platonist in any strict sense. He certainly never shared Plato's disdain for art. With Plato, as with all of his productive reading, the filmmaker seized on phrases and notions that confirmed or extended his own intuitions and speculations. Formulations concerning the soul, eternity, the metaphysical dimensions of Eros, chaos and light, and the ultimate vindication of the Socratic outsider apparently struck a chord in his reading. But above all, it is the form and movement of Plato's dialogues, I believe, that inspired the artist and theoretician. The philosopher's repeated examination of concepts, the tentative or hypothetical status of doctrines, and the conviction that there is always more at stake than can be uncovered in the moment would seem to be important ideas Markopoulos drew from his lifelong reading of Plato.

In the first volume of the notebooks that he called *Chiron*, Markopoulos considered arranging the cycles of *Eniaios* into sections with titles derived mostly from Platonic dialogues and Homer's *Odyssey*: Psyche, *Charmides, Lysis, Phaedrus, Gorgias*, Hades, Selloi, Hagiographia, *Parmenides, Phaedo*, Arhontika, *Alcibiades*, Discord, Charon, Ariston, *Meno*, Kerberos, *Philibos*, [no title], Telemachus, Gibraltar, *Cratylus, Timaeus*, Odysseus, Scylla, Chimera, and Charbydis (I have italicized the titles corresponding to dialogues of Plato).

He avidly researched aspects of Plato's thought and heavily annotated the copy of G. M. A. Grube's *Plato's Thought*, which he acquired in 1985. He seemed quite enthusiastic about this book, but his marginalia call the author to task for his persistent attempts to apologize, downplay, or criticize Platonic pederasty.

Even when he found a book "dull," as he did Reginald Edgar Allen's *Studies in Plato's Metaphysics*, nevertheless he copied out pages of isolated sentences that interested him (*Chiron*, Vol. 25). David Bolton's *Plato's Dialogue on Friendship* (which Beavers gave him in 1990) and Michael Allen's *The Platonism of Marsilio Ficino* (acquired in 1985) are among the eighty or so books he possessed when he died; but, astonishingly, he did not own an edition of any of the dialogues, aside from the text of *Lysis* printed in Bolton's book.

In this extensive and nonstop process of researching aspects of his film-making projects, Markopoulos read to stimulate his creative energies, not for a scholarly, or even objective, view of a subject, as he admits to himself in his notebooks: "I wonder what is more important for my purpose: to read the whole of such a volume [in this case, *Essays on Music in the Byzantine World* by Oliver Strunk]; or, to go through the volume as I have done, + to remain enthralled within myself, the ideas generating towards the work; is it not like the sun shining on the earth?" (*Chiron*, Vol. 17). Foraging in Plato remained a way for Markopoulos to be "enthralled within [him]self." Although he studied the Pre-Socratics and Aristotle, Plato seems to have been the philosopher who most deeply engaged him. I believe the convergence of Greekness and homo-sexuality founded the filmmaker's intense identification with the philosopher. The other philosophers most frequently cited in his notebooks were homosex-uals or sympathetic to the study of homoerotic desire: Arthur Schopenhauer and George Santayana. Furthermore, both of these philosophers were pro-foundly influenced by Plato, especially in their reflections on art, which par-ticularly interested Markopoulos.

Along with Plato, Homer and Euripides provided primary stimuli for Markopoulos's art. He examined the minutest details of their language and their metrics for inspiration in editing *Eniaios*. Among the most heavily anno-tated volumes in his library were *Yale Classical Studies: 20—Homeric Studies* (which Markopoulos purchased in 1967), Euripides's *Heracles* (the Oxford classical text edited by Godfrey W. Bond in 1981 and bought by Markopoulos a year later), and Paolo Vivante's *The Epithets in Homer*[45] (acquired in 1983). The filmmaker made even more extensive use of Charles Mugler's *Dictionnaire historique de la terminologie optique des grecs*.[46] He mined this erudite study of the vocabulary of ancient visual experience for analogies to the filmmaking process, copying many passages from it into his notebooks.

The metaphysical assertions which had always been a factor in Markopoulos's theoretical speculations assumed prophetic proportions by the 1970s. A per-tinent example would be found in "The Intuition Space" (1973), in which he postulates an enigmatic duality in "reality" and suggests that its apocalyptic meaning will be revealed to the initiated through "film as film":

> The Content of a film image is like a magnificent, super terrestrial, chloro-phyllic process (in constant Evolution) which creates, and at the same time

preserves or imbues, enforces, a sense of human reality. A human reality, always, incomprehensible. Incomprehensible because of the existence of the Gigantic Reality; with both Human Reality and the Gigantic Reality forever doomed in a state of Illusion as opposites.

In this state of the Illusion of opposites, the Human Reality retains its state only so long as it remains unresolved; and, the Gigantic Reality forbids any communication with Human Reality, or Meaning itself, until the ultimate moment is achieved or revealed.[47]

Reading through Markopoulos's texts, we come upon two love stories. The first is embedded in the oldest layers of his writings; for, as we read the excerpts from Robert C. Freeman Jr.'s diary of the making of *Swain* we get intimations of his increasing fascination with the filmmaker. Significantly, Markopoulos's extraordinary conviction in the inspired nature of his momentary intuitions and his exploitation of chance events plays a crucial role in Freeman's infatuation. Yet this early romance is of interest only insofar as it anticipates and illuminates the central passion revealed in these essays, Markopoulos's love for Robert Beavers.

His writings on Beavers begin dramatically with the one-word sentence: "Recognition."[48] The older filmmaker finds himself pondering the meaning of recognition in the very act of acknowledging the genius of the young ephebe. To recognize that genius entails seeing an aspect of Orpheus in Beavers, who has left the United States "... in order to exist. This in order to make films. This in order to charm the souls of the beasts who claim that his country is without Song."[49] He also identifies the young filmmaker with Eros, an allegorical figure for the creative spirit of beauty as articulated in Plato's *Symposium* and *Phaedrus*.

In the subsequent decade he devoted an essay to each of Beavers's films (except *The Painting* [1972], which he briefly mentions in "The Complex Illusion") up to the *Sotiros* series (1975–1977). For many years these were the only sustained accounts in print of many of these films. They remain the most valuable guide we have to the evolution of Beavers's working processes and his thought. In writing these essays Markopoulos exemplified the ideal of the film spectator prophesied in his texts on the Temenos. Such a spectator must enthusiastically submit to the autonomy of the film he sees with wonder and without prejudice. In "10th of July, 1967," he clarified the difficulties one filmmaker has watching another work:

I, as a filmmaker, observing Venus' latest born, can only suggest and suggest, I am certain, inaccurately. A filmmaker can never understand during the filming, especially, what another filmmaker is doing. The reason for this being simply put, that the filmmaker observing the film being made, at every turn and twist that the head, elbows, shoulders and legs of the filmmaker at

work make, knows he would do it differently; desires to do it differently; almost urges the filmmaker at work to do it differently.[50]

Nowhere does Markopoulos take any of the credit he deserves for nurturing Beavers's art. He writes as if he were always surprised, enthralled, and
instructed by it.

Beavers's films presented him with occasions to reconsider many of the central themes of his own writings. In fact, he saw within them an evolving theory
of the nature of pure cinema. Reacting, perhaps, to academic interest in film
theory in the early 1970s and its concomitant revival of the writings of Soviet
filmmaker-theoreticians, Markopoulos characteristically dismissed them. In
"In Other Words It Is His Tongue" (1971), he affirmed that *Plan of Brussels*
(1968, revised 2000), *Diminished Frame* (1970, 2001), *Early Monthly Segments*
(then tentatively entitled *Degeneration*; 1968–1970, 2002), and the then recent
From the Notebook of… constituted for those with the perspicacity to see it "a
theory developed and expounded in the total and successful apprehension of
his medium as a cosmos within a cosmos."[51] Similarly, Beavers's innovative deployment of asynchronous sound in film after film spurred on Markopoulos's
speculation on sound and image relationships.

His writings during the period in which he was constructing *Eniaios* tend
to be more allusive, focused on the visionary future of the Temenos rather
than on completed achievements. Generally in the later essays and poems,
Markopoulos positions himself and Beavers as epicenters of the Temenos rather
than as the creators of individual films. The psychic cost of Markopoulos's visionary enterprise, as evidenced by those late writings, was enormous. His enthusiasm for Beavers's work reads like a reflex of his intense, but self-imposed,
isolation. Eventually he dismisses the achievements of his contemporaries and
most of his predecessors in the medium (his attitude toward D. W. Griffith,
though equivocal, seems to be the exception). His conception of the film spectator becomes more and more messianic—an exceptional few or even a single
anointed viewer will appear in the coming Millennium to grasp the salvific
achievements of the two filmmakers, himself and Beavers. Furthermore, the
jeremiad against film institutions, academies, governments, and heterosexual
culture becomes increasingly intense, if cryptic.

In the Temenos archive in Zürich we find Markopoulos's diary, *Ein
Eidelweiss*, in fifty-two volumes, including letters received, thirty volumes of
letters written by Markopoulos, six bound scripts including five notebooks in
preparation for *The Illiac Passion*, the nine notebooks of ἐνιαῖος (*The Divine
Series*), the twenty-five volumes of *Chiron*, three notebooks devoted to the editing of *Eniaios*, a volume of codes for the Greek intertitles, and six concerning
the projection speeds of the film. There are also fifty-four rebound books,
thirty still to be bound (as of 2013), and at least seventeen volumes of photocopied books and articles. In addition to bound volumes there are boxes of

correspondence with his family, Robert C. Freeman, and Robert Beavers and twenty-seven containers for articles, programs, and book chapters devoted to Markopoulos's films.

The centrality of poetry in Markopoulos's thought can be seen in the passages he copied into those notebooks and in his marginalia in his books. In the former instance, I have not come upon a single passage directly cited from a poem, but there are numerous citations from critical and philosophical works touching on the nature of poetry. All of these quotations are directly relevant to the filmmaker's reflection on his cinematic poesis. A prime example would be from Santayana, in which the sentence I have italicized was copied into the twenty-first volume of *Chiron*:

> The organ of thought being in flux, the terms of thought can hardly be re-
> peated…Only in dramatic and lyric poetry do we approach any such effort
> at complete personal expression…*for the function of poetry is not to convey
> information, not even to transmit the attitude of one mind to another, but
> rather to arouse in each a clearer and more poignant view of its own experi-
> ence, longings, and destiny*…Hence the musical, inspired, and untranslat-
> able nature of poetry, which lies more in the assault, relief, and cadence of
> the utterance, carrying with it a certain sensuous thrill and moral perspec-
> tive, than in the definable meaning of a poet's words.[52]

Here Markopoulos appears to be inscribing Santayana's words in his notebooks as a reaffirmation of his own commitment to art as a domain of clarification and as the revelation of destiny, rather than as a means of communication.

But sometimes he seems willing to wrench a passage on poesis out of context, as when he quotes Toynbee, both in ἐνιαῖος *(The Divine Series)* (vol. 2) and *Chiron* (vol. 22): "Poetry comes to light in individual flashes of intuitive insight shooting up out of the Subconscious. One flash will differ from another in degree of brightness, but there is no Time-relation between successive flashes."[53] For Toynbee a "Time-relation" refers exclusively to the historical chronology of a number of poems. He is arguing that unlike science, in which knowledge is sequential and cumulative, the truth of poetry does not depend on when it occurs in time. Markopoulos's use of this citation is enigmatic. On the one hand, he seems to be applying Toynbee's thought to the temporal sequence of images *within* his film under construction, although his primary emphasis is on the metaphor of "brightness," which he takes literally; for he adds in one notebook "My own thought: there are many lights in an image," and in another he writes, over the word *brightness*, "give to *Eniaios*." His disregard of context is transparent when he quotes from the next page of Toynbee's book, on which the historian wrote: "…Science is a cumulative charting of this continually changing picture of the Universe on the Psyche's conscious surface." Markopoulos writes: "the words 'Psyche's conscious surface' use for Amor essay—should be Amor or Eros surface—the screen absorbing and releasing images to the Temenos spectator, etc." Clearly, he is raiding Toynbee's text for phrases to clarify his evolving thought on the operations of the Temenos. His own work so thoroughly occupied his mind that he filtered all of his research and reading through the skein of his project.

For a long time he envisioned using Greek intertitles for the various sections of *Eniaios*. His annotations to the Homeric studies of Kirk, Parry, and Vivante sometimes point to this concept, sometimes to the rhythmic infrastructure of the film itself. Such annotations are particularly copious in his copies of Bond's edition of Euripides' *Heracles* and Mugler's *Dictionnaire historique de la terminologie optique des grecs*. From Kirk and Parry he marked the following passages on Homeric enjambment, often notating "as in film":

> A kind of accumulation occurs whenever progressive enjambment takes place: the singer sings a verse potentially complete in itself, then he qualifies or adds to it in a succeeding verse connected by progressive enjambment....Now a further distinction can be made between purely *supplementary* cumulation, whose principle is solely to supplement (either by decoration or by explanation) what has already been stated in the previous verse, and *transitional* cumulation or *prospective* cumulation, which provides some further description of what has preceded but whose main purpose seems to be to lead into a new thought and a fresh accession of meaning.[54]

The emphasis Markopoulos placed on this passage suggests that he intuited that a comparable prospective "cumulation" might be generated from the rhythmic placement of short film fragments or single frames. This is more explicit in his notes to Vivante, where we find the following passage marked:

> I use the term *representation*...for all expression that touches strongly or swiftly upon its immediate object. In a story or in any account of events, it stands out as a highlight. It is not *about* a certain thing, it identifies the thing. It is evocative rather than descriptive. Brief as it is, it does not break the train of thought but add[s] to its vividness.[55]

At this point the filmmaker writes: "the single frame unit!" For him the single frame has the power and function of the Homeric epithet. So, on page 62 of the same book, he is intrigued by a comment on Homeric pronouns. Vivante writes: "We thus find in Homer ὁ δέ, 'and he,' where, for the sake of practical clarity, we would rather use the proper name...Actions quickly succeeding in close relation with one another leaves no room for the concrete presentation of heroes." Markopoulos asks himself: "Use in complete order of film work?" In the first volume of ἐνιαῖος (*The Divine Series*) he elaborates it thus: "ὁ δέ, 'and he' instead of proper name, use with portraits." Although he eventually abandoned the idea of Greek intertitles, the elaborate research

he did on particles, pronouns, and epithets to be used in the films illuminates some of the mechanisms of its epic construction. In 1988, as he was
completing *Eniaios* and initiating *Asklepiades*, Markopoulos read and annotated David Constantine's *Hölderlin*.[56] German Romanticism had become a
more and more important inspiration for the filmmaker over his decades
of life in Europe. Like Goethe and Schiller and the post-Romantics dear to
Markopoulos—Schopenhauer, Wagner, Nietzsche, George, and Heidegger—
Hölderlin thought of himself as an heir to ancient Hellenic insights into vision, light, landscape, language, and poetry. Markopoulos identified with the
German Romantics' passion for ancient Greece and the imaginative need to
renew Greek ideals through making original artworks. In the annotations to
Constantine's biography and analysis of the poet's writings, he would at times
disregard context to read himself into the text. We can infer that from his
attention to the following on page 282: "The editor's worst problem is not
the deciphering of the words themselves, but to decide, when constituting
a readable text, what to leave out and what to include." If the filmmaker was
thinking of his editing process in making *Eniaiaos* as he read this sentence, as
I suspect he was, he has ignored the issue of how editors dealt with Hölderlin's
manuscripts after his death. Even more interesting is the following sentence
as an analogy to Markopoulos's film editing: "For it was Hölderlin's practice,
in the late poems to a frightening degree, not to erase but rather to leave first
versions and their expansions or replacements standing as long as possible."
On the previous page we find marked: "Hölderlin began to destroy the linguistic homogeneity of his earlier work." It is easy to see that Markopoulos
saw his own cinematic practices anticipated in Hölderlin's poetic strategies,
as Constantine describes them.

For an artist who had been filling page after page of his notebooks with
meticulously planned sequences of black-and-white frames, often inspired by
Greek poetics, Constantine's interpretation of Hölderlin's Pindar translations
struck home.[57] "Altogether, Hölderlin was fascinated by the possibility that certain effects could be arrived at by calculable means. His Pindar translations are,
I think, an attempt to arrive mechanically at a poetic language of his own . . . One
could almost believe that he thought the angle of refraction might be calculable" (p. 123). And when he describes the obscurity of Hölderlin's Homberg
essays on poetry "at the very limits of intelligibility, we might suppose, even
to the author himself," he could as well be describing some of Markopoulos's
speculations. "They are like the Pindar translations in their privacy: they expect
no audience and accommodate themselves to none" (p. 120).

Although the lack of markings or annotations in these pages of Markopoulos's
copy of Constantine's book (which is heavily marked in other parts) might cast
doubt on my hunch that Hölderlin's approach to Pindar influenced the most
"calculable" aspect of *Eniaios*, that is, its projection speeds, the correspondence is too striking to pass unnoticed. In six small notebooks titled ἐνιαῖος

(Visual Speeds), commenced in late October 1990 ("309th Day of Herakles"), he wrote: "There is no reason for film at 24 fr.—*sound defeated...*" Then, forty days later, he interrupted his note taking—largely on Heidegger's ontology from John Sallis's *Delimitations*[58] and David Robinson's *Pindar: A Poet of Eternal Ideas*[59]—to envision new projection speeds for each of the 165 reels which make up the twenty-two cycles of *Eniaios*. Accordingly, the excerpts from *The Illiac Passion* were to run consistently at 24 frames per second (fps); *Eros, O Basileus* was fixed at 16 fps until the final cycle, when the last two parts were to be shown at 12 fps and 8 fps, respectively; and *Twice a Man* and *The Mysteries* at 18 fps. All of the other multireel films varied in their speeds.[60] There is no calculation for the presumed running time of the film if it were to be screened this way; it would surely exceed 100 hours.

By mid-May of 1991 (101st Day of Herakles), the exhibition plan had evolved into a four-year Olympiad. The complex system of alternating speeds would be shown in the first year. The second year he would show the whole film, either from the end of the cycles forward, that is, from the twenty-second to the first, or he would show each cycle backward, that is, from the thirteenth reel of Order I to the first, from the seventh reel of Order II to the first, and so on, at the same speeds. The third year the whole film would be shown from beginning to end at 24 fps. The fourth year there was to be an entirely new order of reels at new speeds, ending with a part of *Eros, O Basileus*.[61] Then the four-year cycle would begin again. The six notebooks contain numerous reworkings of these schemata.

Markopoulos's conception of "film as film" bears distinctive affinities to Hölderlin's conception of poetry, as summarized by Constantine: "Poetry then is an act of translation ('Ubertragung') of Spirit into appropriate form, and the poem itself, in its total working, is a process through which the Spirit may be realized... Hölderlin also believed that the expressiveness of material correlatives in poetry would be increased by their being in some ways at odds with the intangibles they were serving to express. Creative contradiction is at the heart of Hölderlin's poetics" (pp. 124–125). The film-maker had even freely combined Christian ideas and Greek mythology as the German poet had done; for "Hölderlin associated poetry's usual aim (making manifest) with the revelation and incarnation of divinity in material and apprehensible things" (p. 126). A specific example of this fusion can be found in both ἑνιαῖος (*The Divine Series*) and *Chiron*. In the volume of the former dated "9 VII 88," as he was editing the *Chronion* section of the long film, he wrote: "Towards the end of the splicing I was thinking of the sun and made such variations. Also more exactly I was thinking of father, son, and Holy Ghost. Created such variations—the sun, father, son, Holy Ghost elements were introduced with very long white lengths [of film frames]." More elliptically *Chiron*, volume 5, has "Father, Son, Holy Ghost/ Benefactor, Lover, The Beloved Physician" and "Autumn, Spring, Winter/

Father, son, Holy Ghost." In this case, as frequently occurs when we read in Markopoulos's library, there are alternative sources of his Trinitarian thought. He read widely in medieval Islamic theology and poetry, including A. J. Arberry's *Sufism*[62] in which we find an account of the "mystical trinity of Love, Lover, and Beloved" in Ahmad Ghazzali's *Sawānih*.

Markopoulos did not expect his viewers to recognize a Trinity in the rhythmic alternation of white and black leader into which he embedded frames from the films he had shot. Yet he may have anticipated, or desired, a viewer such as Constantine who would treat *Eniaios* in the same way that the biographer approached Hölderlin's poems and theoretical essays. Constantine tells us: "The articulation of tones in words, as [Hölderlin] imagined it in his doctrine of the 'Wechsel der Töne', is a near analogy of the entire poetic undertaking in which the Spirit would be made manifest in tangible form. Listening for the tones, then, is an attempt to attend to the poem's endeavor at its most abstract level" (p. 231). But he warns us:

> Poems are not crosswords, and difficulties in them are not there to be conclusively solved... It is quite salutary to forget what one thought a difficult passage meant. The poem, as Hölderlin conceived of it, seeks to realize the condition of immanence. In an ideal reading it would take place in us, even *as we read*. In that experience retained knowledge may be more of a hindrance than a help. (p. 242)

That same year, when Markopoulos read Ian Gibson's new biography of Federico García Lorca, he paid more attention to Gibson's account of Lorca's creative processes than to the poems, although he did check lines from the "Ode to Salvador Dalí," which Gibson called "perhaps the finest paean to friendship ever written in Spanish" (p. 161). "Friendship" had always been a key term in Markopoulos's vocabulary. It encompassed intellectual understanding, erotic love, and Platonic metaphysics, which may have been the sources for the elliptical reflection in *Chiron* (volume 9): "For film as film, what is the attitude of the spectator, and is there, can there be any attention? My always present theory of the role of homosexual thought." (The filmmaker made frequent marginalia critical of Gibson's unsympathetic treatment of Lorca's homosexuality.) In his discussion of the "Ode to Salvador Dalí", Gibson reads Lorca's speech "The Poetic Image in Don Luis de Góngora" (written at the same time) as a key to the poem, as if in writing of Góngora he were speaking for himself:

> Lorca expresses his admiration for Góngora's pursuit of "objective beauty, beauty pure and useless", free of personal confessions and sentimentality; for his fashioning of a highly original mode of linguistic expression, "a new model of the language"; and for the self-imposed limitations with which the poet chose to work, his efforts to control and shape the metaphorical

exuberance of his extravagant imagination. Góngora, he notes, hated those "obscure forces" of the mind that defy encapsulation, seeking above all clarity, measure and order. And if the *Soledades* are difficult, this is not the result of deliberate, perverse pursuit of obscurity for the sake of obscurity, but of the imperious task the poet had set himself of finding "new perspectives."[63]

For Góngora, read not García Lorca but Markopoulos; for *Soledades*, not "Ode to Salvador Dalí" but *Eniaios* (and its extraordinary path to "clarity, measure and order"); as, by the last decade of his career, the filmmaker had mentally separated his work from that of the rest of cinema (excepting always the work of Beavers). Instead, he drew encouragement, and sometimes inspiration, from reading himself and his project into the lives of earlier poets and composers.

The theoretical foundation for these acts of identification came from the philosophical reading he did, especially in Schopenhauer and his exegetes. There are numerous passages from *On the Fourfold Root of the Principle of Sufficient Reason* and *The World as Will and Representation*, quoted in both ἐνιαῖος *(The Divine Series)* and *Chiron*. He also read attentively Bryan Magee's *The Philosophy of Schopenhauer*. The attraction to Schopenhauer was over-determined. He was both the first modern philosopher to put art at the center of his speculations and the first to examine the nature of homosexual desire. Furthermore, he introduced ideas from Eastern religions—one of Markopoulos's preoccupations—into western philosophy. Perhaps most important of all, he was the theoretical source to which Markopoulos's chief role model, Richard Wagner, turned. Magee clearly points out how Plato's aversion to art did not deter Schopenhauer. Through his reading of Kant, he realized that "[t]his was because of [Plato's] mistaken view that works of art are imitations of things and events in the phenomenal world."[64] Rather, the different arts reveal "the Platonic Ideas *inherent* in"[65] stone, painted images, and words. But "[m]usic, by contrast, does not represent anything in the phenomenal world, or have anything to do with it as far as its content goes...music by-passes the Platonic Ideas; so whereas all the other arts speak of the noumenal indirectly, via them, music speaks of it directly."[66] If, as I suspect, Markopoulos came more and more to think of his editing of black and white leader as the noumenal or musical work of "film as film," he believed that the eighty-hour-long matrix of *Eniaos* transcended the glimpses of the phenomenal world that he had culled from almost all the films he had shot. This was a cinematic music he could intuit in his imagination, so that he was not deterred by the merely phenomenal threat that he might not live to see it projected.

After Plato, Schopenhauer, and Santayana, Martin Heidegger was the most important philosopher in Markopoulos's reading. When he worked out the projector speeds for the four-year cycles, the passages he copied from Sallis's *Delimitations* into the notebooks of ἐνιαῖος *(Visual Speeds)* give indications that he took Heidegger's metaphorical language literally, as a guide to the elements of his Temenos and *Eniaios*. He was particularly interested in Sallis's readings of the way Heidegger interpreted Plato. For instance, when he marks Sallis's sentence, "The Socratic turn thus differentiates between things in their immediate sensible presence and those things in their original truth, in their originary presence..." (p. 5), I take it he is thinking of his own efforts to ground the editing of *Eniaios* in a tension between phenemonal and noumenal revelations. Similarly, the visual metaphor in Sallis's description of the unveiling of Platonic ideas may have been what held the filmmaker's attention when he read: "The force of the Platonic determination: Being is determined as εἶδος or ἰδέα, as the pure look of whatever would be offered up to vision, the sheer aspect of whatever would present itself to intuition" (p. 25). The Heideggerian terms *Lichtung* [Clearing] and *Entwurf* [Projection] (pp. 119–127, heavily annotated by Markopoulos) seem to have evoked the open field of the Temenos and its film projector. Heidegger used *Umwendung* [Turning-around], according to Sallis, to describe "a movement, a displacement, from the domain of man's ordinary dealings with things to another domain in which things show themselves as they properly are, in their look, their outward appearance..., i.e. in their εἶδος, their ἰδέα" (p. 172). Markopoulos's marginalium, however, reads: "Turning around equals reels projected from end to beginning": his all-absorbing concern for the cycles of *Eniaios* reshaped everything he read!

He was even heartened near the end of his life, when he knew that he would not survive to see *Eniaios*, to refer to the pleasure Anton von Webern had in composing and hearing music in his head. In the late 1960s he had read, in *Anton Webern Perspectives*, Cesar Bresgen's recollection of the composer's last years: "He explained to me once, too, that he no longer needed to hear his works performed; the work sounds 'in itself'—he himself could hear it completely with his inner ear.... It seems certain that Webern committed no works to paper at that time"[67] (p. 111). The astonishing confidence Markopoulos had in his genius and in his vocation as an Asclepian "physician of the future" gave him a comparable satisfaction in editing *Eniaios* and planning for the Temenos screenings. That confidence assured him that his study of the classics and of philosophy always took place within what Messaien called "the climate of poetry."

{ APPENDIX }

Eniaios scheme with reference to original films
(x) based on completed films, previously exhibited (21)
(**x**) films not in filmography, new to *Eniaios* (55)
(*x*) based on films edited but not printed (6)
82 films
142 segments in all

ἑνιαῖος (Unity/Uniqueness)

δή (indeed/now)
ὅδε αἰῶν (this age/ this period of time)

Pyra Heracleos (**1**)
I τὰ τῆς ψυχῆς ὄμματα (The Eyes of the Soul)

> Psyche (1)
> Lysis (2)
> Charmides (3)
> Illiac Passion 1 (4)

II ὁ τὴς ὄψεως κόσμος (The Cosmos of Sight)

> Ming Green (5)
> Parker Tyler [Galaxie] (6)
> Mark Turbyfill (7)
> Sorrows (8)
> Kirby Siber [Political Portraits, hereafter PP] (9)
> Franco Quadri [PP] (9)
> Giorgio Frapolli [PP] (9)
> Klaus Schoenherr [PP] (9)
> Illiac Passion 2 (4)

III σχήματα τοῦ στόματος (Shapes of the Mouth)

> Gilbert & George (**2**)
> Genius (*1*)
> Marcia Haydee [PP] (9)
> Barbara Hepworth [Moment] (11)
> Hulda Zumsteg [PP] (9)
> Eduard Roditi [Aleph] (2)
> Illiac Passion 3 (4)
> The Mysteries 1 (12)

IV νεφέλη φωτός (Cloud of Light)

> Giorgio De Chirico [PP] (9)
> Bliss (13)
> Cimabue! Cimabue! (3)
> Alberto Moravia [Olympian](14)
> Illiac Passion 4 (4)
> Eros, O Basileus 1 (15)
> Chronion 1 (**3**)
> Twice a Man 1 (16)

V τὸ μέγα χάσμα (The Great Chasm)

> Hagiographia (**4**)
> Illiac Passion 5 (4)
> Epidaurus 1 (**5**)
> The Mysteries 2 (12)

VI χρόνῳ οὐδέν οὖσα (Not Being in Time)*

> Diamantis Diamantopoulos (**6**)
> Chartres (**7**)
> Painting & Studio-Diamantopoulos (**8**)
> Illiac Passion 6 (4)
> Eros, O Basileus 2 (15)
> Himself as Herself 1 (17)

VII φωνὴ φωνῶν (Voice of Voices)

> Georges Auric (**9**)
> Punschun (**10**)

Alberto Cavalcanti (**11**)
Illiac Passion 7 (4)
Olympia 1 (**12**)

VIII οὐρανοβάτης (Skyclimber)

Odyseus Elytis (**13**)
Vassili Tsindoukidis (**14**)
Valerio Adami (**15**)
Illiac Passion 8 (4)
Eros, O Basileus 3 (15)
Twice a Man 2 (16)

IX μιαρὰ ἡμέρα (Polluted Day)

Mrs. Giedeon-Welker [Doldertal 7] (4)
Nina Kandinsky [35, Boulevard General Koenig] (5)
Mycenae (**16**)
Patricia Highsmith (**17**)
Illiac Passion 8 (4)
Himself as Herself 2 (17)

X τὰ ὑπό γῆς (The [Things] Under the Earth)

Hadjikiriakos Ghikas (**18**)
Arhontika Spitia (**19**)
Catherine Gide (**20**)
Illiac Passion 9 (4)
Himself as Himself 1 (**21**)

XI ἡδέα καὶ ἀηδέα (Sweet and Not Sweet)

Lilika Nakou (**22**)
Dodona (**23**)
Yannis Tsarouchis (**24**)
Illiac Passion 10–11 (4)
Delphi (**25**)
Swain 1–2 (18)

XII οἱ δέ (And They)

    Lucebert (**26**)
    Marguerite Maeght (**27**)
    Cinders (**28**)
    Byzantios (**29**)
    Felix Baumann [PP] (**9**)
    Illiac Passion 12–13 (**4**)
    Swain 3–4 (**18**)

XIII ὕστερος χρόνος (Later Time)

    Jasper Johns [Galaxie] (**6**)
    Roccasinabala [Gammalion] (**30**)
    Peggy Guggenheim (**31**)
    Illiac Passion 14 (**4**)
    Eros, O Basileus 4 (**15**)

XIV φάναι φόνοι καὶ τάφοι (Murders and Graves to Appear)**

    Jonas Mekas [Galaxie] (**6**)
    Robert Liddell (**32**)
    Evangelos Pappanoutsos (**33**)
    Eleusis (**34**)
    Lambros Eutaxias (**35**)
    Illiac Passion 15 (**4**)
    The Mysteries 3 (**12**)

XV ὕπνον ὕπνον (Sleep Sleep)

    Ben Weber [Galaxie] (**6**)
    Eugene Ionesco (**36**)
    Anton Bruckner (**37**)
    Mark Tobey (**38**)
    Illiac Passion 16 (**4**)
    Eros, O Basileus 5 (**15**)
    Epidauros 2 (**5**)
    Twice a Man 3 (**16**)

XVI μνήμης καὶ σοφίας φάρμακον (Drug of Memory and Wisdom)

    Tinos Malanos (**39**)
    Ithomi (**40**)
    Oskar Kokoschka (**41**)

Illiac Passion 17 (4)
The Mysteries 4 (12)

XVII ἀκίνητα κατὰ κύκλον ([Things] Not Moving towards the Circle)

Ernst Fuchs (**42**)
Hans Richter (Index-Hans Richter) (19)
Benna Premsela (**43**)
W. H. Auden's House (**44**)
Illiac Passion 18 (4)
Eros, O Basileus 6 (15)
Himself as Himself 2 (17)

XVIII ἀρίστον φωτός (Best of Light)

Paul Thek [Galaxie] (6)
W. H. Auden [Galaxie] (6)
Dionysos Theater (**45**)
Frederick Ashton (**46**)
Rudolph Nureyev [PP] (9)
Illiac Passion 19 (4)
Olympia 2 (**12**)

XIX ὅρον τῆς οὐσίας (Boundary of Being)

Eduardo Arroyo (**47**)
Herakles (6)
Krzysztof Penderecki (**48**)
Harold Acton [Saint Acteon] (20)
Illiac Passion 20 (4)
Eros, O Basileus 7 (15)
Chronion 2 (**3**)
Twice a Man 4 (16)

XX τα οἰκεῖα ἤθη (The Familiar Customs)

Basil Wright (**49**)
Freya Stark (**50**)
Bassae (**51**)
Graham Sutherland (**52**)
Illiac Passion 21 (4)
Himself as Herself 3 (17)

XXI ἀθάνατος ἀρετή (Deathless Honor)

    Carl Jacob Burckhardt (**53**)
    Love's Friendship (**54**)
    Otto von Habsburg [Meta] (**7**)
    Illiac Passion 22 (**4**)
    Himself as Himself 2 (**21**)

XXII τὸ εἶ (The One) ***

    Eugenio Montale (**55**)
    Illiac Passion 23 (**4**)
    Eros, O Basileus 8 (**15**)
    Illiac Passion 24 (**4**)
    Eros, O Basileus 9 (**15**)
    Illiac Passion 25 (**4**)
    Eros, O Basileus 10 (**15**)
    Illiac Passion 26 (**4**)
    Figalia (**56**)

---

    * Literally "in time nothing being"
    ** If Markopoulos's accentuation is correct it would be rendered
       literally "murders and graves to say"
    ***The Greek orthography is ambiguous and the meaning uncertain.
       Markopoulos's Greek is a fusion of classical and modern diction
       with some neologisms. In classical Greek εἶ can mean 'you [singular]
       are' or 'you go'. In modern Greek one is usually written εις or ένας.

{ NOTES }

Introduction

1. Of course, my career as a follower of Tyler has been influenced as well by the literary criticism I absorbed with great enthusiasm: the work of Maurice Blanchot, Kenneth Burke, Leo Spitzer, René Girard, and my teachers, Adam Parry, Eric Havelock, Harold Bloom, Paul de Man, and John Freccero. Albert Merriman may have given me more than anyone else when, in a Latin course on Livy, he assigned me to produce a term paper on the historian's use of the present participle. I struggled mightily and eventually handed him a mediocre essay. But later, when I read Spitzer on the relationship of linguistic history to the explication of texts and delighted in his achievements, I realized that by forcing me to concentrate on a grammatical detail, Merriman had influenced the way I repeatedly isolated cinematic rhetoric—shot-countershot, camera movements, superimpositions, etc.—as the key to defining a filmmaker's style and its evolution.

2. Parker Tyler, *The Three Faces of the Film* (New York: Thomas Yoseloff, 1960) p. 79.

3. Ibid., p. 69.

4. Ibid., p. 71.

5. Ibid., p. 73.

6. Several of these contributions are included in the first book I edited, *The Film Culture Reader*.

7. Ken Kelman, "Film as Poetry," *Film Culture* 29 (Summer 1964), p. 23.

8. Noel Burch, *Theory of Film Practice*, trans. Helen Lane (New York, Praeger, 1973).

9. Stig Björkman, Torsten Manns, Jonas Sima, *Bergman on Bergman: interviews with Ingmar Bergman*, translated from the Swedish by Paul Britten Austin (New York: Simon and Schuster, 197#). Bergman said: "No other art medium—neither painting nor poetry—can communicate the specific quality of the dream as well as film can" (p. 44).

10. Ingmar, Bergman, *Images: My Life in Film*, trans. by Marianne Ruuth (New York, Arcade, 1994), p. 73.

11. Ibid., p. 97.

12. Suranjan Ganguly, "All That Is Light: Brakhage at 60," *Sight and Sound* 3, no. 10 (1993), p. 21.

13. "Stan Brakhage, OJ Simpson and the Democracy of the Whole Organism: Stan Brakhage at Millennium, May 18th, 1996," *Millennium Film Journal*, Nos. 47/48/49 (2007), p. 129.

Chapter 1

1. John David Rhodes, "Pasolini's Exquisite Flowers: The 'Cinema of Poetry' as a Theory of Art Cinema," in *Global Art Cinema: New Theories and Histories*, ed. Rosalind Galt and Karl Schoonover (New York: Oxford University Press, 2010) p. 145. Teresa de Lauretis

opens "Re-Reading Pasolini's Essays on Cinema" (*Italian Quarterly* 21–22, Fall 1980–Winter 1981: pp. 159–166) with the sentence "That Pier Paolo Pasolini was a man of contradiction, and a figure in excess of its cultural ground, is worth repeating."

2. See Zygmunt Baranski, "Pier Paolo Pasolini: Culture, Croce, Gramsci," in *Culture and Conflict in Postwar Italy: Essays on Mass and Popular Culture*, ed. Zygmunt Baranski and Robert Lumley (Houndmills, Basingstoke, Hampshire, UK: Macmillan, 1999) pp. 139–159; Joseph Francese, "The Latent Presence of Crocean Aesthetics in Pasolini's 'Critical Marxism' "; Sam Rohdie, "Neo-Realism and Pasolini: The Desire for Reality"; and Christopher Wagstaff, "Reality into Poetry: Pasolini's Film Theory," all in *Pasolini Old and New: Surveys and Studies*, ed. Zygmunt Baranski (Dublin: Four Courts Press, 1999); and especially Patrick Keating, "Croce and the Cinema of Poetry," *Scope* (June 2001), www.scope.nottingham.ac.uk.

3. Benedetto Croce, "Expression Pure and Otherwise" in Croce, *Philosophy, Poetry, History: An Anthology of Essays*, trans. Cecil Sprigge (London: Oxford University Press, 1966) pp. 282, 287.

4. Martin Heidegger, "The Origin of the Work of Art," in *Poetry, Language, Thought*, trans. with introduction by Albert Hofstader (New York: Harper & Row, 1971) p. 72.

5. Pier Paolo Pasolini, *Heretical Empiricism* (hereafter HE), trans. L. Barnett and B. Lawton, (Bloomington: Indiana University Press, 1988) p. 82. Italics in original.

6. Pier Paolo Pasolini, *Saggi sulla letteratura e sull'arte*, tomo secondo, ed. Walter Siti and Silvia De Laude, (Milano: Mondadori, 1999) pp. 2946–2947.

7. Pier Paolo Pasolini, *Empirismo eretico*, (Milano: Garzanti, 1972) p. 173.

8. Pasolini, *HE*, p. 171.

9. Pasolini, *Empirismo eretico*, p. 173.

10. Oswald Stack, *Pasolini on Pasolini: Interviews with Oswald Stack*, (London: Thames and Hudson, 1969) pp. 153–154.

11. Pasolini's argument for this eccentric claim would not appear until the December 1965 issue of *Paragone* (15, no. 190) in the controversial article "La volontà di Dante à essere poeta."

12. The date of publication raises questions about the timing of the journal. Pasolini delivered his text on the last day of May at the Pesaro festival. That is acknowledged both at the head and at the end of the *Filmcritica* publication. The "Speciale" edition of the journal may have actually appeared after June 1965. It is possible, of course, that the author provided copy for the journal before its public presentation.

13. Pier Paolo Pasolini, *Le belle bandiere: Dialoghi 1960–65*, ed. Gian Carlo Ferretti, (Rome: Riuniti, 1977) pp. 286–287. My translation.

14. Barnett and Lawson translate *insistenze* (which Pasolini isolates in quotation marks) as "insistent pauses."(HE, p. 180) I do not believe the idea of pauses is justified here; Pasolini seems to be referring to obsessive acts of emphasis.

15. Pasolini, *HE*, p. 219.

16. Rhodes, "Pasolini's Exquisite Flowers," pp. 152–153.

17. *Filmcritica* 156–157 (16, April–May 1965), p. 250. The dactyloscript of "Di un possible discorso libero indiretto nel cinema"—probably the initial draft of "Il 'cinema di poesia' "— in the Gabinetto Viesseux in Florence refers explicitly to *A bout de souffle*. The later versions make no mention of specific Godard films.

18. The final term of this poem-song, "mon semblable," will be repeated in the quotation of Charles Baudelaire's "Au lecteur" which Godard invokes several times in *2 ou 3 choses que je sais d'elle* (1967) in the coffee cup scene. In that sequence Godard himself whispers a commentary fusing allusions to Wittgenstein, Heidegger, Genesis, and Sartre, as well as Baudelaire.

The brief philosophical-poetic meditation on the cup of espresso, "taking the side of" a thing in a cinematic adaption of the mode of Francis Ponge, is the filmmaker's most eloquent film poem "made for the pure pleasure of restoring a reality fragmented by technique."

Chapter 2

1. Richard Abel, *French Cinema: The First Wave 1915–1929* (Princeton, NJ: Princeton University Press, 1984), pp. 396–397, 400.

2. Marcel Lapierre, "Opinions de Cinéastes: Dimitri Kirsanoff," *Cinéa-Ciné-pour-tous*, no. 127 (15 Fev. 1929): p. 12.

3. "Film sans sous-titre—Film d'avant-garde: *L'Ironie du destin*," *Cinéa-Ciné-pour-tous*, no. 7 (15 Fev. 1924): pp. 20–21.

Chapter 3

1. Robert C. Gordon, *Pasolini: Forms of Subjectivity* (Oxford: Clarendon Press, 1996), p. 234. Gordon's invaluable study examines the film theory after, and to some extent as an appendix to, his reading of Pasolini's poetry. Although I concur with his identification of "a repressed subconscious" in Pasolini's adaptation of "free indirect subjective," I do not find an explicitly "psychoanalytic vocabulary" in the film essays. I take Gordon to be referring to Pasolini's evocation of cinema's "irrational, oneiric, elementary, and barbaric elements...forced below the level of consciousness" (HE, p. 172).

2. P. Adams Sitney, *Modernist Montage: The Obscurity of Vision in Cinema and Literature* (New York: Columbia University Press, 1990).

3. Henry Edelheit, "Crucifixion Fantasies and their Relation to the Primal Scene," *International Journal of Psycho-Analysis* 55, no. 2 (1974): pp. 193–199; "Mythopoeisis and the Primal Scene," *Psychoanalytical Study of Society* 5 (1972): pp. 212–233.

4. Jacob Arlow, "The Revenge Motif in the Primal Scene," *Journal of American Psychoanalytical Association* 38 (1980): pp. 28–51.

5. Edelheit, "Crucifixion Fantasies and the Relation to the Primal Scene," p. 194.

6. Ingmar Bergman, *Four Stories*, trans. Alan Blair (Garden City, NY: Anchor Books, 1976), p. 60.

7. Frank Gado, *The Passion of Ingmar Bergman* (Durham, NC: Duke University Press, 1986), p. 408.

8. Bruno Bettelheim, *The Uses of Enchantment: The Meaning and Importance of Fairy Tales* (New York: Vintage, 1977). Much of what I shall have to say regarding the magic lantern show in *Viskningar och rop* grew out of a reading of this book while I was thinking about Bergman's film.

9. Peter Cowie, *Ingmar Bergman* (New York: Limelight Editions, 1992), p. 8. Cowie draws this observation from Jörn Donner's 1975 film, *Three Scenes with Ingmar Bergman*.

10. See Frank Gado, *Passion of Ingmar Bergman*, pp. 497–499, for a concise summary of autobiographical details in the film.

11. Ingmar Bergman, *The Magic Lantern: An Autobiography*, trans. Joan Tate (New York: Viking, 1988), p. 19.

12. Ingmar Bergman, *Fanny and Alexander* (New York: Pantheon, 1982), pp. 13–14.

13. Gado, *Passion of Ingmar Bergman*, pp. 499, 500, 502, 505.

Chapter 4

1. Susan Howe, "Sorting Facts; or, Nineteen Ways of Looking at Marker," in *Beyond Document: Essays on Nonfiction Film*, ed. Charles Warren, pp. 295–344 (Hanover, NH: Wesleyan University Press, 1966). Howe's essay on Chris Marker, Dziga Vertov, and Andrey Tarkovsky is the strangest and most original (and therefore the best) text I have found on the documentary material in *Mirror*. My epigraph is from page 332.

2. Andrey Tarkovsky, *Sculpting in Time: Reflections on the Cinema*, trans. Kitty Hunter-Blair (Austin: University of Texas Press, 1986), p. 18.

3. Ibid., p. 20.

4. Ibid., p. 21.

5. Ibid., p. 38.

6. Ibid., p. 21.

7. Ibid., p. 66.

8. Ibid., pp. 69, 224.

9. Stan Brakhage, "Brakhage Pans Telluride Gold," *Rolling Stock* 6, (1983) pp. 11–14.

10. Maya Deren, "Cinematography: The Creative use of Reality," *Deadalus: The Visual Arts Today* 89 (1960): p. 159.

11. Tarkovsky, *Sculpting in Time*, p. 62.

12. Vida T. Johnson and Graham Petrie, *The Films of Andrei Tarkovsky: A Visual Fugue* (Bloomington: University of Indiana Press, 1994), p. 116.

13. Natasha Synessios, *Mirror, KINOfiles Film Companion* 6 (London: Tauris, 2001), p. 103.

14. Alexandra Smith, "Andrei Tarkovsky as Reader of Arsenii Tarkovsky's Poetry in the Film *Mirror*," *Russian Studies in Literature* 40, no. 3 (Summer 2004): p. 54. She proposed that the likely addressee is his third wife Tat'iana Alekseevna Ozerskaia-Tarkovskaia.

15. Tarkovsky, *Sculpting in Time*, p. 29.

16. Synessios, pp. 112–113; Robert Bird, *Andrei Tarkovsky: Elements of Cinema* (London: Reaktion Books, 2008). Bird traces this story to Vasilii Grossman's novel, *Life and Fate*, p. 136. Sean Martin (*Andrei Tarkovsky*. Hampenden, UK: Pocket Essentials, 2005) recognizes it as an urban legend (p. 143) in his account of pseudo-autobiographical moments in the film, but he is silent on the grenade story.

17. I recall a moralizing television episode from the late 1950s in which a group of GIs bully a clumsy recruit by tossing a dummy grenade at him in order to see his panic. Instead, he throws himself on it to save their lives.

18. Robinson, *Sacred Cinema*, p. 416, observes: "The abundant water of the earlier hair-washing scene, which was aligned with Maria's sexual relations, has now run dry."

19. Claire Devarrieux, "The Artist Lives Off His Childhood Like a Parasite: An Interview with the Author of *The Mirror*," trans. Susana Rossberg, in *Andrei Tarkovsky Interviews*, ed. John Gianvito, p. 44 (Jackson: University of Mississippi Press, 2006).

20. See Jacob Arlow, chap. 3, n. 4. in which the author examines *Blow-Up*, and P. Adams Sitney, *Modernist Montage*, pp. 125–145 (see chap. 4, n. 2), in which I discuss *Persona*, following Arlow's lead.

21. Synessios, p. 98.

22. Johnson and Petrie, *Films of Andrei Tarkovsky*, p. 209.

23. Sean Martin, *Andrei Tarkovsky*, p. 136.

24. Arseny Tarkovsky played a large role in ensuring that Akhmatova received an Orthodox funeral, which was massively attended. One would like to imagine the second woman as a figure for the other great woman poet of twentieth-century Russia, Marina Tsvetaeva (1892–1941), who adored the young Arseny Tarkovsky and dedicated her last poem to him; he in turn wrote an important cycle of poems for her. However, I can find no evidence to connect her to the elderly woman in an apron. Alexandra Smith, "Andrei Tarkovsky as Reader," p. 56, interprets the spilled milk scene, along with "First Meetings," as an allusion to Tsvetaeva in a reading that is daring but unconvincing.

25. Robinson, p. 419, claims that Tarkovsky denied that the figure represented Akhmatova, but he does not cite his source.

26. Andrei Tarkovsky, *Sculpting in Time*, p. 130. Quoted by Synessios, p. 63.

27. See Synessios, pp. 53–54, for an account of how his film editor, Liudimila Feiginova, got Tarkovsky to consider this solution.

28. Here, as elsewhere, I have relied on the translations of Virginia Rounding in Arseny Tarkovsky, *Life, Life: Selected Poems* (Kent, UK: Crescent Moon, 2000), p. 66.

29. Synessios, p. 112, note 37.

30. Tarkovsky, *Sculpting in Time*, p. 195.

31. Bird, *Andrei Tarkovsky: Elements,* p. 138, quoting Andrei Tarkovskii, *Zapechatlemnoe vremia,* in *Andrei Tarkovskii: Arkhivy, Dokumenty. Vospoominaniia,* ed. P. D. Volkova (Moscow: Eskmo Press, 2002) pp. 72, 73.

32. Synessios, p. 76, reveals that the filmmaker "sublimated" the memory of his sister threatening to disclose that he stole a book from a family friend to make paper soldiers.

33. Tarkovsky, *Sculpting in Time*, p. 108.

34. Ibid., p. 221.

35. Martin, p. 141: "the sense here is of Alexei's exclusion from the parents' conjugal bed."

36. Synessios, p. 75.

37. Johnson and Petrie, p. 217.

38. Synessios, pp. 107–108.

39. Bird, pp. 127–128.

40. Ibid., p. 128, translating Tarkovsky's statement from Olga Surkova, *S Tarkovskim I o Tarkovskom*, 2nd ed. (Moscow: Raduga, 2005), p. 132.

41. Nicolas Berdyaev, *The Russian Idea* (New York: Macmillian, 1948), p. 193.

42. Tarkovsky, *Sculpting in Time*, p. 241.

43. See George P. Fedotov, *The Russian Religious Mind* (Cambridge, MA: Harvard University Press, 1946).

44. Tarkovsky, *Sculpting in Time*, p. 213. Ellipses in text.

45. Ibid., p. 224. This may be another allusion to his meeting with Stan Brakhage.

46. Ibid., p. 216.

47. Ibid.

Part II

1. Gilles Deleuze, *Cinéma 2: L'image-temps* (Paris: Éditions de minuit, 1985), pp. 50–52. Although I have largely reproduced the translation of Hugh Tomlinson and Robert Galeta (Deleuze, *Cinema 2: The Time-Image* [Minneapolis: University of Minnesota Press, 1989], pp. 34–36). I have altered the translation of some words and phrases.

2. The description he offers matches Mekas's film more than any other work shown in Italy at that time: "one glimpses blue skies with black, chopped-off branches, New York under snow, a good Negro who goes down into the subway, girls who dance dances which go out of style in a month, etc., etc." (HE, p. 251). He repeats this description, somewhat amplified, in an excerpt from "Perché quella di Edipo è una storia" (unpublished in his lifetime and collected in *Saggi sulla letteratura e sul arte*, vol. 1, p. 1665), in which he names Mekas as the filmmaker who thus creates "a character from a novel for school girls."

3. Pasolini's reuse of titles for his essays can cause confusion. This essay originally appeared as "La Paura del naturalismo (Osservazioni sul piano-sequenza)" in *Nuovi Argomenti*, no. 6, aprile 1967; that is, *before* the Terza Mostra Internazionale del Nuovo Cinema at Pesaro (May 27–June 4, 1967) as the second part of the text Pasolini presented at Pesaro and later published separately in *Empirismo eretico* as "Osservazioni sul Piano-sequenza." The essay titled "La Paura del naturalismo" in *Empirismo eretico* was initially published along with the scenario of *Edipo re* as a section of "Perché quella di Edipo è una storia."

4. While Mekas was in Rome, Gideon Bachmann invited him and Pasolini to his apartment, where they recorded a conversation on the American avant-garde cinema and the New Left: "Does the 'Third Alternative' Need an Ideology?" It remains unpublished, as the seventh part of Bachmann's volume of conversations with film directors, *The Human Dream and the Human Condition: The Conflict of the Artist and the Society*. Mekas dominates the dialogue at first, explaining how the American filmmakers are anarchic, wanting to destroy the situation in which they find themselves. Pasolini, talking at cross-purposes, infrequently intervenes until he is able to turn the conversation to his notions of ideology and religion in America, speaking of his hope for the invention of a new ideology that would bring on a civil war, which would save America from assuming the heritage of Nazi Germany through its mystical religion of spiritual well-being. (Typescript in archives of Jonas Mekas.)

5. R. Bruce Elder, *Body of Vision: Representations of the Body in Recent Film and Poetry* (Waterloo, Ontario, Canada: Wilfried Laurier University Press, 1997), pp. 36–65. For "Mozart," he heard "Mossod"; for "Rodin," "zoa"; for "featherbed," "cerebed"; for "Anadyomene," "Andromeda"; for "seventh parallel," "17th parallel"; for "stance," "stomp"; and for "Astarte! Astarte! Astarte!" "hastato, hastato hastate." See *Filmwise* 5–6, Marie Menken/ Willard Maas (1964), pp. 4–5, for George Barker's script.

Chapter 5

1. Catalogue of the exhibition "Fantastic Art, Dada, Surrealism," ed. Alfred H. Barr, Jr. (New York: Museum of Modern Art, 1936), p. 266. Biography presumably based on a questionnaire (now lost) completed by the artist. His birth year is actually 1903.

2. Published in Julien Levy, *Surrealism* (New York: Black Sun Press, 1936), pp. 77–88; reprinted in *The Avant-Garde Film: A Reader of Theory and Criticism*, ed. P. Adams Sitney (New York: New York University Press, 1978), pp. 51–59.

3. *Dance Index* 4, no. 9 (September 1945), pp. 155–159.

4. The five images appeared in the copy of the scenario Cornell gave to Marcel Duchamp (Art Institute of Chicago). At least three other copies of the manuscript with stereopticon views exist. They are reproduced, along with the text of "Monsieur Phot," in *Avant-Garde Film*.

5. Joseph Cornell, "Monsieur Phot," *Avant-Garde Film*, p. 58.

6. *Dance Index*, pp. 155, 158.

7. Ibid., pp. 158–159.

8. Ibid., p. 139.

9. Draft of a letter to Claude Serbanne, March 26, 1946. Joseph Cornell Collection, Anthology Film Archives, New York. This collection contains letters, film stills, and books related to cinema given to Anthology Film Archives by Cornell's sister, Elizabeth Cornell Benton, after the artist's death. In 1969 Cornell himself gave the Archives a collection of his films, both those he made and those he assembled for his own amusement and that of his brother Robert. The collection contains many of the early French trick films described.

10. Letter to Serbanne. Annette Michelson makes a similar observation in her analysis of René Clair's *Paris qui dort* in "Dr. Crase and Mr. Clair," *October*, no. 11 (Winter 1979). Michelson has written an important study of Cornell's cinema in "*Rose Hobart* and *Monsieur Phot*: Early Films from Utopia Parkway," *Artforum* 11, no. 10 (June 1973): pp. 47–57.

11. Letter to Serbanne. There are no accents marks in Cornell's French text. The French passage may be translated: "Sometimes her face is something rare on the screen today. At first there are some passages where she endows the close-ups with an eloquence that recalls the heroic age of silent cinema. Here there are rare flashes of the lyrical [undecipherable] of Falconetti. However without the depth. For myself, at least."

12. Joseph Cornell, "'Enchanted Wanderer': Excerpt from a Journey Album for Hedy Lamarr," *View*, series 1, nos. 9–10 (December 1941–January 1942), p. 3.

13. Ibid.

14. Controversy has arisen over the printing of *Rose Hobart*. When Cornell showed the film, he projected it through a deep-blue glass plate. Yet when Anthology Film Archives offered to make a color print, he selected a purple tint.

15. Letter to Serbanne.

16. Letter dated November 13, 1936, Archives of The Museum of Modern Art, New York.

17. Mary Baker Eddy, *Science and Health* (Boston, 1875; reprint, 1971), pp. 305, 312.

18. Bettelheim, See Chapter 3, note 8, pp. 76–77.

19. Federico Garcia Lorca, "Your Childhood in Menton," *The Poet in New York*, trans. Ben Belitt (New York: Grove Press, 1955), p. 13.

20. Federico Garcia Lorca, "Your Childhood in Menton," in *The Selected Poems of Federico Garcia Lorca*, eds. Francisco Garcia Lorca and Donald M. Allen, trans. Edwin Honig, p. 111 (Norfolk, CT: New Directions, 1955).

21. Garcia Lorca, *Poet in New York*, p. 14.

22. Garcia Lorca, *Selected Poems*, p. 113.

23. Dated note, November 15, 1963, Cornell Collection, Anthology Film Archives.

Chapter 6

1. Jordan reedited many of his earliest films several times, sometimes giving them new titles or combining them into series; for instance, four films from 1958 (*Madonna, Desertlight, Skylight*, and *Portrait of John Reed*) became *Triptych in Four Parts*, which has been dated both 1958 and 1959; *Man Is in Pain* is usually dated 1954 or 1955, although in an "Autobiographical Note" from around 1958, Jordan wrote: "there [San Francisco] [he] made what he considered his first film, *Man Is in Pain*. Years later a sound track was made from the reading of lines of a poem by Philip Lamantia. The film also took its name from the poem." [Reprinted in *Larry Jordan Retrospective*, ed. P. Adams Sitney, Anthology Film Archives, 1976].

2. *Fictive Certainties: Essays by Robert Duncan* (New York: New Directions, 1986), p. 4, 6, 54.

3. Paul Karlstrom, "Oral history interview with Larry Jordan, 1995 Dec. 19—1996 July 30," http://www.aaa.si.edu/collections/collection5.htm.

4. G. T. Collins, "Larry Jordan's Underworld," *Animation Journal* (Fall 1997): pp. 54–69.

5. When I inquired why he had not included the film in *The Lawrence Jordan Album*, he said he may have made a mistake in excluding some short films that were "not very exciting" or that he may have been "a little enthusiastic" about *The Seasons' Change* when he wrote me the note. [Telephone conversation March 1, 2009].

6. Karlstrom.

7. Ibid.

8. I am grateful to Courtney Banks at *Artforum*, who identified the background plate as an illustration of the "mishkan." She also pointed out Blake's *The Great Red Dragon and the Woman Clothed with Sun* and corrected several errors in my ms. of an earlier version of this chapter.

9. Karlstrom.

10. In the Karlstrom interview, Jordan also credits Max Ernst, Wallace Berman, and George Herms as major influences. Lawrence Jordan sent me this corrective note on April 23, 2014 in response to an earlier publication of this chapter:

> Who are my guides through the underworld? Literary guides, that is. There is of course Virgil, whom I read in his native tongue. And Homer as expounded by [M. I.] Finley in the Harvard Hall as he strode the boards with long hair, speaking half in English and half in ancient Greek, voice thundering with Zeus recalled. There is George MacDonald in the Visionary Novels. There is Edgar Allan Poe and ratiocination. And with Charles Baudelaire, having read the whole of *Les Fleurs du Mal* aloud to Joanna [McClure], I know whereof I speak. And Stéphane Mallarmé and Guillaume Apollinaire, William Blake.
>
> And fairy tales of all countries, and L. Frank Baum
>
> The Arabian Nights, Lewis Carroll, James Stephens, A. Merritt, H.P. Lovecraft, Pierre Louys.
>
> The Sacred books of Babylonia, Assyria, Egypt, Hebrews, Arabia, Persia, India, China, Japan.
>
> Robert Graves, James G. Frazer, Sax Rohmer.
>
> Robert Duncan, Jess, and Joseph Cornell do not actually influence my films. But Duncan lends support when he says that the realm of imagination is as real as the world of cars and stop lights.
>
> Emerson has never influenced my work, but his glorious essay, "The Over-Soul," nails much of my other-world view.

11. Ralph Waldo Emerson, "Nature," in *Essays and Poems* (New York: Library of America), pp. 33–34.

Chapter 7

1. Bruce McPherson, ed., *Essential Brakhage: Selected Writings on Filmmaking by Stan Brakhage* (Kingston, NY: Documentext, 2001), pp. 182–183.

2. Ezra Pound, *The Cantos* (New York: New Directions, 1973), pp. 605–606. Brakhage later titled a hand-painted film *Yggdrasail: Whose Roots Are Stars in the Human Mind* (1997).

3. Gertrude Stein, *Stanzas in Meditation (The Corrected Edition)*, (New Haven, CT: Yale University Press, 2010), p. 203. The original edition, which Brakhage possessed, misprinted *now* for *not* in the fourth line and *can* for *may* in the eighth.

4. Ezra Pound, "How to Read," in *Literary Essays of Ezra Pound*, ed. T. S. Eliot, p. 25 (New York: New Directions, 1968).

5. Ezra Pound, "The Wisdom of Poetry," in *Selected Prose 1909–1965*, ed. William Cookson, p. 360 (New York: New Directions, 1970).

6. I believe the term is my coinage, but the concept can be found in Parker Tyler's writings on avant-garde cinema, particularly in *The Three Faces of the Film*. Tyler recognizes the centrality of the figure of the somnambulist, Cesare, from *Das Cabinet of Dr. Caligari* to this mode of filmmaking. He also explores the crucial influence of Jean Cocteau's *Le sang d'un poète*.

7. Gertrude Stein, *Writings 1903–1932* (New York: Library of America, 1998), p. 308.

8. Gertrude Stein, "Natural Phenomena," in *Painted Lace and Other Pieces 1914–1937*, p. 182 (New Haven, CT: Yale University Press, 1955).

9. Stan Brakhage, *Metaphors on Vision* (New York: Film Culture, 1963).

10. Philip Taaffe, *Composite Nature: A Conversation with Stan Brakhage* (New York: Peter Blum Editions, 1998), p. 116.

11. Robert Duncan, *Fictive Certainties* (New York: New Directions, 1985), pp. 61–62.

12. R. Bruce Elder, *The Films of Stan Brakhage in the American Tradition of Ezra Pound, Gertrude Stein, and Charles Olson* (Waterloo, Ontario, Canada: Wilfrid Laurier University Press, 1998), pp. 255–257.

13. Hollis Frampton, *Circles of Confusion: Film/Photography/Video Texts 1968–1980* (Rochester, NY: Visual Studies Workshop Press, 1983), pp. 82–83.

14. *Film-Makers' Cooperative Catalogue No. 7* (New York, 1989), p. 63.

15. Suranjan Ganguly, "Stan Brakhage—the 60th Birthday Interview," *Film Culture* 78 (Summer 1994): p. 27.

16. Adrian Leverkühn renounced his Faustian gifts of musical talent and success in these terms in Mann's novel, after his beloved nephew dies of a disease caught from him. I was unaware of the quotation when I wrote *Visionary Film* and even misquoted the film from faulty memory. The correct attribution first appeared in William Wees's essay "Words and Images in Stan Brakhage's *23rd Psalm Branch*," *Cinema Journal* 27, no. 2 (Winter 1988): p. 43.

17. A fragment of the script appears in Stan Brakhage, *Metaphors on Vision*.

18. Telephone interview with Joel Haertling, February 8, 1996.

19. Robert Duncan, *Faust Foutu* (Stinson Beach, CA: Enkidu Surrogate, 1960), p. 57.

20. Ganguly, p. 27.

21. Brakhage refers to *Mr. Frenhofer and the Minotaur* as Peterson's "greatest work" in "Sidney Peterson. A Lecture by Stan Brakhage, The Art Institute of Chicago, 1973" (*Film Culture* 70–71, 1983, p. 35), from which the chapter in *Film at Wit's End* was edited. Brakhage did not discuss the film in detail in the lecture, and allusions to it did not remain in the edited book.

22. Stan Brakhage, *Film at Wit's End: Eight Avant-Garde Filmmakers* (Kingston, NY: Documentext, McPherson & Company, 1989), p. 59.

23. *Canyon Cinema Film/Video Catalog 7* (San Francisco: Canyon Cinema, 1992), p. 57. The claim of incorporating a female point of view reaffirms earlier statements of the role Jane Collom Brakhage played in his filmmaking.

24. Paul Valéry, *Plays*, trans. David Paul and Robert Fitzgerald (New York: Pantheon, 1960), 45:3, p. 3.

25. Joel Haertling understands the title to refer to Emily. Telephone interview, February 9, 1996.

26. Stan Brakhage, *Metaphors on Vision*, from "His Story" chapter.

27. See Benjamin Bennett, *Goethe's Theory of Poetry: Faust and the Regeneration of Language* (Ithaca, NY: Cornell University Press, 1986), for an illuminating discussion of the role of masturbation in Goethe's *Faust*.

28. Ganguly, p. 28.

29. Stan Brakhage, "*The Dominion of Picture*," pp. 2, 16. Robert Haller of Anthology Film Archives made his copy of the typescript available to me in 1996.

30. Ganguly, pp. 29–30.

31. *Canyon*, p. 57.

32. Stan Brakhage, *Telling Time: Essays of a Visionary Filmmaker* (Kingston, NY: Documentext, 1993), pp. 85–86. James Strachey coined the word *cathexis* to translate Freud's *Besetzung* (which means a charge or an act of occupation). Brakhage may not have been aware of the controversy over Strachey's adaptation of the Greek κάθεξις ("holding") with its scientific tone to render Freud's more ambiguous, common German noun. Following the Freudian analogy, the visual cathexis Brakhage theorizes would be an optical equivalent to an affect attached to instances of sight.

33. Elder, p. 170.

34. Stan Brakhage, *Telling Time*, pp. 135–136.

35. Fred Camper, "Stan Brakhage: New Films," http://www.fredcamper.com/Film/Brakhage2.html#GodofDay.

36. See Stan Brakhage, "Chicago Review Article," for a discussion of the poets who influenced him. He cites Johnson, McClure, and Lisa Jarnot as "the three today" "who contribute directly to my filmmaking" (p. 38). *Chicago Review* 47–48 (Winter 2001–Spring 2002): pp. 38–41.

37. R. Bruce Elder discusses Brakhage's reading of *ARK* extensively in "Brakhage Poesis" in *Stan Brakhage: Filmmaker,* ed. David E. James, pp. 88–106 (Philadelphia: Temple University Press, 2005).

38. Although Brakhage has affirmed that Michael McClure's poetry continued to inspire him during this period, the lines of connection are not obvious, as they had been during the period of his marriage to Jane Collom, whose remarkable empathy for animals resonated with McClure's ecstatic evocation of "beast language." The influence of McClure's prose is evident in the essays collected in *Telling Time*, especially in the ontological category Brakhage calls "meat-ineffable."

39. Ganguly, p. 18.

40. Paul Arthur, "Becoming Dark with Excess of Life: The Vancouver Island Films," in *Stan Brakhage: Filmmaker,* ed. David E. James, pp. 210, 212–213.

41. Ganguly, p. 19.

42. Arthur, p. 212.

43. Stan Brakhage and Ronald Johnson (with Jim Shedden), "Another Way of Looking at the Universe (1997)," *Chicago Review,* 47–48 (Winter 2001—Spring 2002): pp. 33–35; ellipses mine.

44. Fred Camper, however, finds phallic images particularly prominent in *The Mammals of Victoria*. See his essay "Brakhage's Contradictions" in the *Chicago Review* 47–48: pp. 69–96.

45. See Fred Camper, p. 80, for an elaboration of the paradoxical representation of a self in the Vancouver Island films. He precedes me in recognizing the relation to *Anticipation of the Night*.

46. Bart Testa, "Late and Somewhere Film: Notes on Brakhage's Vancouver Island Films," *Canadian Review of Film Studies* 14, no. 1 (Spring 2005): pp. 12–25.

47. Camper, p. 86, fn. 13. He notes, "in many of Brakhage's... cuts the two joined shots are separated by one or two frames of darkness... [the shots are] separated by a little 'blink,' contributing to the sense that each shot occupies its own space."

48. Brakhage, *Telling Time*, p. 74.

49. Ibid., p. 36. With my ellipses I have moved this phrase out if its context, in which the author is discussing prenatal vision.

50. Brakhage, *Film at Wit's End*, p. 29.

51. Ganguly, p. 29.

52. "Marilyn Brakhage on Stan Brakhage, Interview with Rick Raxlen, October 2005," http://vantagepointmagazine.worldpress.com/2008/01/03/marilyn-brakhage-on-stan-brakhage-interview-with-rick-raxlen-0.

53. Ibid., p. 21.

54. Brakhage, *Film at Wit's End*, p. 15,

55. Ibid., p. 86.

56. Brakhage, *Telling Time*, p. 138.

57. *Millennium Film Journal: Words of Stan Brakhage* (guest editor Mike Hoolbloom) 47–48–49 (Fall–Winter 2007–2008): p. 147.

58. Stan Brakhage, "Mortality: Stan Brakhage at Millennium—April 1st, 2000," *Millennium Film Journal* 47–48–49: p. 147.

59. Yet even more than Pound or Johnson, it is Olson who comes closest to the tone and complex concatenation of valediction and prophetic energy of the film in his late Maximus poem, "I am going to hate to leave this Earthly Paradise."

60. Kenneth Patchen, *Panels for the Walls of Heaven* (Berkeley, CA: Ben Porter, 1946), p. 66.

61. See Brakhage's radio broadcasts, *The Test of Time*, transcribed by Fred Camper http://www.fredcamper.com/Brakhage/TestofTime.html], especially Programs 5 and 6.

62. Fred Camper, "A Review of Stan Brakhage's Last Films," http://www.fredcamper.com/Film/Brakhage3.html.

Chapter 8

1. Mary Kite, "A Conversation with Nathaniel Dorsky," *Poetry Project Newsletter* 187 (February/March 2001): p. 7.

2. Scott MacDonald, ed., *A Critical Cinema 5: Interviews with Independent Filmmakers* (Berkeley: University of California Press, 2006), p. 87.

3. Max Goldberg, "The Inmost Leaf: An Article and Interview with Nathaniel Dorsky," *Cinema Scope* 3 (2011).

4. Goldberg, "The Inmost Leaf."

5. Wheeler W. Dixon, *The Exploding Eye: A Re-visionary History of 1960s American Experimental Cinema* (Albany: State University of New York Press, 1997); MacDonald, *A Critical Cinema 5*.

Chapter 9

1. Robert Beavers, Email to P. Adams Sitney, April 30, 2014.

2. Claude Samuel, *Entretains avec Messiaen* (Paris: Pierre Belfond, 1967), p. 121, translation mine.

3. This passage can be found in volume 21 of Markopoulos's handwritten notebook series, Chiron. See pp. 242–243 for a description of the Temenos Archive where Chiron and other manuscripts are held.

4. *Yale Classical Studies: Volume Twenty/ Homeric Studies*, ed. G. S. Kirk and Adam Parry (New Haven, CT: Yale University Press, 1966), p. 86.

5. Gregory Markopoulos, *Film As Film: The Collected Writings of Gregory J. Markopoulos*, ed. Mark Webber (London: The Visible Press, 2014), p. 102 Hereafter FAF.

6. FAF, p. 102.

7. FAF, p. 151.

8. FAF, p. 133.

9. FAF, p. 470.

10. I had never been able to attend the Temenos sessions held between 1980 and 1986. The early September screenings always conflicted with the beginning of the academic year and my teaching responsibilities, but I had seen all the films shown in that period when only completed films by Markopoulos and Beavers were screened at Temenos.

11. FAF, pp. 385–387.

12. FAF, pp. 376–379.

13. FAF, p. 379.

14. Karl Kerényi, *Asklepios; Archetypal Image of the Physician's Existence*. Trans. By Ralph Manheim (New York: Pantheon, 1959).

15. Emma J. Edelstein and Ludwig Edelstein, *Asclepius: Collection and Interpretation of the Testimonies* / by (Baltimore, MD: Johns Hopkins University Press, 1945).

16. Gregory Vlastos, "Religion and Medicine in the Cult of Asclepius: A Review Article," *Review of Religion* 13, no. 3 (1949), pp. 269–290.

17. FAF, pp. 207–208. Originally in *Film Culture*, Winter 1963–1964.

18. FAF, p. 275.

19. FAF, pp. 275–276.

20. FAF, p. 276.

21. FAF, p. 347.

22. In my *Eyes Upside Down* I explore the Emersonian trope of upside-down vision in the work of several of Markopoulos's contemporaries and epigones.

23. FAF, pp. 178–179.

24. FAF, p. 199.

25. FAF, p. 212.

26. FAF, p. 150.

27. FAF, p. 68.

28. FAF, p. 486.

29. FAF, pp. 105-106.

30. FAF, p. 66.

31. FAF, p. 131.

32. FAF, p. 136.

33. FAF, p. 68. Markopoulos invokes the category of "Eternity" as a superlative frequently in his writings.

34. FAF, p. 142, footnote 5.

35. FAF, p. 207.

36. Jonas Mekas did not begin to use the single-frame mechanism of his Bolex camera in recording his cinematic diaries until after 1963, to the best of my knowledge. Markopoulos's discussion of "the premise to taking short phrases" is especially relevant to the style Mekas would find for his cinematic diaries.

37. FAF, p. 245.

38. FAF, p. 234.

39. FAF, p. 236–237.

40. FAF, p. 182.

41. FAF, pp. 359–360.

42. FAF, p. 251.

43. FAF, p. 350.

44. FAF, p. 333.

45. Paolo, Vivante, *The Epithets in Homer: a Study in Poetic Values* (New Haven, CT: Yale University Press, 1982).

46. Charles Mugler, *Dictionnaire historique de la terminologie optique des Grecs; douze siècles de dialogues avec la lumière* (Paris, Klincksieck, 1964).

47. FAF, p. 75.

48. FAF, p. 285.

49. FAF, p. 286.

50. FAF, p. 287.

51. FAF, p. 309.

52. George Santayana, *The Realm of Essence: Book First of Realms of Being* (London: Constable, 1936), pp. 110-111, my ellipses.

53. Arnold Toynbee, *An Historian's Approach to Religion* (London: Oxford University Press, 1956), p. 121.

54. Kirk and Parry, *Yale Classical Studies,* p. 114.

55. Vivante, p. 18.

56. David Constantine, *Hölderlin* (Oxford, UK: Clarendon Press, 1988).

57. However, there are no markings between pp. 120 and 126 in Markopoulos's copy of the book.

58. John Sallis, *Delimitations—Phenomenology and the End of Metaphysics* (Bloomington, IN: Indiana University Press, 1986).

59. David M. Robinson, *Pindar, a Poet of Eternal Ideas* (Baltimore, MD: Johns Hopkins University Press, 1936).

60. In the second notebook, year 4 seems to be made up of selected reels: Order IV, reel 10; VIII, 8; XV, 8; XIX, 7, all at 12 frames per second; then VI, 7; IX, 5; IX, 6; XVII, 6; XVII, 7; XX, 6, at 12 fps; III, 7; V, 11; XIV, 5; XV1, 6, all at 12 fps; then all 24 reels of *The Illiac Passion* at 18 fps interrupted after XII by *Swain* from XI, 8 (16 fps); XI, 9 (8 fps); *Pyra Heracleos, Swain* XII, 7 (8 fps); XII, 8 (16 fps); and finally *Figalia* XXII, 10 (12 fps); XXII, 11 (24 fps); and all 19

reels of *Eros, O Basileus* (there is no mention of speed, but notes on inserting reels of *Swain* and *The Illiac Passion*), followed by many variations.

61. Noted in *Chiron*, vol. 24.

62. A. J. Arberry, *Sufism: An Account of the Mystics of Islam* (London, Allen & Unwin, 1950), p. 102.

63. Ian Gibson, *Federico García Lorca: A Biography* (London: Faber and Faber, 1989), p. 158.

64. Bryan Magee, *The Philosophy of Schopenhauer* (New York: Oxford University Press, 1983), p. 174. Apparently Markopoulos did not possess a copy of this book. He copied out several passages from it in *Chiron*, vol. 20, but those are not the passages quoted here. He did own a special issue of *Opera Quarterly* devoted to Wagner (1/3/1983), which contained a chapter of Magee's book devoted to Schopenhauer and Wagner. Markopoulos annotated it heavily and wrote a note to himself to obtain the book.

65. Ibid., p. 174.

66. Ibid., p. 182.

67. Cesar Bresgen, "Webern's Last Months in Mittersill," in *Anton Webern Perspectives*, ed. Demar Irvine, comp. Hans Moldenhauer, (Seattle: University of Washington Press, 1966) p. 111. Beavers recalled Markopoulos quoting this passage with approval.

{ INDEX }